# FAIRY TAIL

フェアリーテイル

20

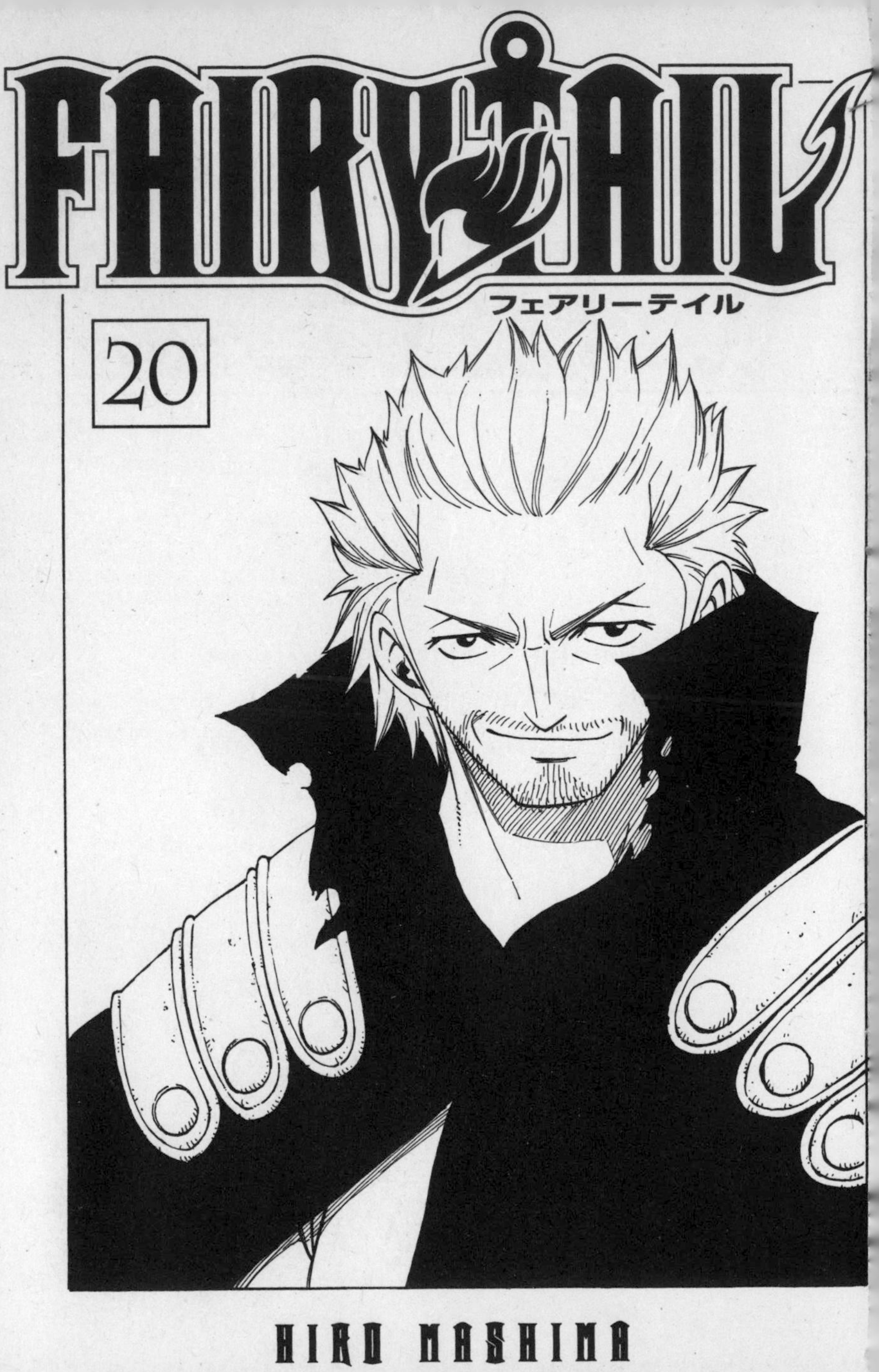

HIRO MASHIMA

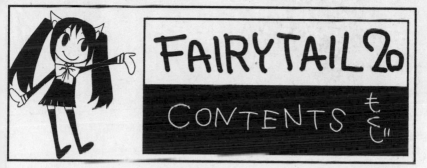

# FAIRYTAIL 20

## CONTENTS もくじ

Published in serial form by Weekly Shōnen Magazine 2009 Volume 53 and 2009 Volumes 1 - 9

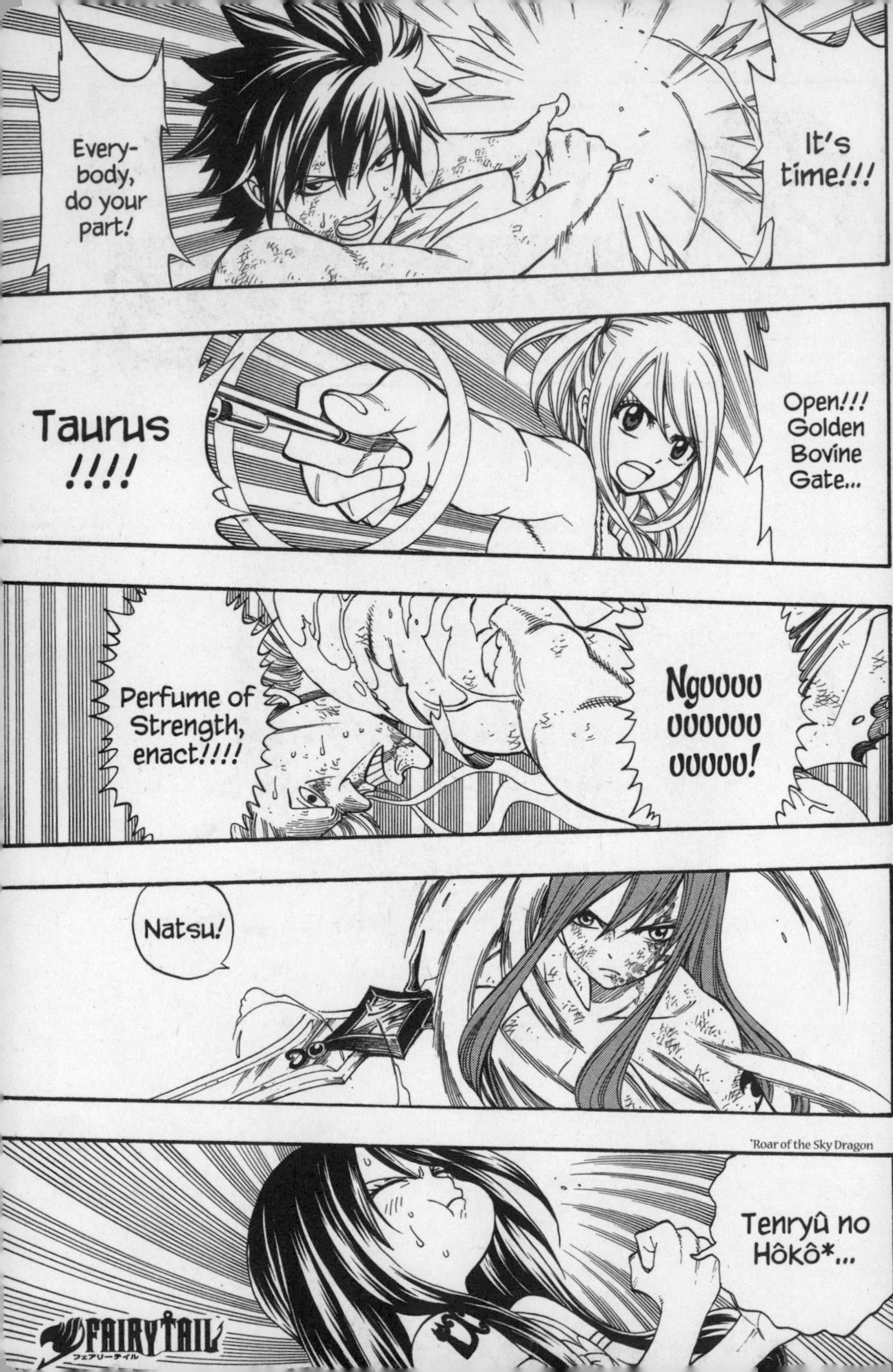
It's time!!!
Every-body, do your part!
Open!!! Golden Bovine Gate...
Taurus!!!!
Nguuuu uuuuuu uuuuu!
Perfume of Strength, enact!!!!
Natsu!
Tenryû no Hôkô*...

*Roar of the Sky Dragon

# Chapter 161, Fight for Right

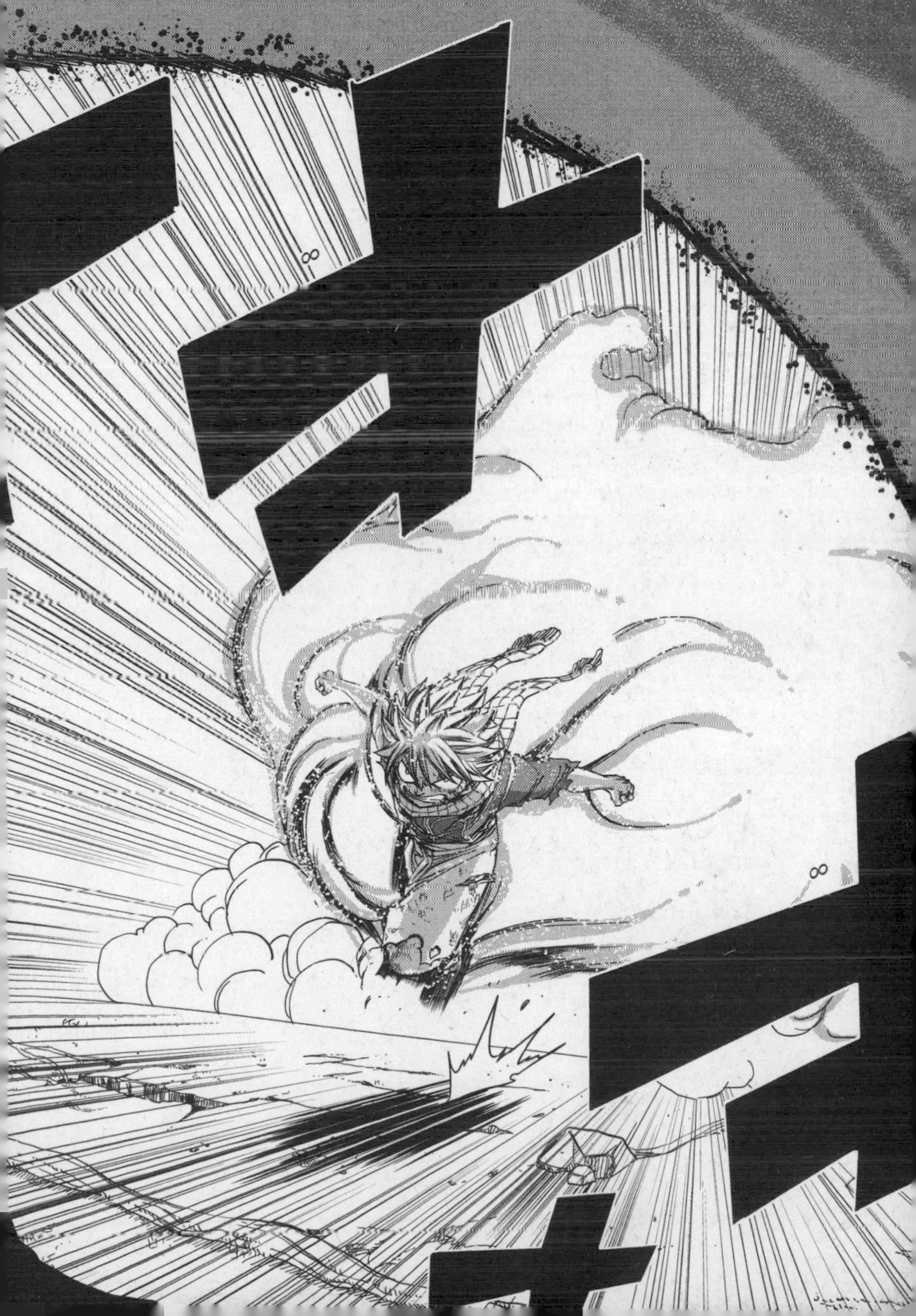

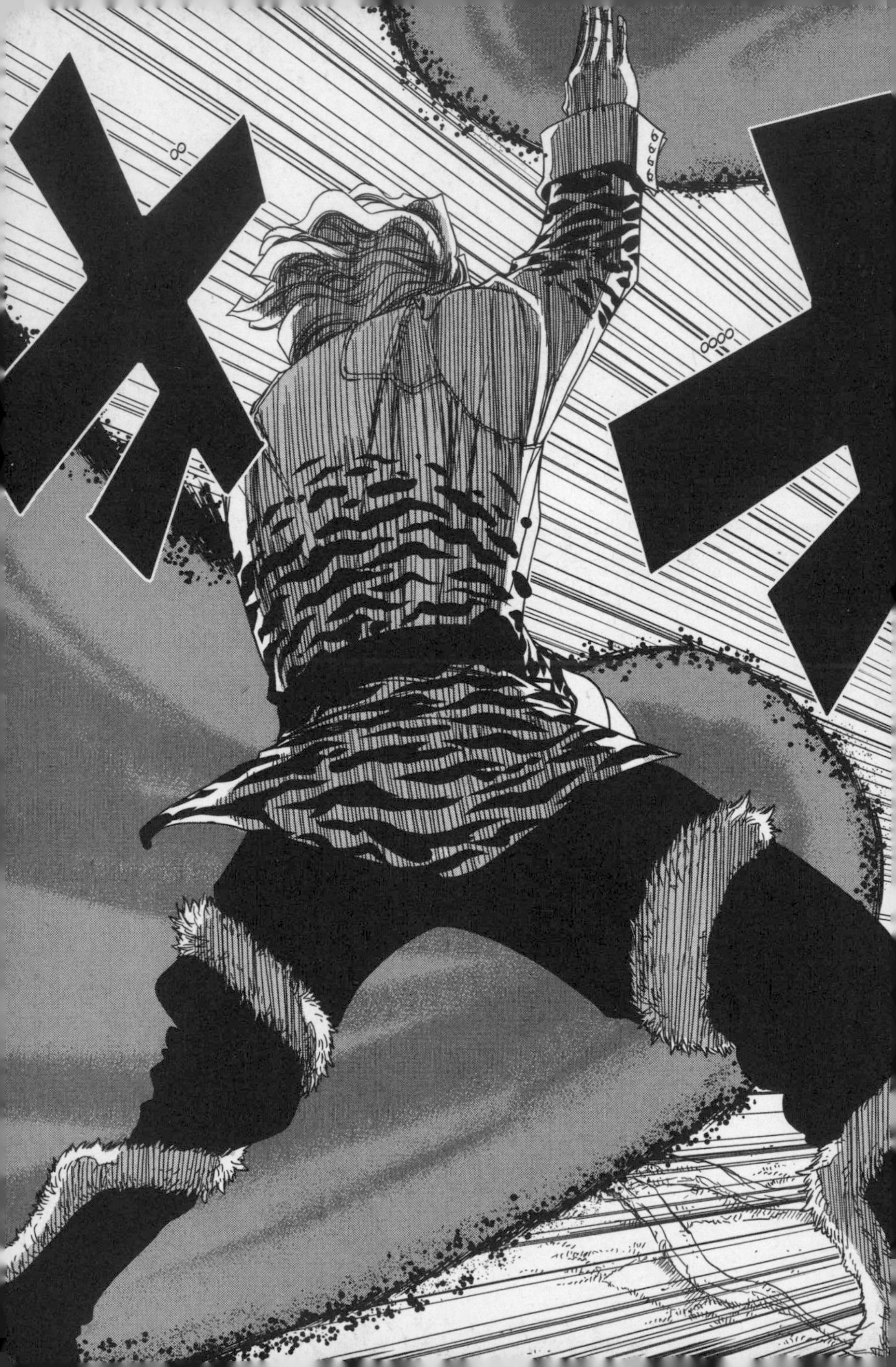

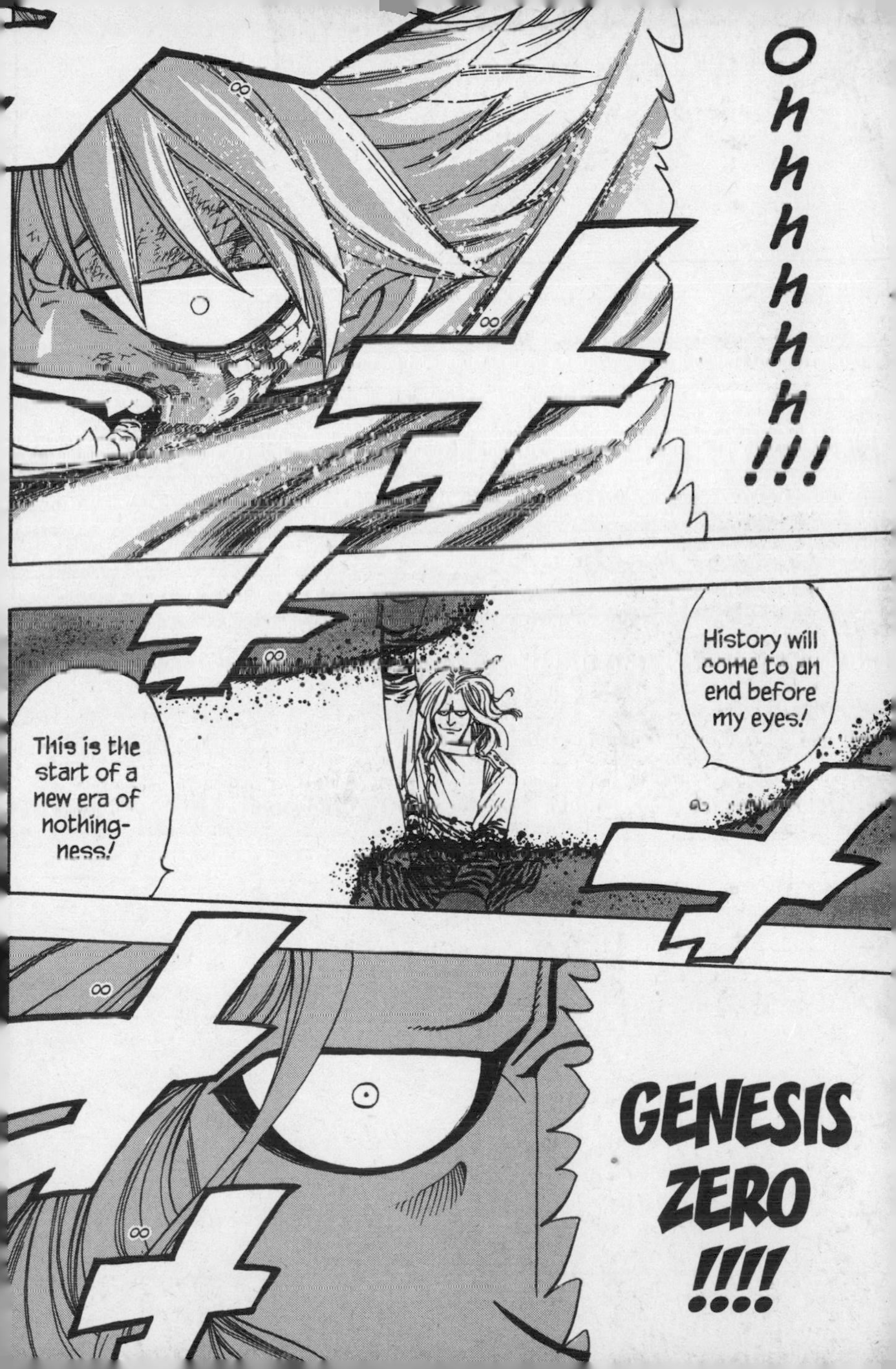
Ohhhhhh!!!
History will come to an end before my eyes!
This is the start of a new era of nothing-ness!
GENESIS ZERO!!!!

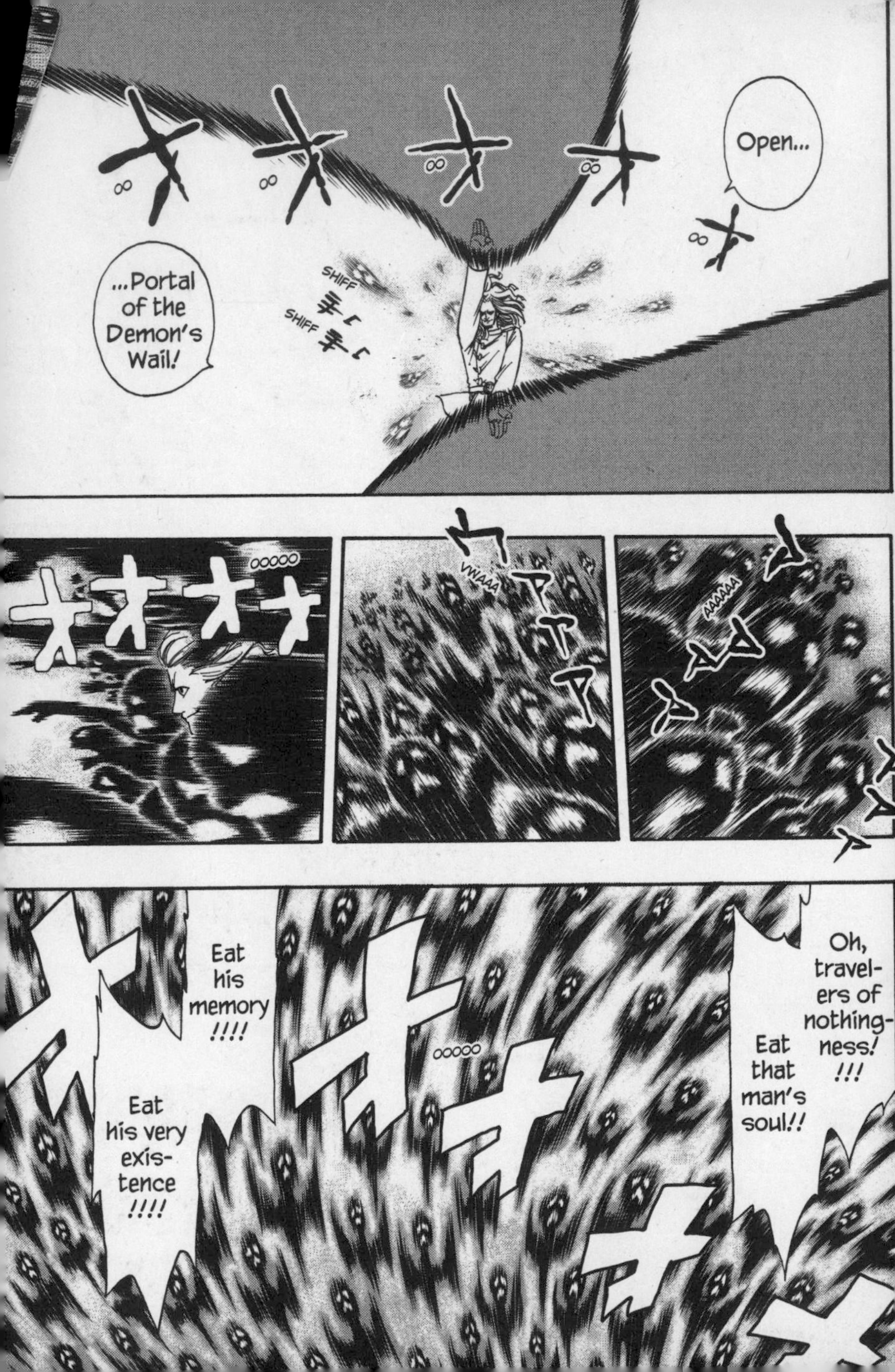
Open...
...Portal of the Demon's Wail!
SHIFF
SHIFF
AAAAAA
VWAAA
OOOOO
Oh, travelers of nothingness!!!
Eat that man's soul!!
OOOOO
Eat his memory!!!!
Eat his very existence!!!!

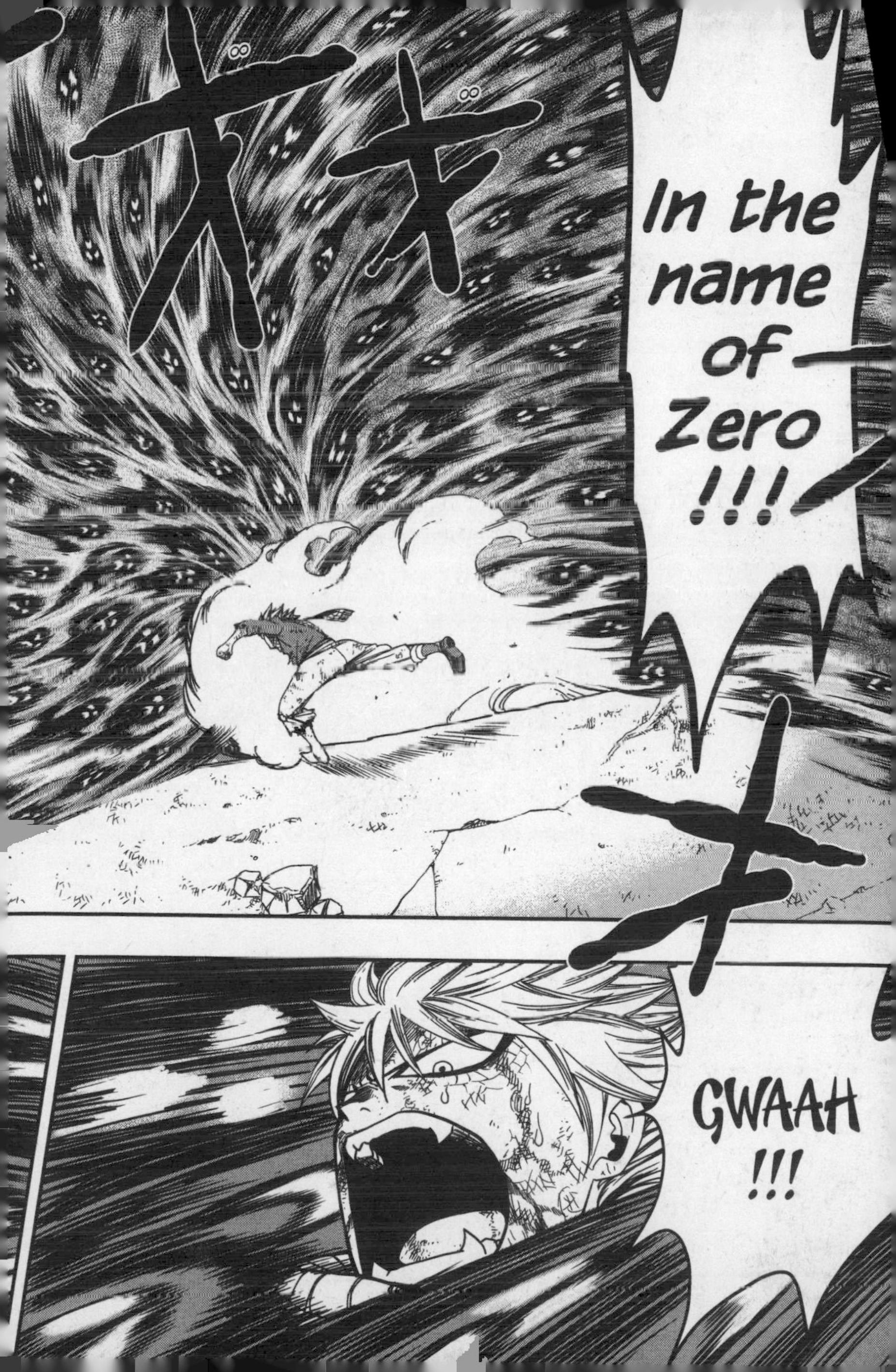
In the name of Zero!!!
GWAAH!!!

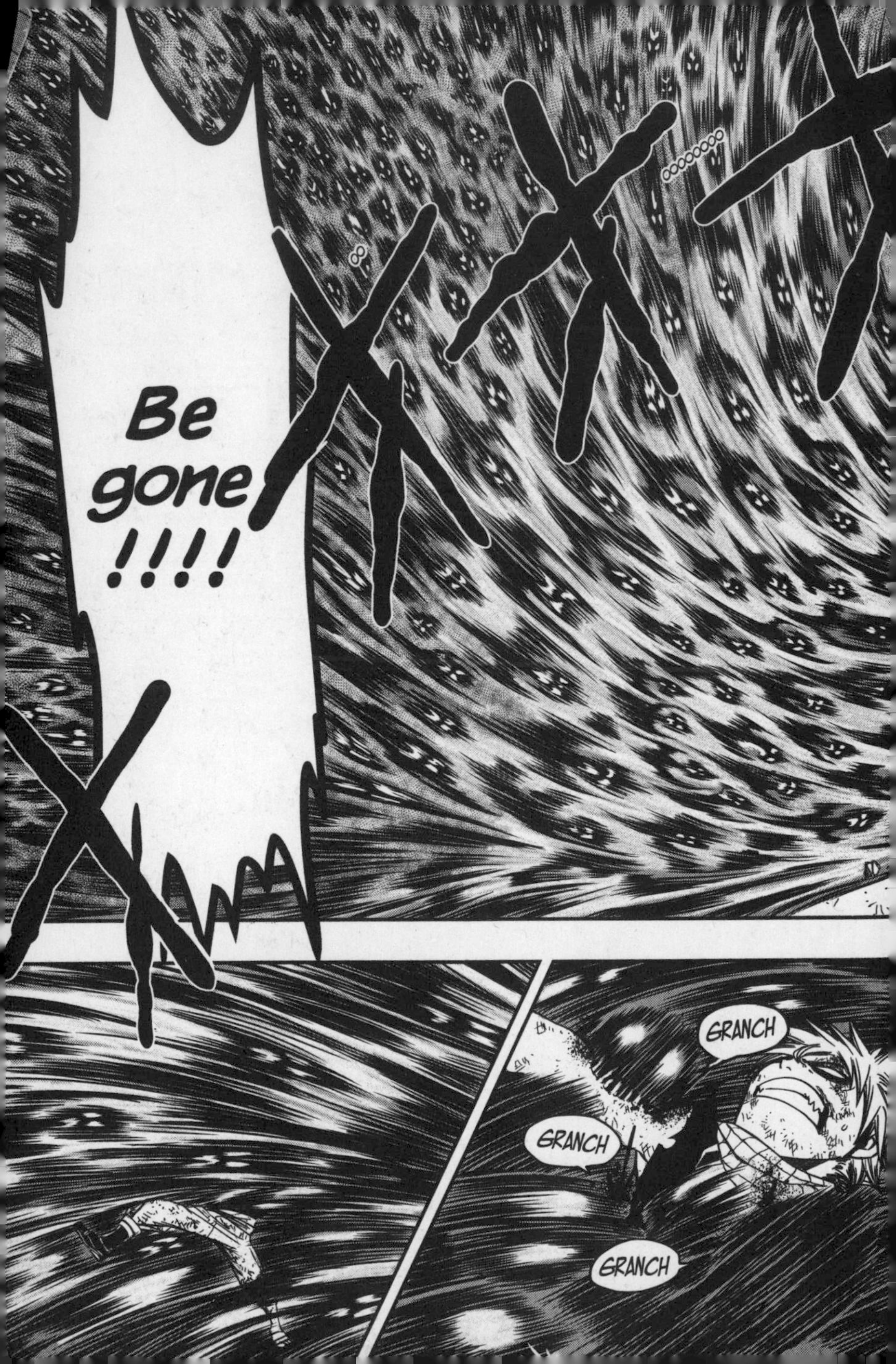
Be gone !!!!
GRANCH
GRANCH
GRANCH

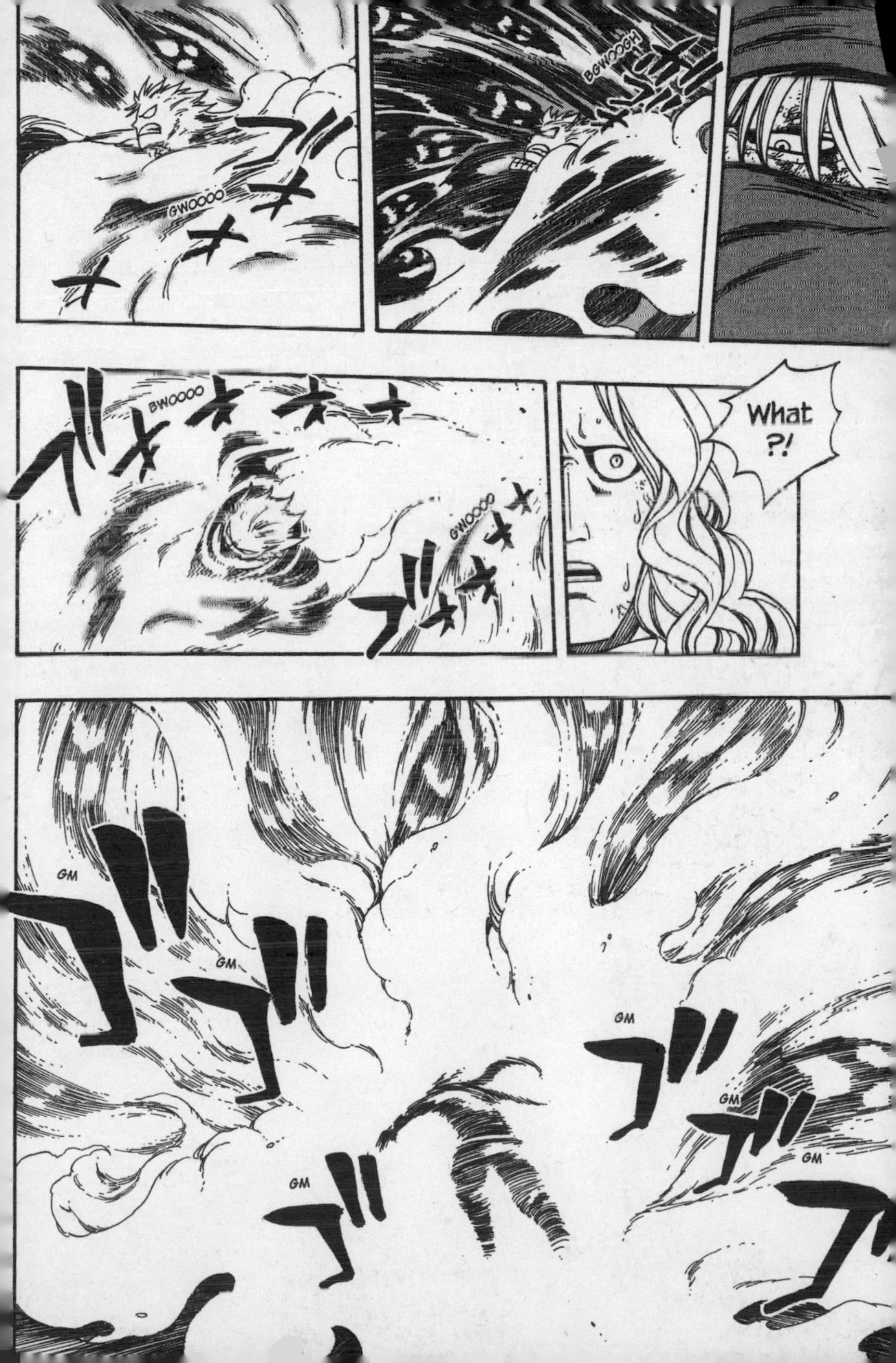
BGWOOGH
GWOOOO
What ?!
BWOOOO
GWOOOO
GM
GM
GM
GM
GM
GM

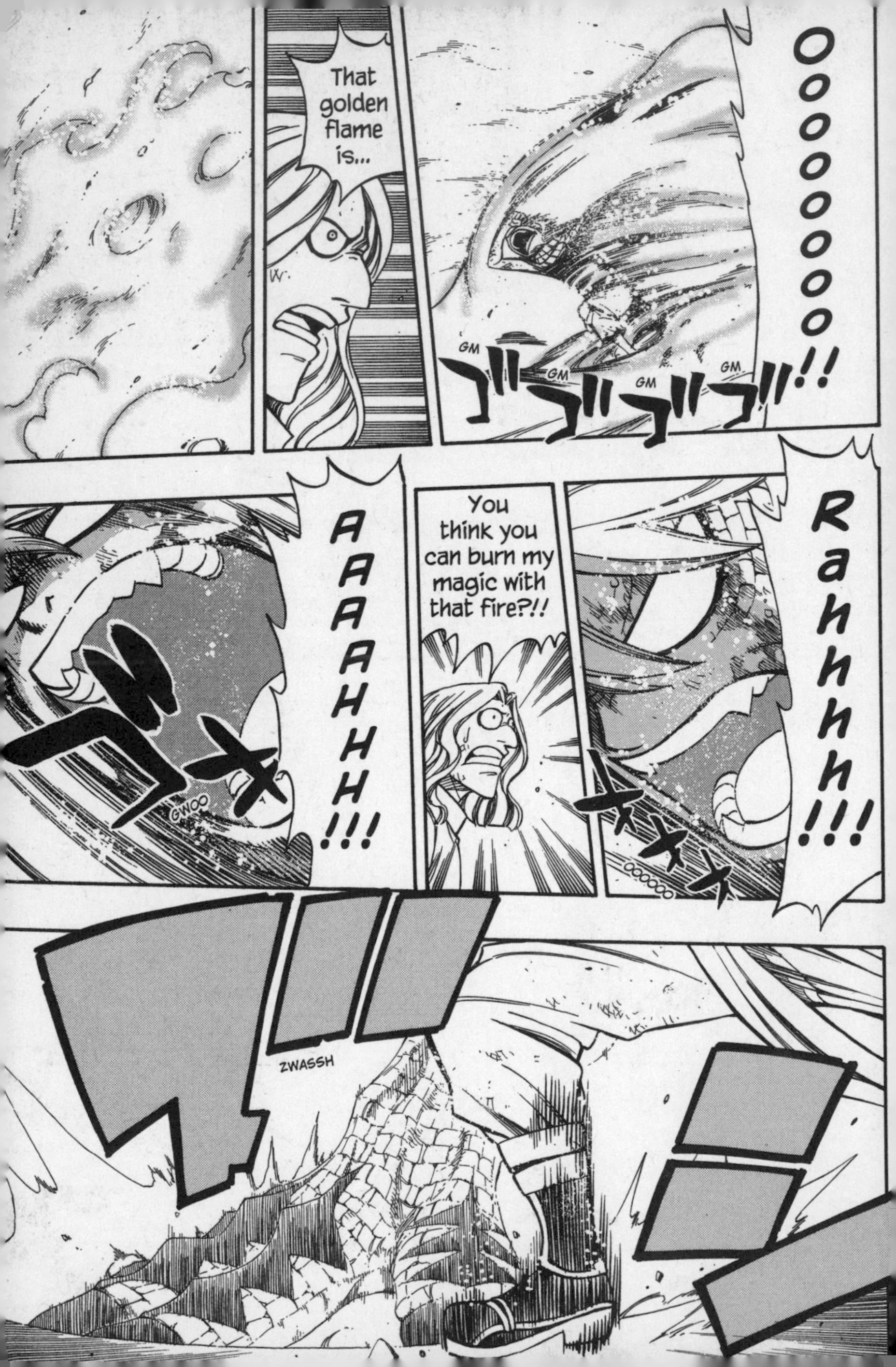

Oooooooooo!!
GM
GM
GM
GM
That golden flame is...
Rahhhhh!!!
OOOOOO
You think you can burn my magic with that fire?!!
AAAAHHH!!!
GWOO
ZWASSH

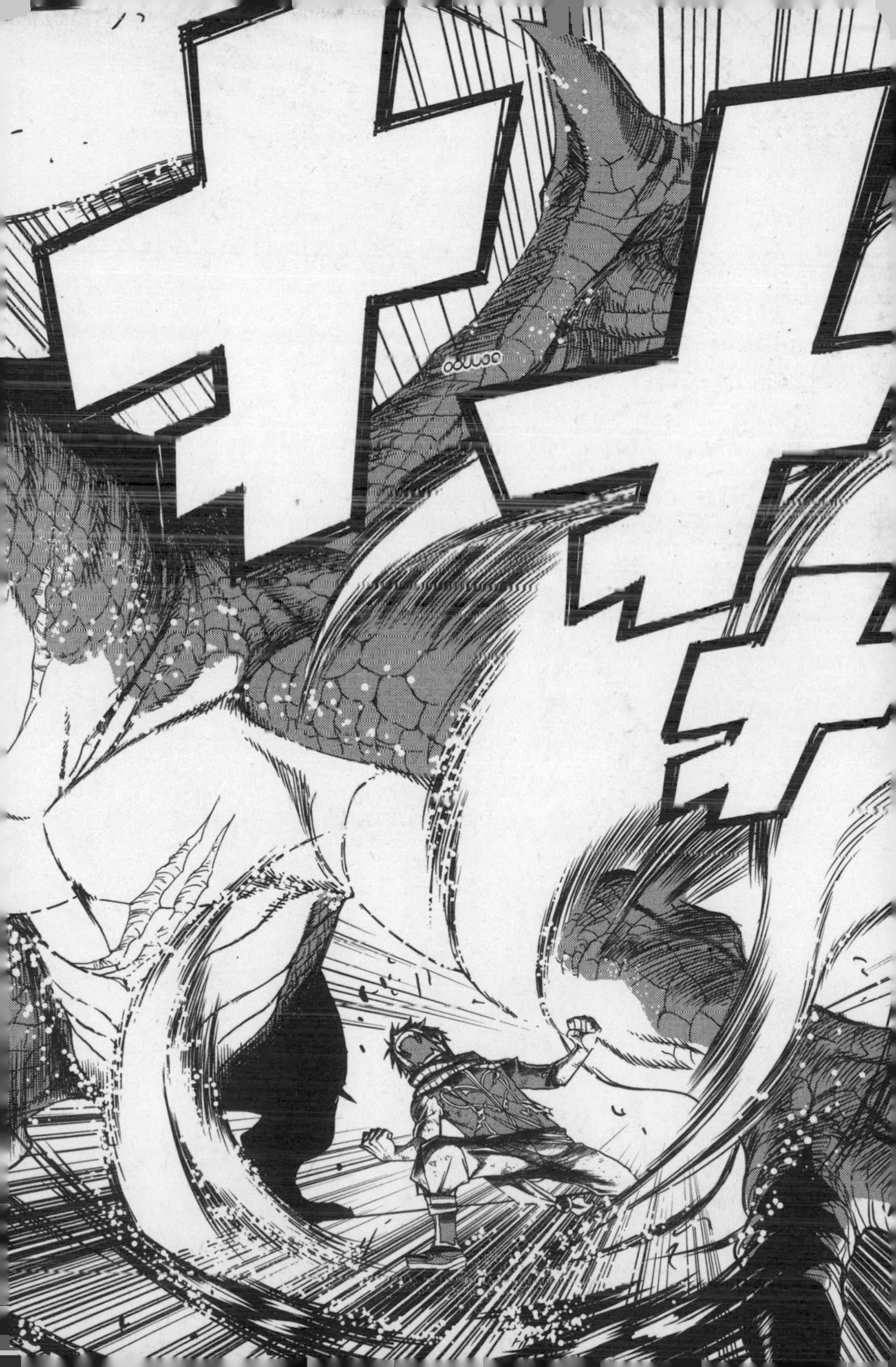

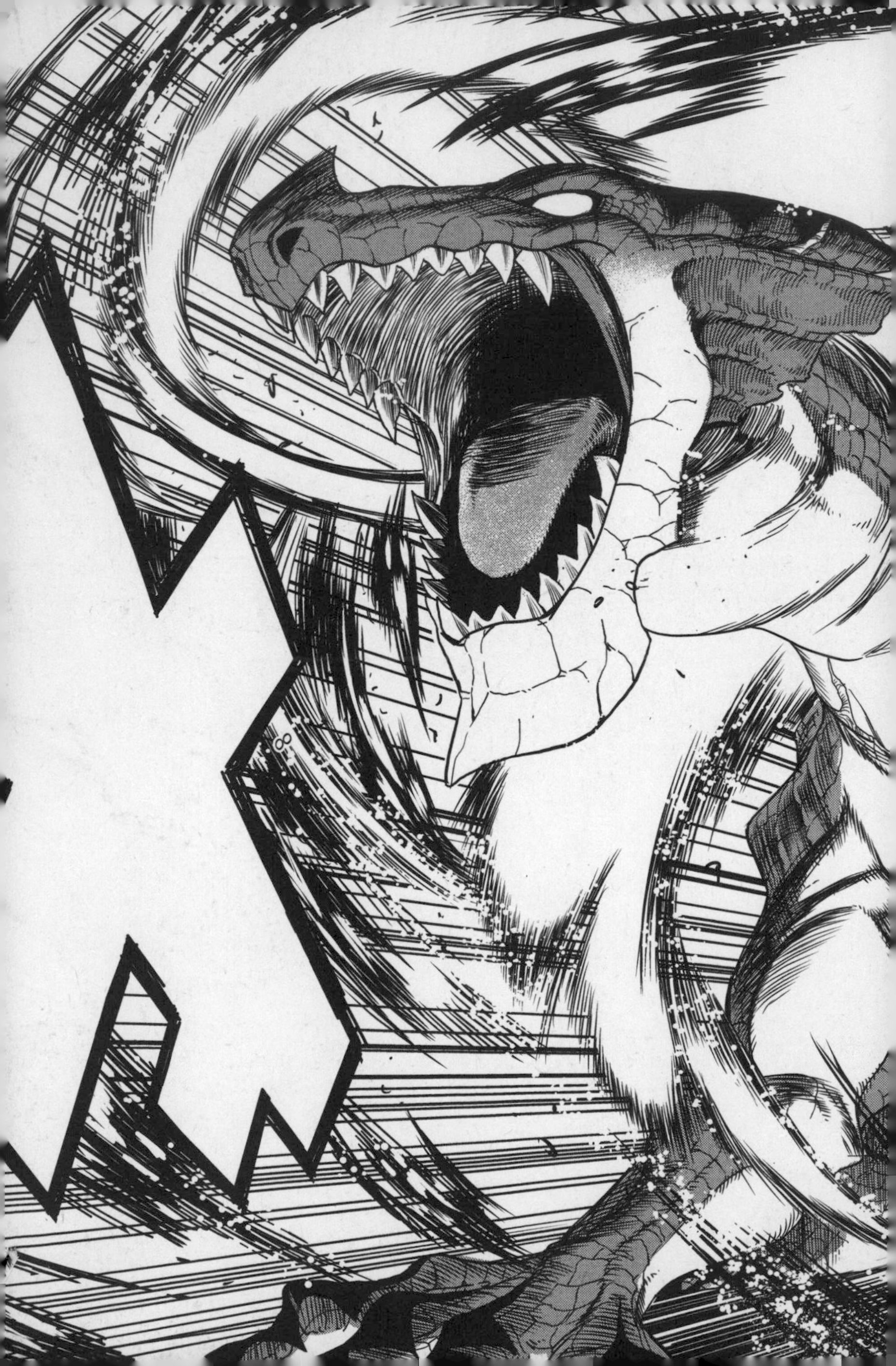

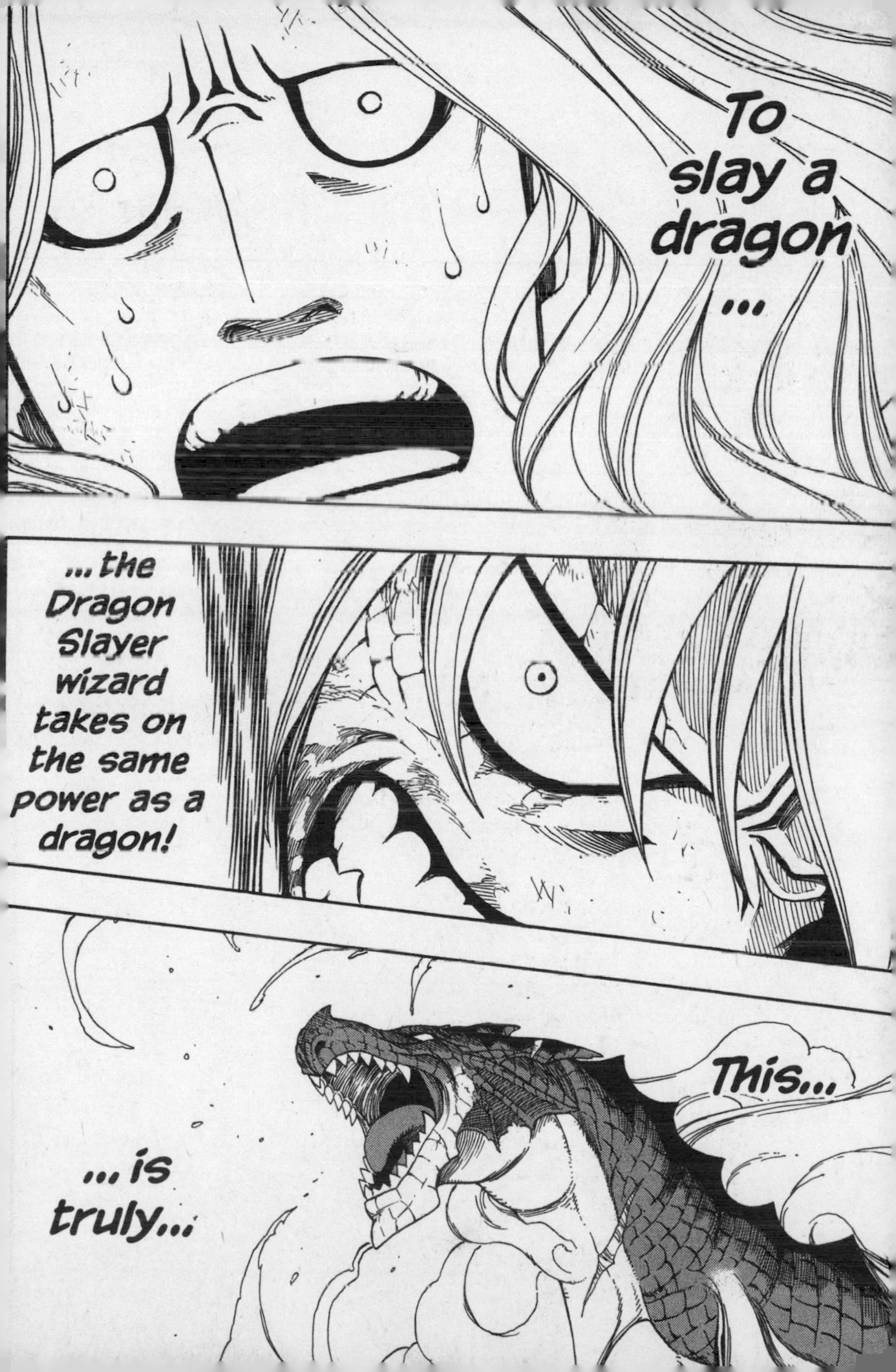
To slay a dragon ...
...the Dragon Slayer wizard takes on the same power as a dragon!
This...
...is truly...

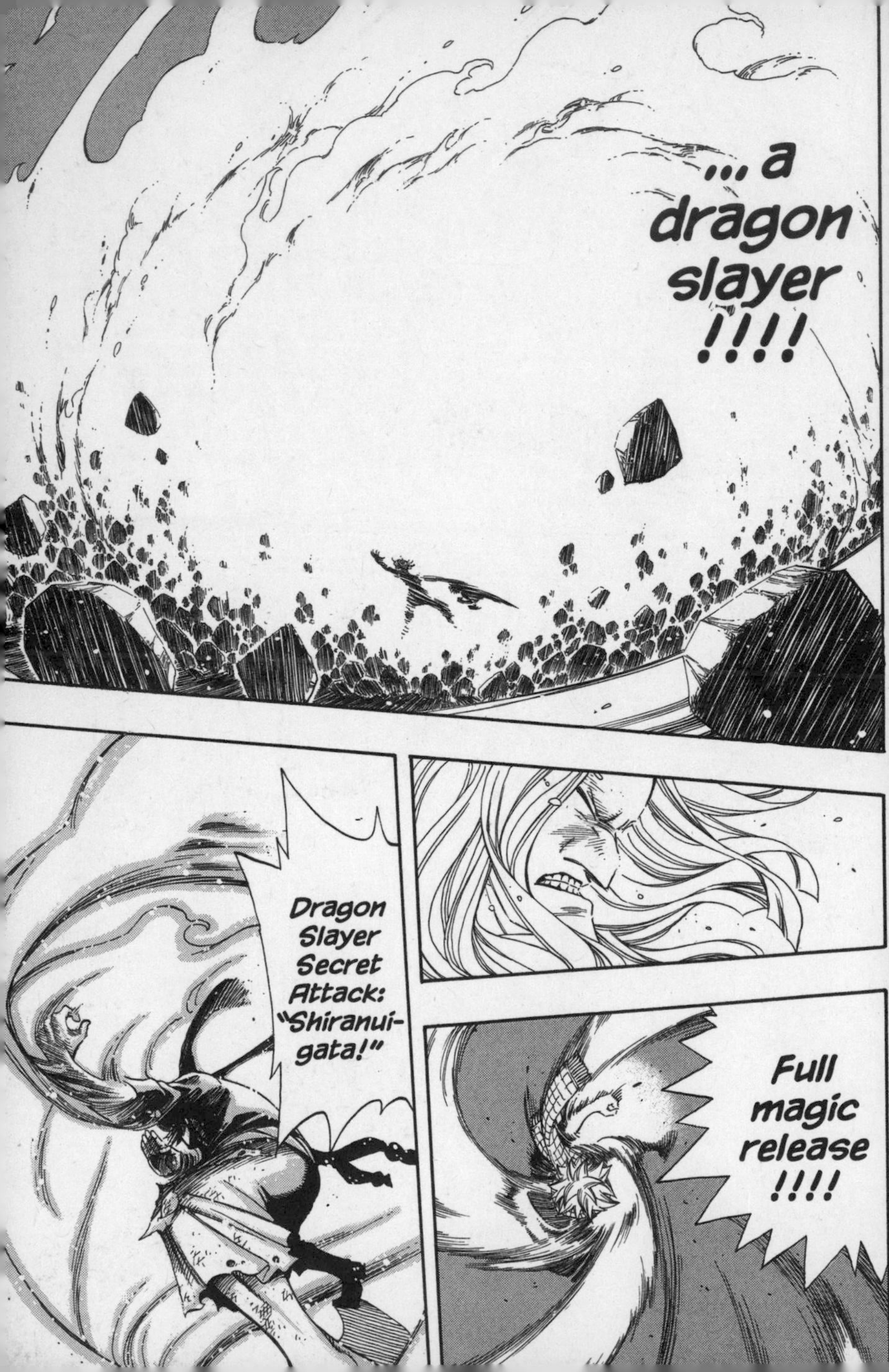
...a dragon slayer !!!!
Full magic release !!!!
Dragon Slayer Secret Attack: "Shiranui-gata!"

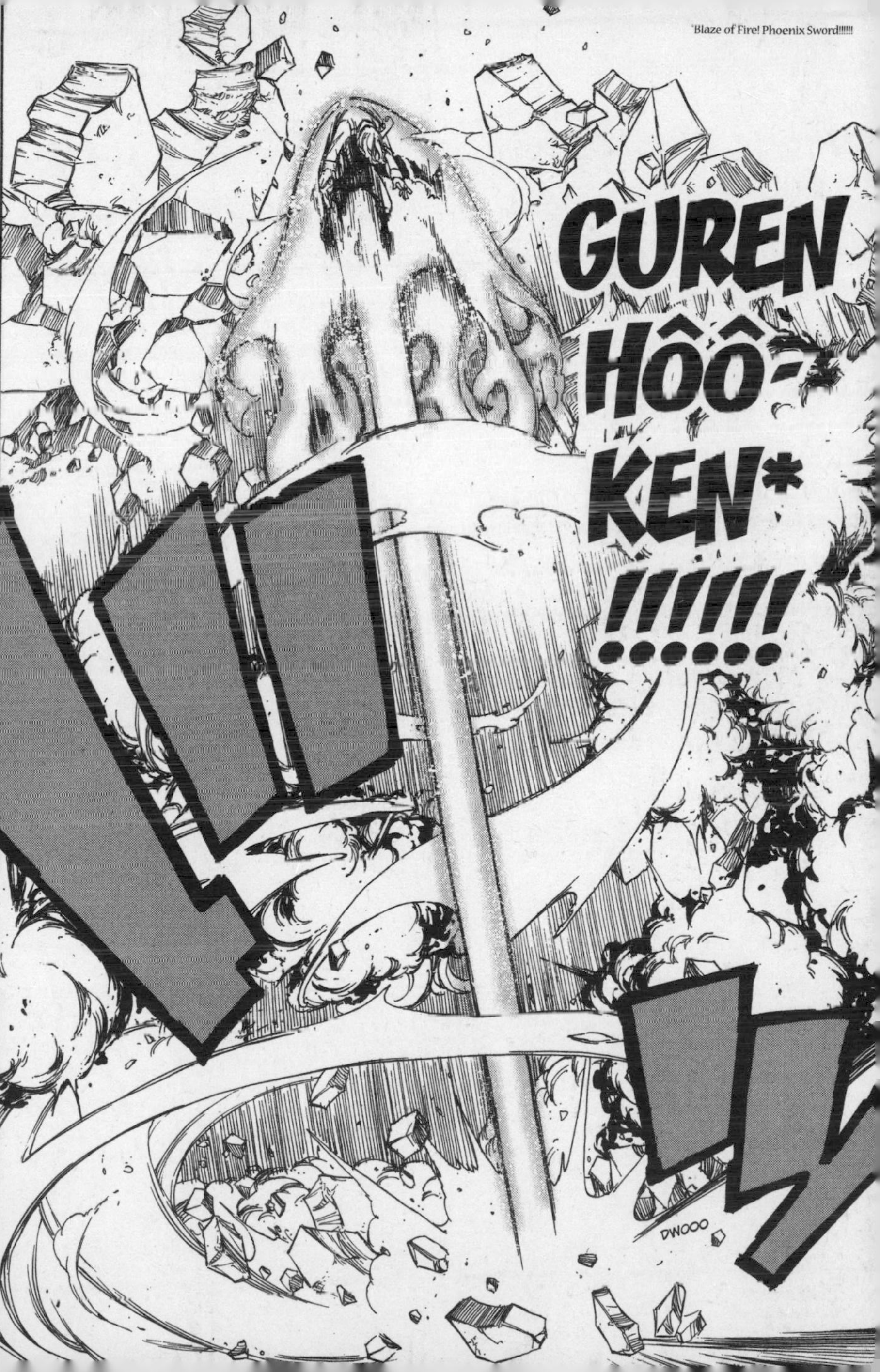
GUREN HÔÔ-KEN*!!!!!!!
DWOOO
*Blaze of Fire! Phoenix Sword!!!!!!

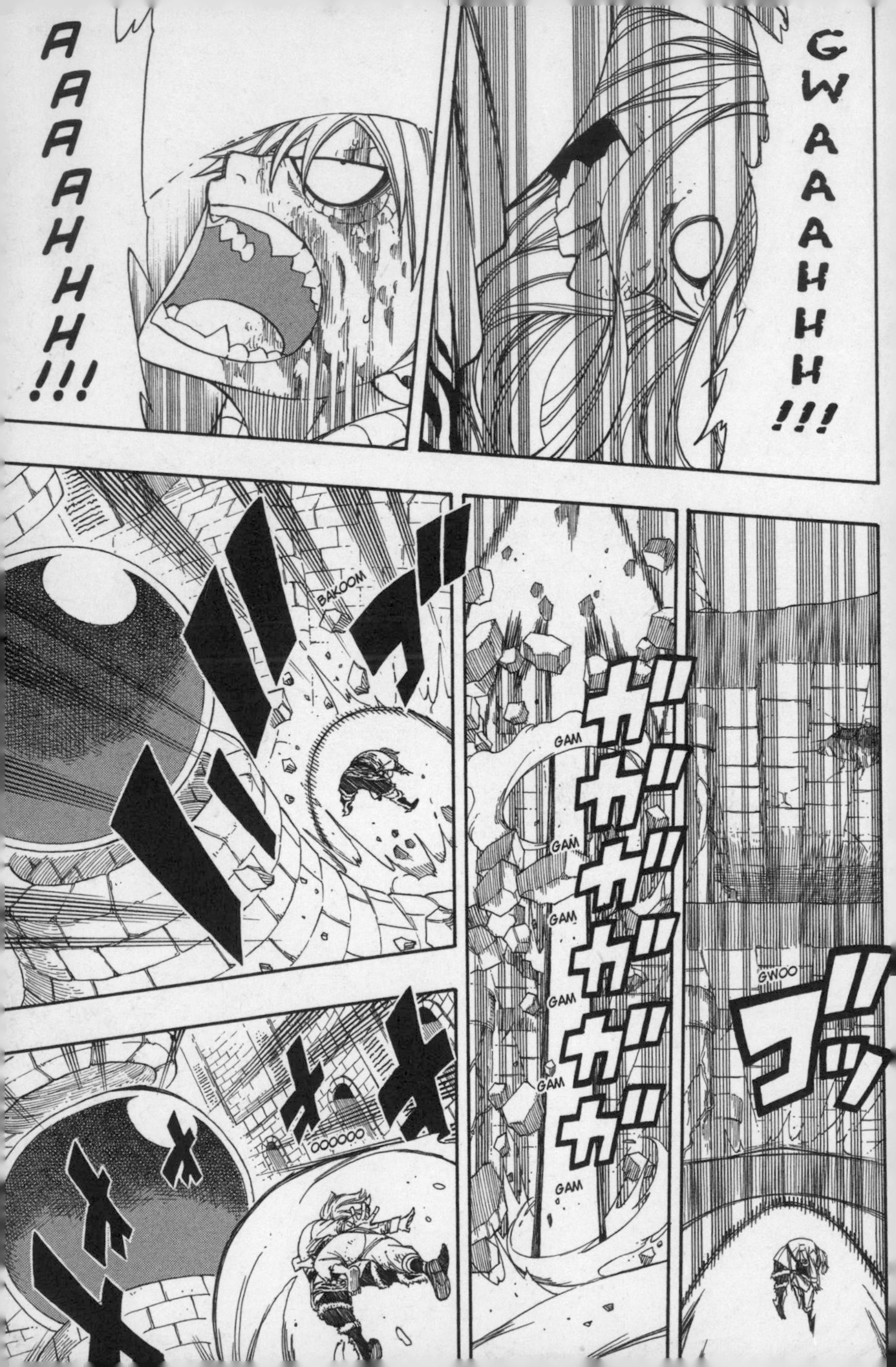
GWAAAHHH!!!
AAAAHHH!!!
GWOO
ゴッ
GAM
GAM
GAM
GAM
GAM
GAM
BAKOOM
OOOOOO

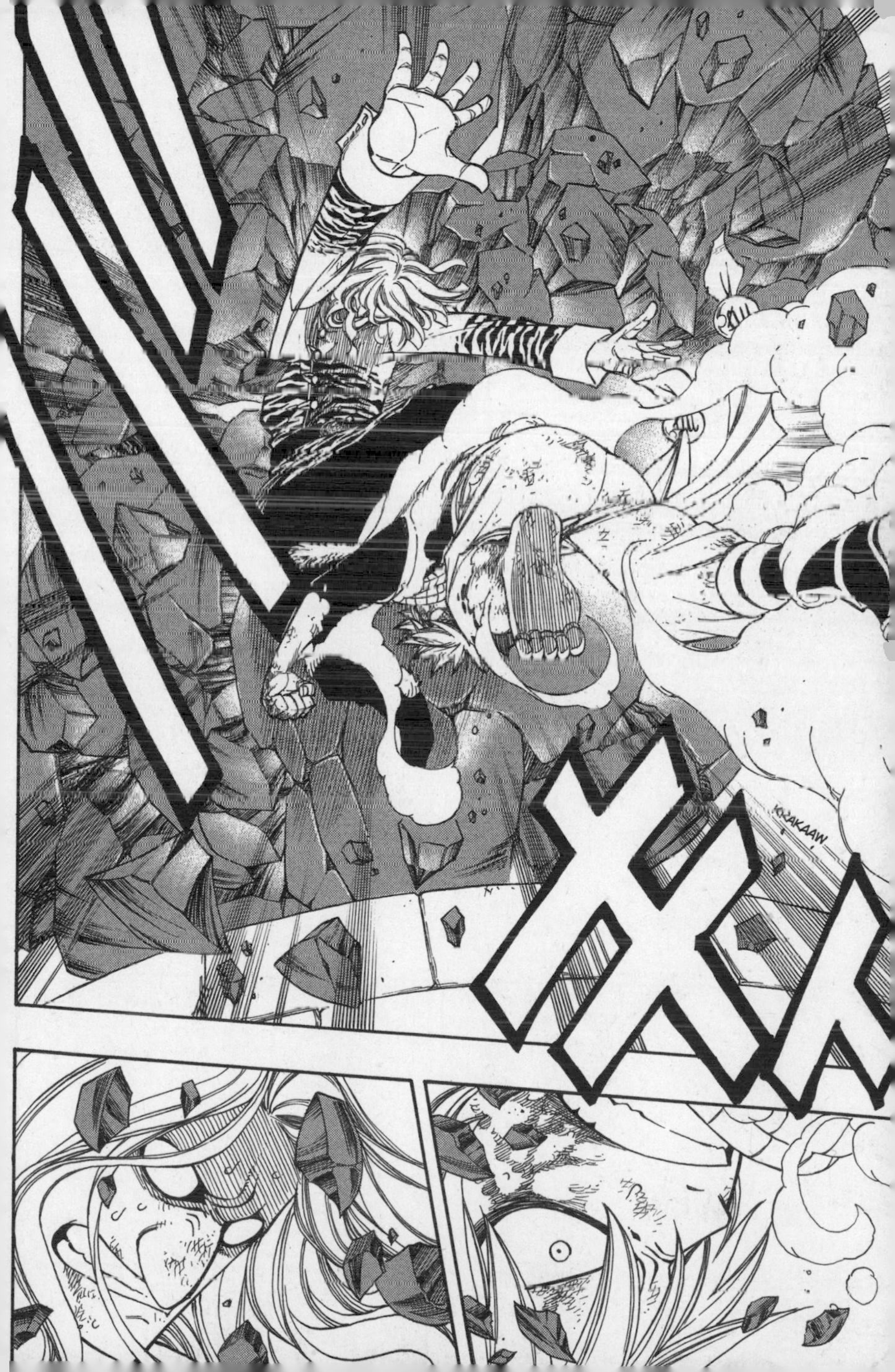
KRAKAAW

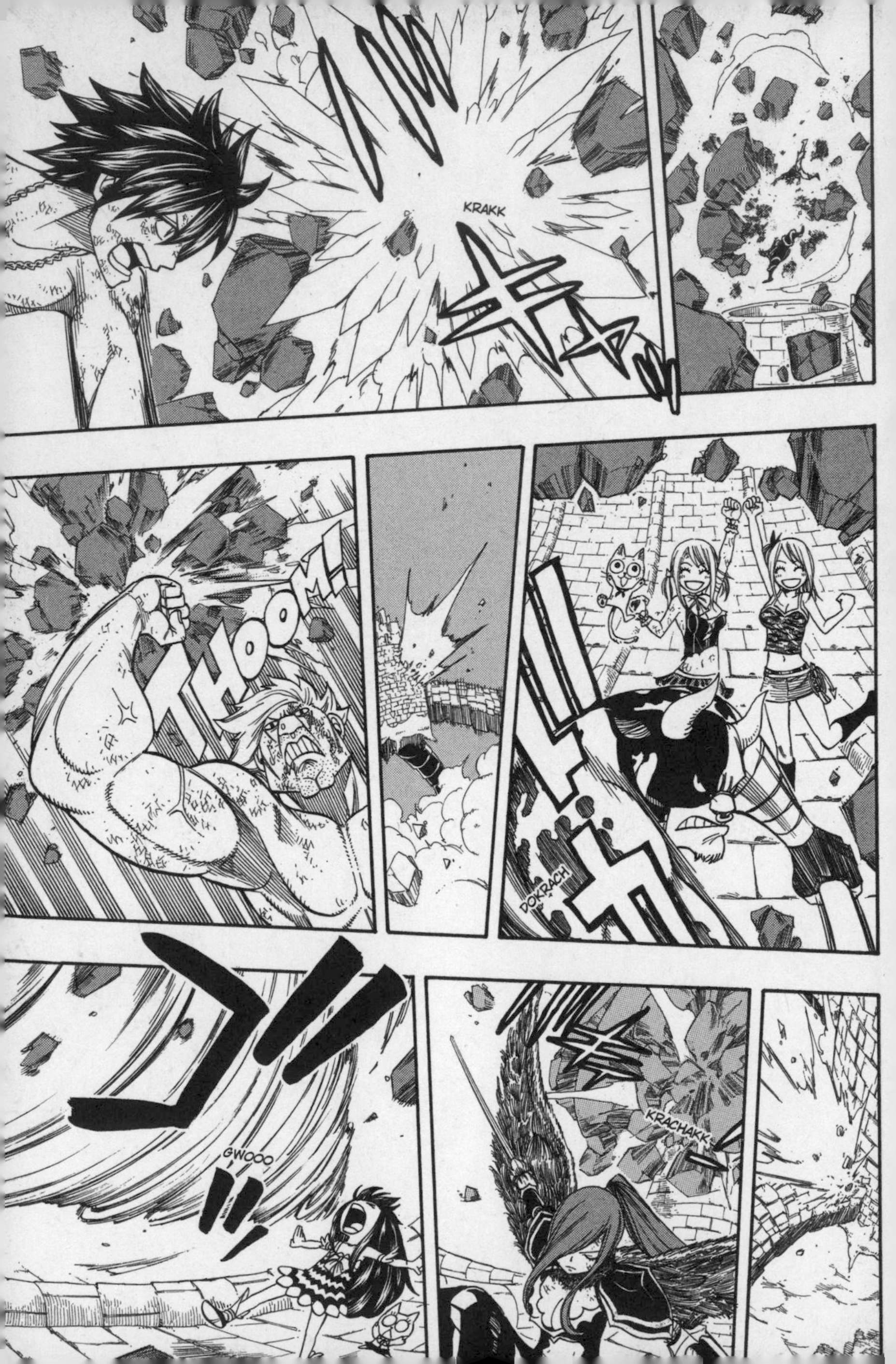
KRAKK
DOKRACH
THOOM!
KRACHAKK
GWOOO

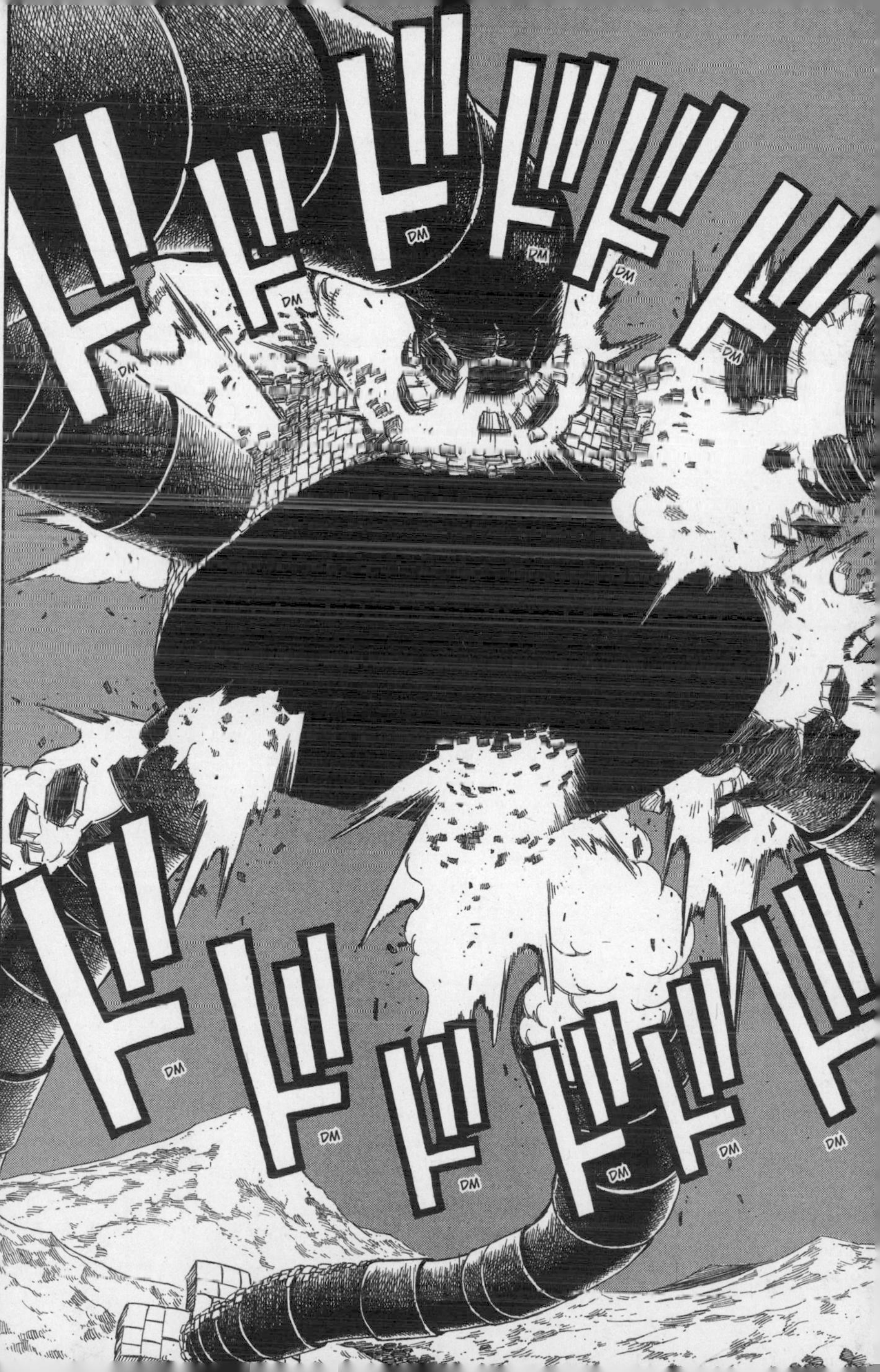

ドドドドドド
DM DM DM DM DM DM
ドドドドドド
DM DM DM DM DM DM

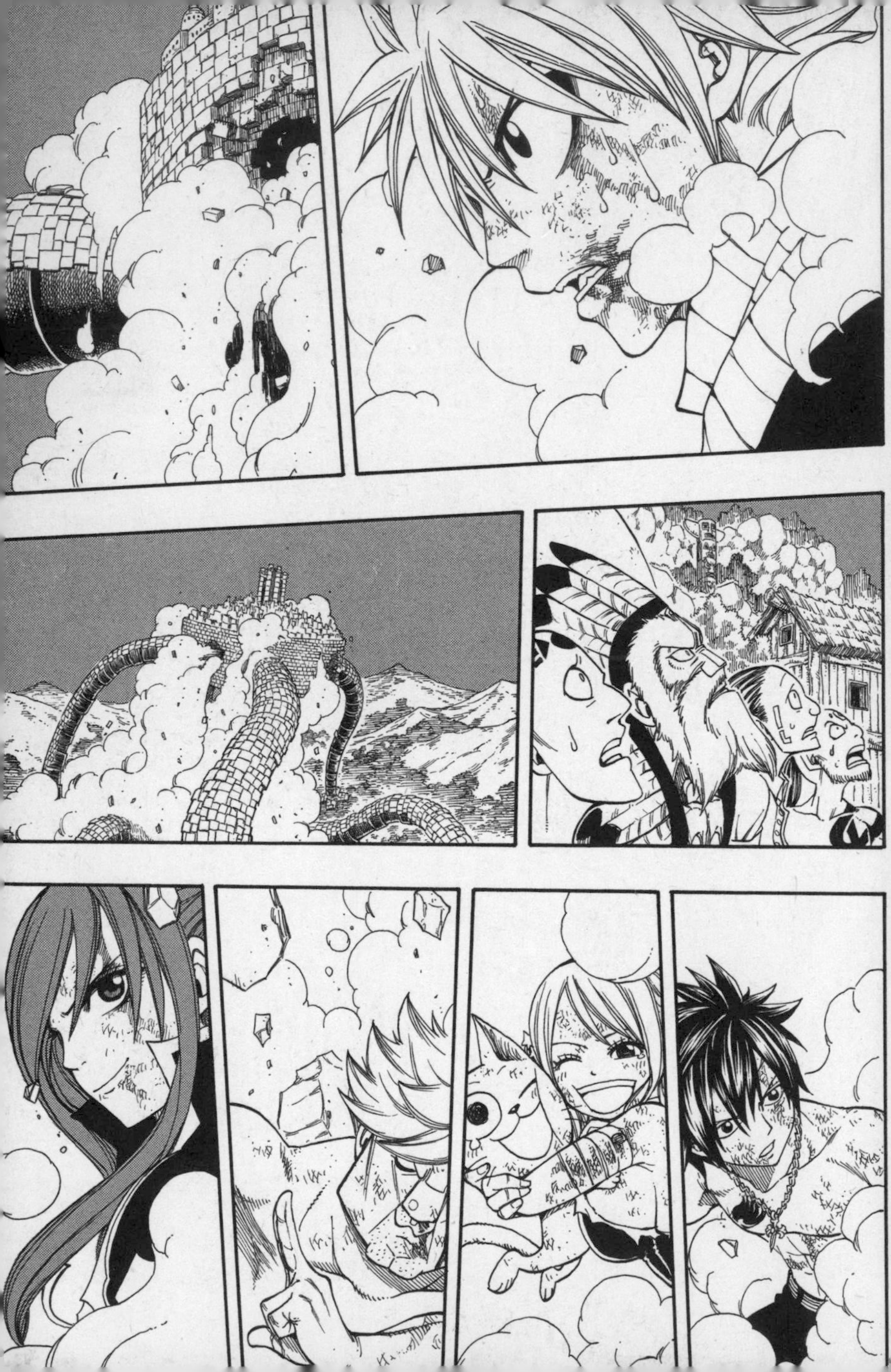

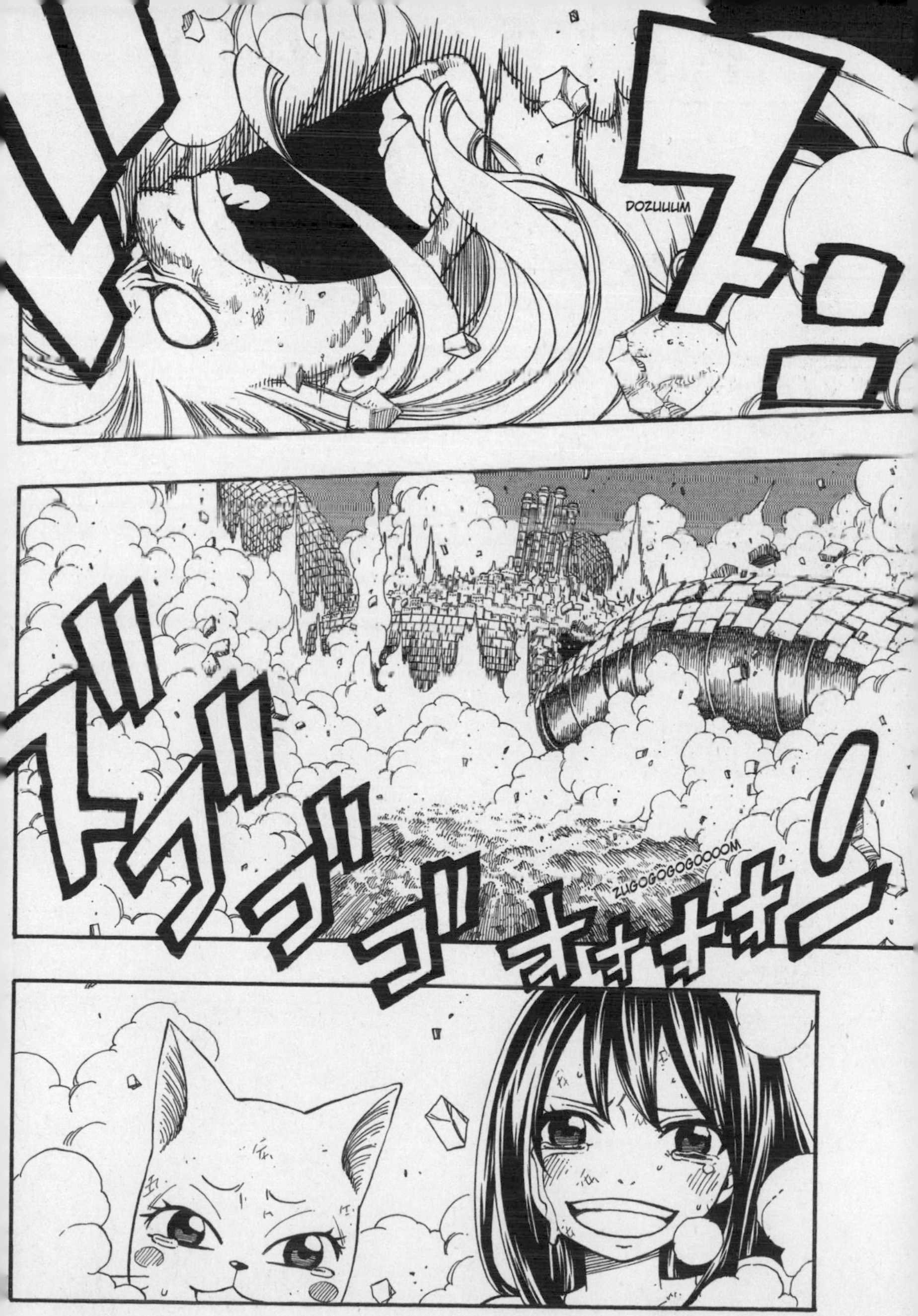
DOZUUUM
ZUGOGOGOGOOOOM

FAIRY TAIL

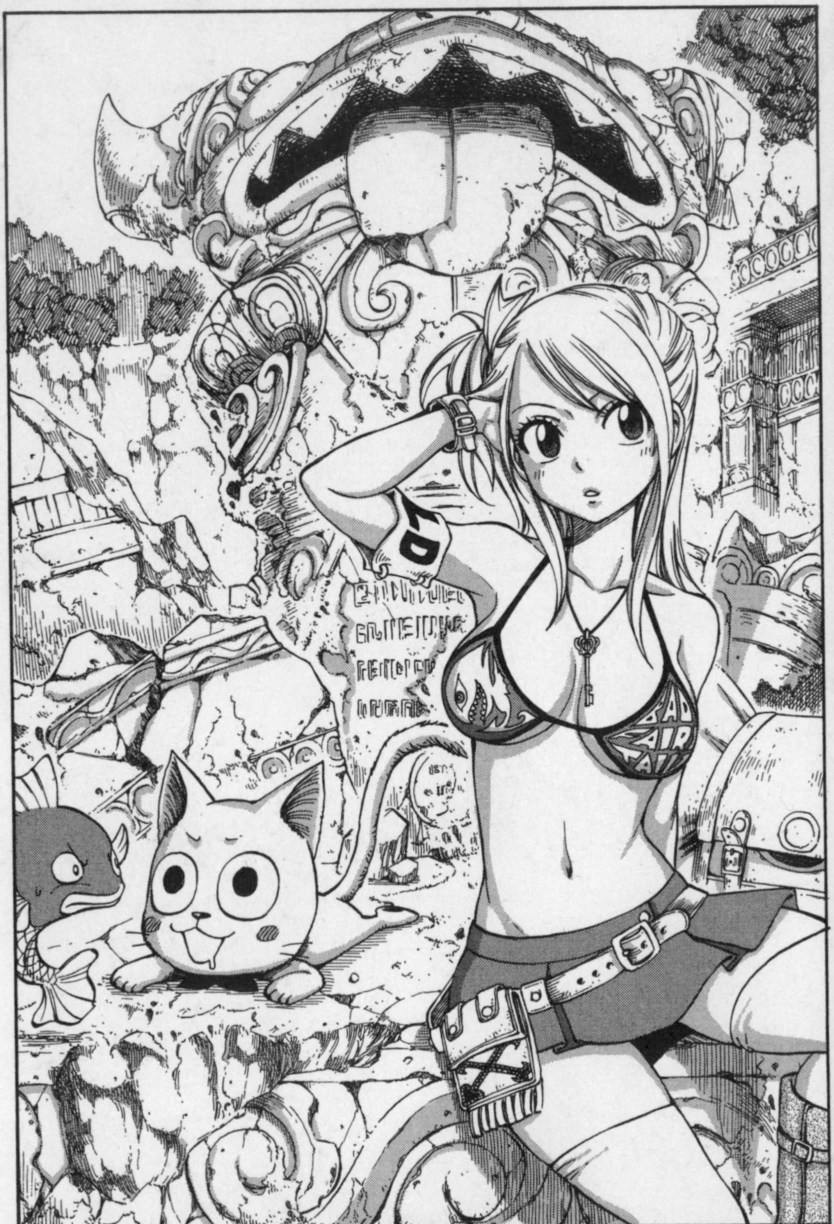

# Chapter 162, I'm by Your Side

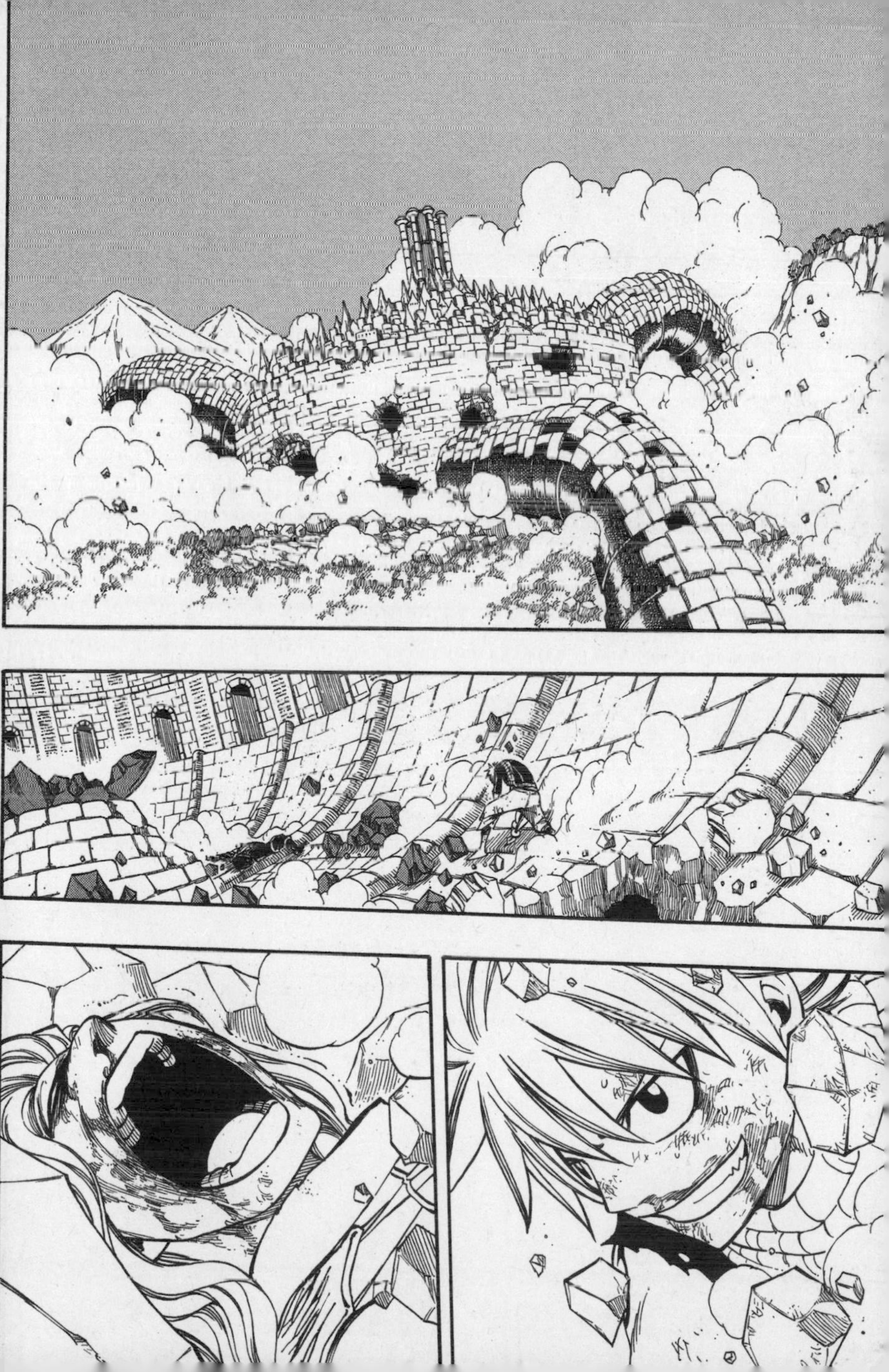

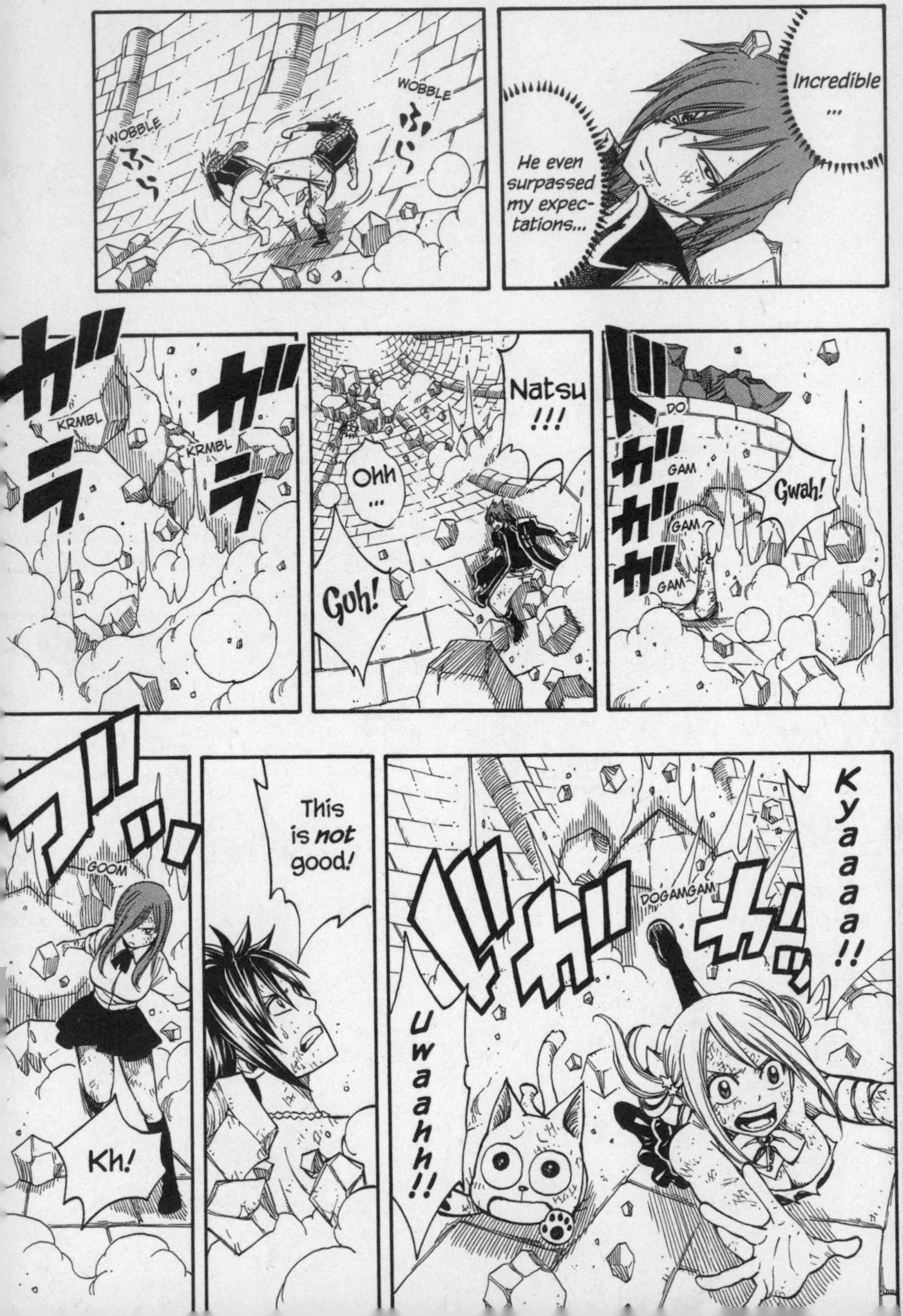

Incredible...
He even surpassed my expectations...
WOBBLE
ふら
WOBBLE
ふら
DO
GAM
GAM
GAM
Gwah!
Natsu!!!
Ohh...
Guh!
KRMBL
ガラ
KRMBL
ガラ
Kyaaaa!!
DOGAMGAM
Uwaahh!!
This is *not* good!
GOOM
Kh!

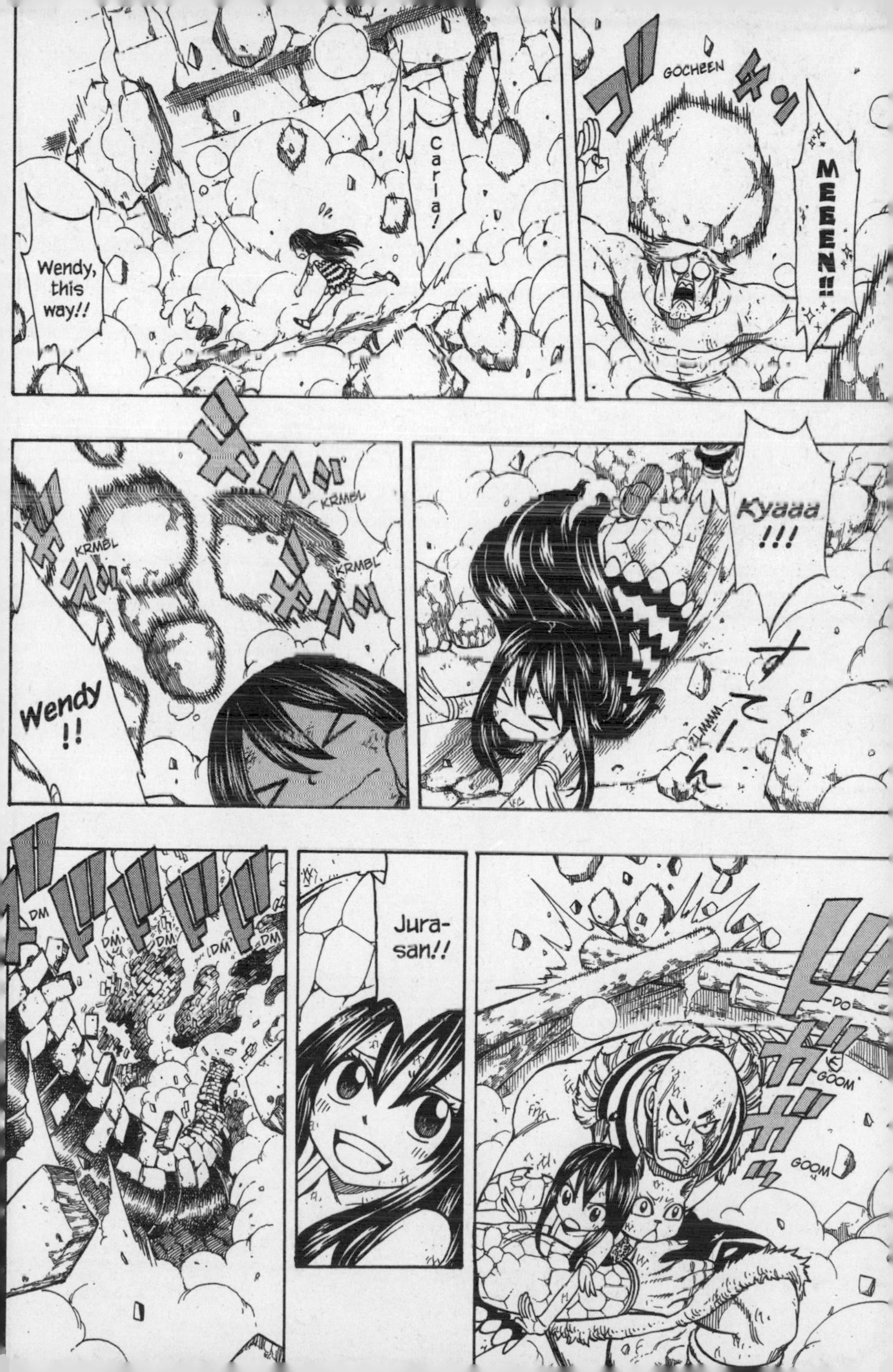

GOCHEEN
MEEEN!!
Carla!
Wendy, this way!!
Kyaaa !!!
すてーん
KRMBL
KRMBL
KRMBL
Wendy !!
DO
GOOM
GOOM
Jura-san!!
DM
DM
DM
DM
DM

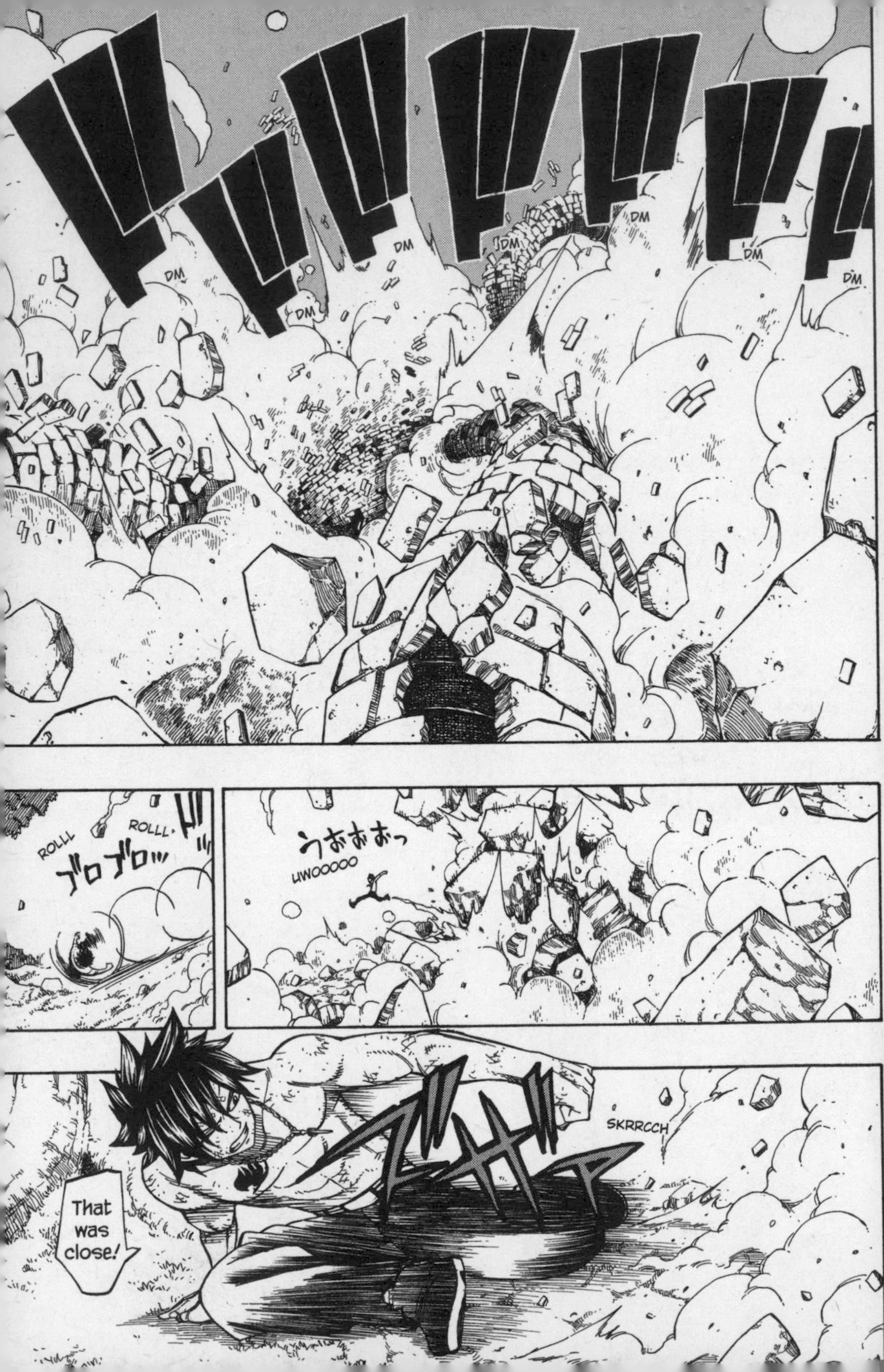
DM
DM
DM
DM
DM
DM
DM
DM
うおおおっ
UWOOOOO
ROLLL
ROLLL
ゴロゴロッ
SKRRCH
That was close!

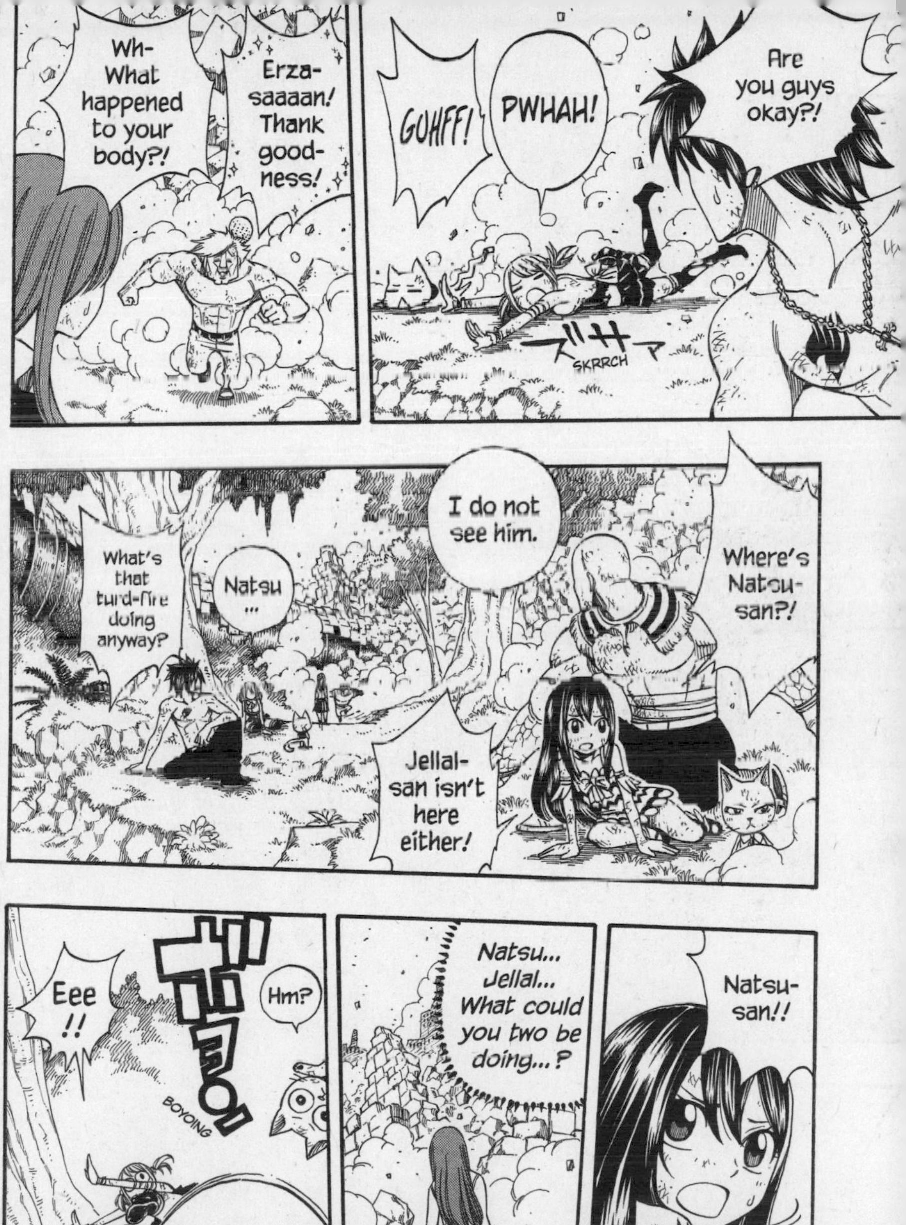
Are you guys okay?!
PWHAH!
GUHFF!
SKRRCH
Erza-saaaan! Thank goodness!
Wh-What happened to your body?!
Where's Natsu-san?!
I do not see him.
Jellal-san isn't here either!
Natsu ...
What's that turd-fire doing anyway?
Natsu-san!!
Natsu... Jellal... What could you two be doing...?
Hm?
Eee !!
BOYOING

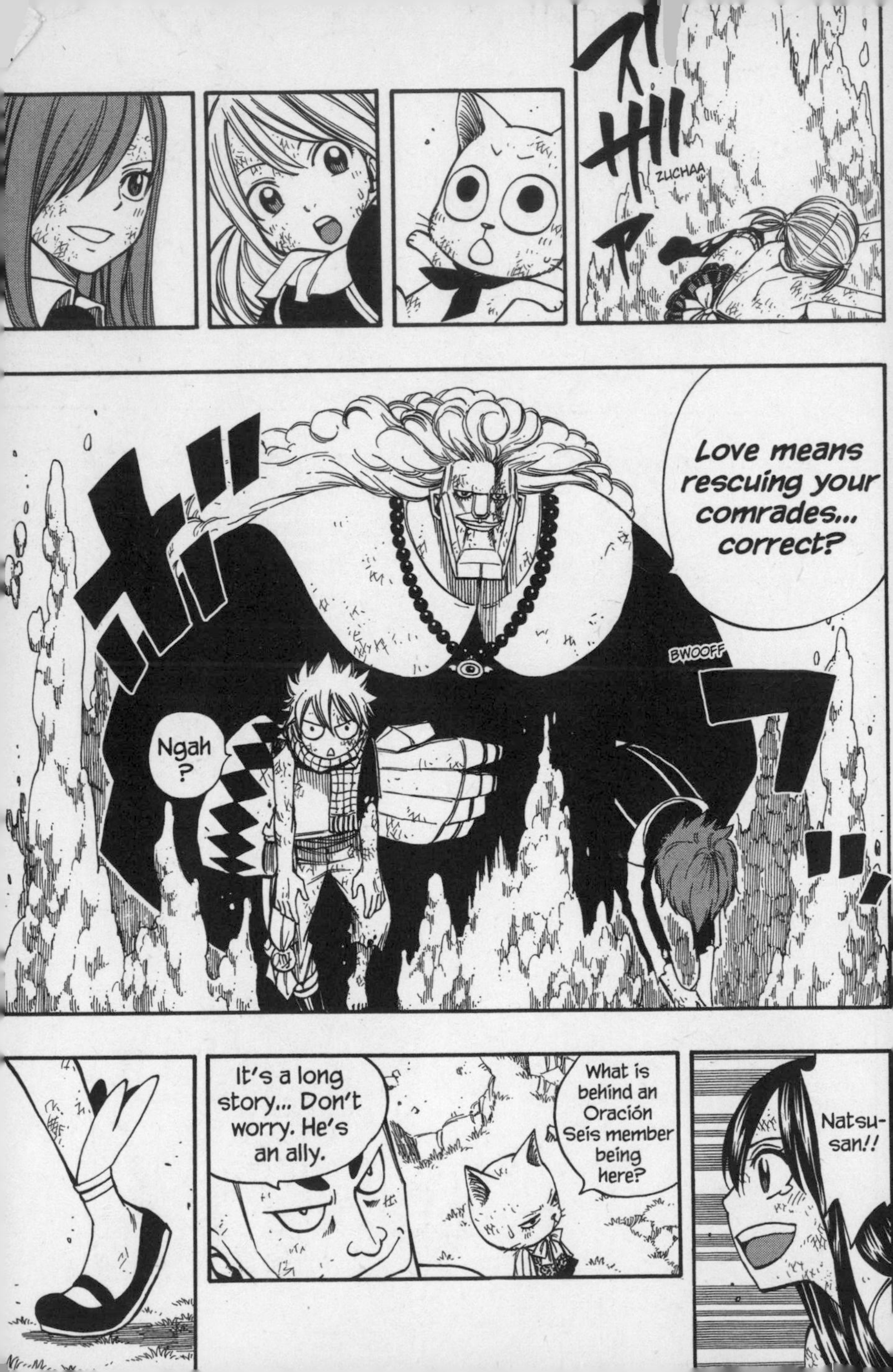
ZUCHAA
Love means rescuing your comrades... correct?
BWOOFF
Ngah?
Natsu-san!!
What is behind an Oración Seis member being here?
It's a long story... Don't worry. He's an ally.

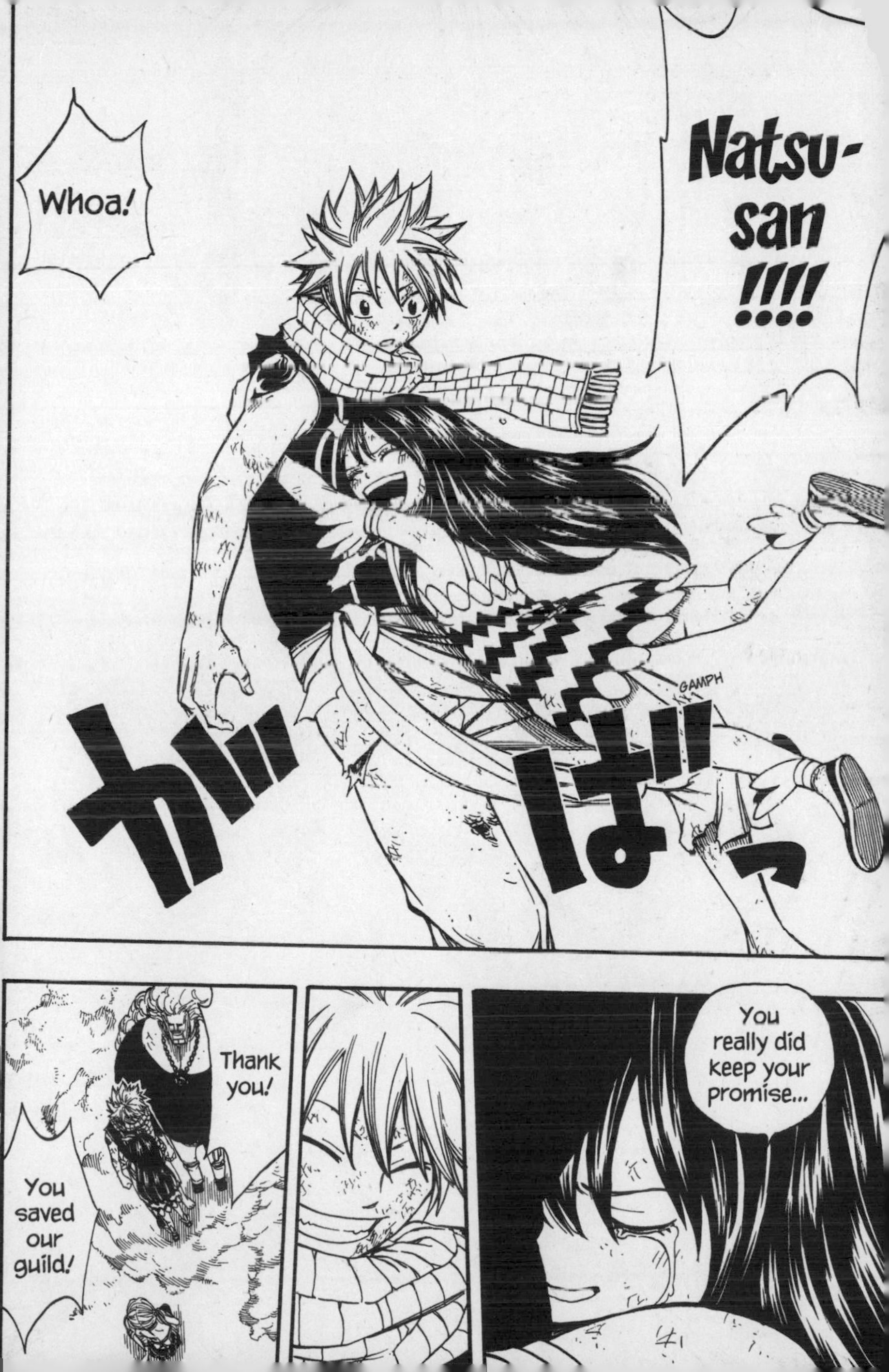

Natsu-san!!!!
Whoa!
GAMPH
ガばっ
You really did keep your promise...
Thank you!
You saved our guild!

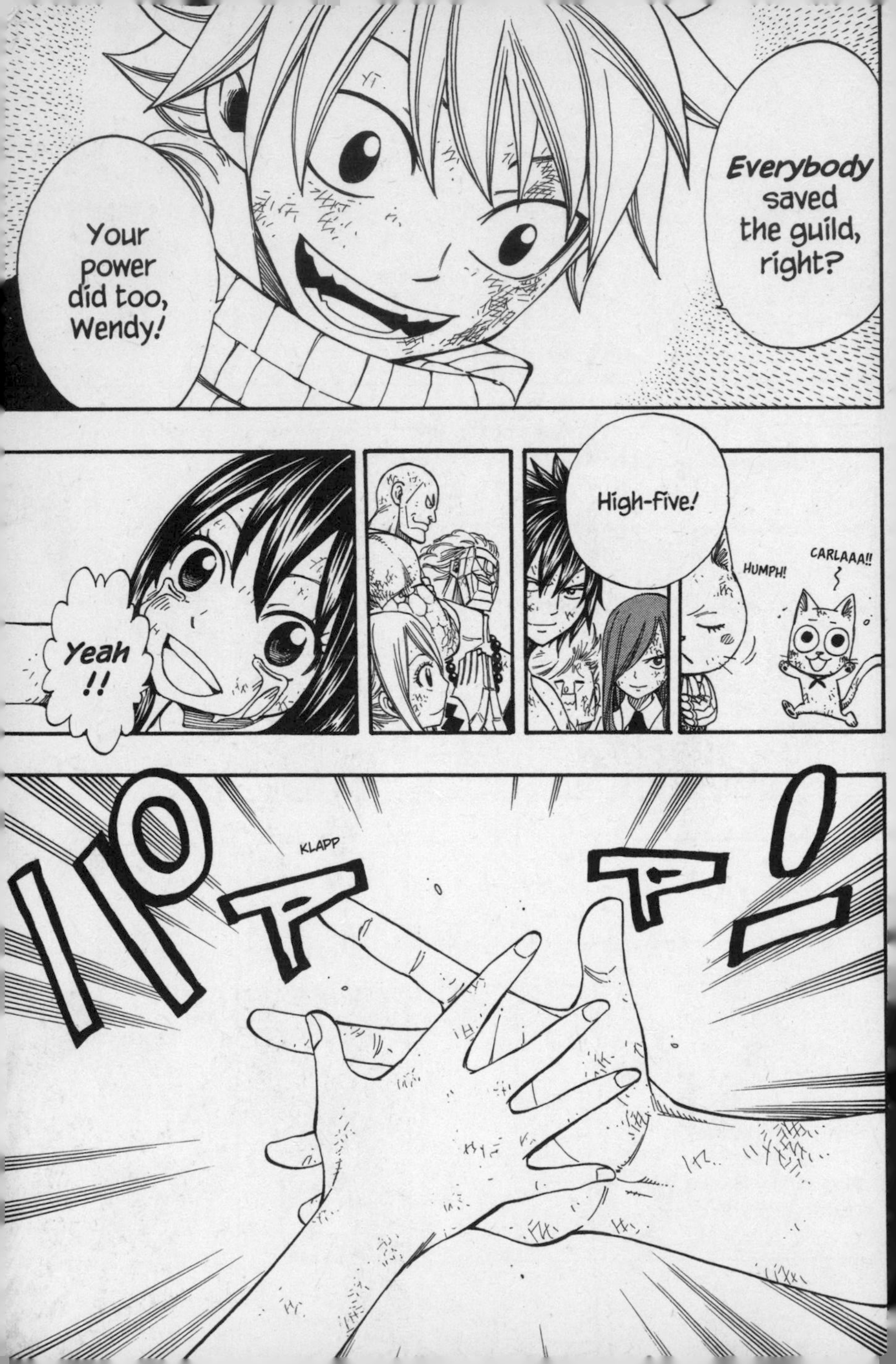
Everybody saved the guild, right?
Your power did too, Wendy!
CARLAAA!!
HUMPH!
High-five!
Yeah!!
KLAPP

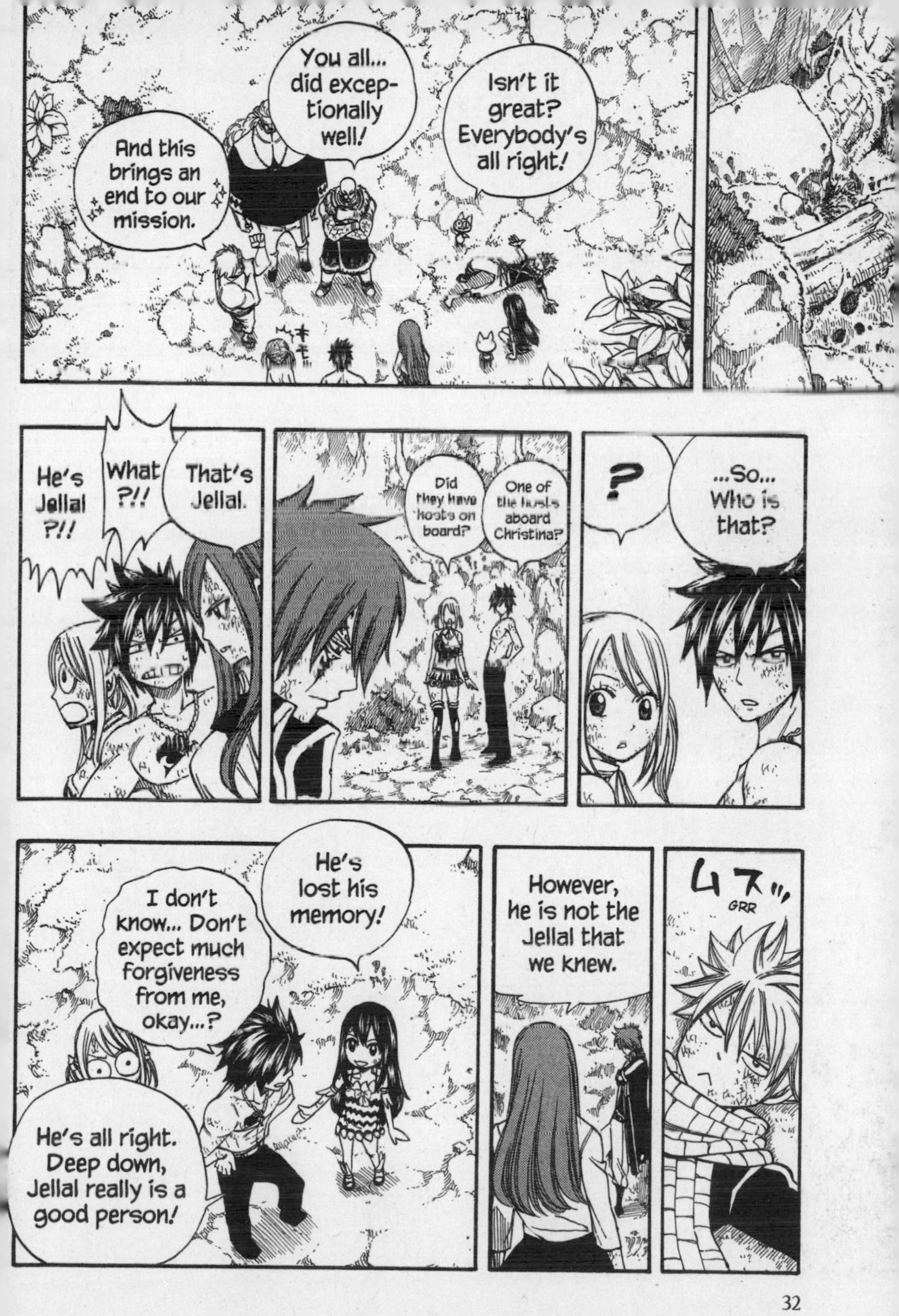
Isn't it great? Everybody's all right!
You all... did exceptionally well!
And this brings an end to our mission.
...So... Who is that?
?
One of the hosts aboard Christina?
Did they have hosts on board?
That's Jellal.
What?!!
He's Jellal?!!
ムス
GRR
However, he is not the Jellal that we knew.
He's lost his memory!
I don't know... Don't expect much forgiveness from me, okay...?
He's all right. Deep down, Jellal really is a good person!

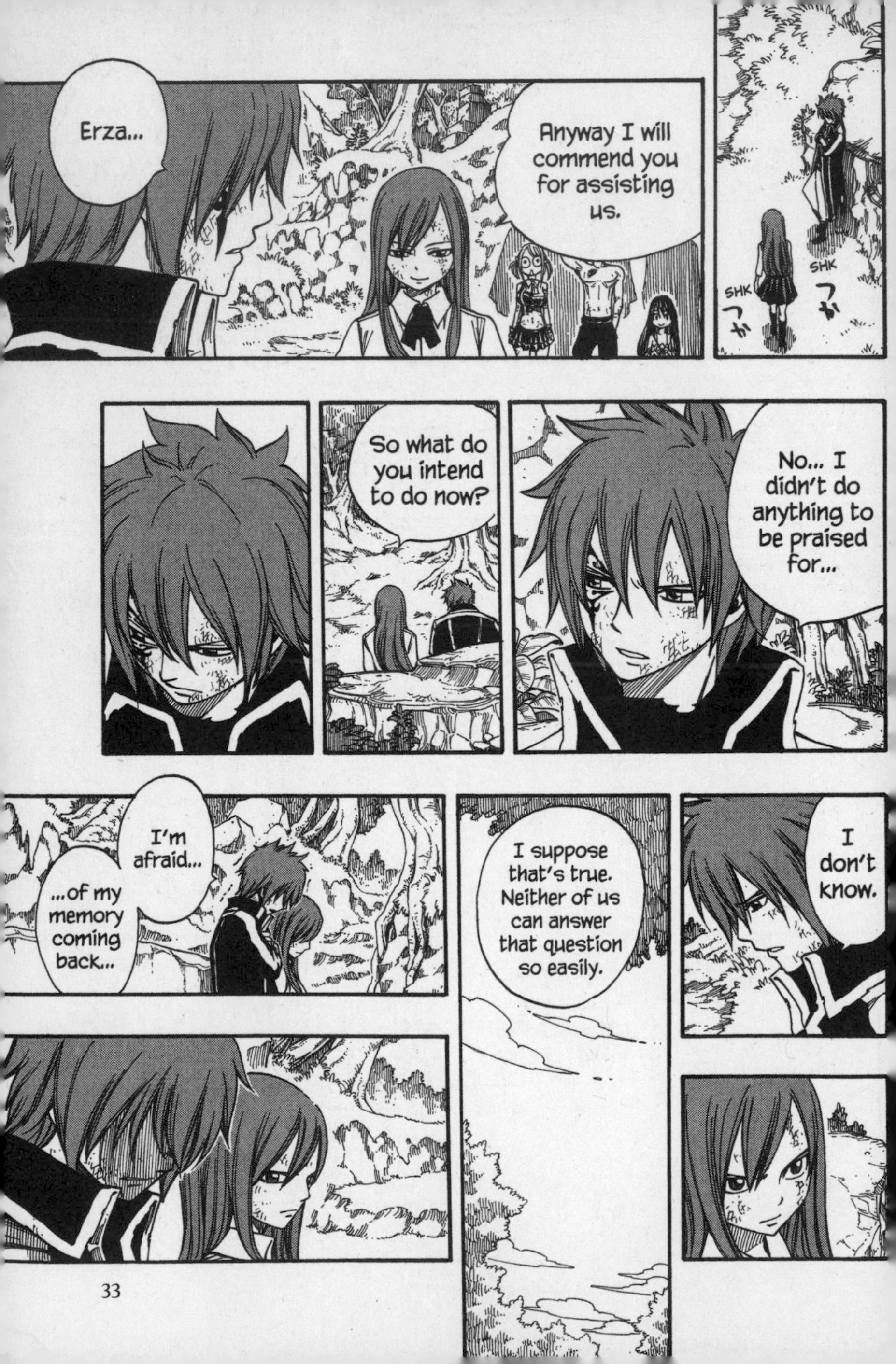
SHK
つか
SHK
つか
Anyway I will commend you for assisting us.
Erza...
No... I didn't do anything to be praised for...
So what do you intend to do now?
I don't know.
I suppose that's true. Neither of us can answer that question so easily.
I'm afraid...
...of my memory coming back...

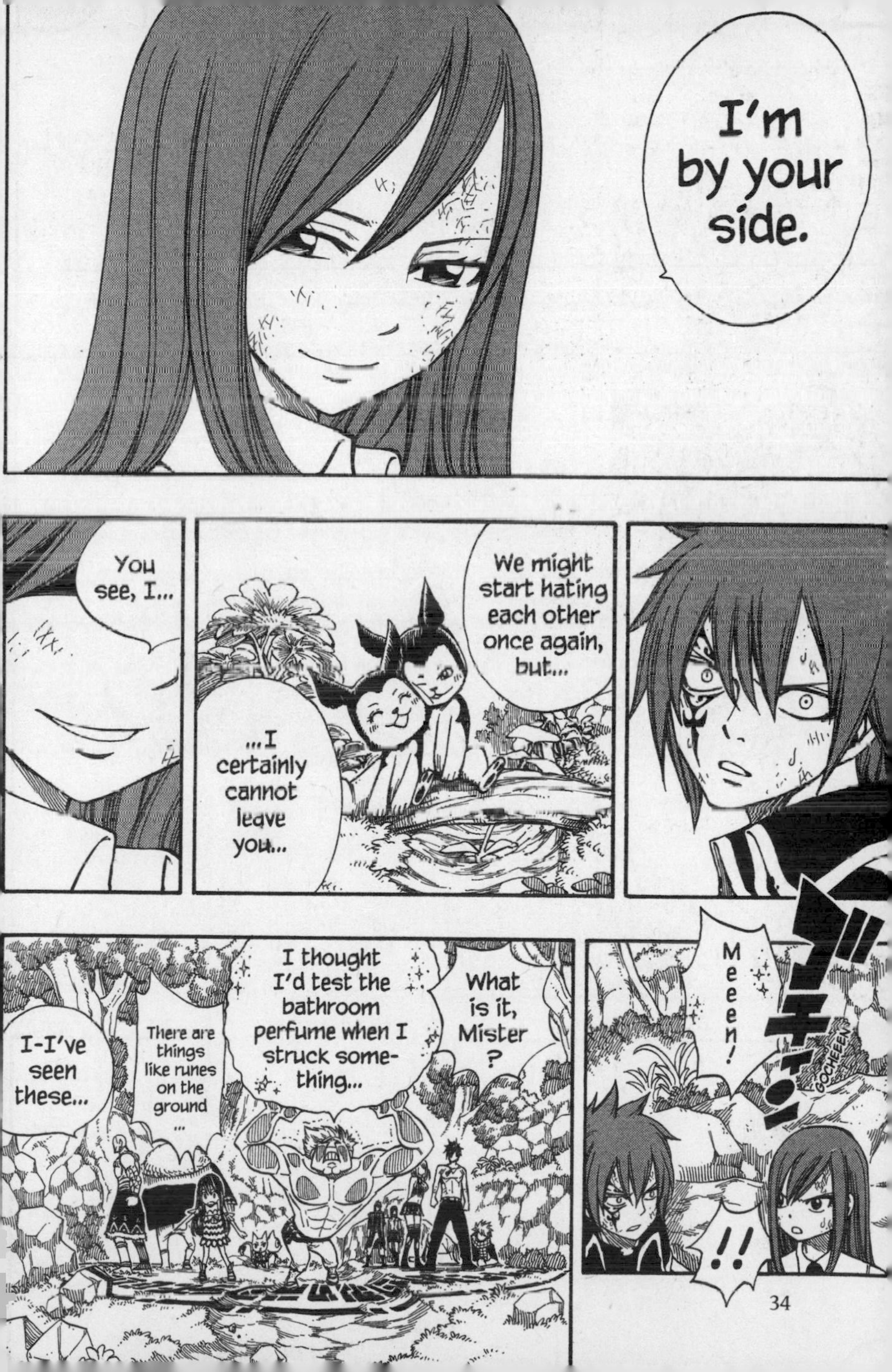
I'm by your side.
We might start hating each other once again, but...
...I certainly cannot leave you...
You see, I...
Meeen!
GOCHEEEN
!!
What is it, Mister?
I thought I'd test the bathroom perfume when I struck something...
There are things like runes on the ground...
I-I've seen these...

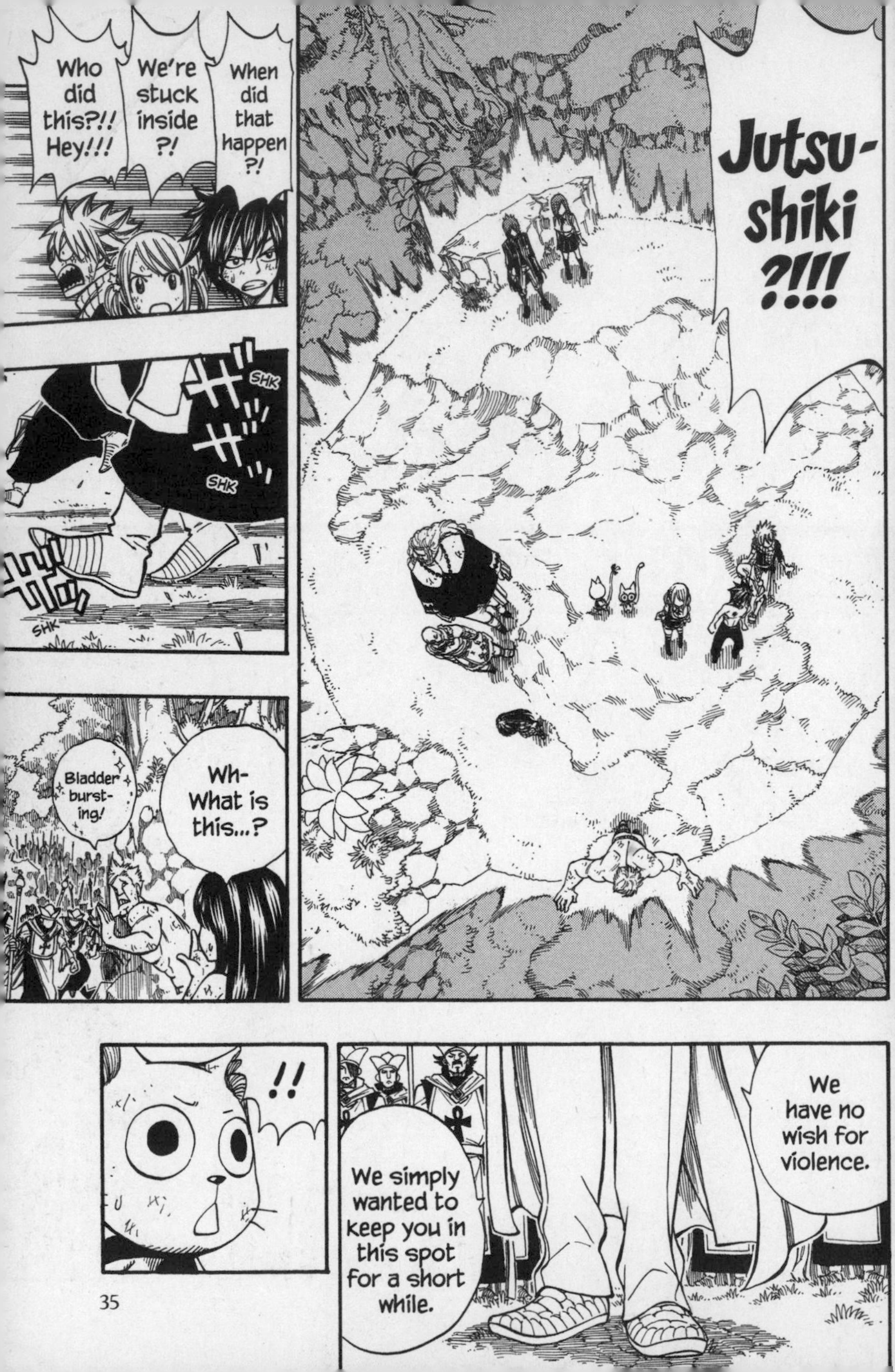
Jutsu-shiki?!!!
When did that happen?!
We're stuck inside?!
Who did this?!! Hey!!!
SHK
SHK
SHK
Wh-What is this...?
Bladder burst-ing!
We have no wish for violence.
We simply wanted to keep you in this spot for a short while.
!!

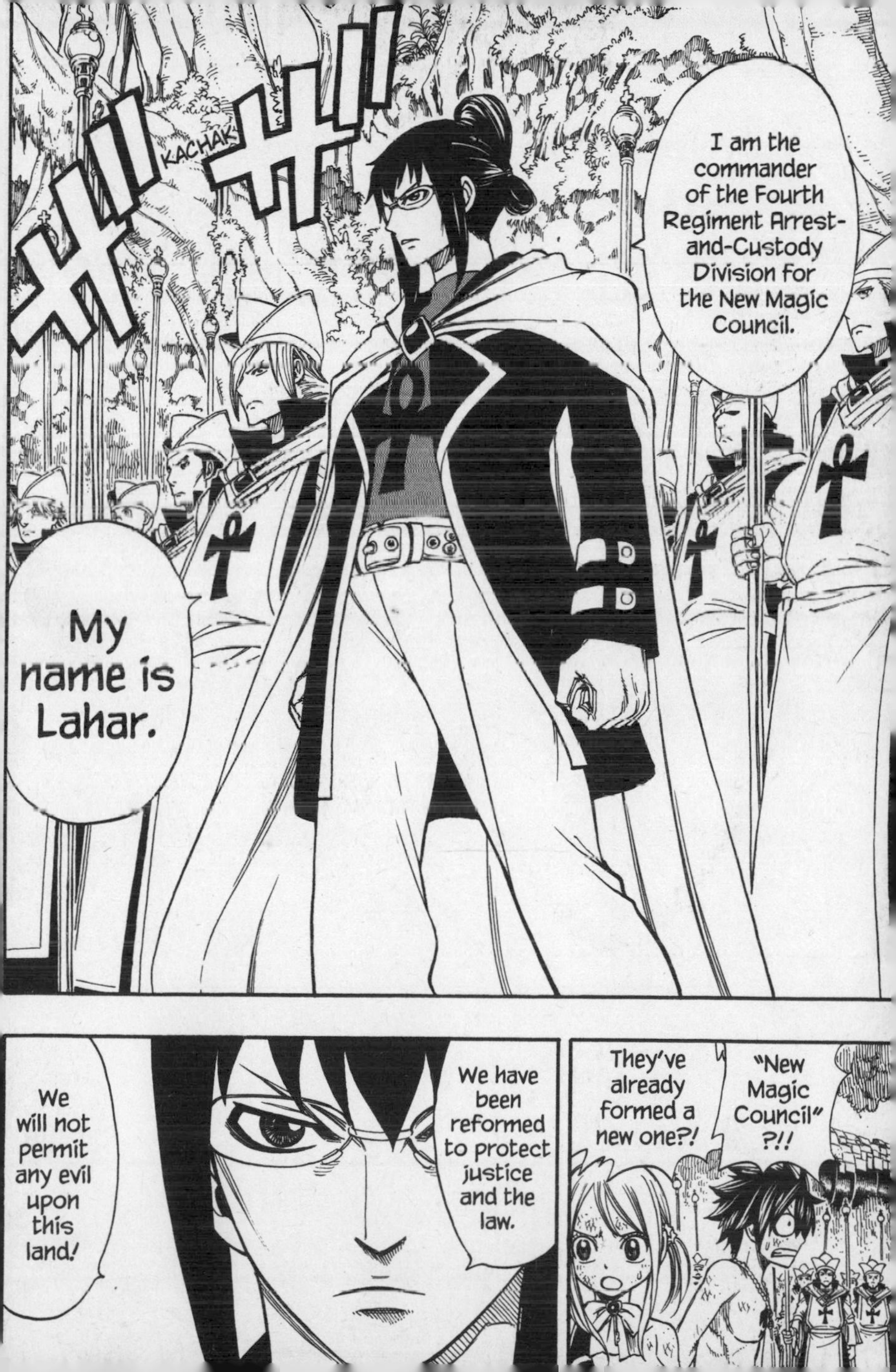
I am the commander of the Fourth Regiment Arrest-and-Custody Division for the New Magic Council.
KACHAK
My name is Lahar.
"New Magic Council"?!!
They've already formed a new one?!
We have been reformed to protect justice and the law.
We will not permit any evil upon this land!

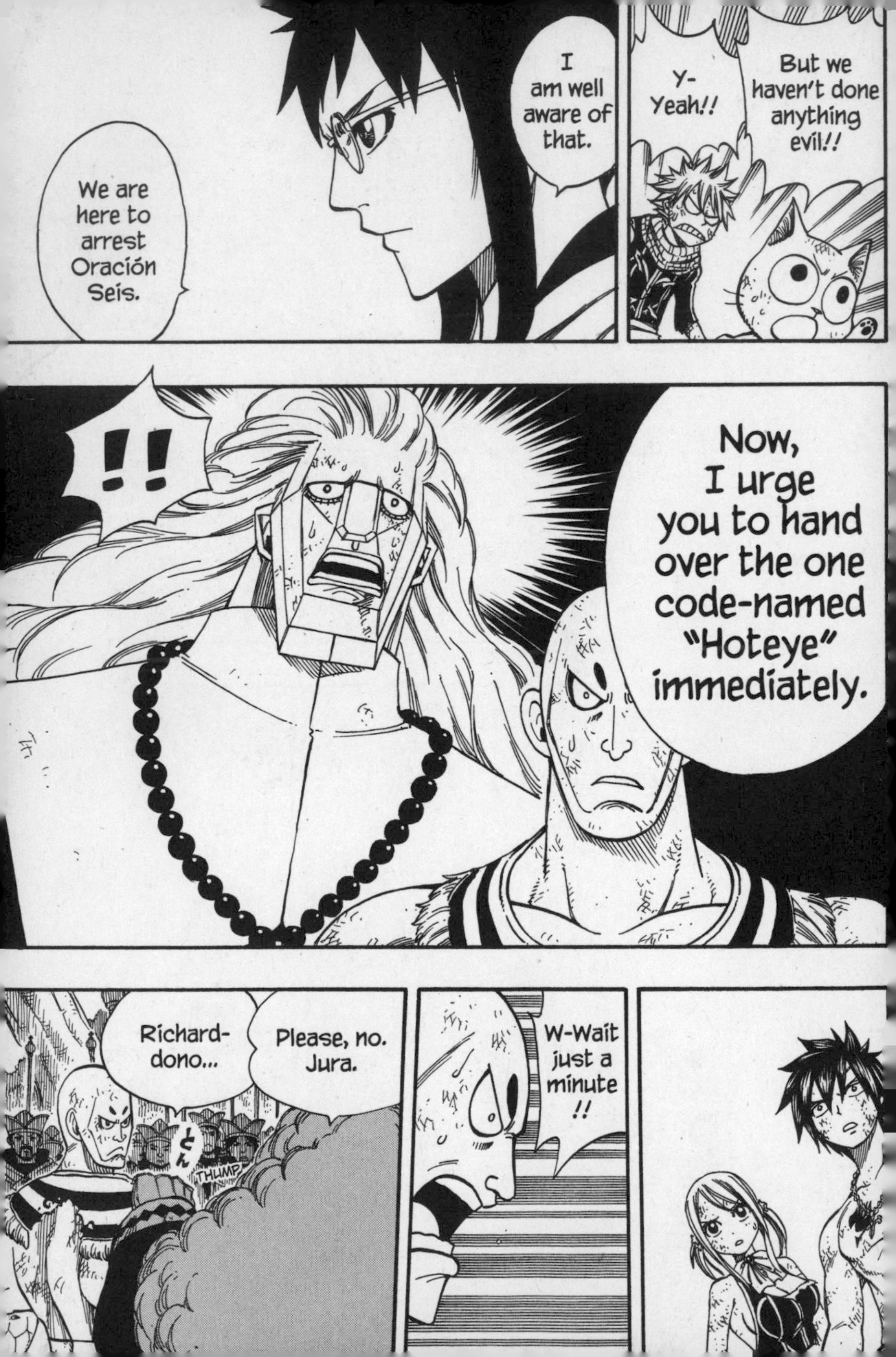
But we haven't done anything evil!!
Y-Yeah!!
I am well aware of that.
We are here to arrest Oración Seis.
Now, I urge you to hand over the one code-named "Hoteye" immediately.
!!
W-Wait just a minute!!
Please, no. Jura.
Richard-dono...
とん
THUMP

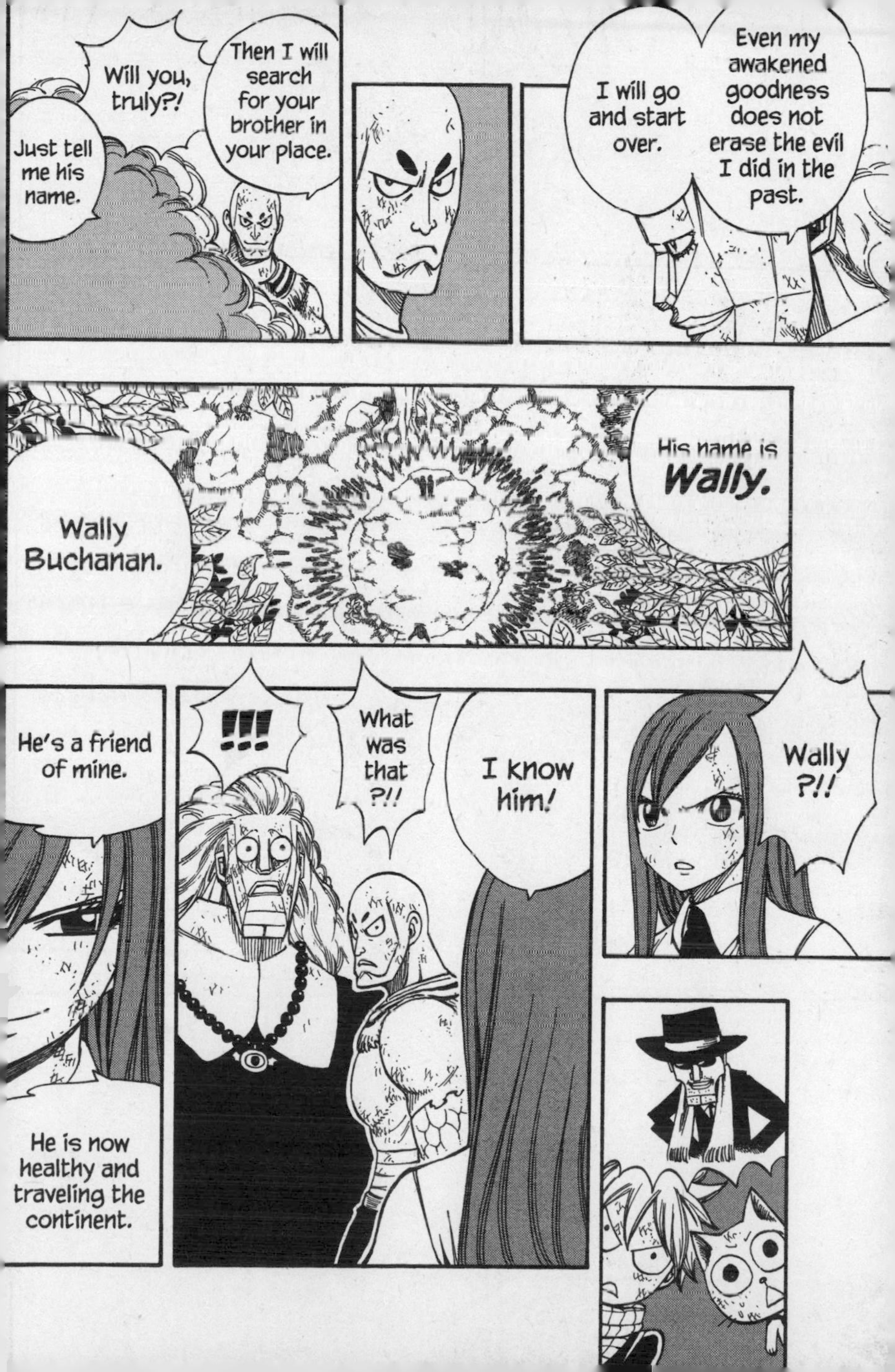
Even my awakened goodness does not erase the evil I did in the past.
I will go and start over.
Then I will search for your brother in your place.
Will you, truly?!
Just tell me his name.
His name is Wally.
Wally Buchanan.
Wally ?!!
I know him!
What was that ?!!
!!!
He's a friend of mine.
He is now healthy and traveling the continent.

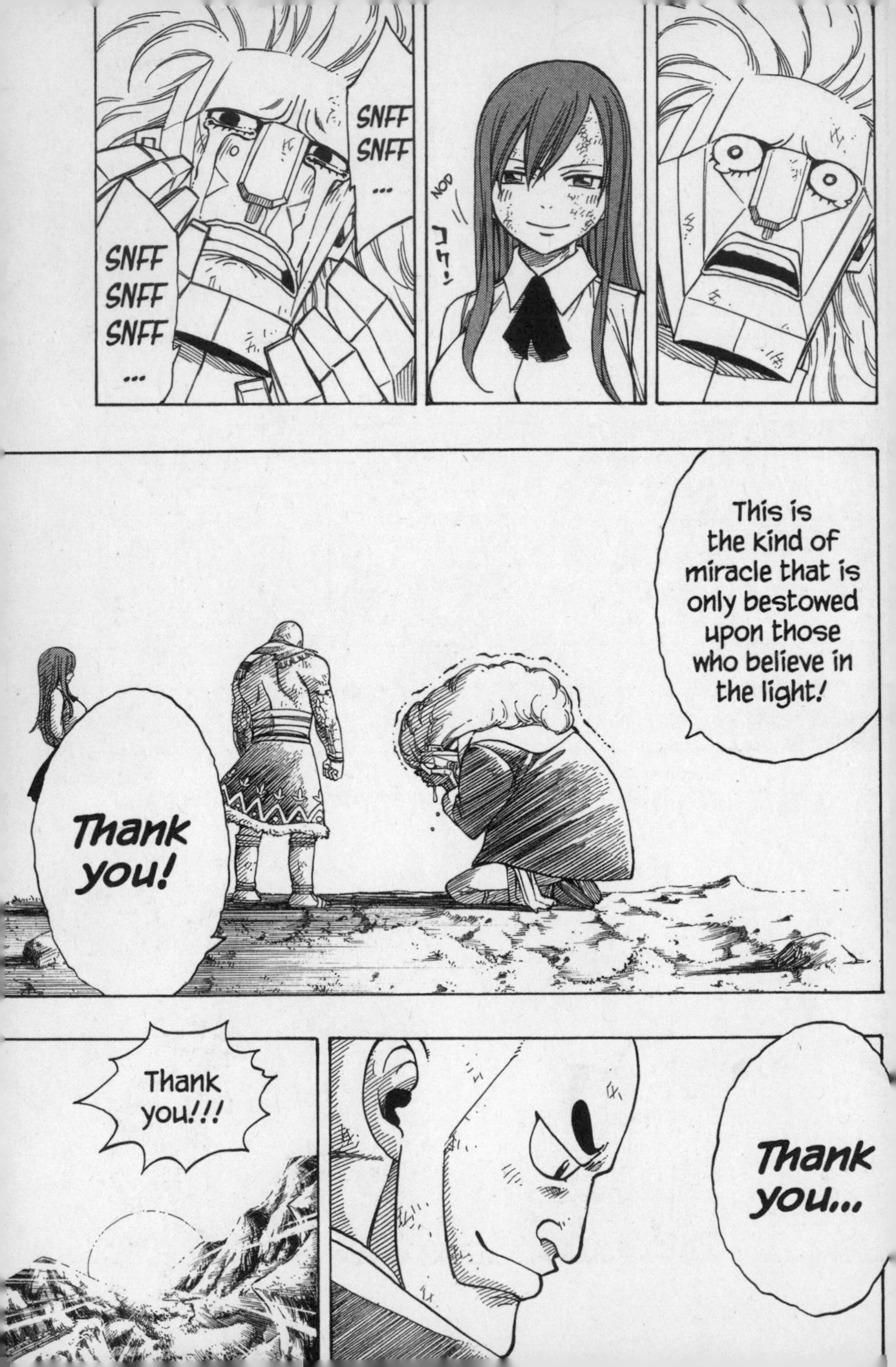
NOD
SNFF SNFF ...
SNFF SNFF SNFF ...
This is the kind of miracle that is only bestowed upon those who believe in the light!
Thank you!
Thank you...
Thank you!!!

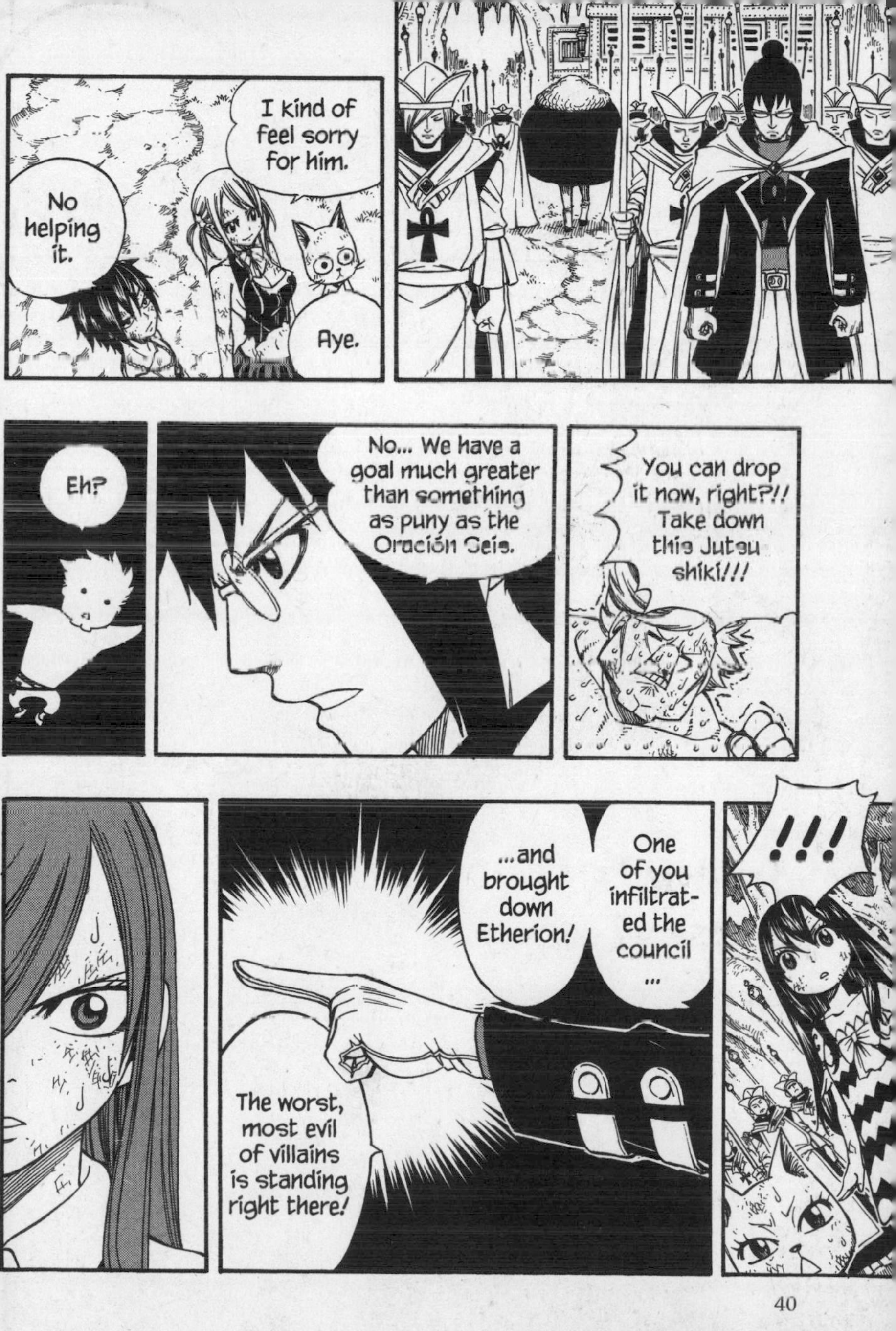
I kind of feel sorry for him.
No helping it.
Aye.
You can drop it now, right?!! Take down this Jutsu shiki!!!
No... We have a goal much greater than something as puny as the Oración Seis.
Eh?
!!!
One of you infiltrat-ed the council ...
...and brought down Etherion!
The worst, most evil of villains is standing right there!

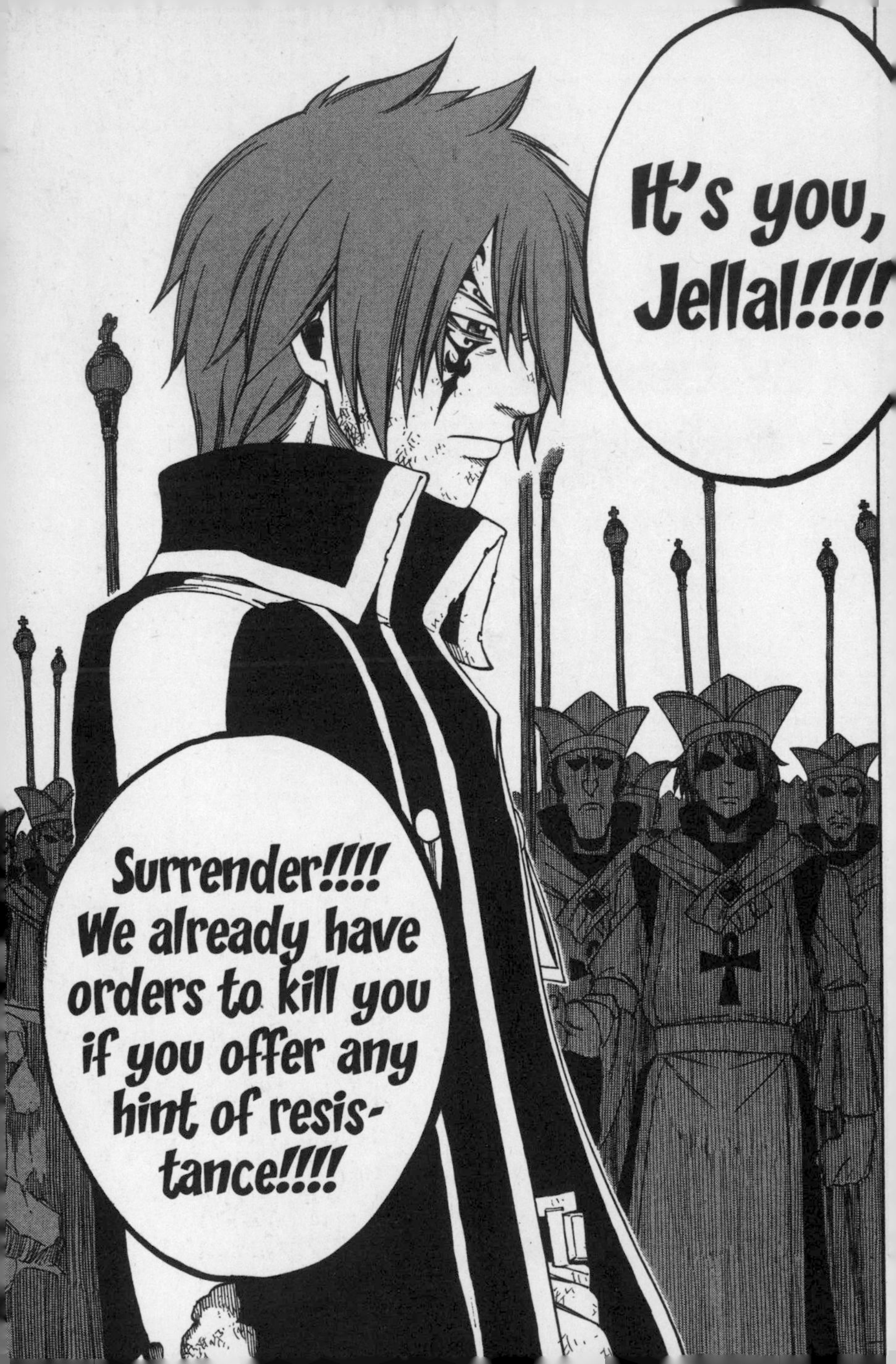
It's you, Jellal!!!!
Surrender!!!! We already have orders to kill you if you offer any hint of resis-tance!!!!

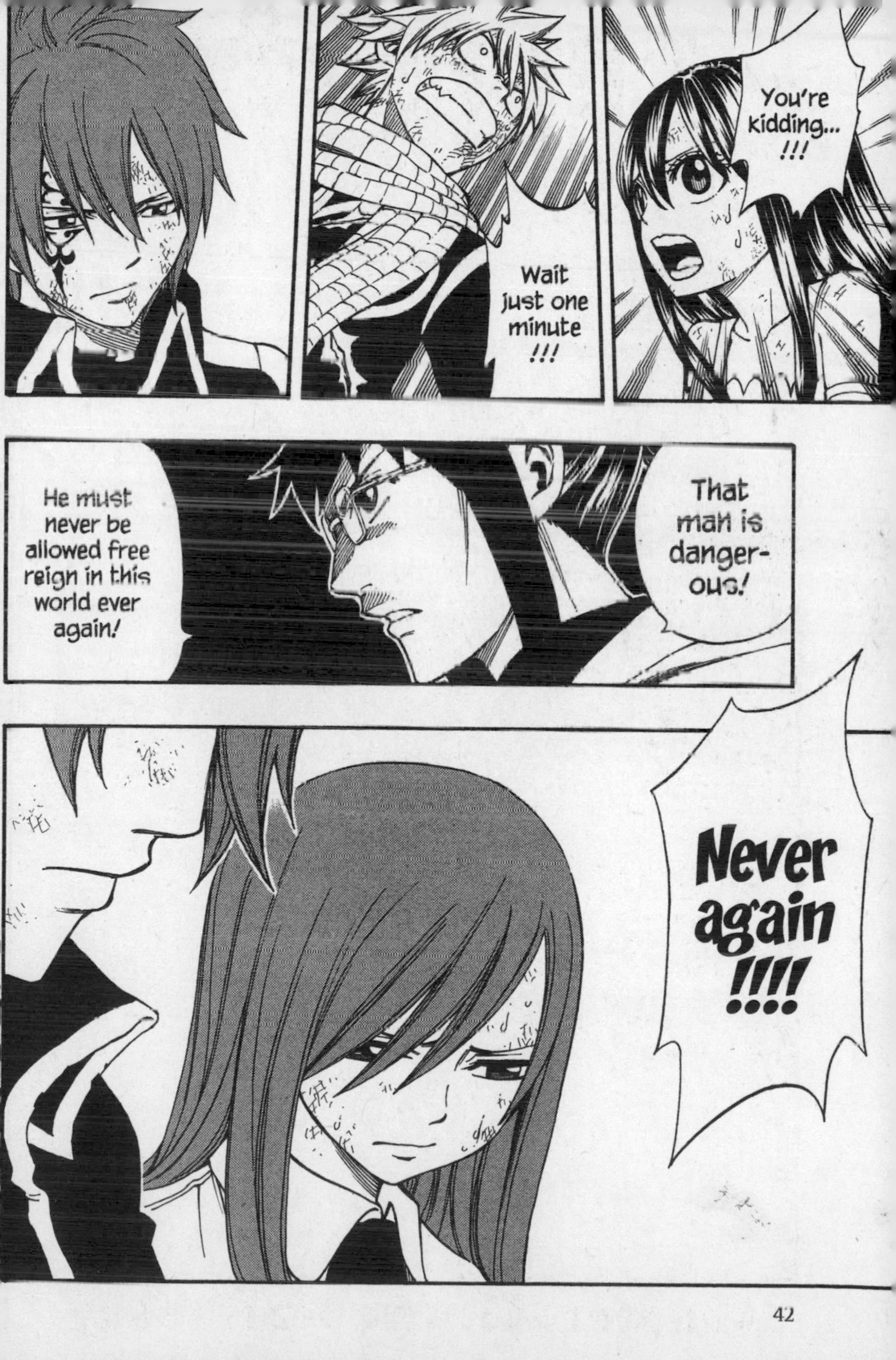
You're kidding... !!!
Wait just one minute !!!
That man is danger- ous!
He must never be allowed free reign in this world ever again!
Never again !!!!

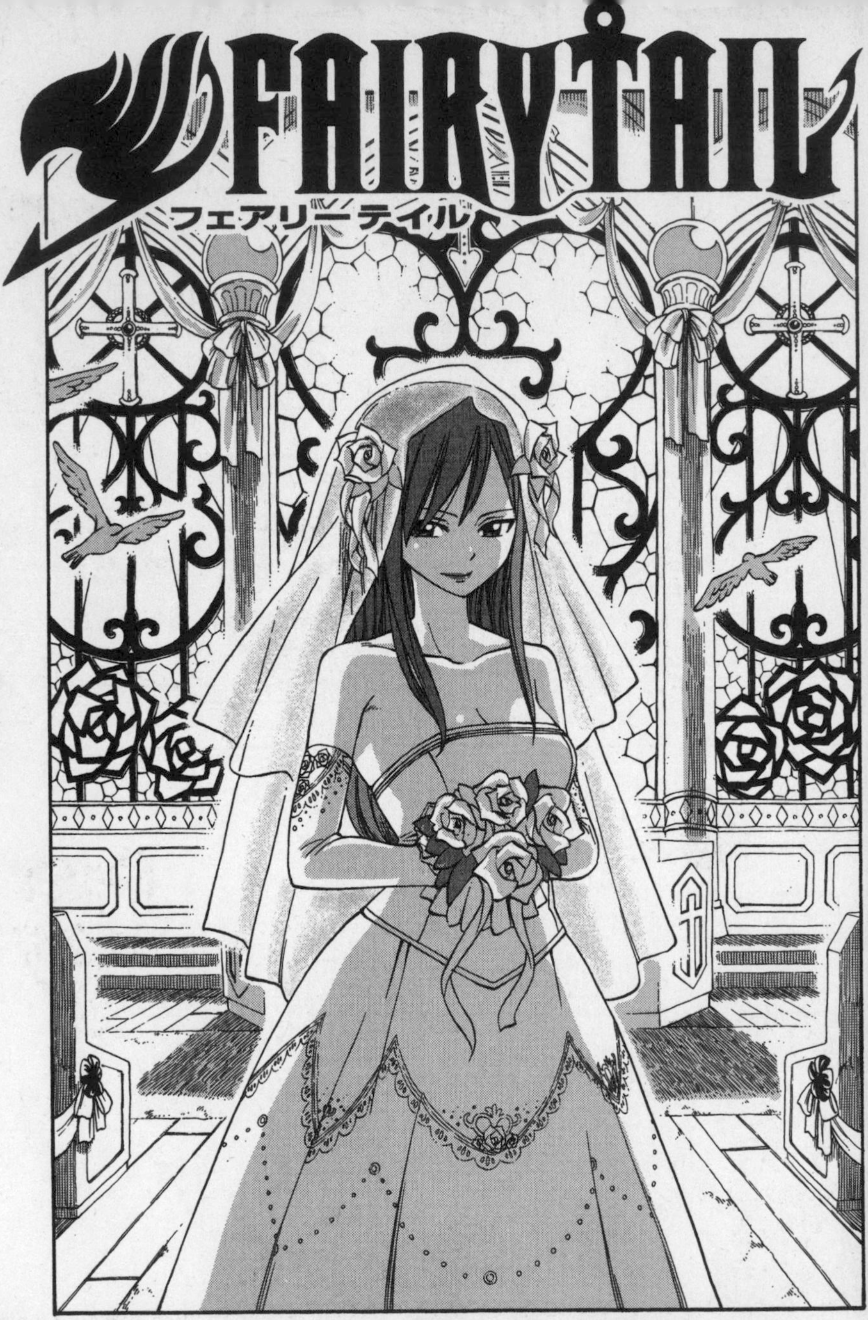
FAIRY TAIL
フェアリーテイル

## Chapter 163, The Scarlet Sky

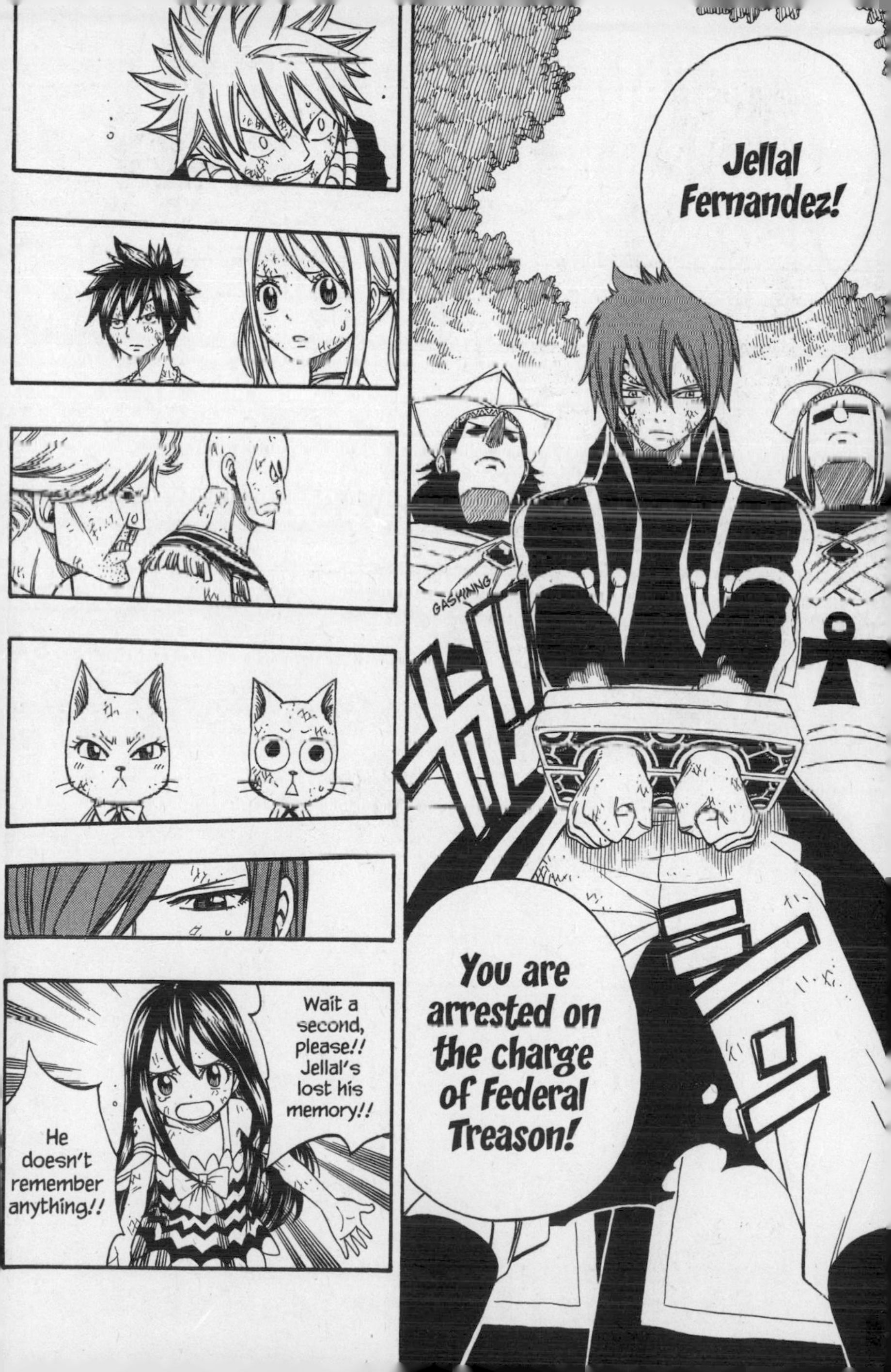
Jellal Fernandez!
GASHINNG
You are arrested on the charge of Federal Treason!
Wait a second, please!! Jellal's lost his memory!!
He doesn't remember anything!!

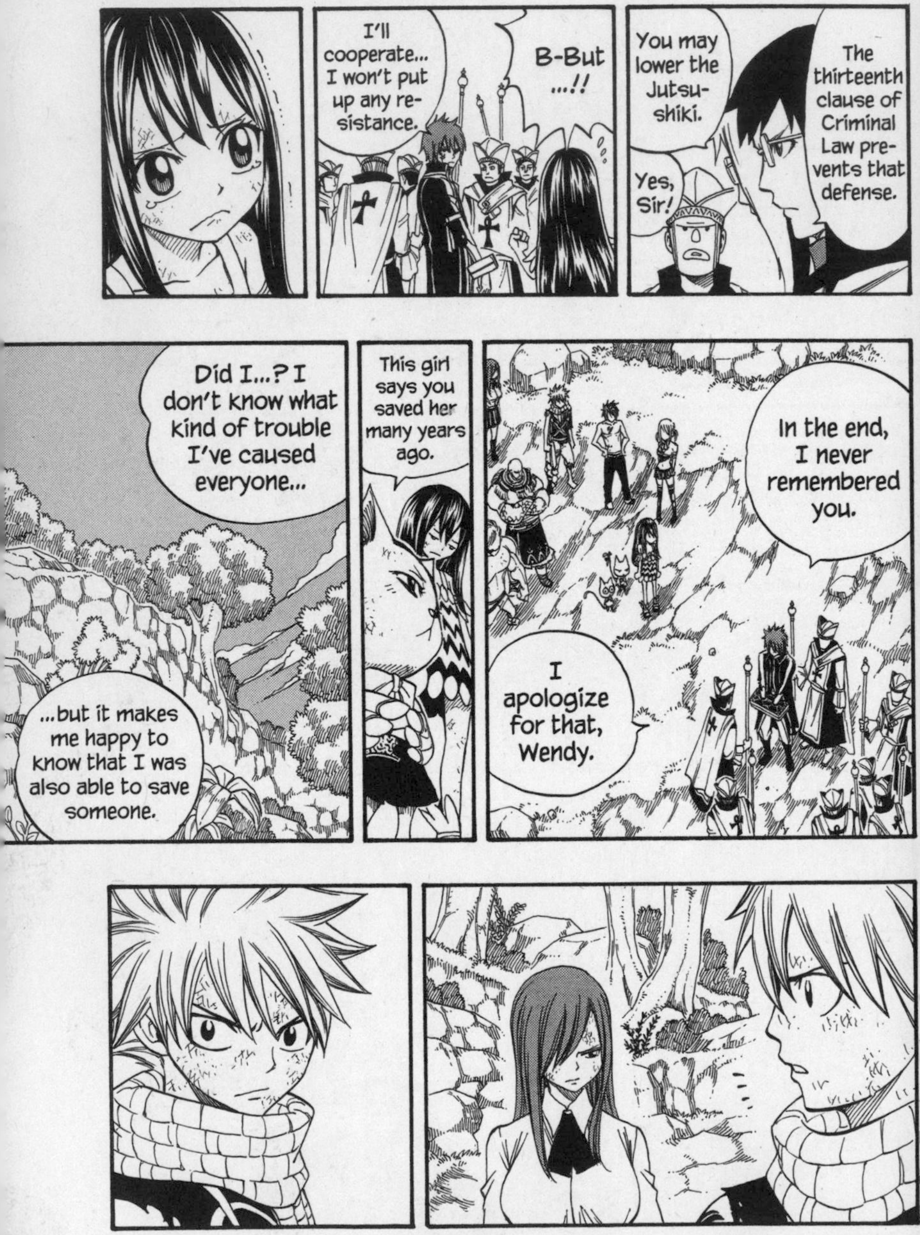
The thirteenth clause of Criminal Law prevents that defense.
You may lower the Jutsu-shiki.
Yes, Sir!
B-But ...!!
I'll cooperate... I won't put up any resistance.
In the end, I never remembered you.
I apologize for that, Wendy.
This girl says you saved her many years ago.
Did I...? I don't know what kind of trouble I've caused everyone...
...but it makes me happy to know that I was also able to save someone.

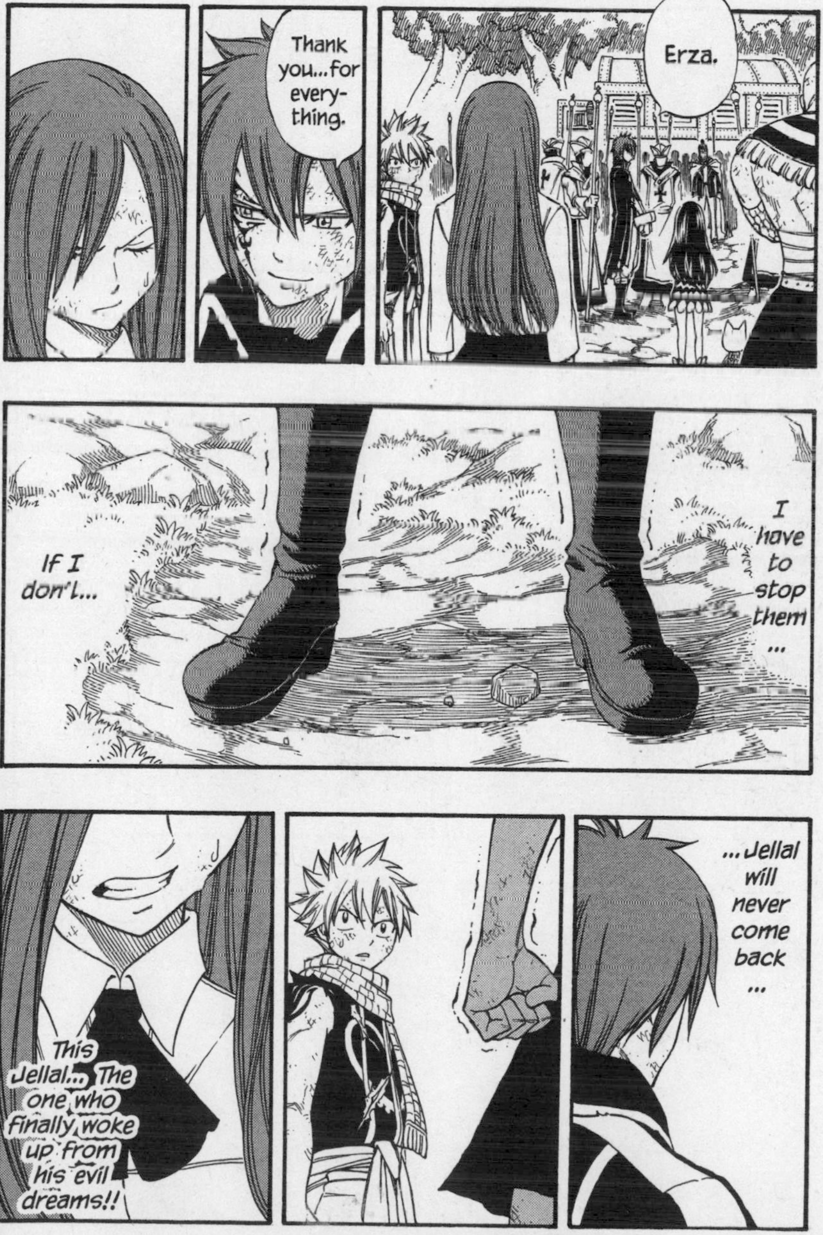
Erza.
Thank you...for every-thing.
I have to stop them...
If I don't...
...Jellal will never come back...
This Jellal... The one who finally woke up from his evil dreams!!

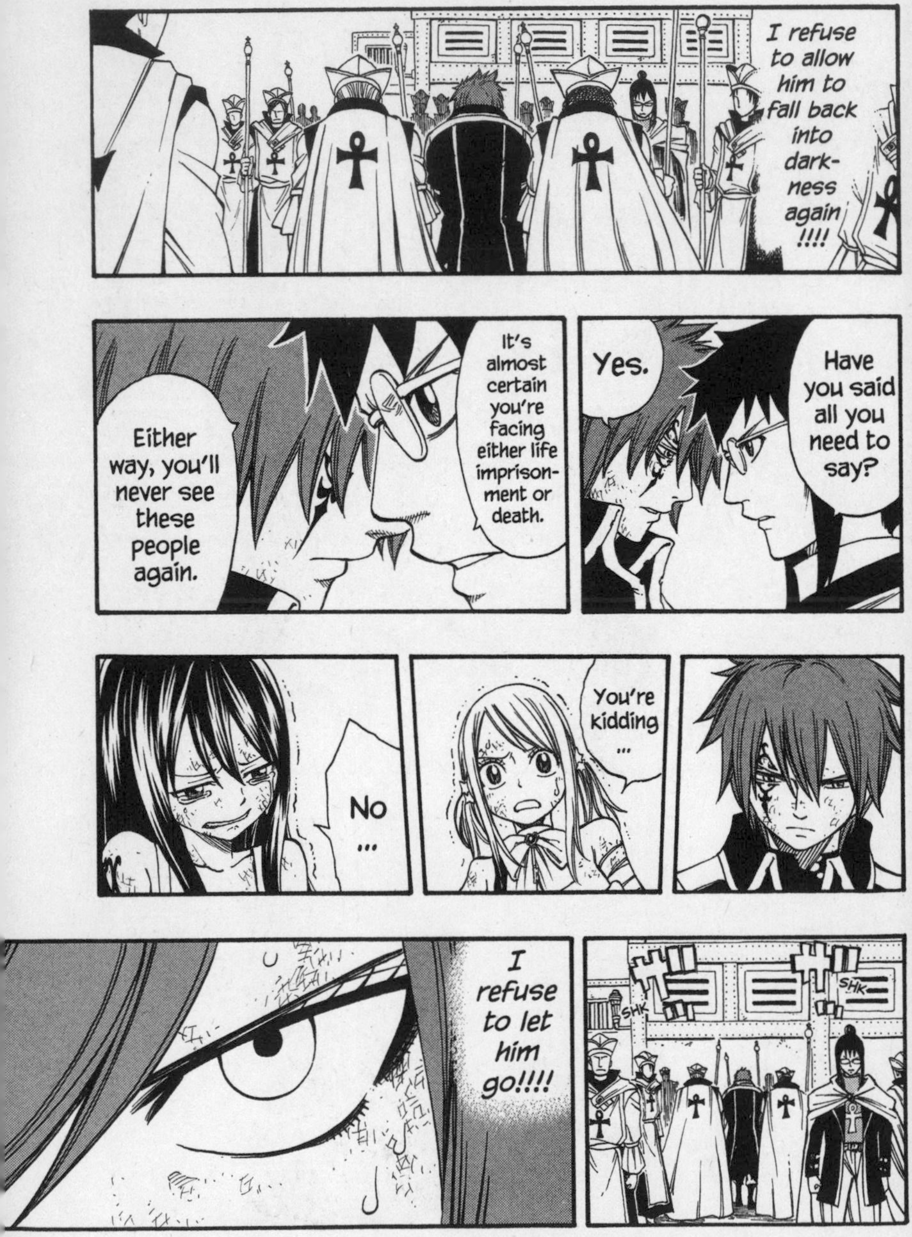
I refuse to allow him to fall back into darkness again!!!!
Have you said all you need to say?
Yes.
It's almost certain you're facing either life imprisonment or death.
Either way, you'll never see these people again.
You're kidding...
No...
SHK
SHK
I refuse to let him go!!!!

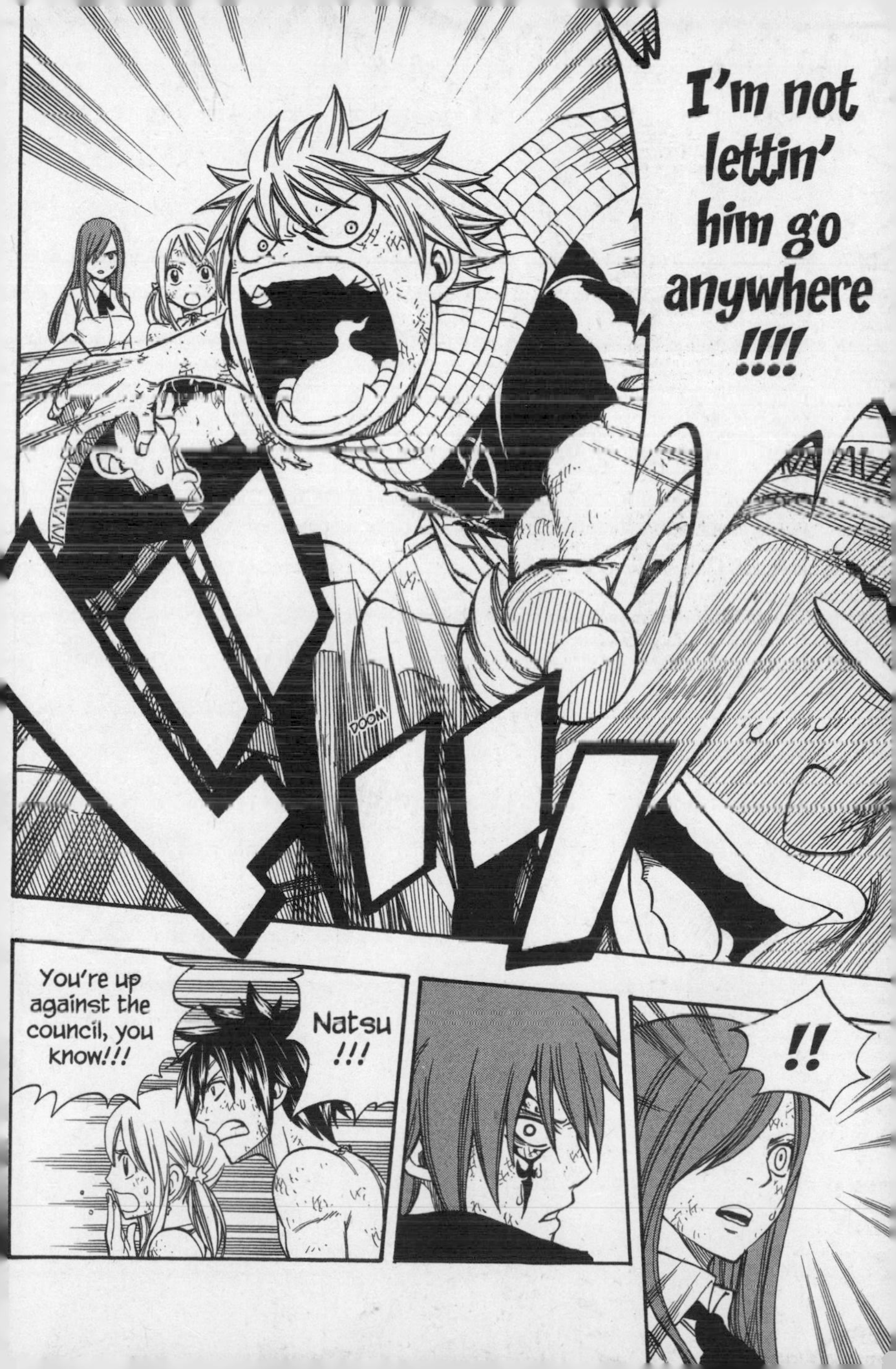

I'm not lettin' him go anywhere!!!!
DOOM
!!
Natsu!!!
You're up against the council, you know!!!

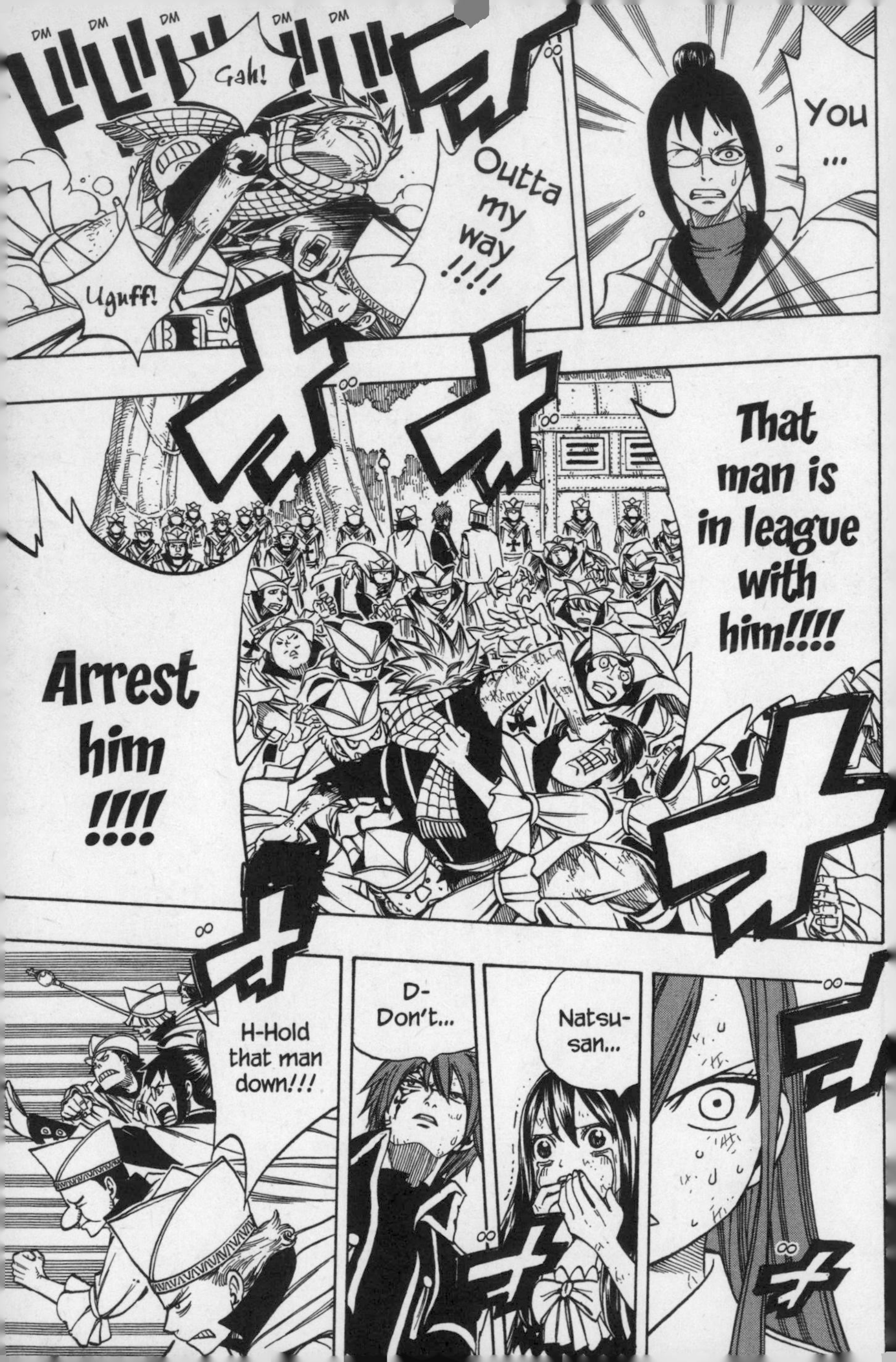

You ...
DM DM DM DM DM
Gah!
Outta my way!!!!
Uguff!
That man is in league with him!!!!
Arrest him!!!!
Natsu-san...
D-Don't...
H-Hold that man down!!!

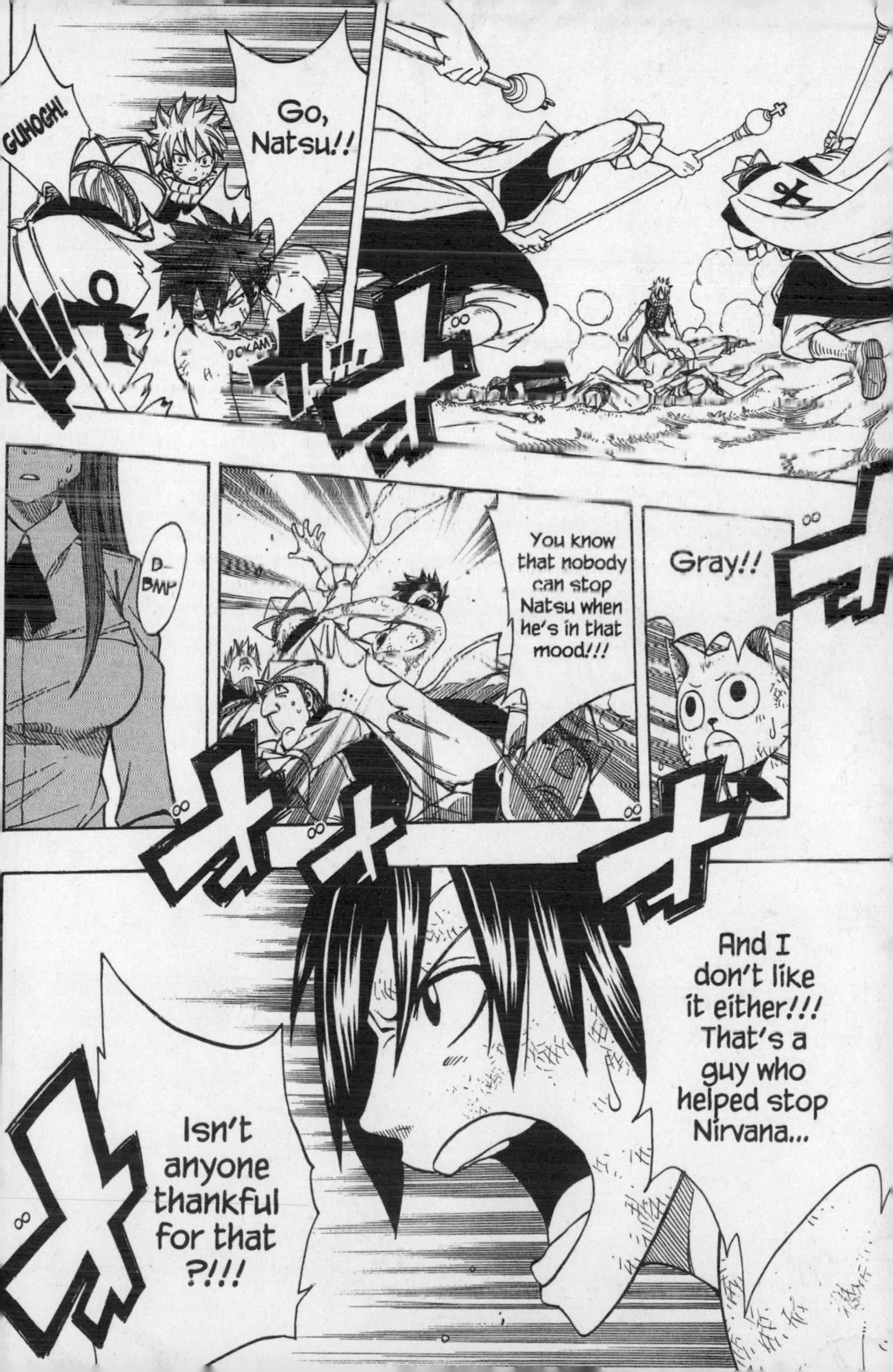
Go, Natsu!!
GUHOGH!
DOKAM
Gray!!
You know that nobody can stop Natsu when he's in that mood!!!
D-BMP
And I don't like it either!!! That's a guy who helped stop Nirvana...
Isn't anyone thankful for that ?!!!

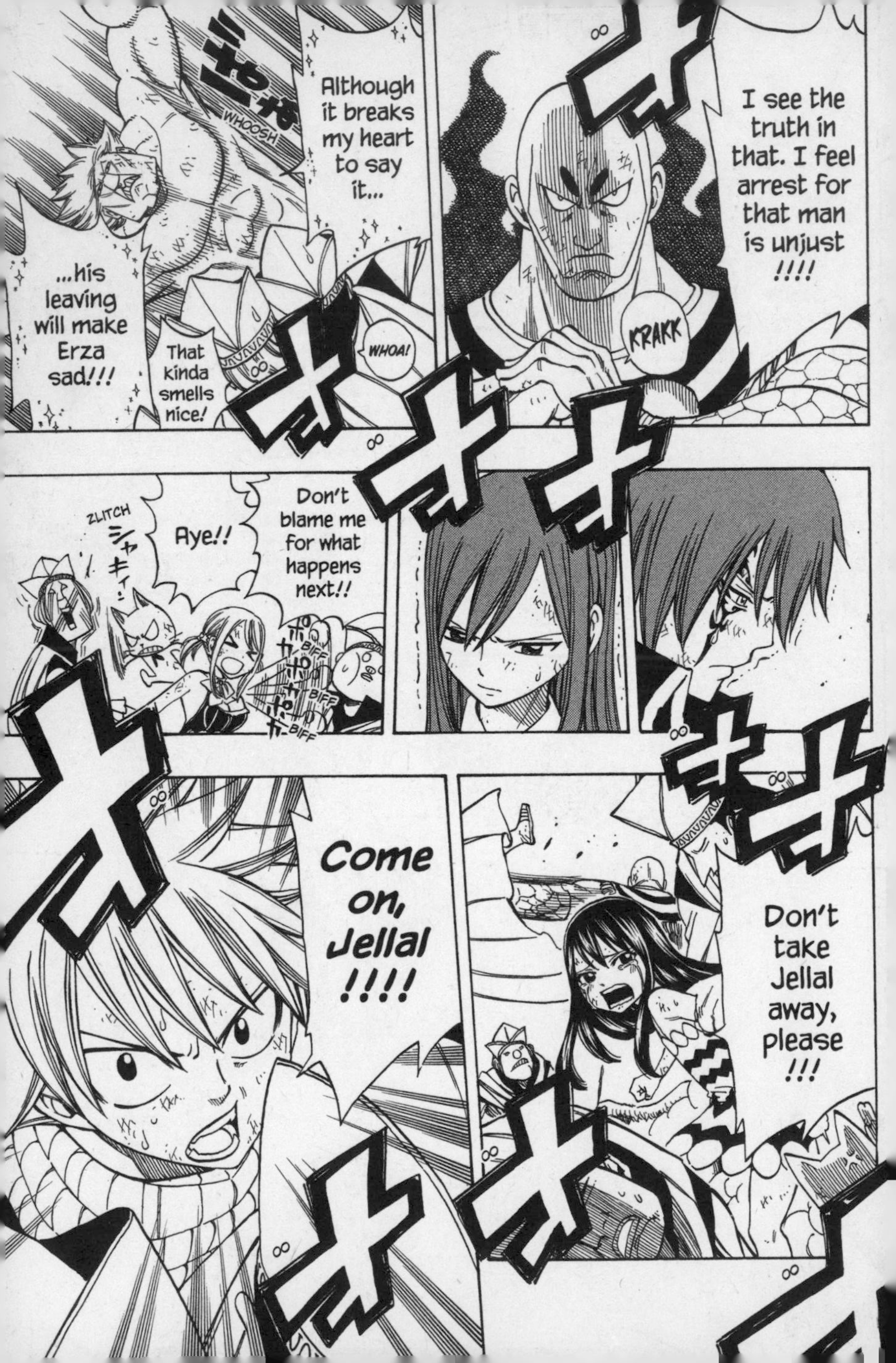
I see the truth in that. I feel arrest for that man is unjust!!!!
KRAKK
Although it breaks my heart to say it...
...his leaving will make Erza sad!!!
WHOOSH
WHOA!
That kinda smells nice!
Don't blame me for what happens next!!
Aye!!
ZLITCH
BIFF
BIFF
BIFF
Don't take Jellal away, please!!!
Come on, Jellal!!!!

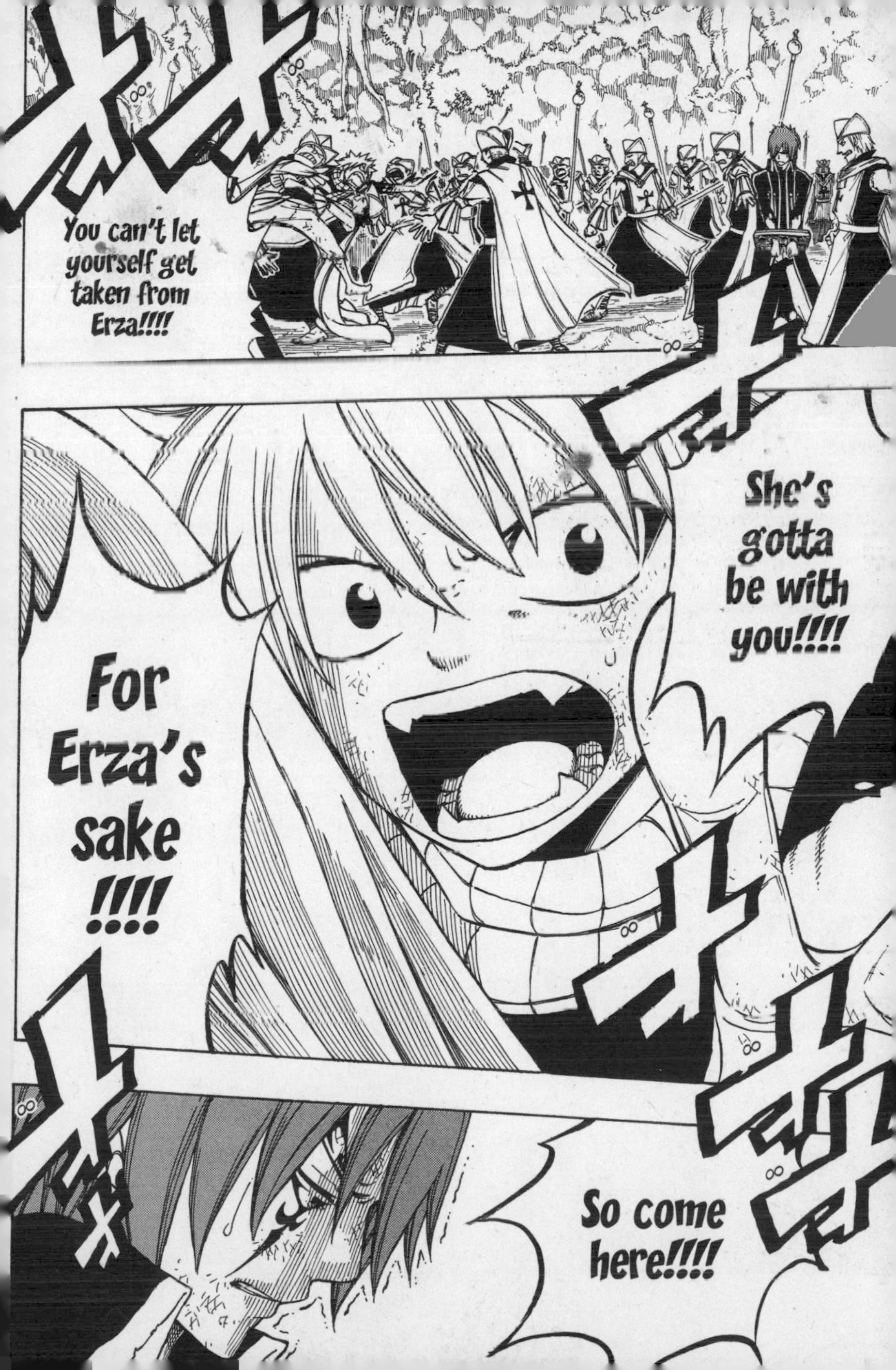
You can't let yourself get taken from Erza!!!!
She's gotta be with you!!!!
For Erza's sake !!!!
So come here!!!!

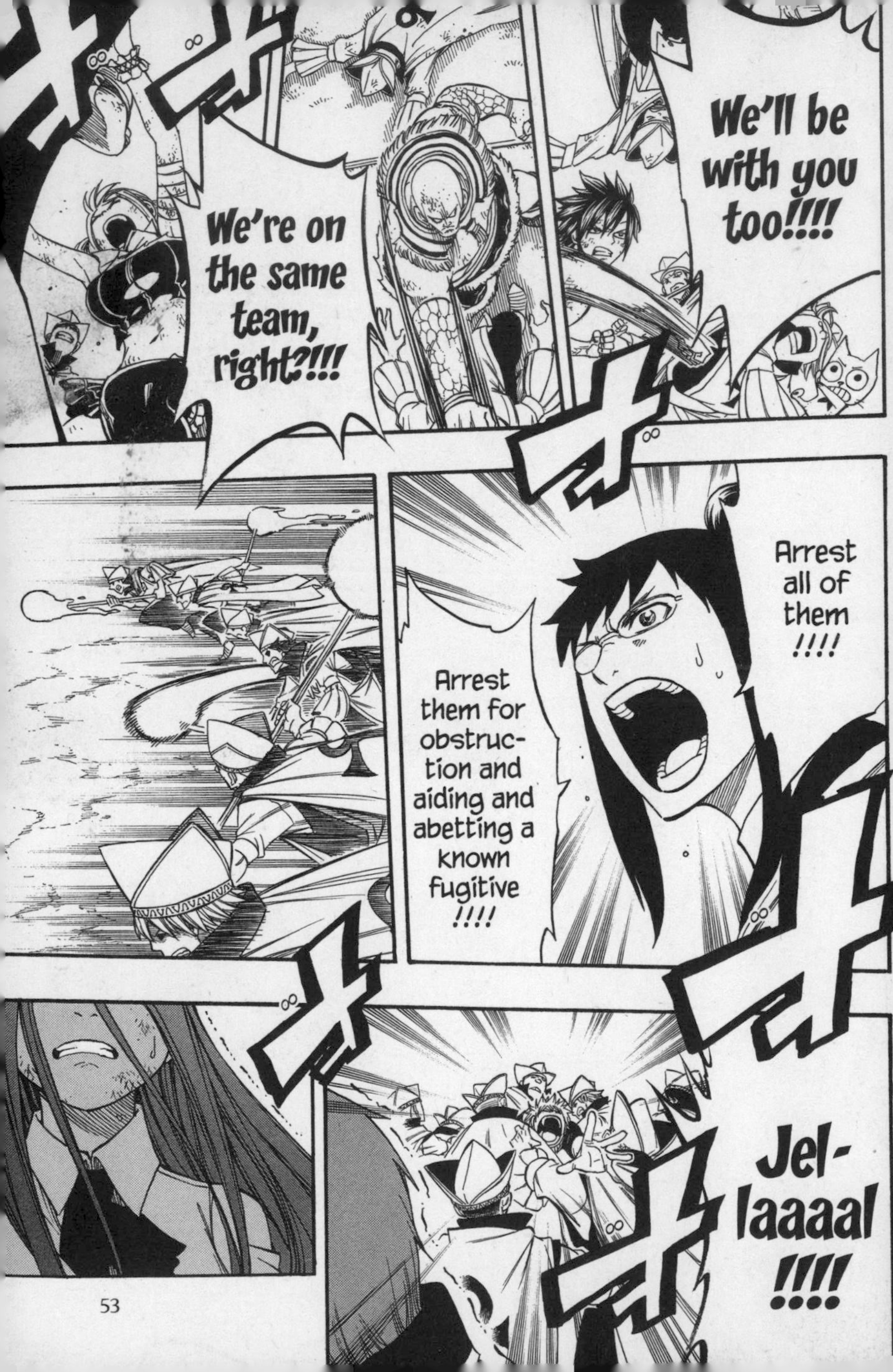
We'll be with you too!!!!
We're on the same team, right?!!!
Arrest all of them !!!!
Arrest them for obstruction and aiding and abetting a known fugitive !!!!
Jel-laaaal !!!!

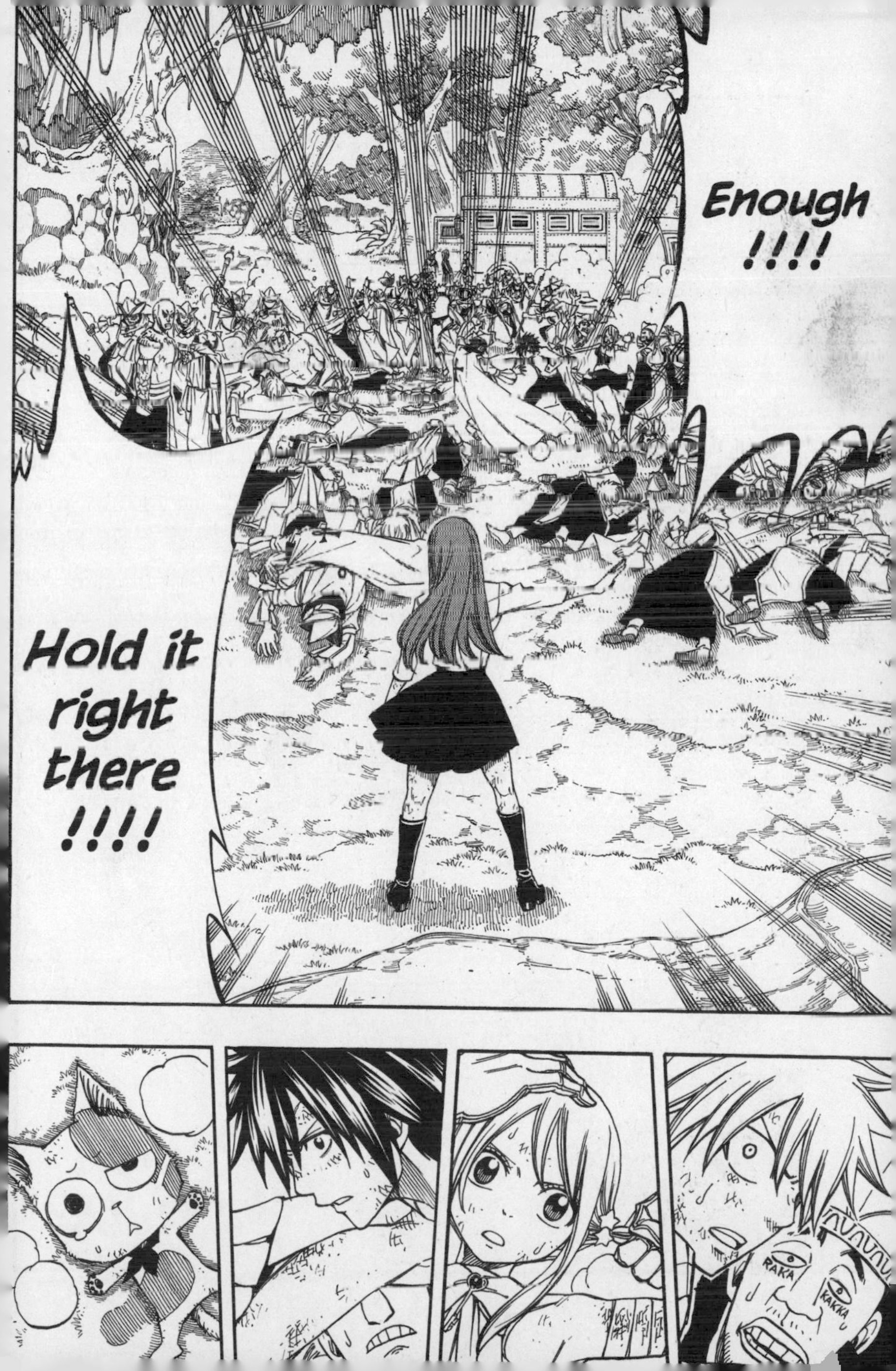
Enough !!!!
Hold it right there !!!!
RAKA
KAKKA

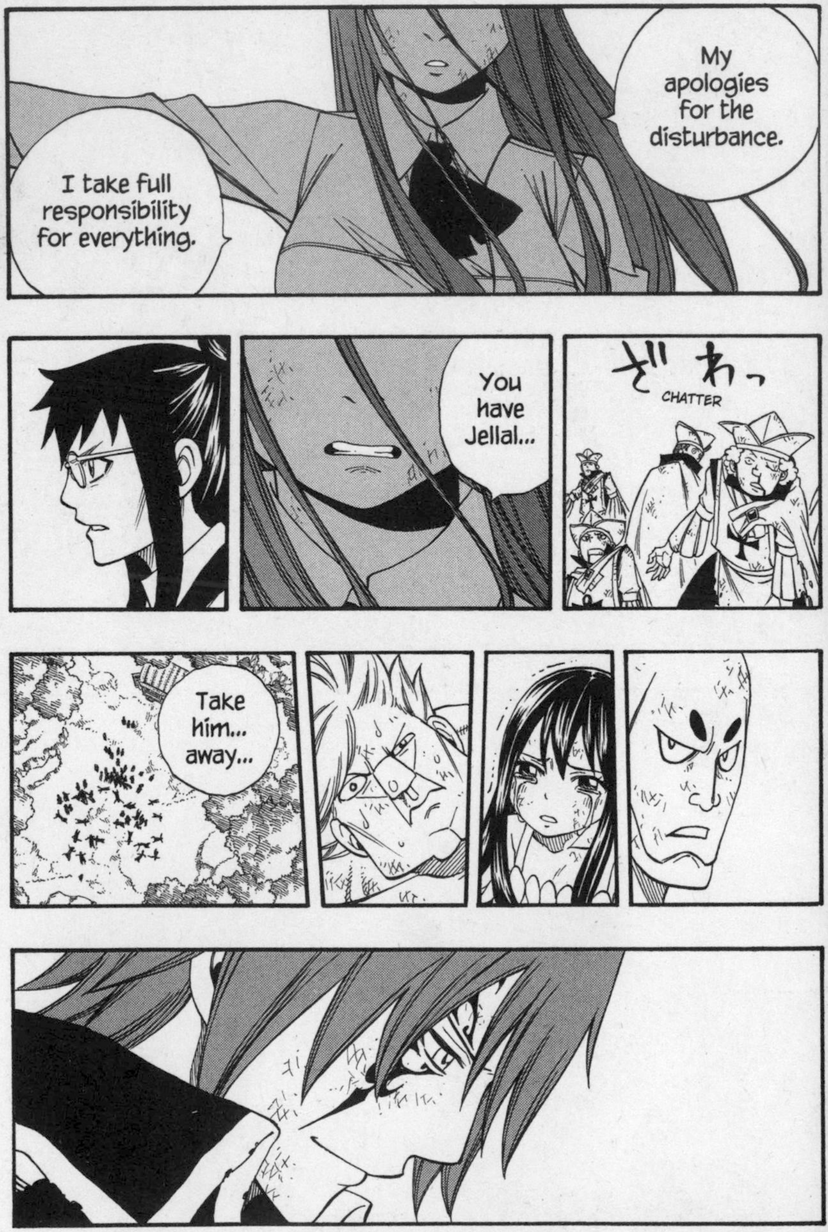

My apologies for the disturbance.
I take full responsibility for everything.
ざわっ
CHATTER
You have Jellal...
Take him... away...

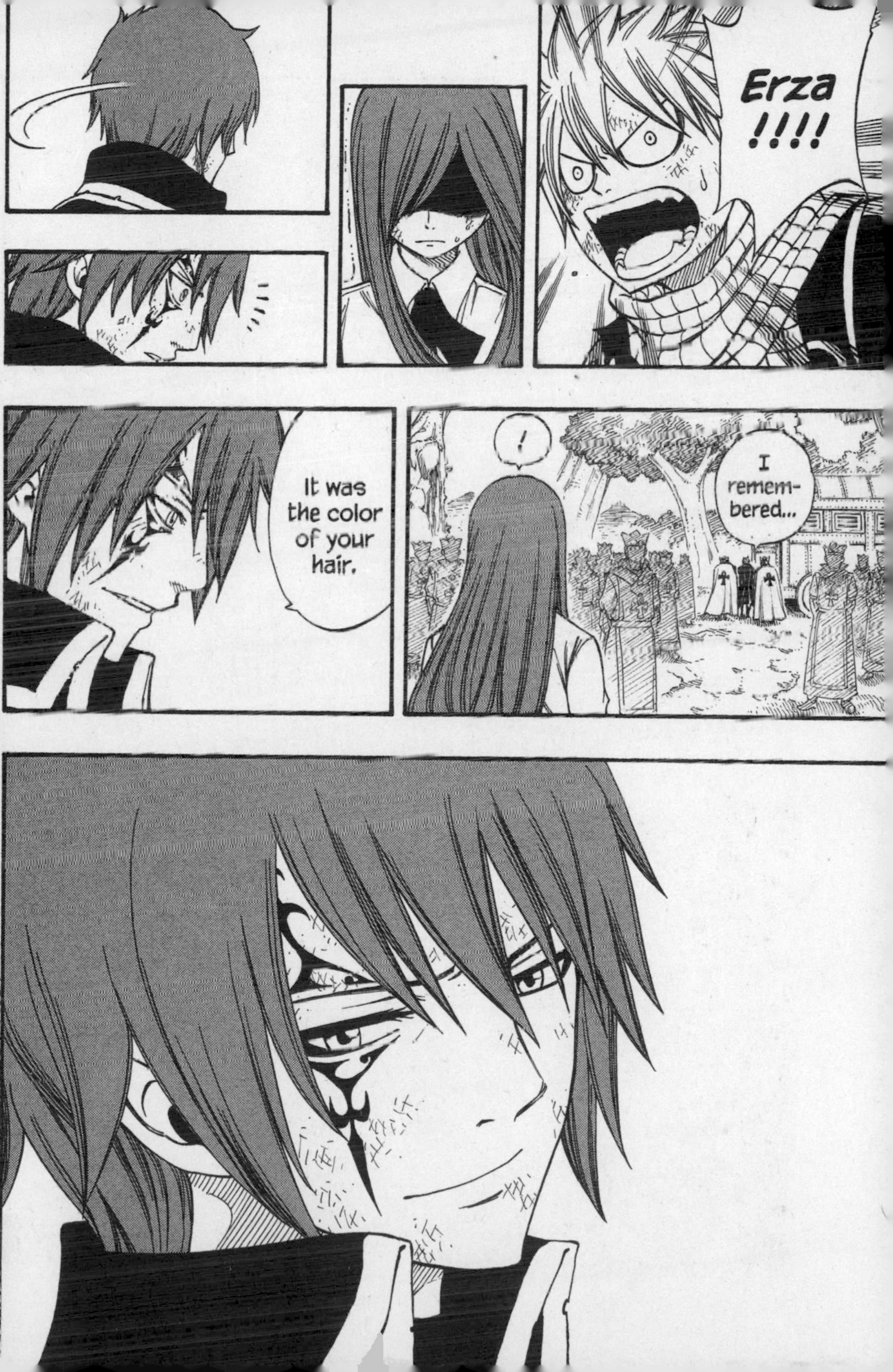
Erza!!!!
!
I remem-bered...
It was the color of your hair.

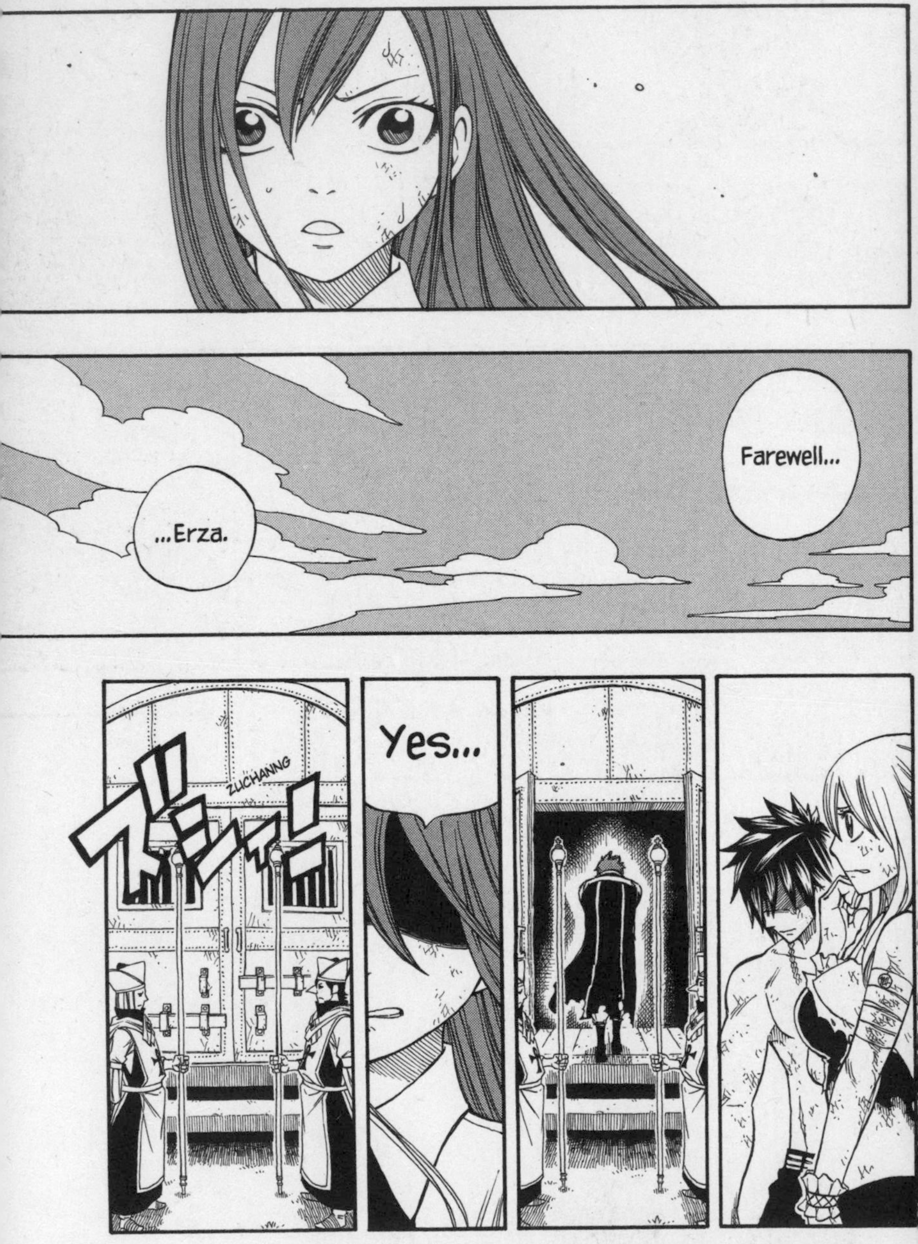
Farewell...
...Erza.
Yes...
ZUCHANNG

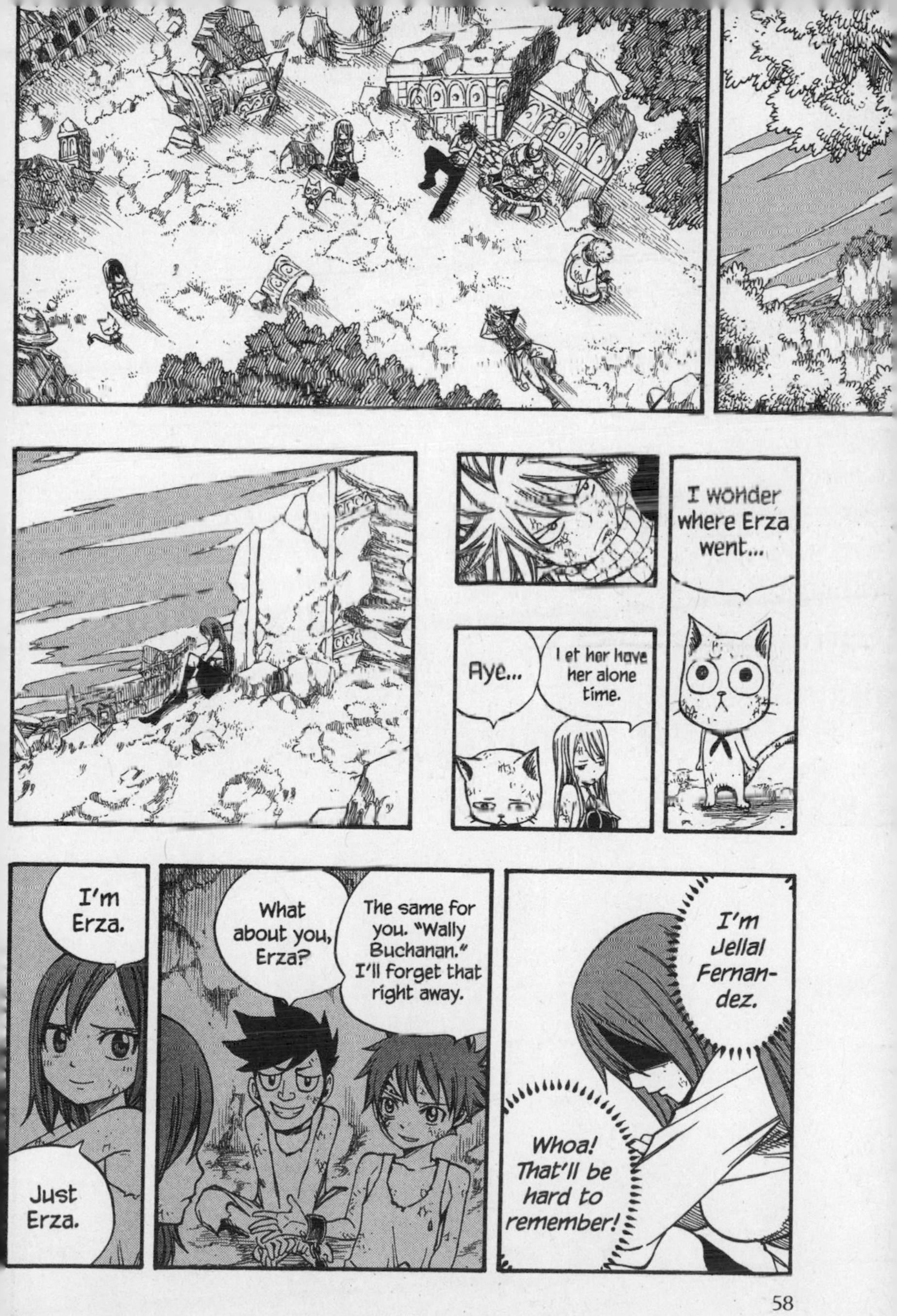
I wonder where Erza went...
Let her have her alone time.
Aye...
I'm Jellal Fernandez.
Whoa! That'll be hard to remember!
The same for you. "Wally Buchanan." I'll forget that right away.
What about you, Erza?
I'm Erza.
Just Erza.

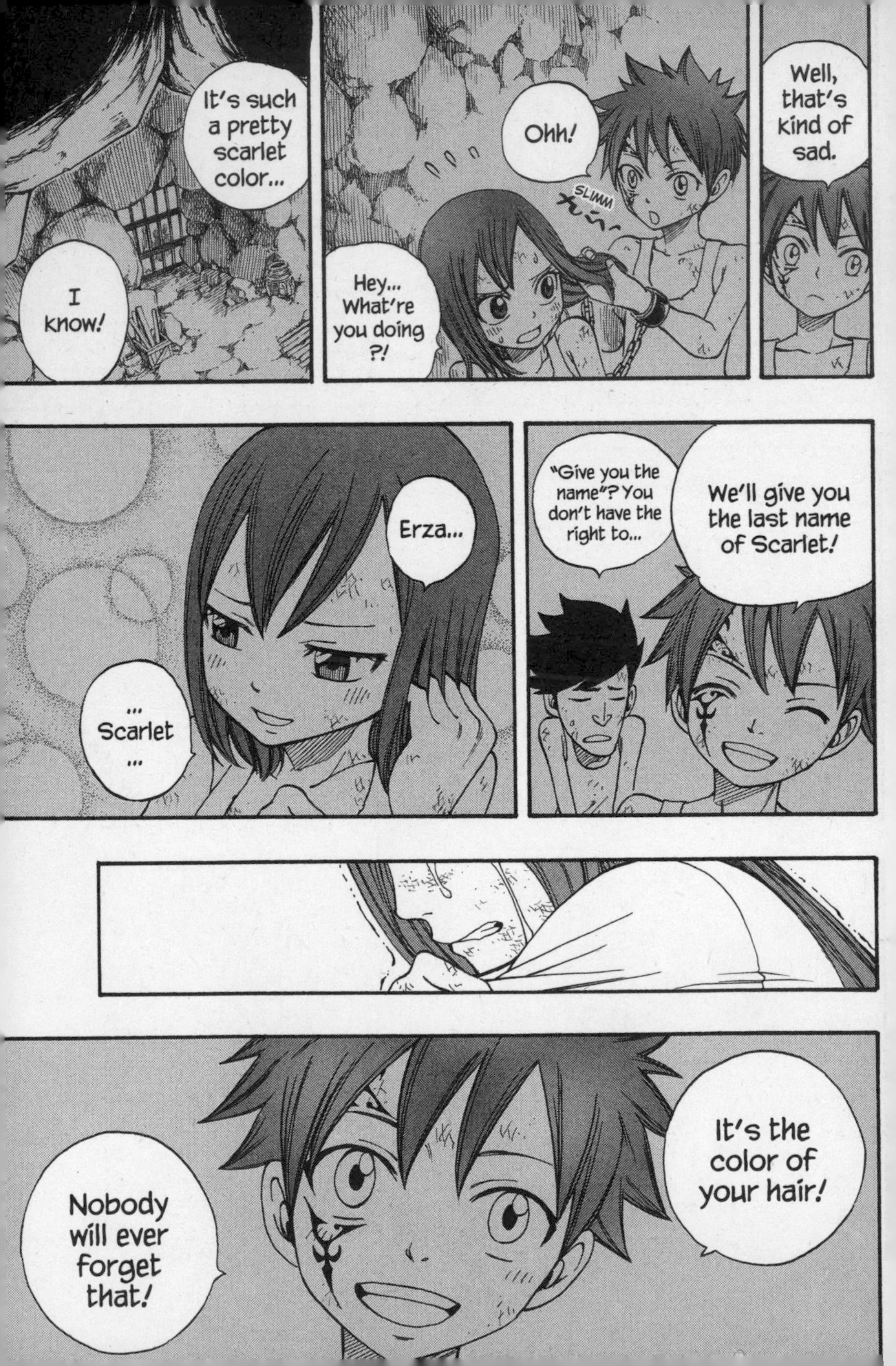
Well, that's kind of sad.
Ohh!
SLIMM
Hey... What're you doing ?!
It's such a pretty scarlet color...
I know!
We'll give you the last name of Scarlet!
"Give you the name"? You don't have the right to...
Erza...
... Scarlet ...
It's the color of your hair!
Nobody will ever forget that!

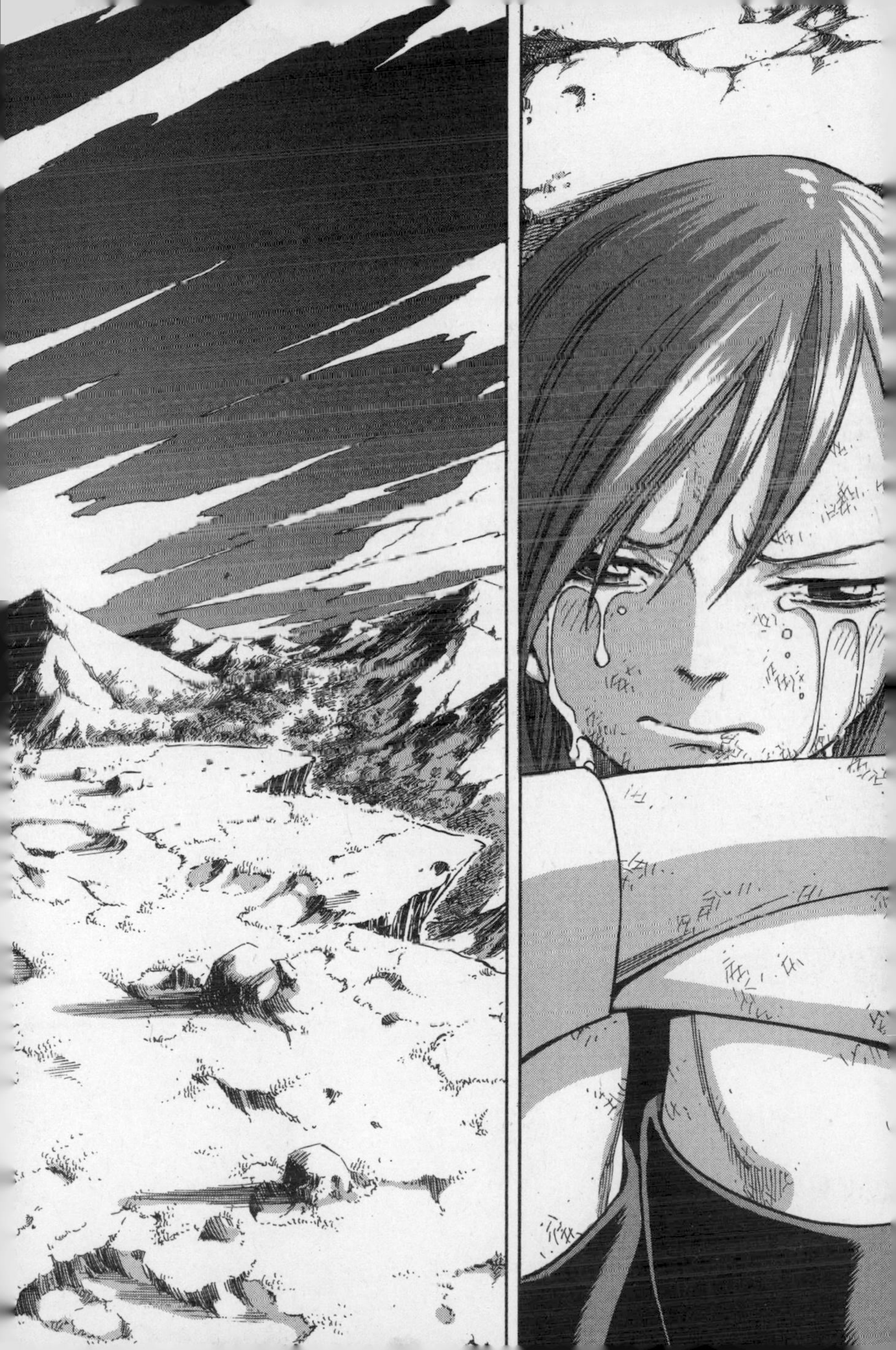

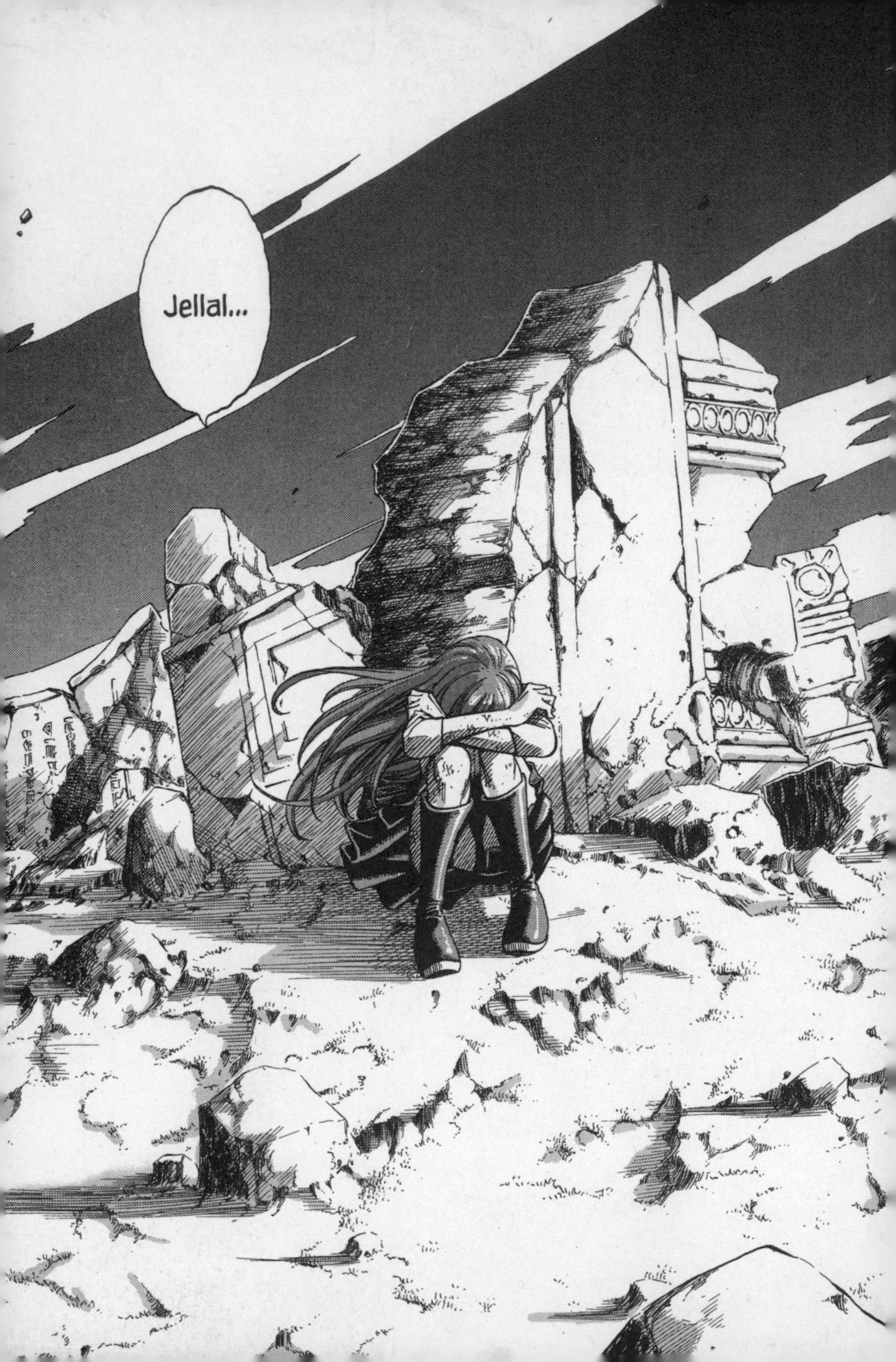
Jellal...

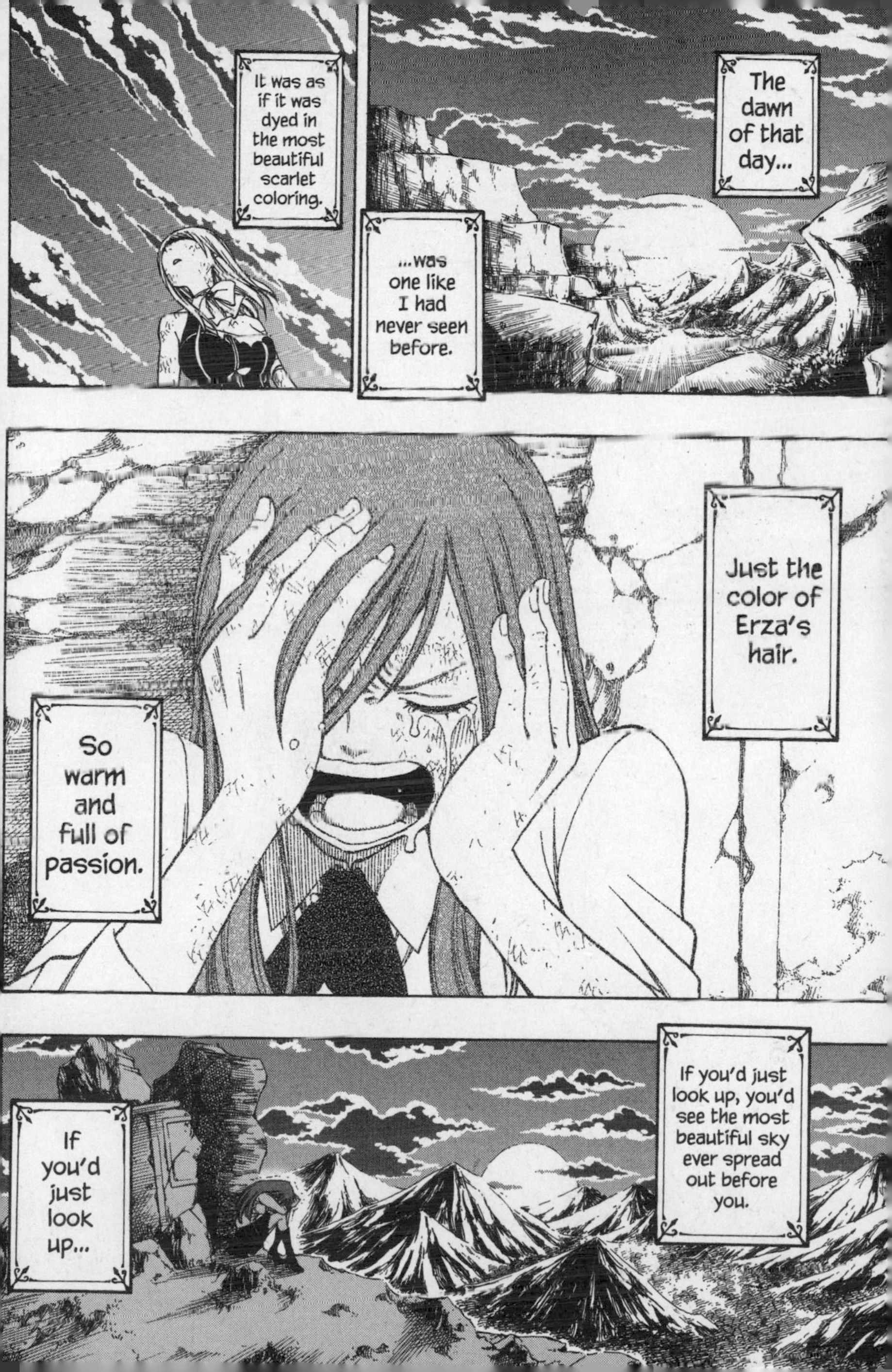
The dawn of that day...
...was one like I had never seen before.
It was as if it was dyed in the most beautiful scarlet coloring.
Just the color of Erza's hair.
So warm and full of passion.
If you'd just look up, you'd see the most beautiful sky ever spread out before you.
If you'd just look up...

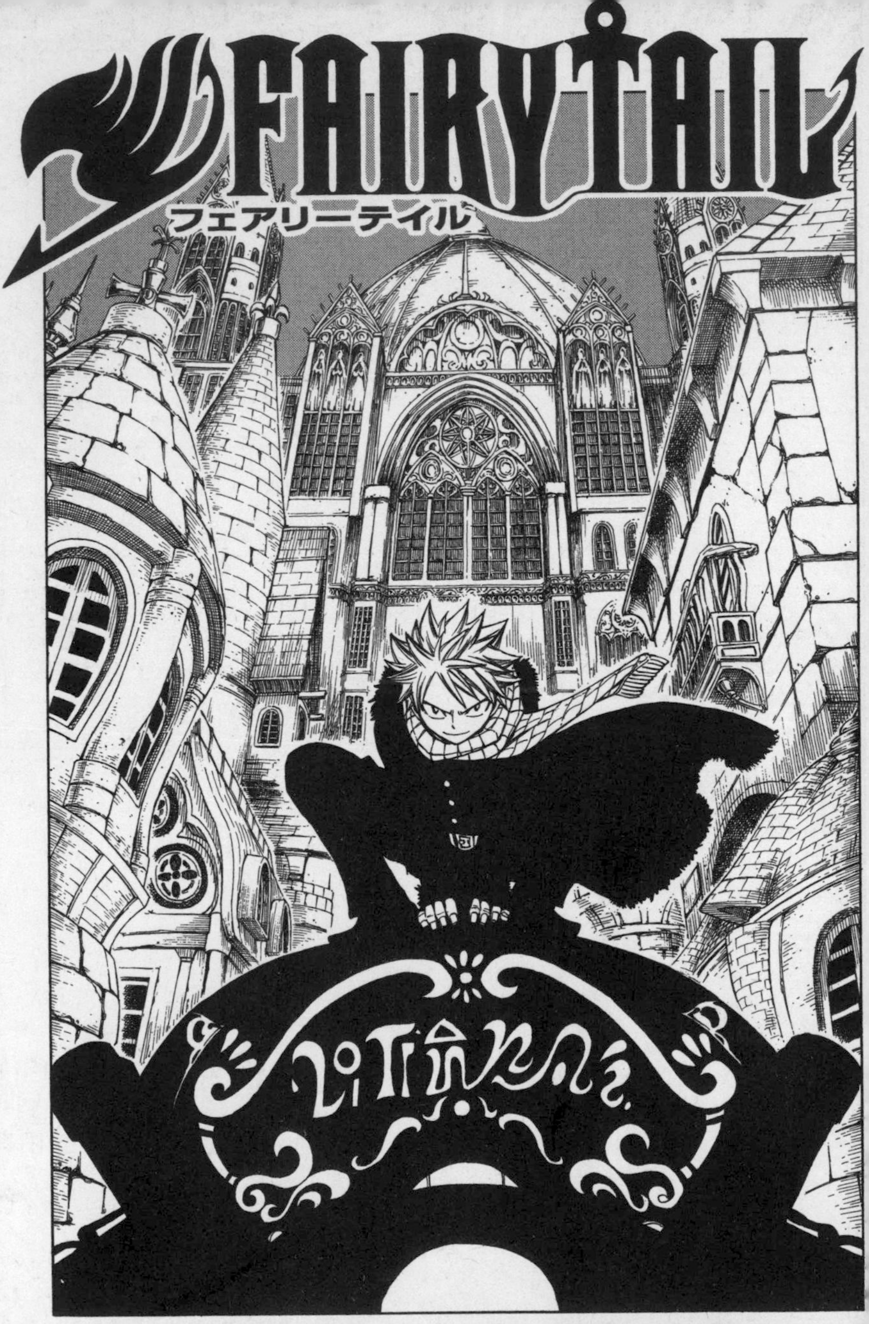
FAIRY TAIL
フェアリーテイル

# Chapter 164, A Guild of One

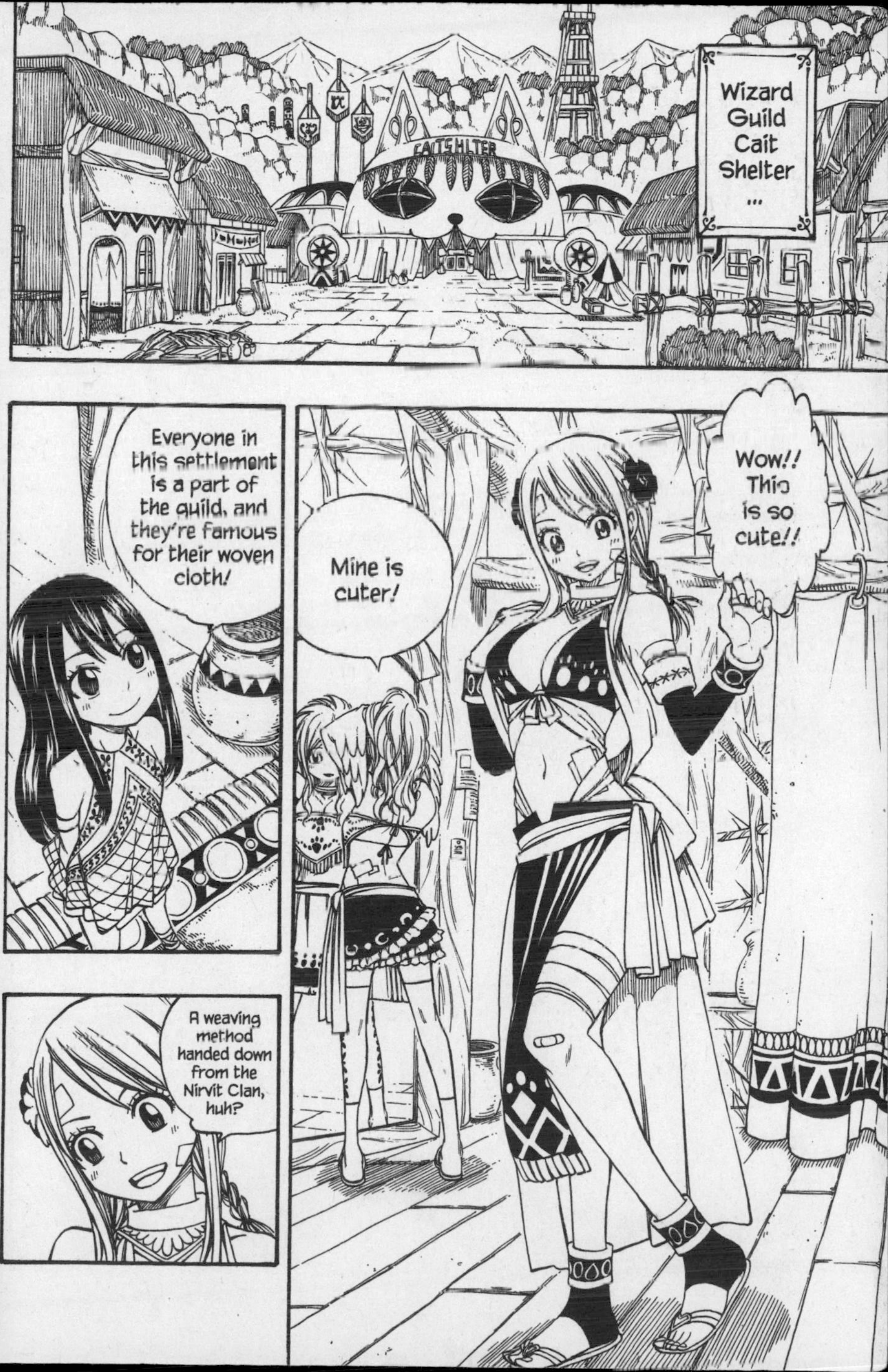
Wizard Guild Cait Shelter …
Wow!! This is so cute!!
Mine is cuter!
Everyone in this settlement is a part of the guild, and they're famous for their woven cloth!
A weaving method handed down from the Nirvit Clan, huh?

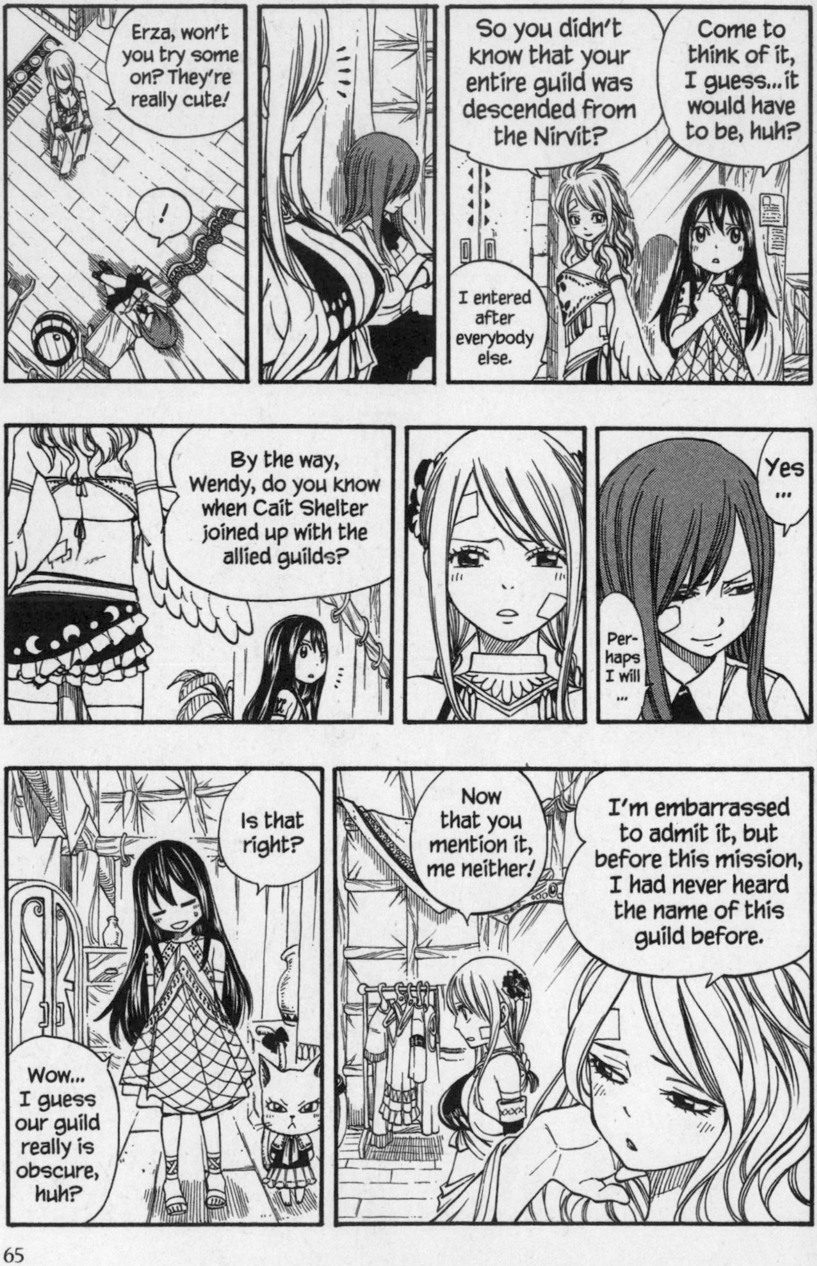
Come to think of it, I guess...it would have to be, huh?
So you didn't know that your entire guild was descended from the Nirvit?
I entered after everybody else.
Erza, won't you try some on? They're really cute!
!
Yes...
Perhaps I will...
By the way, Wendy, do you know when Cait Shelter joined up with the allied guilds?
I'm embarrassed to admit it, but before this mission, I had never heard the name of this guild before.
Now that you mention it, me neither!
Is that right?
Wow... I guess our guild really is obscure, huh?

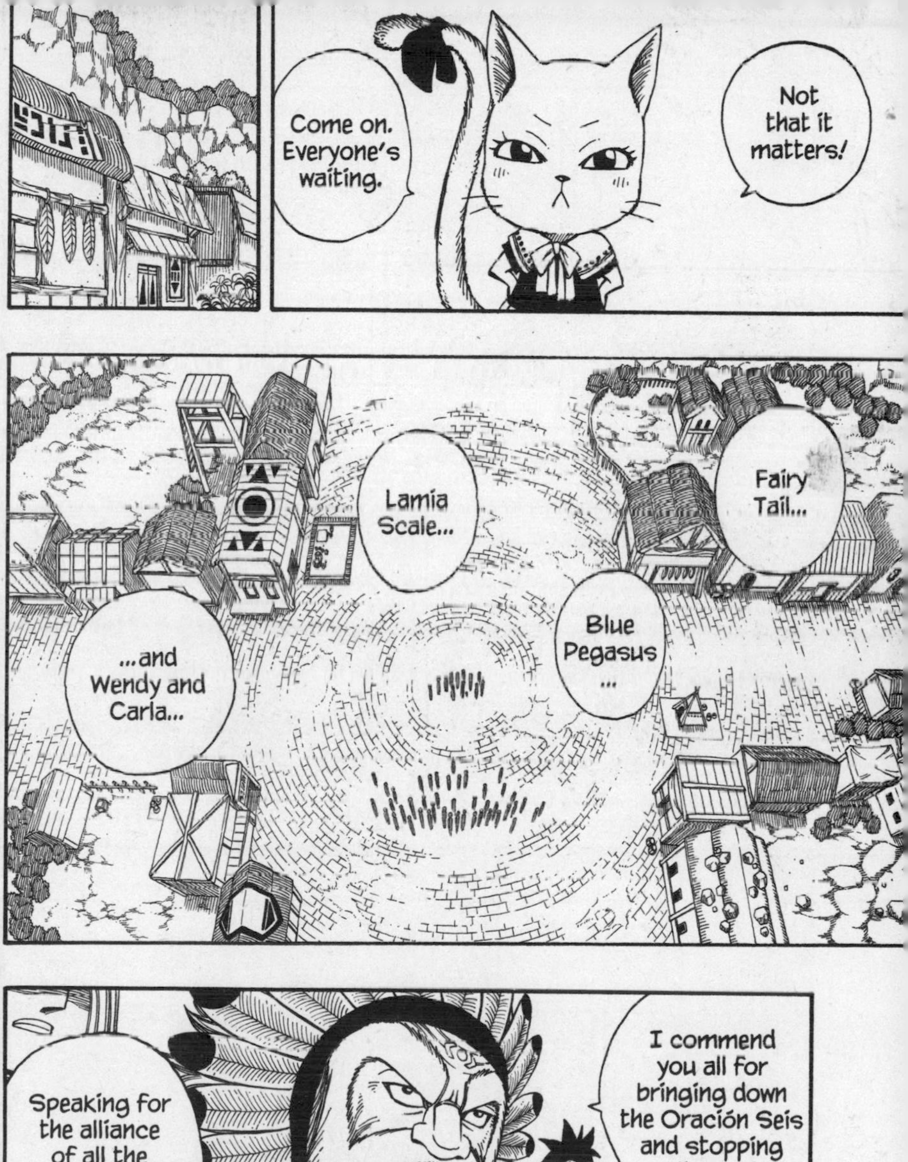
Not that it matters!
Come on. Everyone's waiting.
Fairy Tail...
Blue Pegasus...
Lamia Scale...
...and Wendy and Carla...
I commend you all for bringing down the Oración Seis and stopping Nirvana!
Speaking for the alliance of all the regional guilds, I, Robaul, express our gratitude!

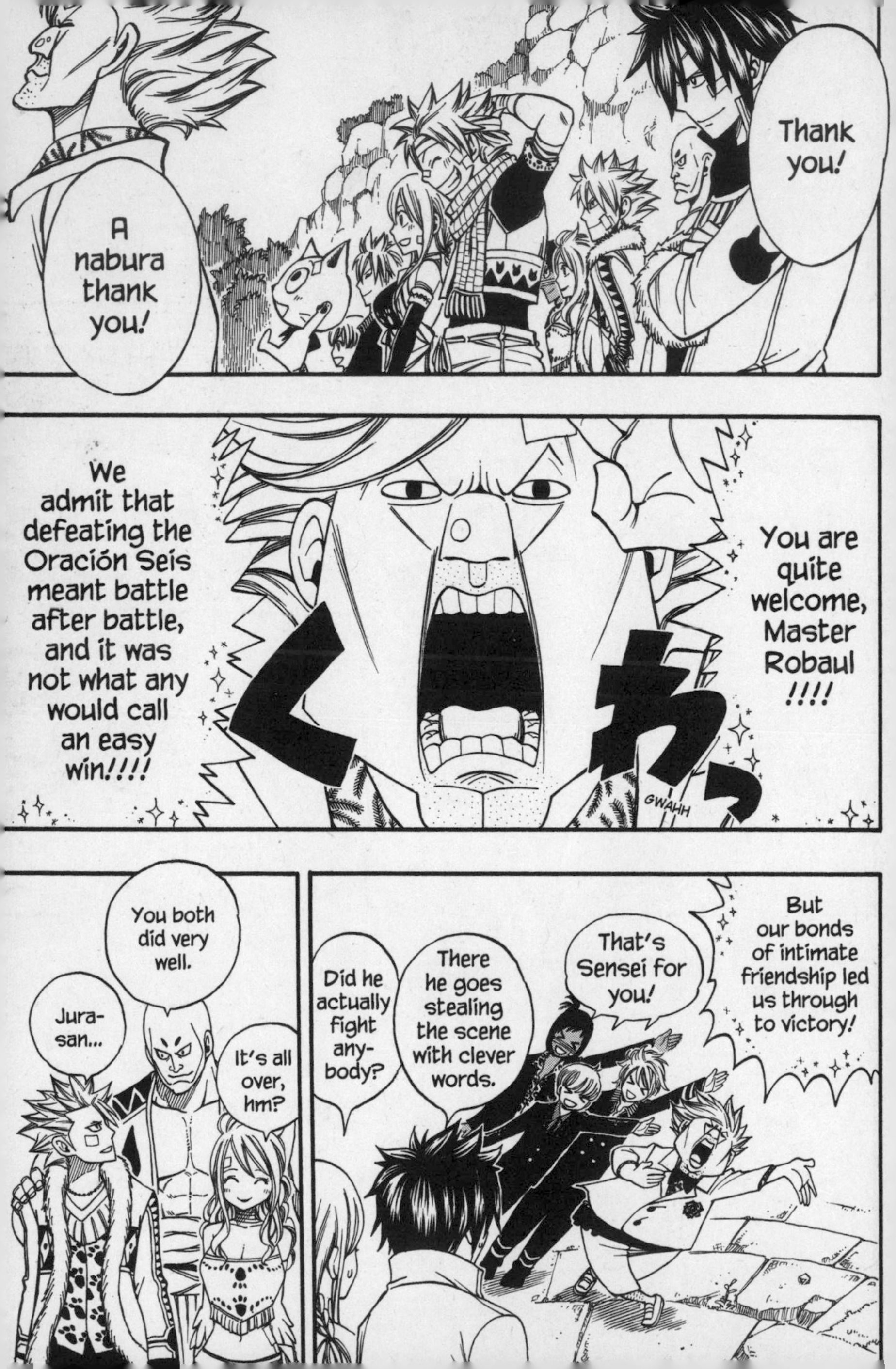
Thank you!
A nabura thank you!
You are quite welcome, Master Robaul !!!!
We admit that defeating the Oración Seis meant battle after battle, and it was not what any would call an easy win!!!!
GWAHH
But our bonds of intimate friendship led us through to victory!
That's Sensei for you!
There he goes stealing the scene with clever words.
Did he actually fight any-body?
You both did very well.
Jura-san...
It's all over, hm?

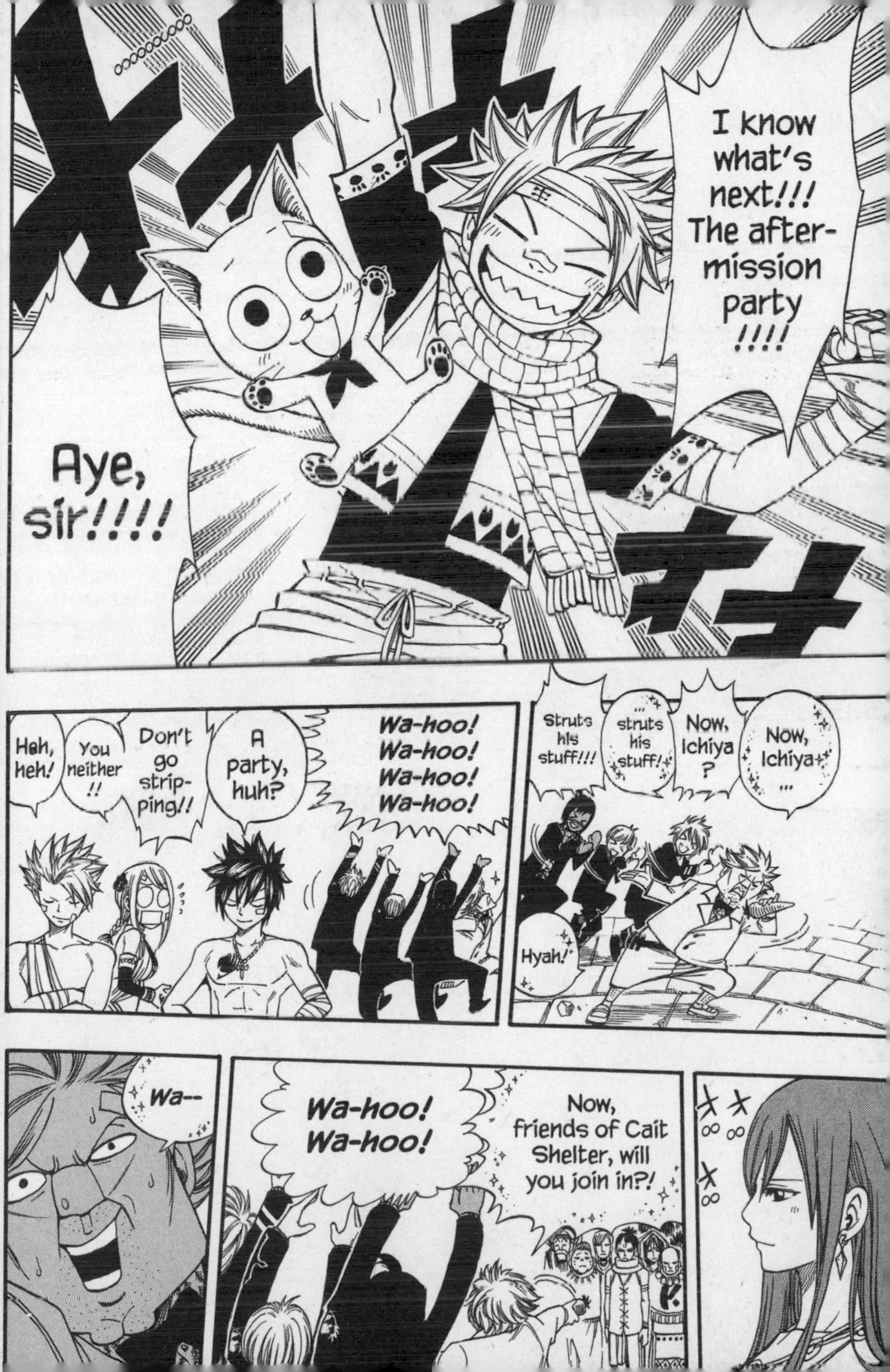
I know what's next!!! The after-mission party!!!!
Aye, sir!!!!!
Now, Ichiya...
Now, Ichiya?
...struts his stuff!
Struts his stuff!!!
Hyah!
Wa-hoo! Wa-hoo! Wa-hoo! Wa-hoo!
A party, huh?
Don't go strip-ping!!
You neither!!
Heh, heh!
Now, friends of Cait Shelter, will you join in?!
Wa-hoo! Wa-hoo!
Wa--

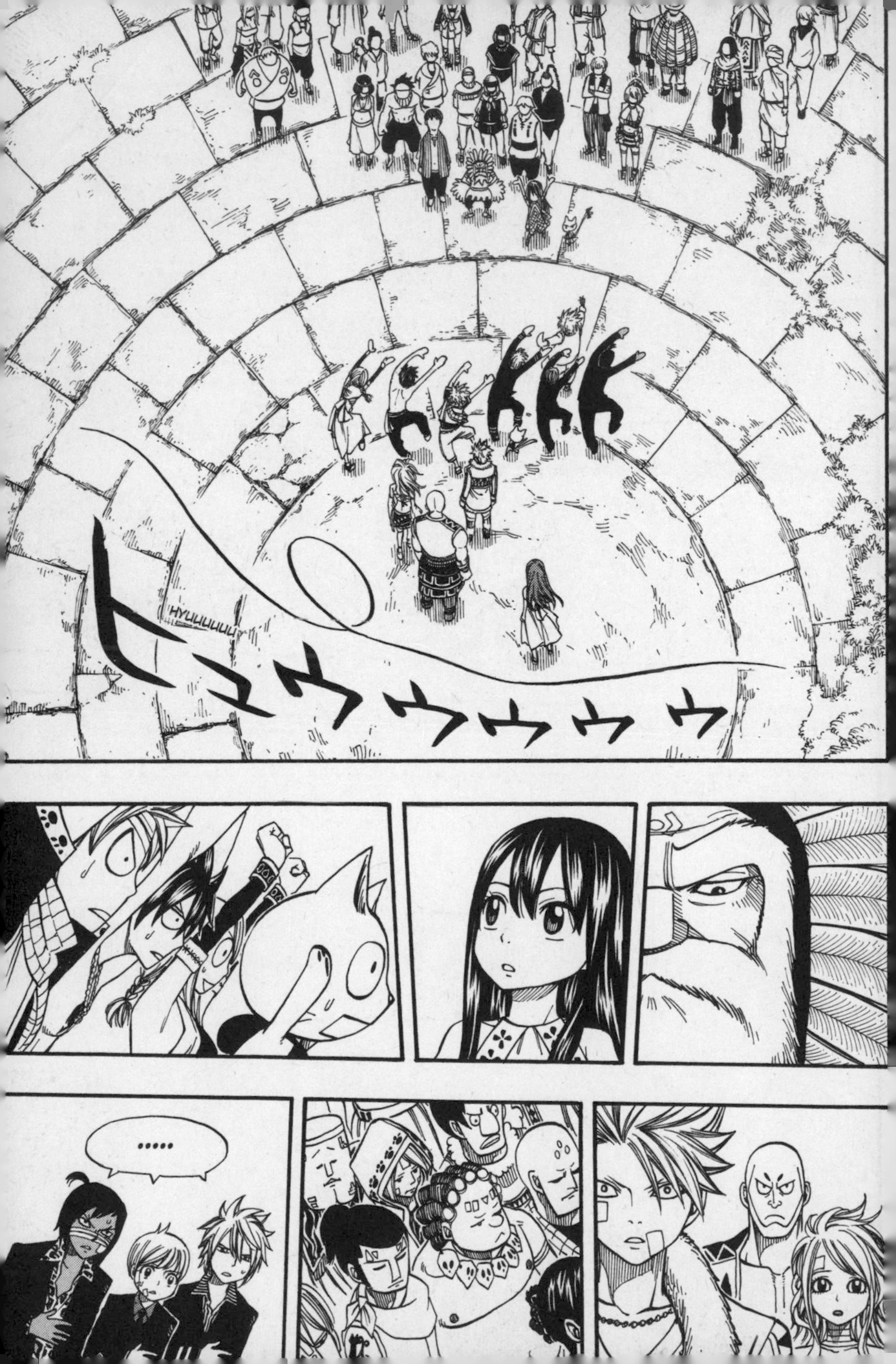
HYUUUUUU
ヒュウウウウウウ
.....

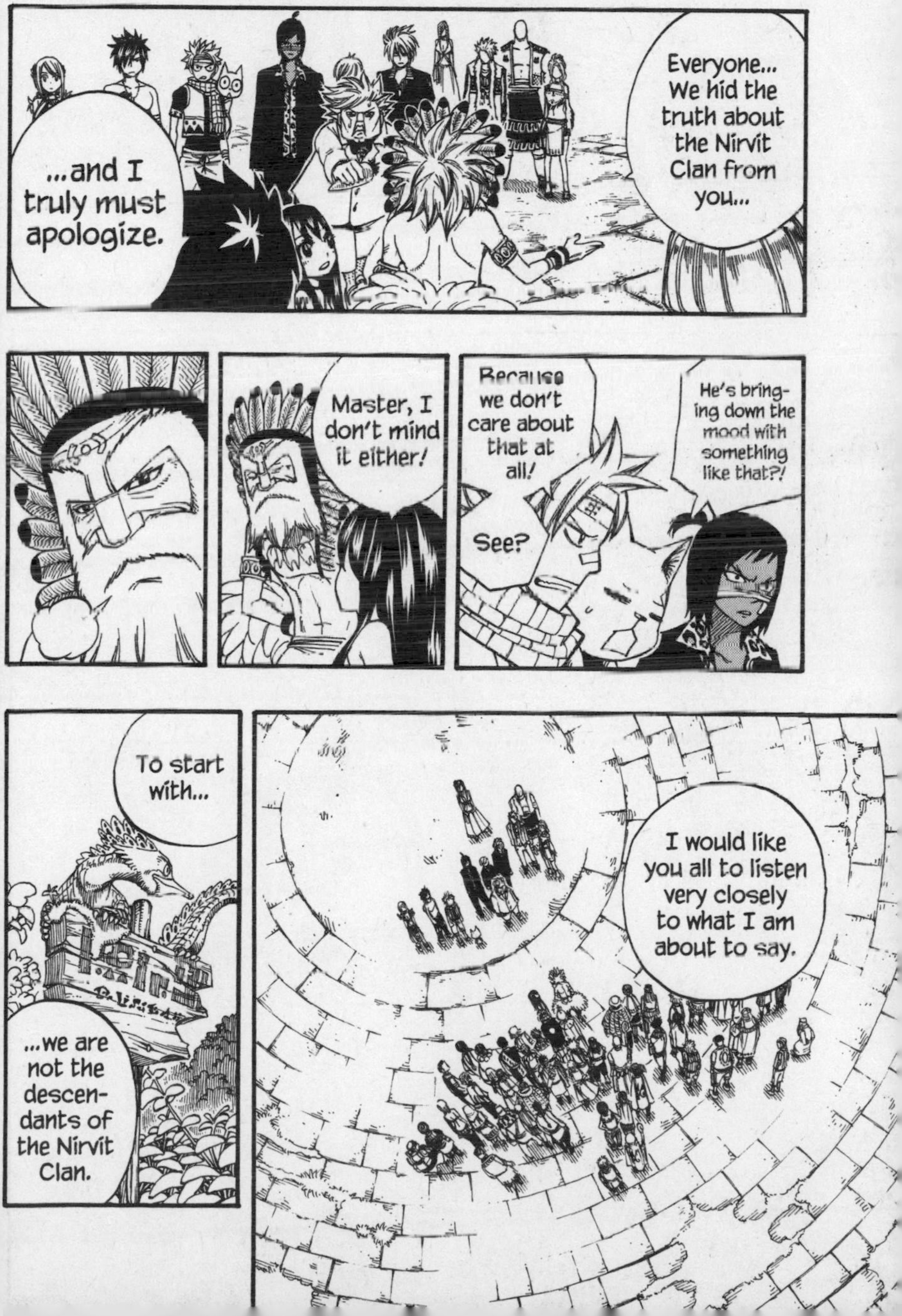
Everyone... We hid the truth about the Nirvit Clan from you...
...and I truly must apologize.
He's bring-ing down the mood with something like that?!
Because we don't care about that at all!
See?
Master, I don't mind it either!
I would like you all to listen very closely to what I am about to say.
To start with...
...we are not the descen-dants of the Nirvit Clan.

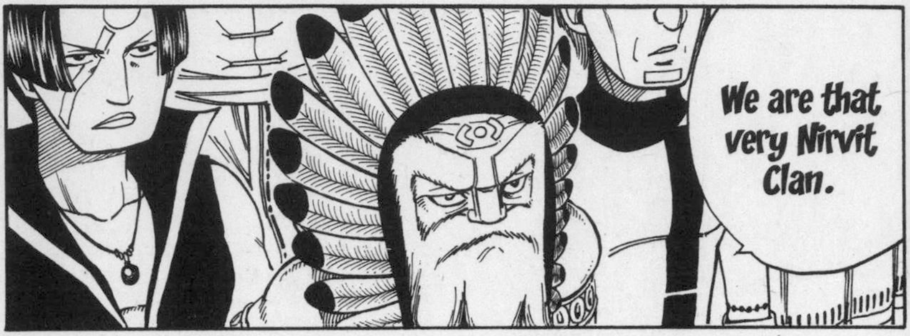
We are that very Nirvit Clan.

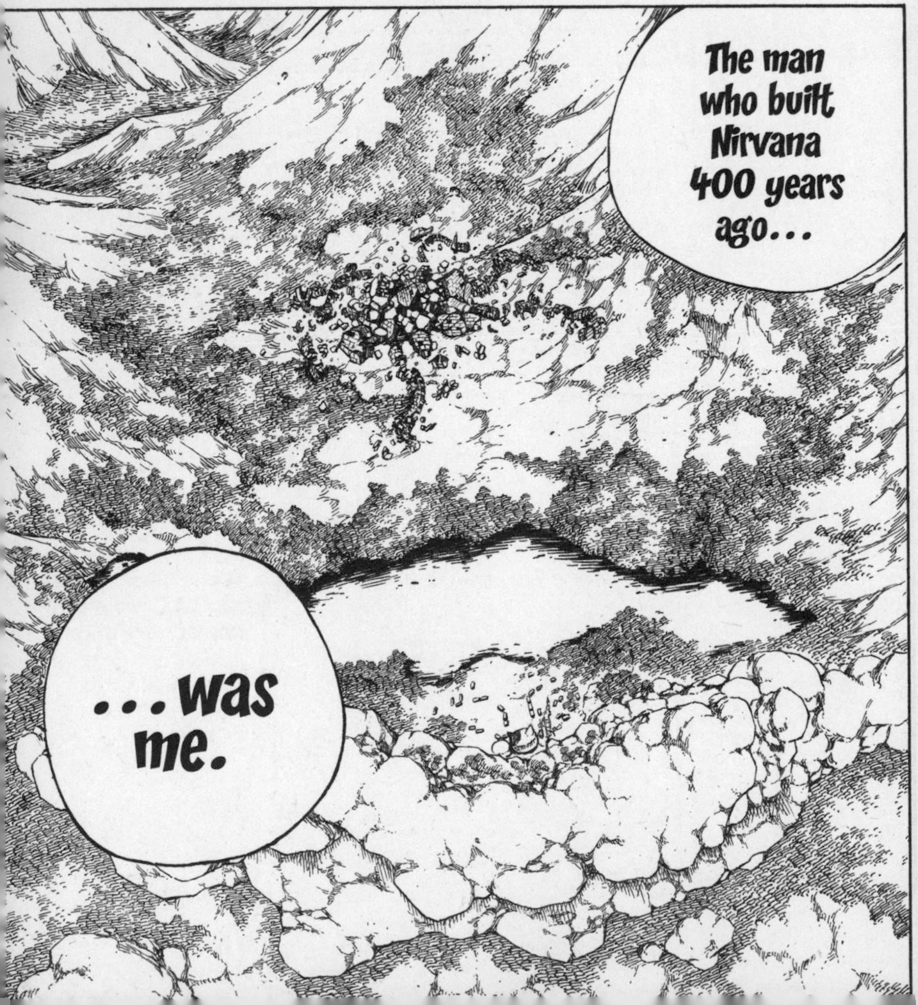
The man who built Nirvana 400 years ago...
...was me.

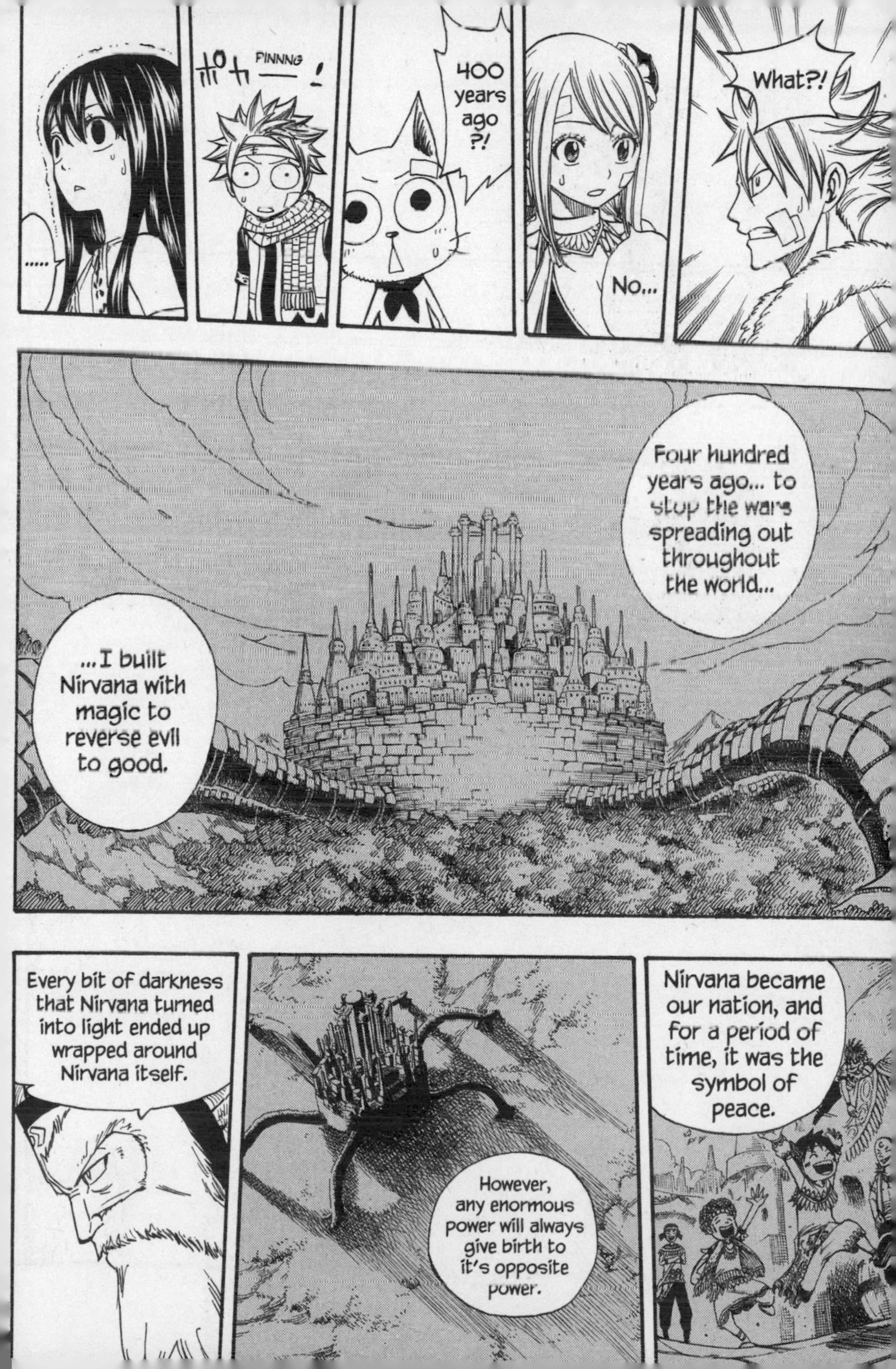
What?!
No...
400 years ago ?!
PINNNG —!
.....
Four hundred years ago... to stop the wars spreading out throughout the world...
...I built Nirvana with magic to reverse evil to good.
Nirvana became our nation, and for a period of time, it was the symbol of peace.
However, any enormous power will always give birth to it's opposite power.
Every bit of darkness that Nirvana turned into light ended up wrapped around Nirvana itself.

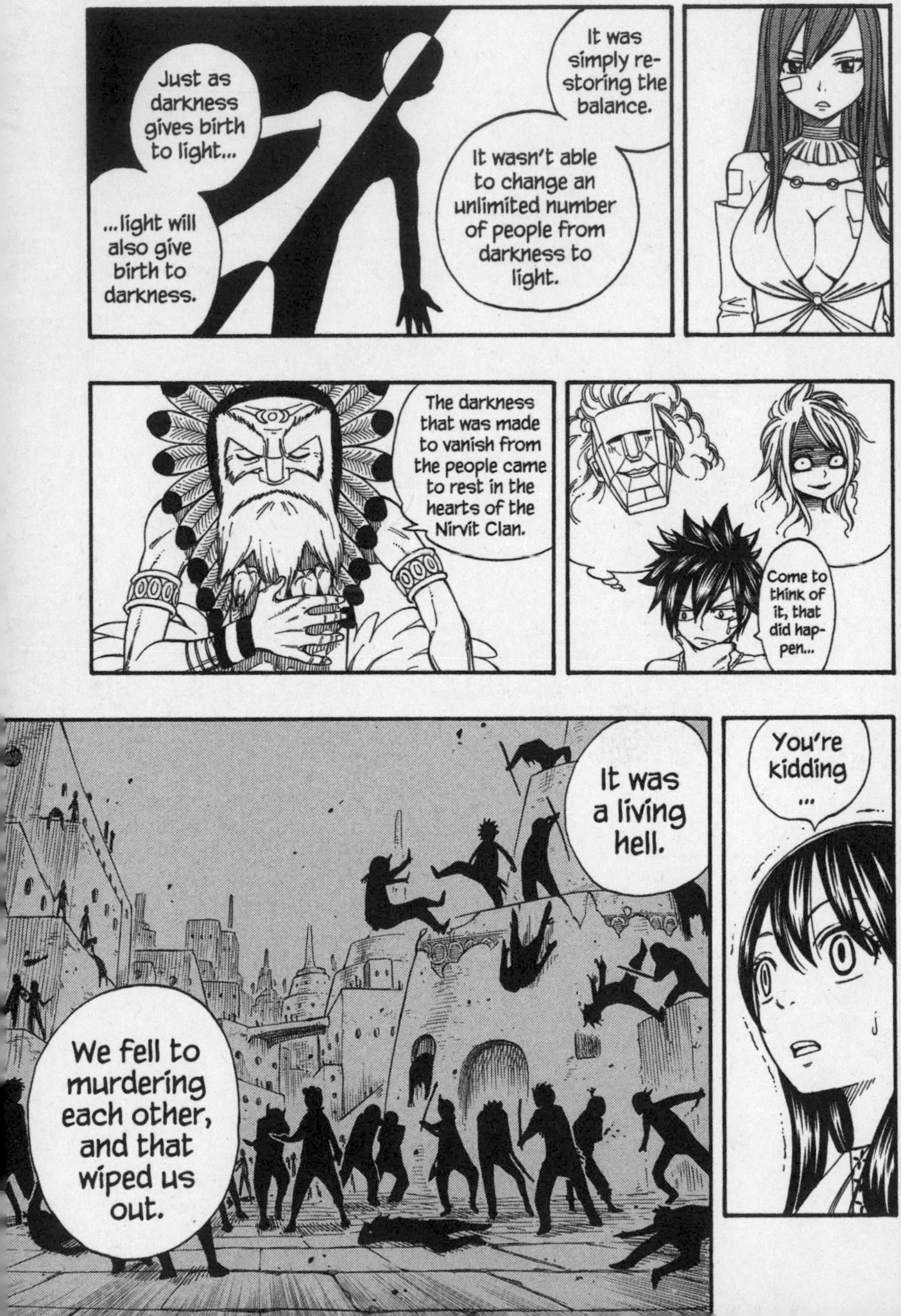
It was simply re-storing the balance.
It wasn't able to change an unlimited number of people from darkness to light.
Just as darkness gives birth to light...
...light will also give birth to darkness.
Come to think of it, that did hap-pen...
The darkness that was made to vanish from the people came to rest in the hearts of the Nirvit Clan.
You're kidding ...
It was a living hell.
We fell to murdering each other, and that wiped us out.

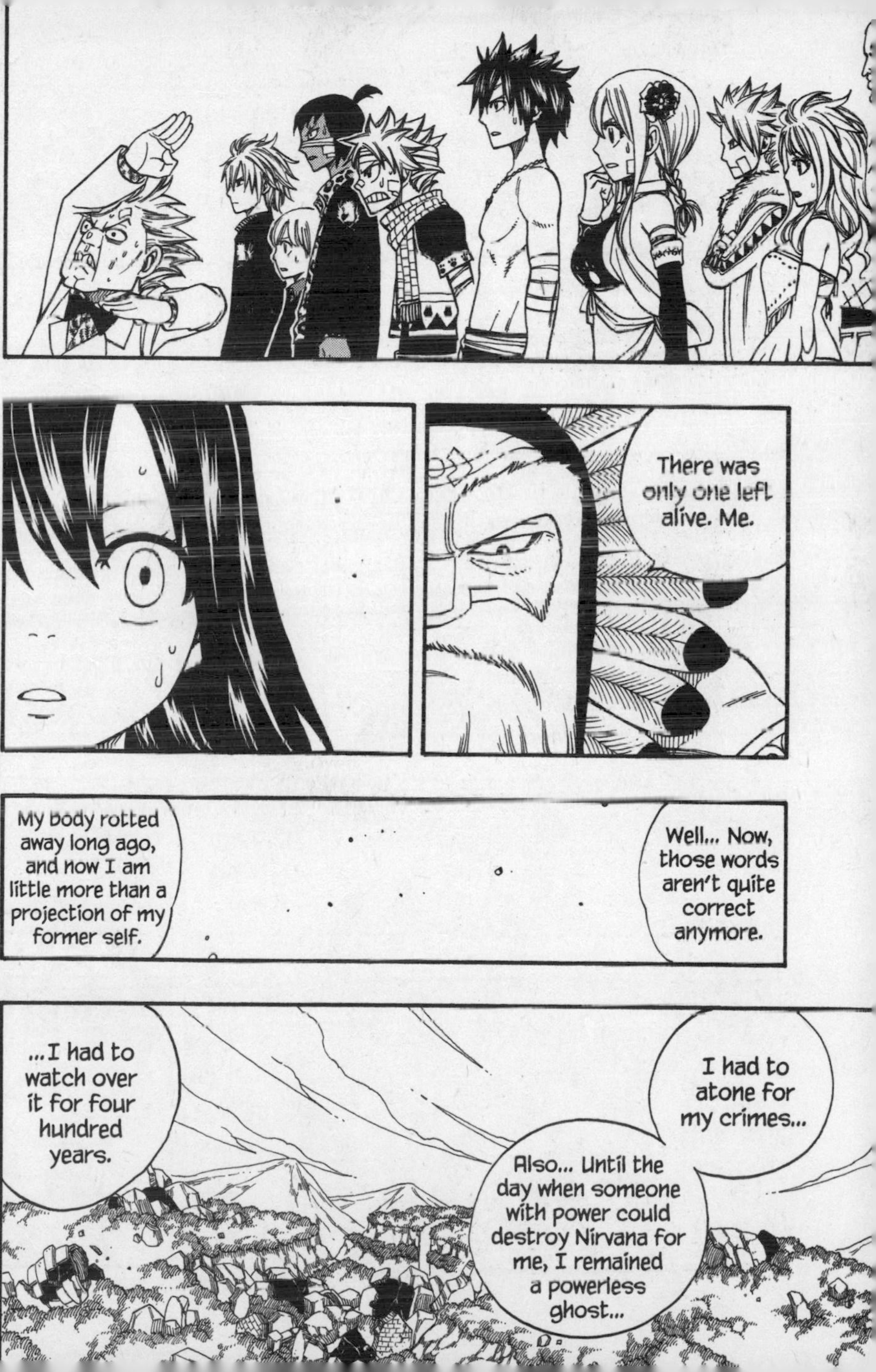
There was only one left alive. Me.
Well... Now, those words aren't quite correct anymore.
My body rotted away long ago, and now I am little more than a projection of my former self.
I had to atone for my crimes...
Also... Until the day when someone with power could destroy Nirvana for me, I remained a powerless ghost...
...I had to watch over it for four hundred years.

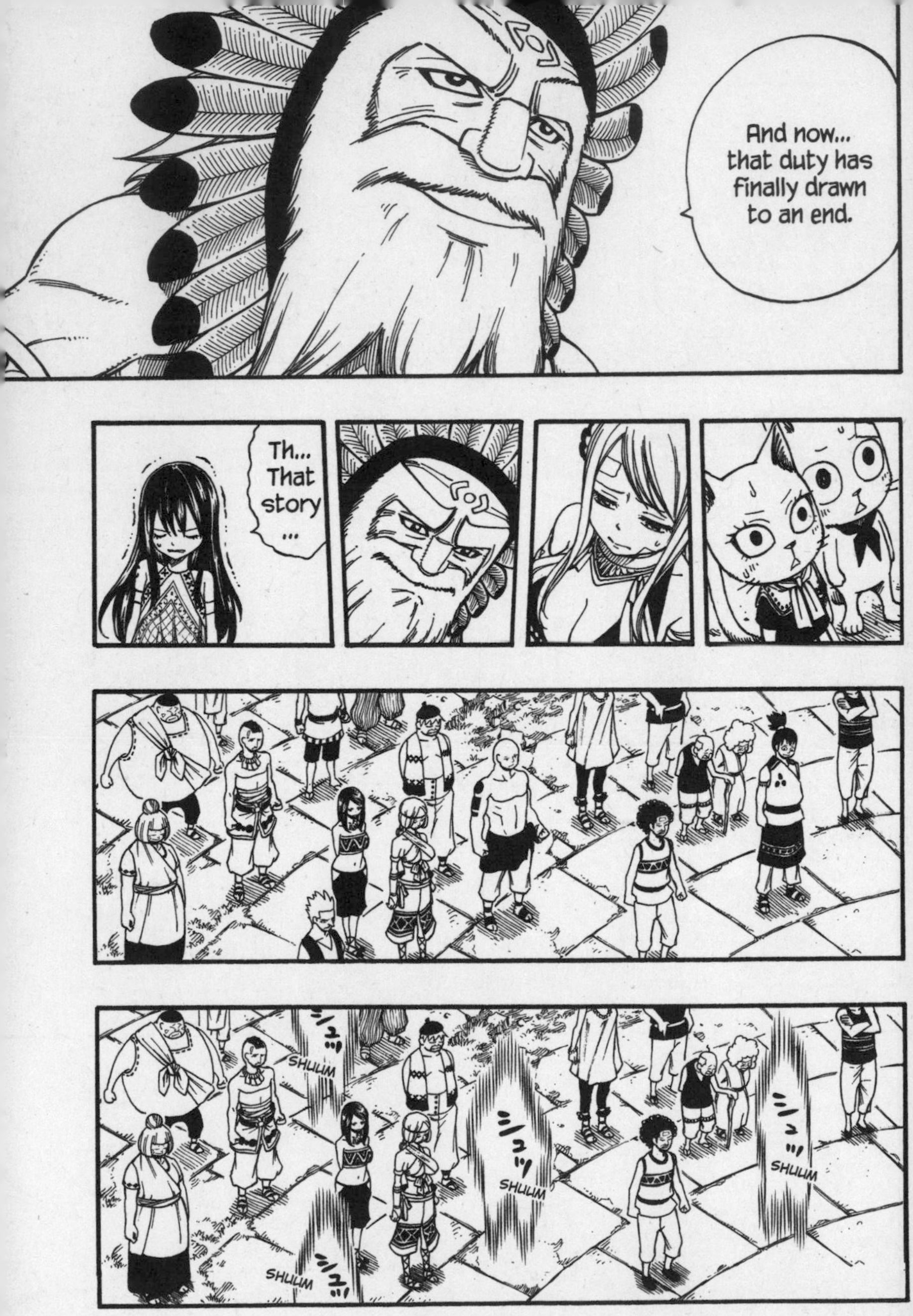
And now... that duty has finally drawn to an end.
Th... That story ...
SHUUM
SHUUM
SHUUM
SHUUM

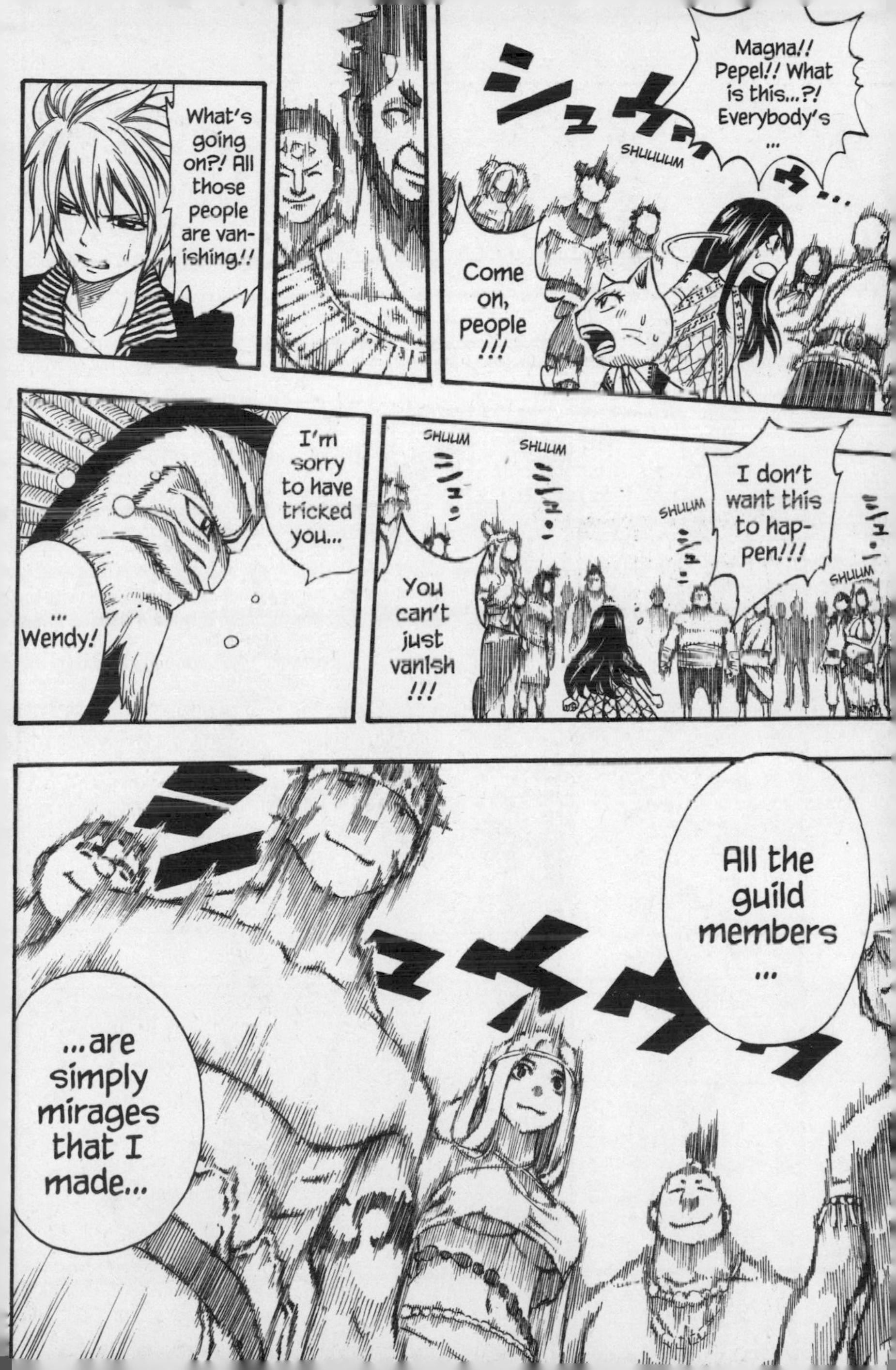
Magna!! Pepel!! What is this...?! Everybody's ...
SHUUUUM
Come on, people!!!
What's going on?! All those people are vanishing!!
SHUUM
SHUUM
SHUUM
SHUUM
I don't want this to happen!!!
You can't just vanish!!!
I'm sorry to have tricked you...
...Wendy!
All the guild members ...
...are simply mirages that I made...

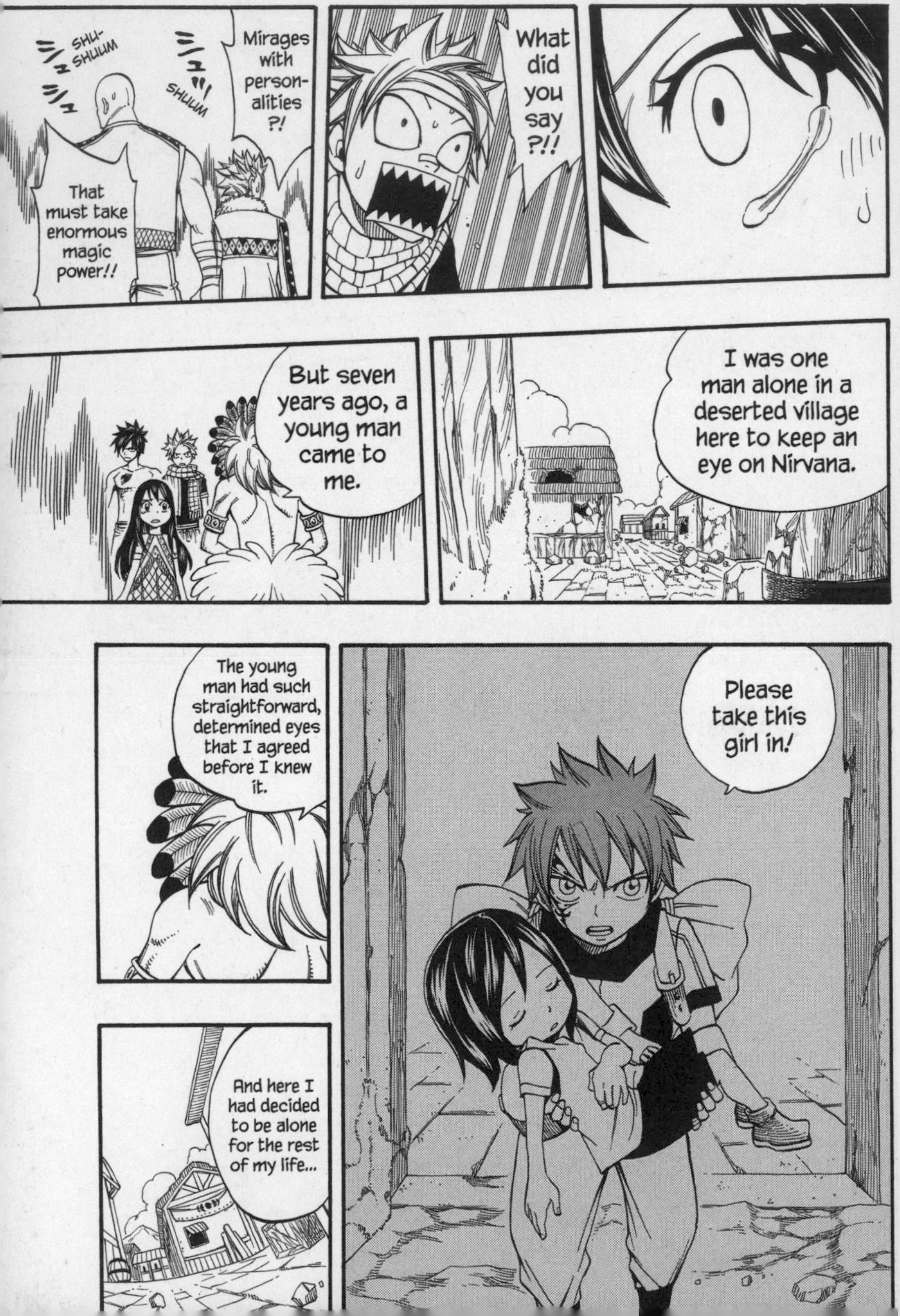

What did you say ?!!
Mirages with personalities ?!
SHU-SHUUM
SHUUM
That must take enormous magic power!!
I was one man alone in a deserted village here to keep an eye on Nirvana.
But seven years ago, a young man came to me.
Please take this girl in!
The young man had such straightforward, determined eyes that I agreed before I knew it.
And here I had decided to be alone for the rest of my life...

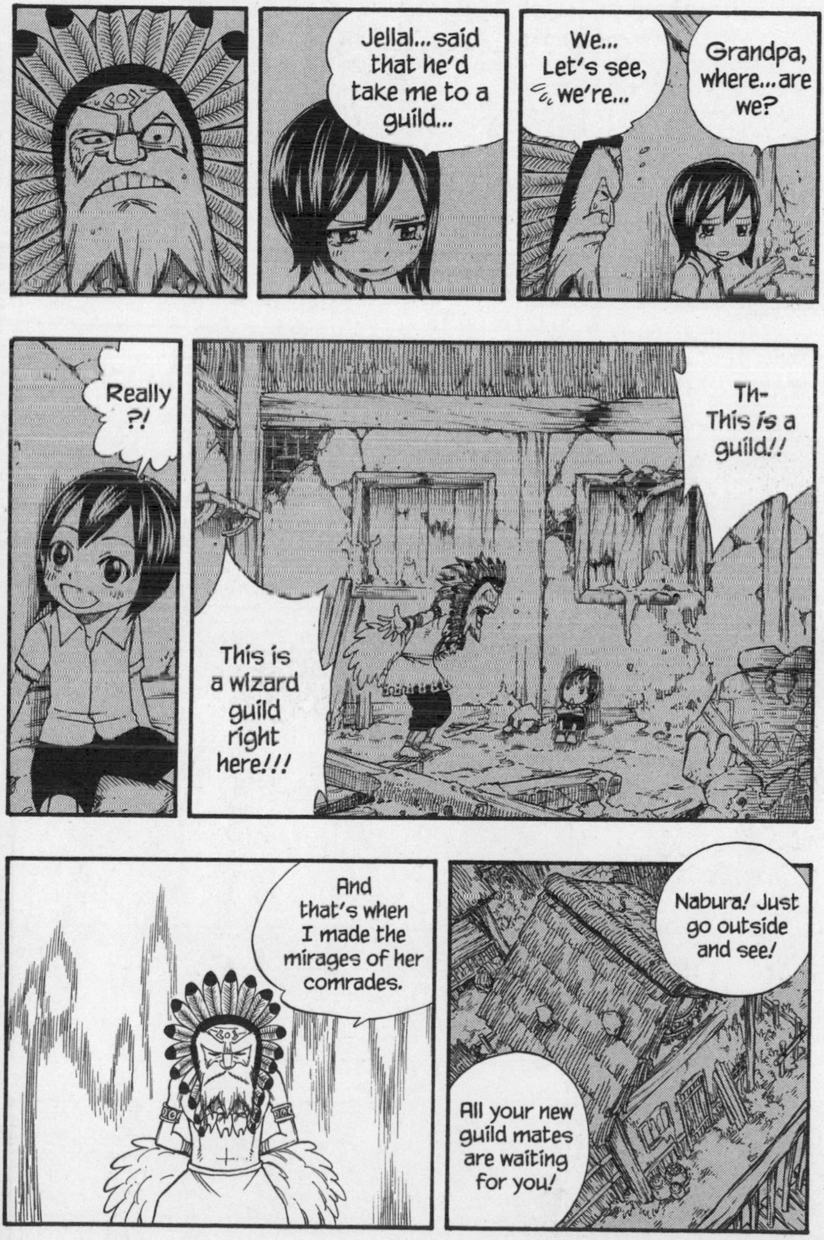
Grandpa, where...are we?
We... Let's see, we're...
Jellal...said that he'd take me to a guild...
Th- This *is* a guild!!
This is a wizard guild right here!!!
Really ?!
Nabura! Just go outside and see!
All your new guild mates are waiting for you!
And that's when I made the mirages of her comrades.

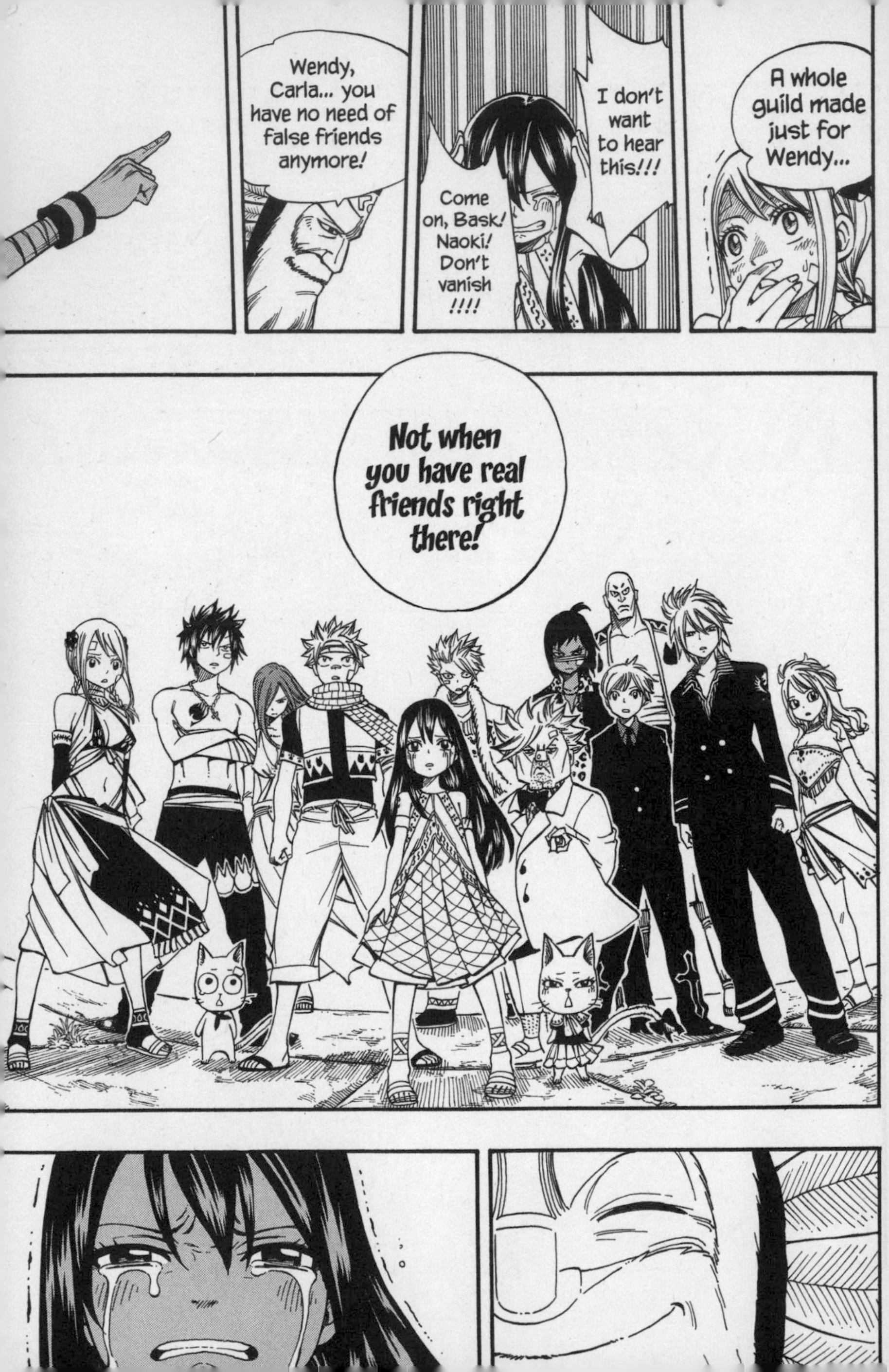
A whole guild made just for Wendy...
I don't want to hear this!!!
Come on, Bask! Naoki! Don't vanish!!!!
Wendy, Carla... you have no need of false friends anymore!
Not when you have real friends right there!

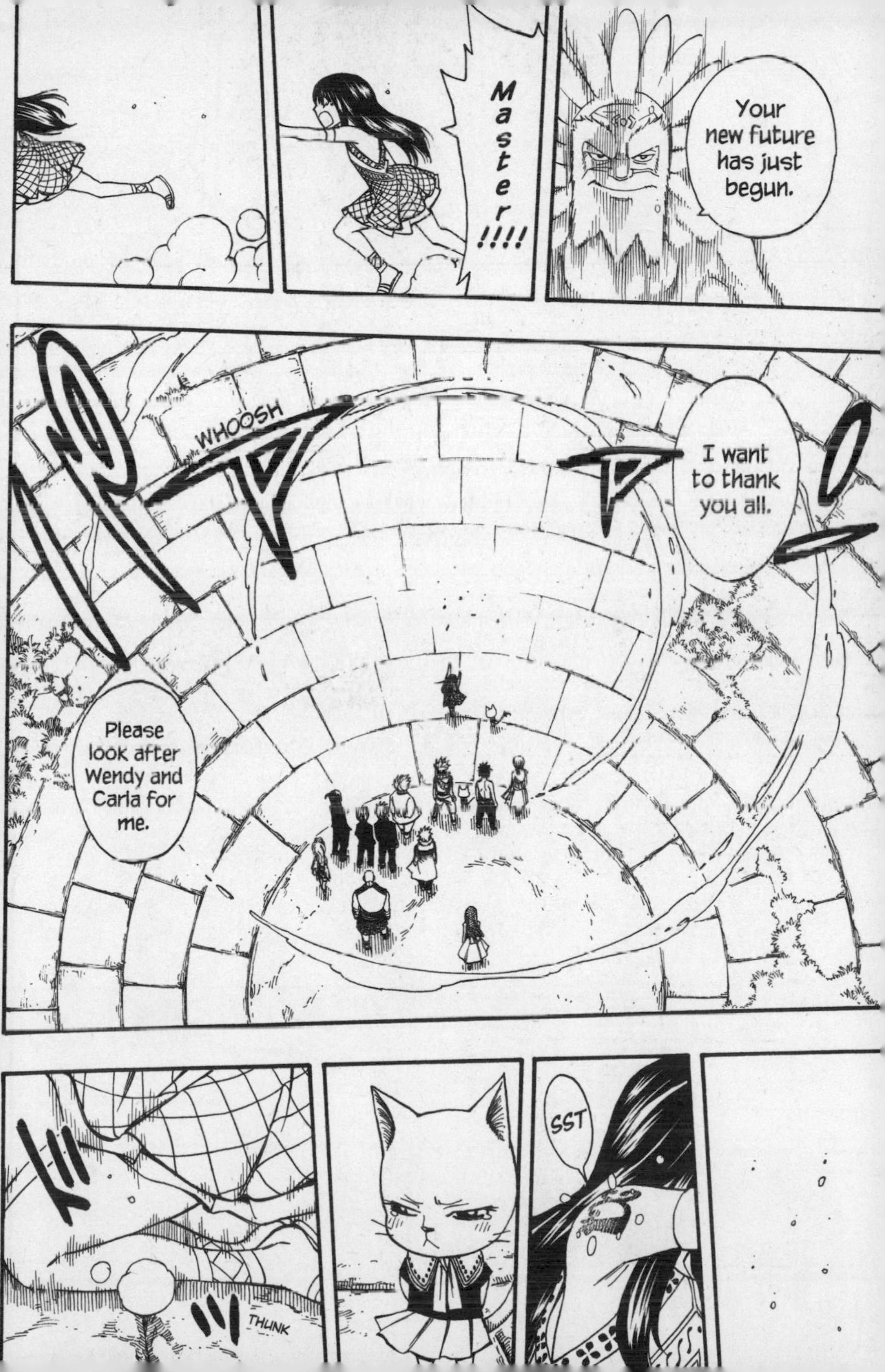
Your new future has just begun.
Master!!!!
I want to thank you all.
WHOOSH
Please look after Wendy and Carla for me.
SST
THUNK

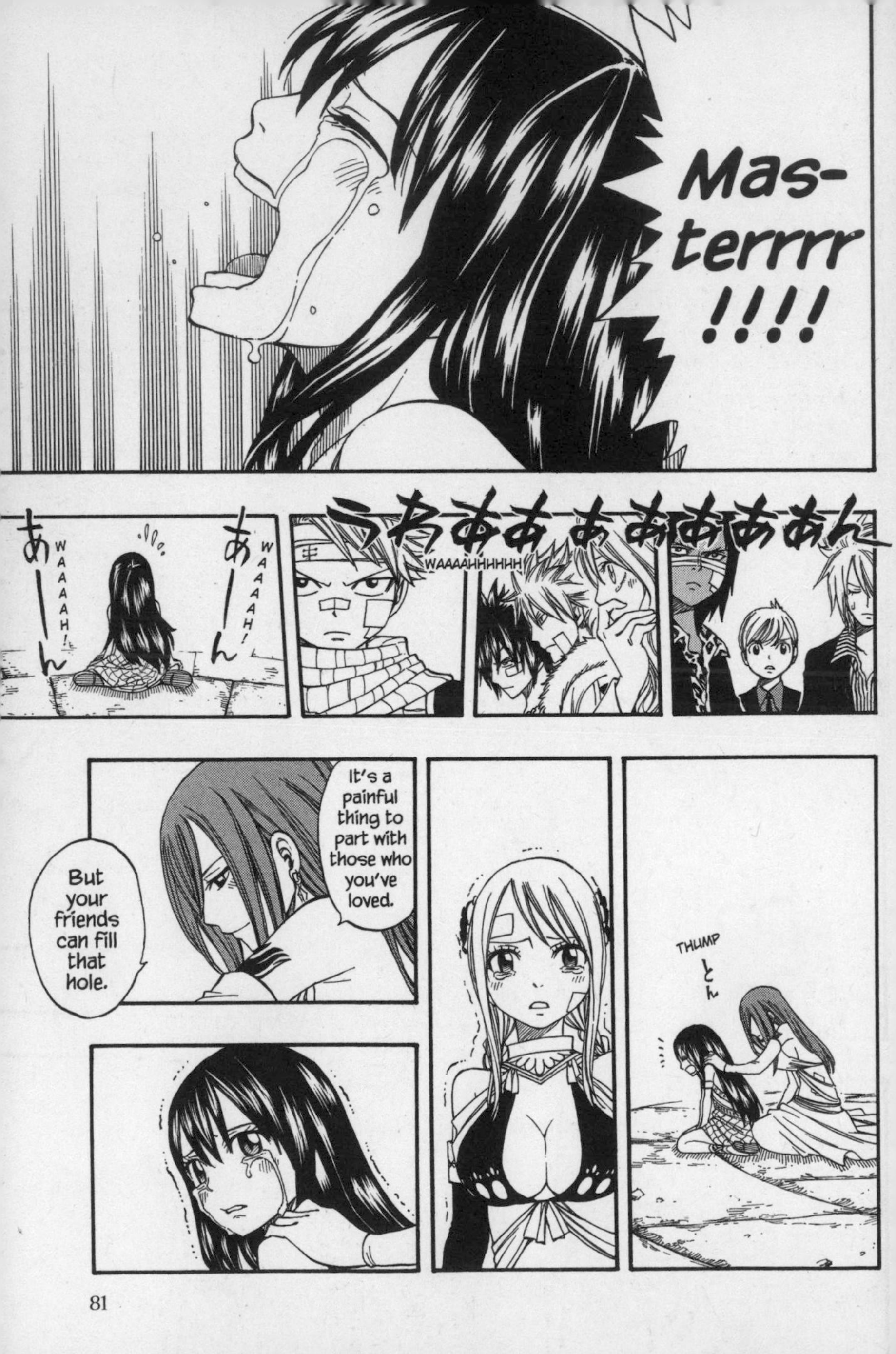

Mas-terrrr!!!!
うわああああああああん
WAAAAHHHHHH
あーん
WAAAAAH!
あーん
WAAAAAH!
THUMP
とん
It's a painful thing to part with those who you've loved.
But your friends can fill that hole.

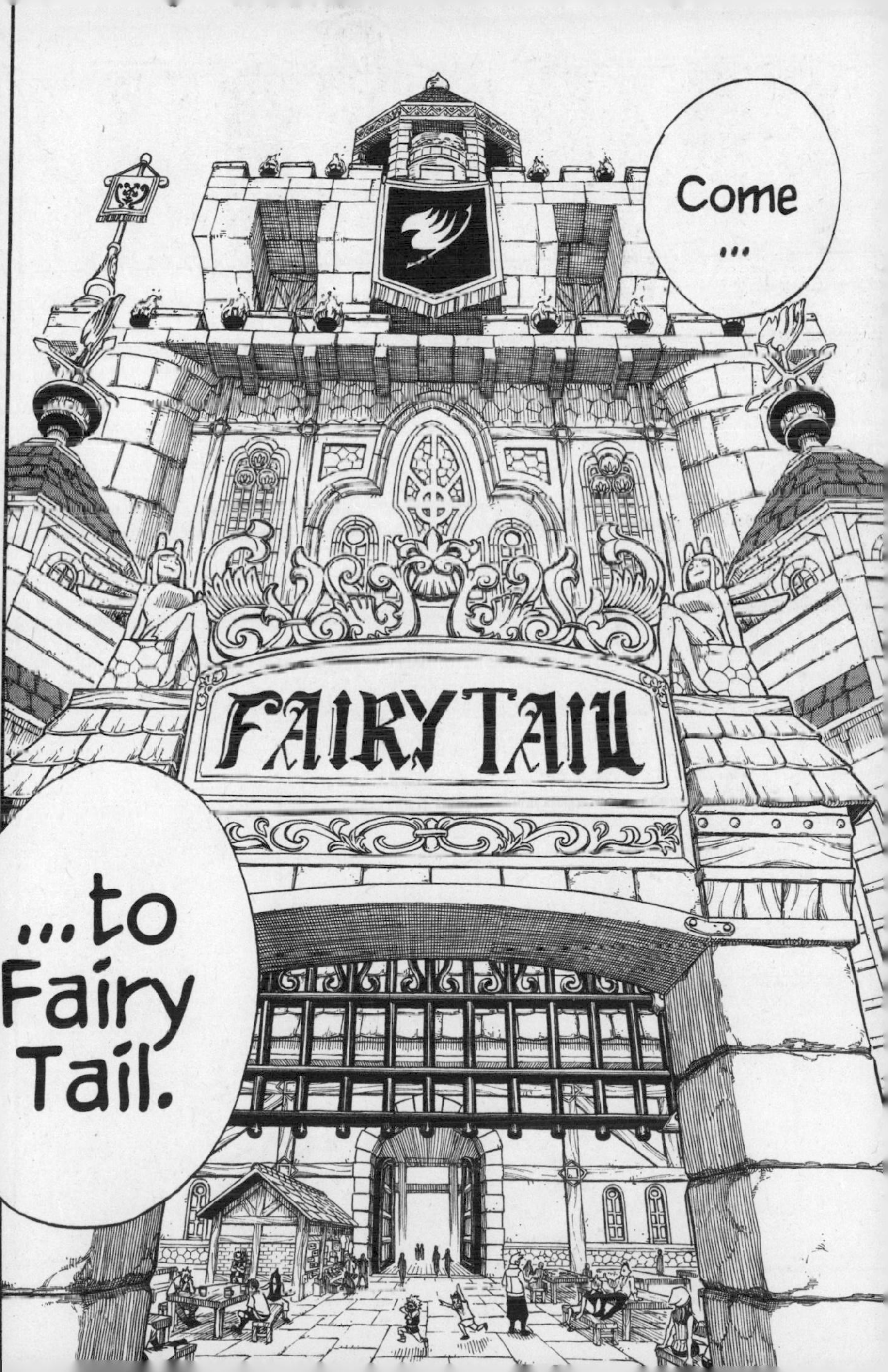
Come ...
FAIRY TAIL
... to Fairy Tail.

# FAIRY TAIL

フェアリーテイル

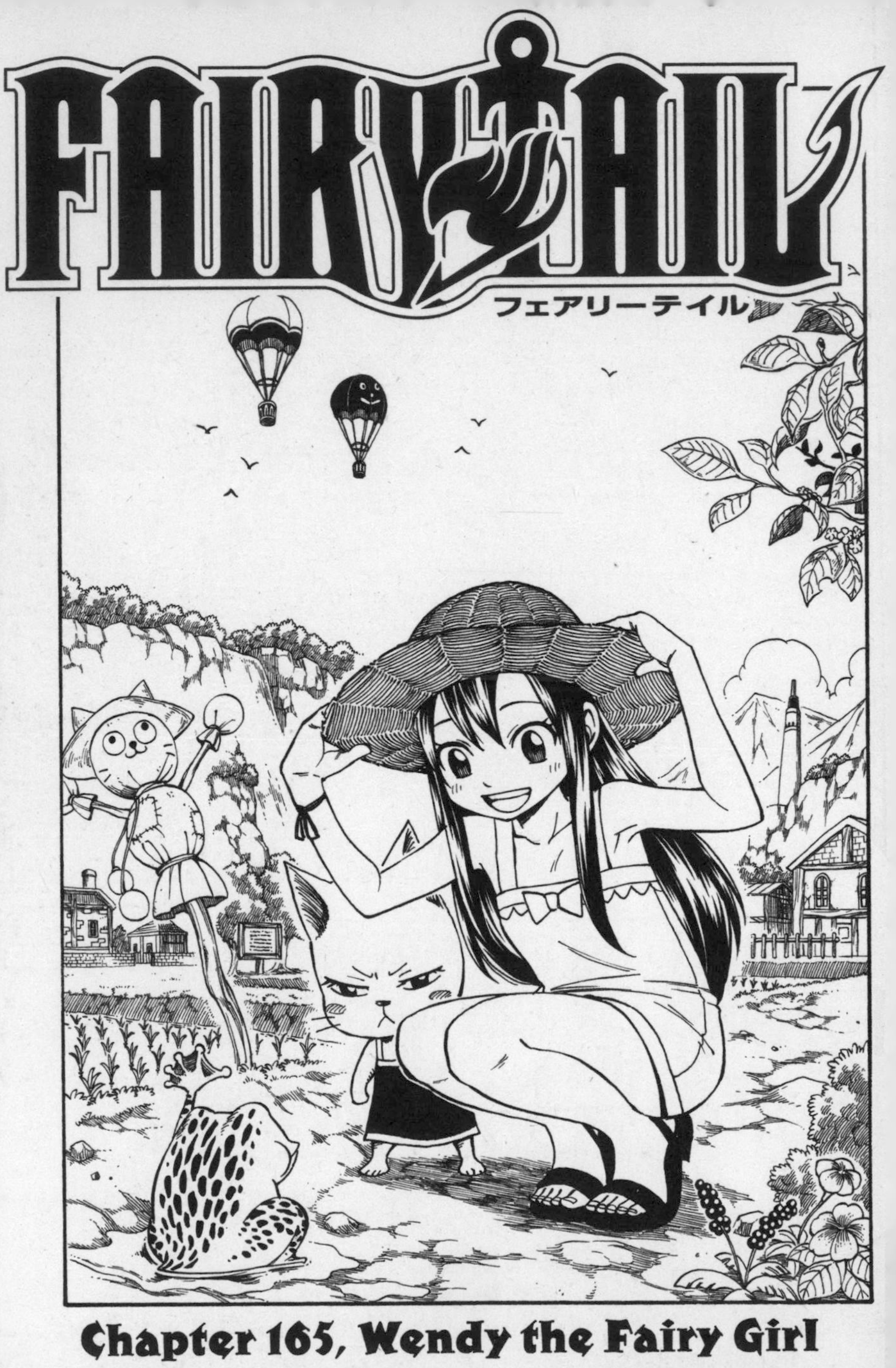

## Chapter 165, Wendy the Fairy Girl

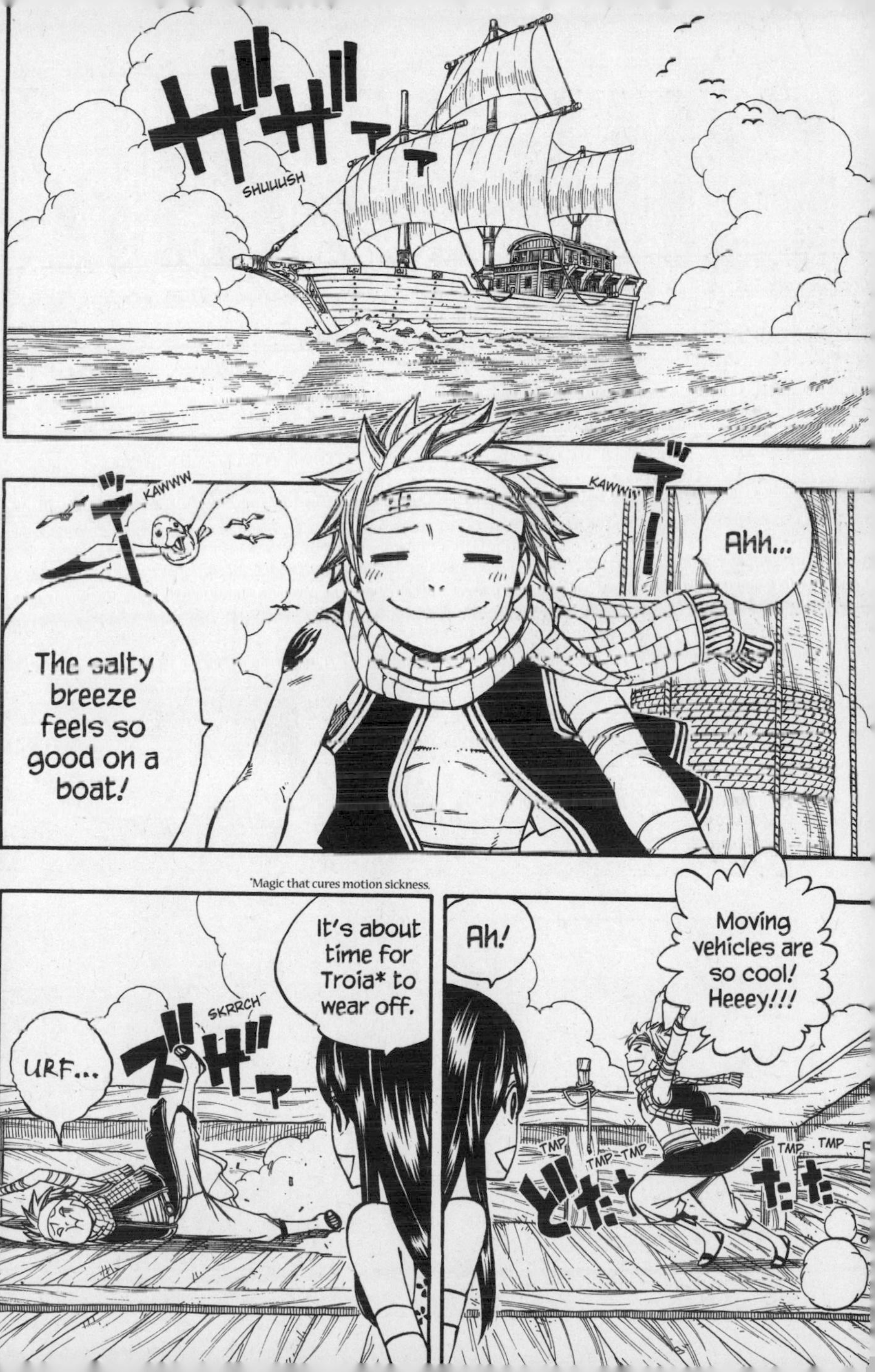
SHUUUSH
Ahh...
KAWWW
KAWWW
The salty breeze feels so good on a boat!
Moving vehicles are so cool! Heeey!!!
TMP TMP
TMP-TMP
TMP
Ah!
It's about time for Troia* to wear off.
SKRRCH
URF...

*Magic that cures motion sickness.

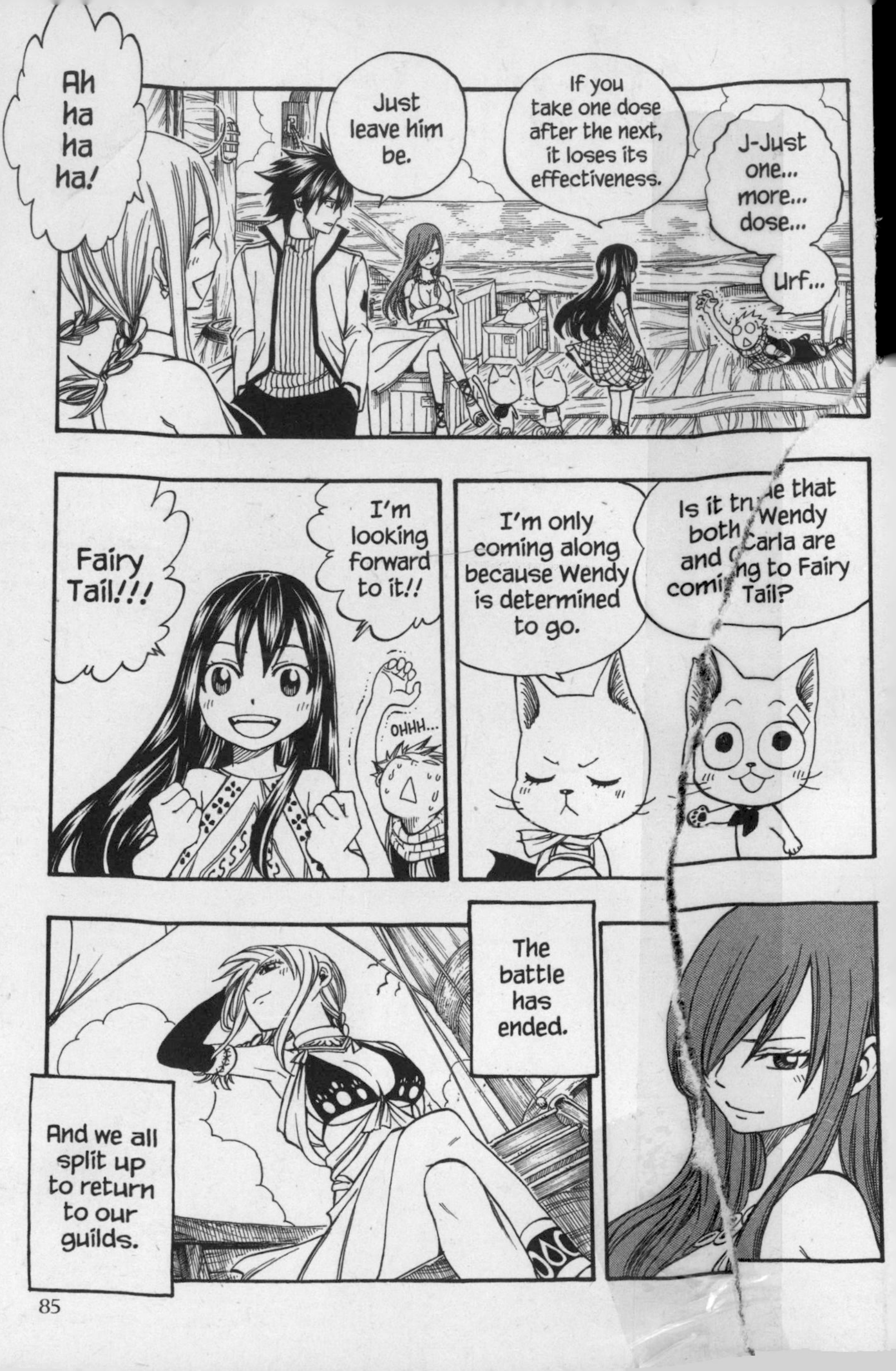
J-Just one... more... dose...
Urf...
If you take one dose after the next, it loses its effectiveness.
Just leave him be.
Ah ha ha ha!
Is it true that both Wendy and Carla are coming to Fairy Tail?
I'm only coming along because Wendy is determined to go.
I'm looking forward to it!!
OHHH...
Fairy Tail!!!
The battle has ended.
And we all split up to return to our guilds.

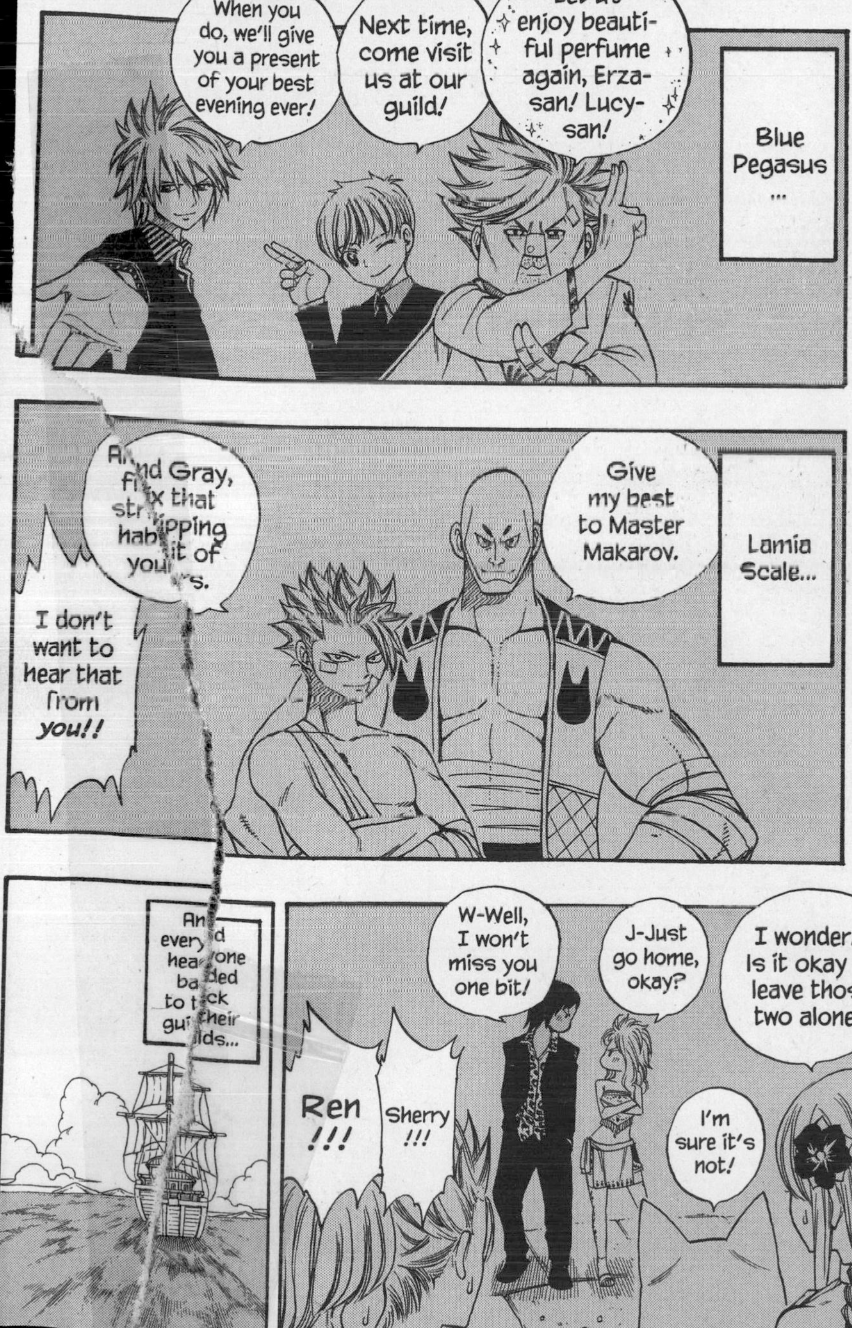

Blue Pegasus...
Let us enjoy beautiful perfume again, Erza-san! Lucy-san!
Next time, come visit us at our guild!
When you do, we'll give you a present of your best evening ever!
Lamia Scale...
Give my best to Master Makarov.
And Gray, fix that stripping habit of yours.
I don't want to hear that from you!!
I wonder... Is it okay to leave those two alone?
I'm sure it's not!
J-Just go home, okay?
W-Well, I won't miss you one bit!
Sherry!!!
Ren!!!
And everyone headed back to their guilds...

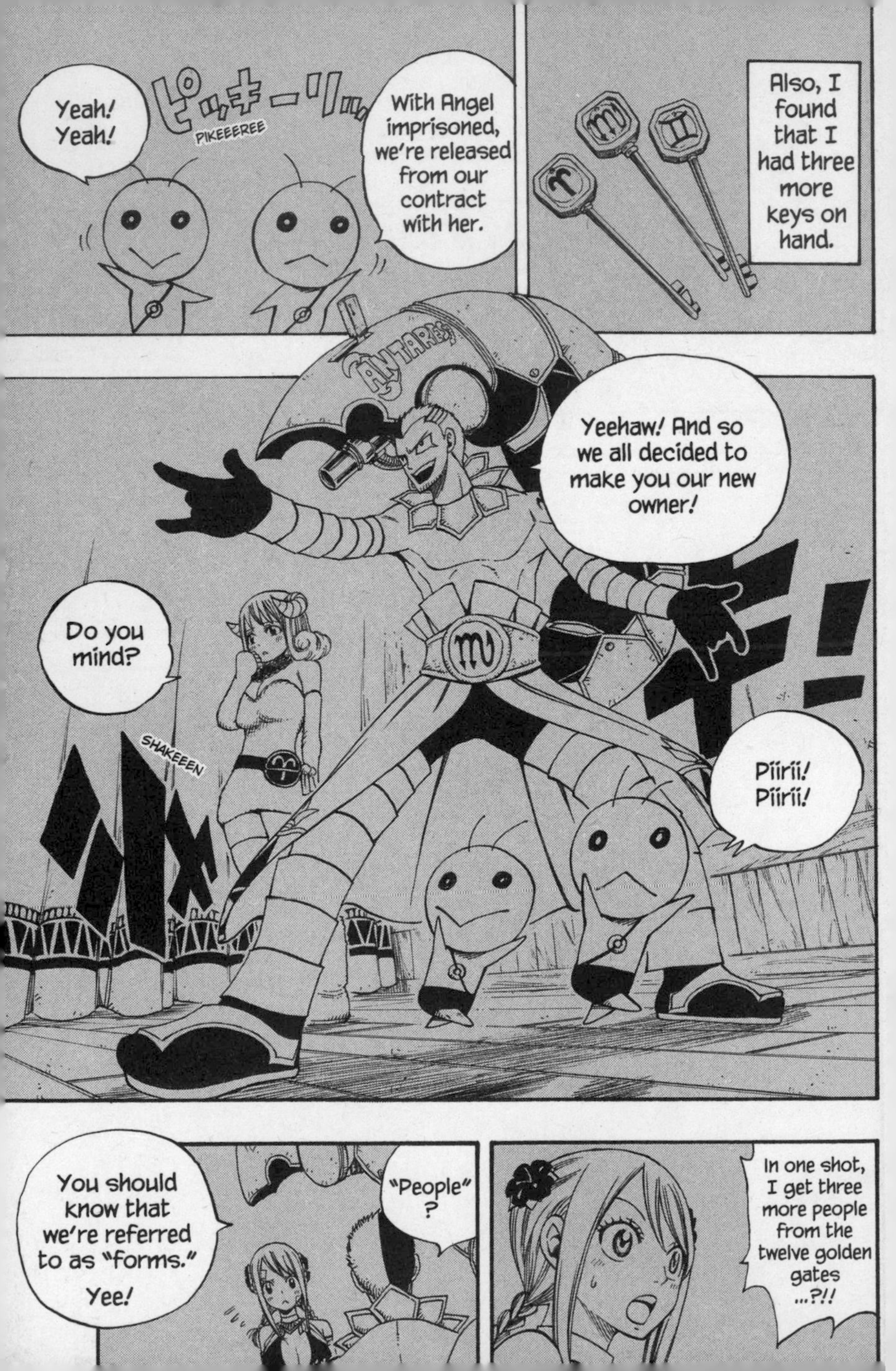

Also, I found that I had three more keys on hand.
With Angel imprisoned, we're released from our contract with her.
PIKEEEREE
Yeah! Yeah!
Yeehaw! And so we all decided to make you our new owner!
Piirii! Piirii!
Do you mind?
SHAKEEEN
In one shot, I get three more people from the twelve golden gates ...?!!
"People"?
You should know that we're referred to as "forms."
Yee!

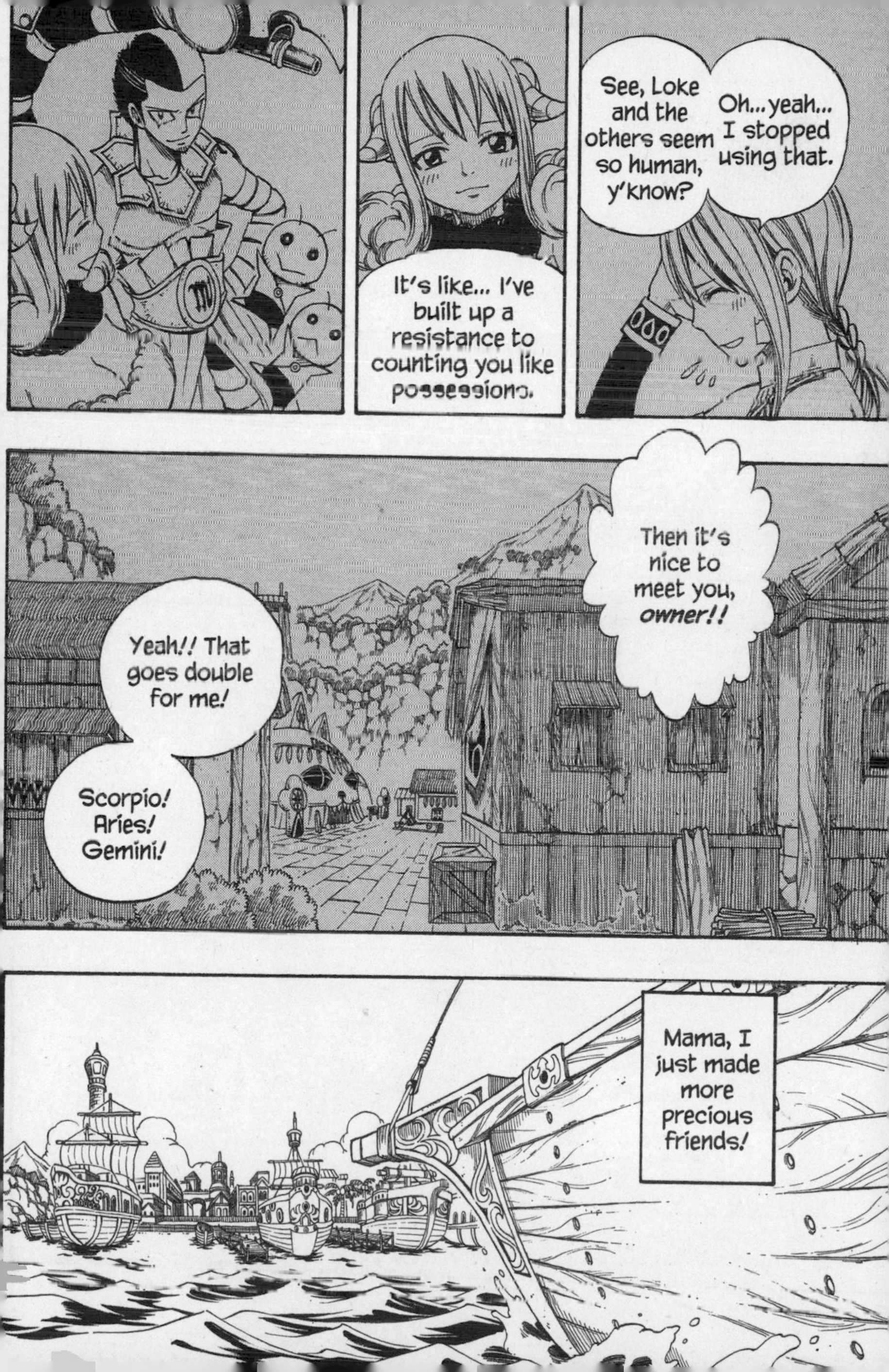
Oh... yeah... I stopped using that.
See, Loke and the others seem so human, y'know?
It's like... I've built up a resistance to counting you like possessions.
Then it's nice to meet you, *owner!!*
Yeah!! That goes double for me!
Scorpio! Aries! Gemini!
Mama, I just made more precious friends!

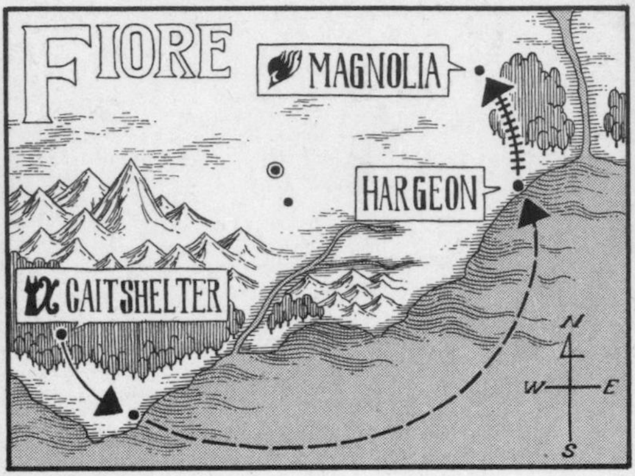
FIORE
MAGNOLIA
HARGEON
CAITSHELTER
N
W
E
S
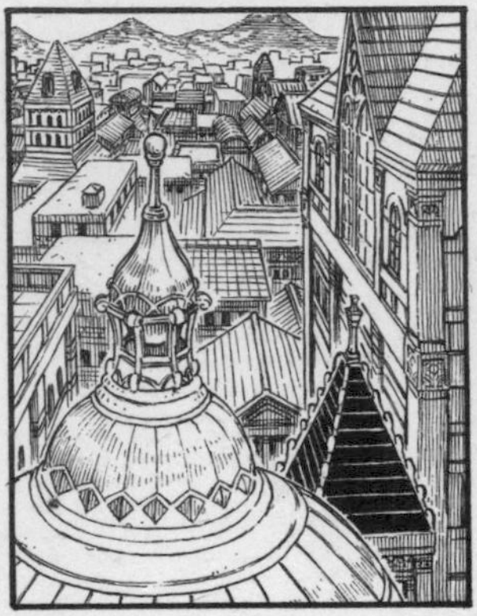
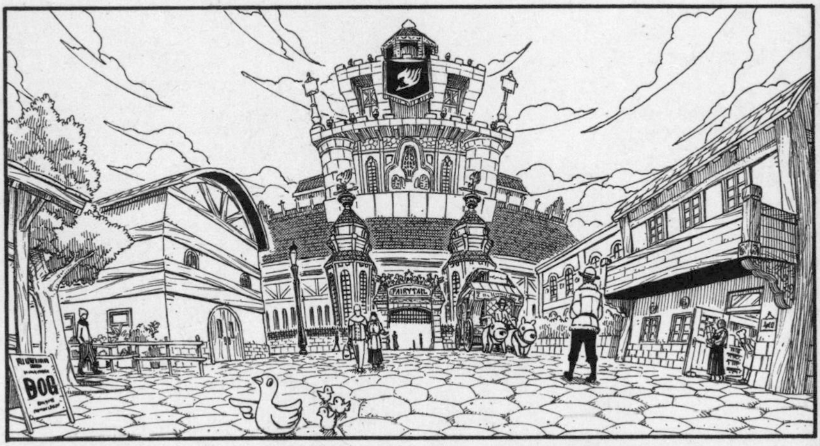
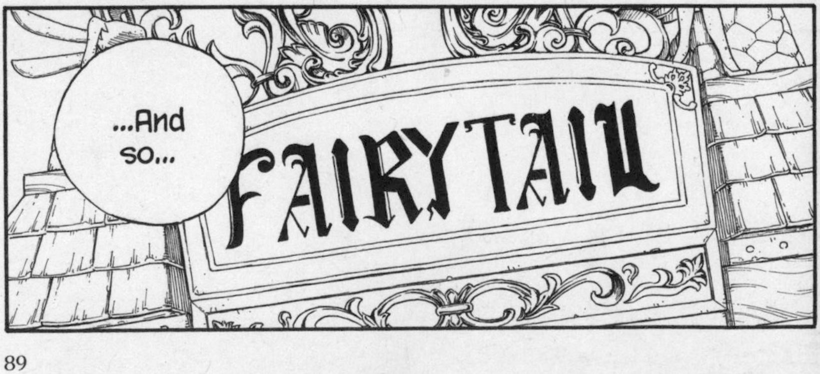
...And so...
FAIRYTAIL

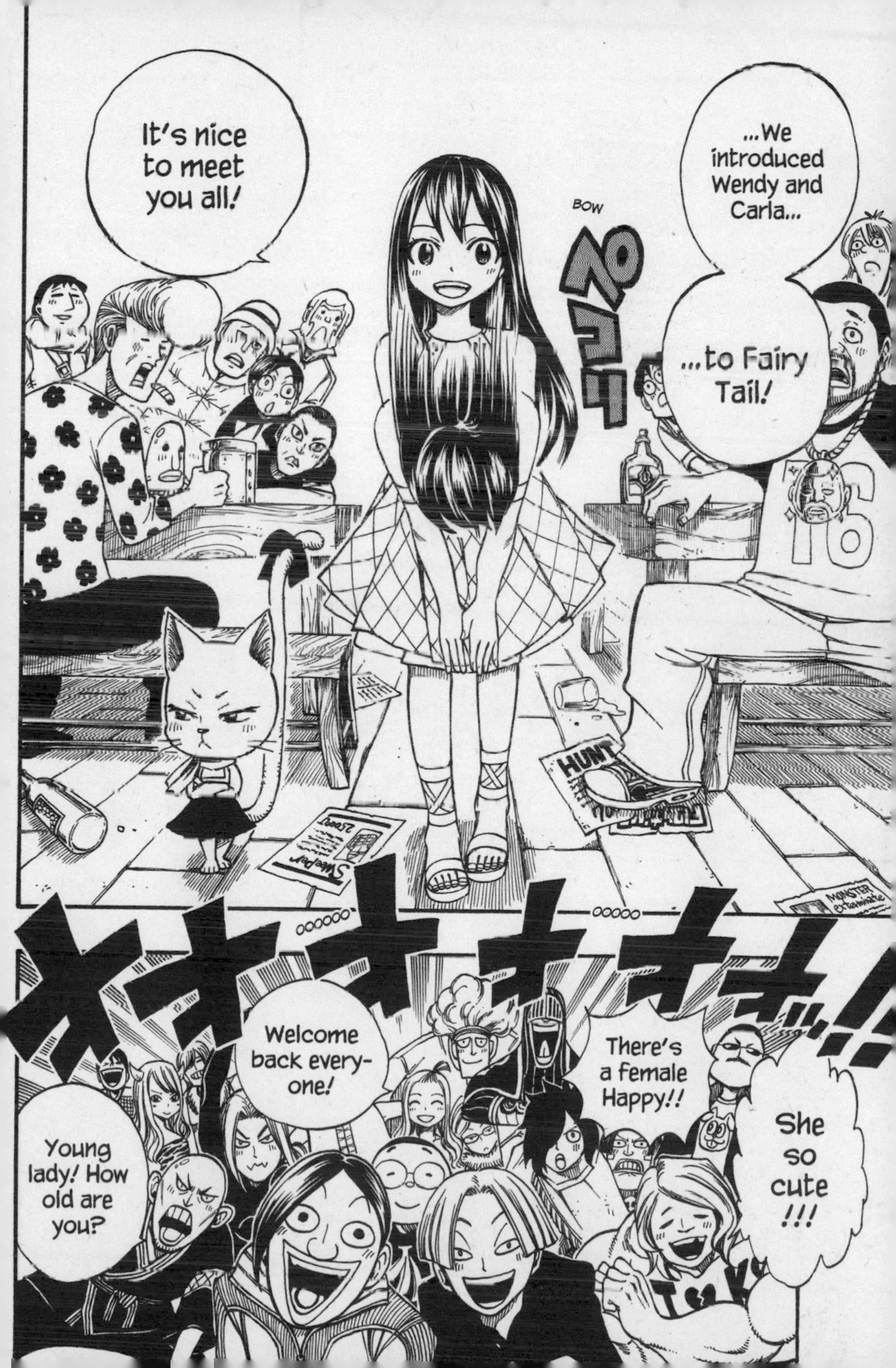
...We introduced Wendy and Carla...
...to Fairy Tail!
BOW
It's nice to meet you all!
HUNT
16
ooooo
oooooo
She so cute!!!
There's a female Happy!!
Welcome back every-one!
Young lady! How old are you?

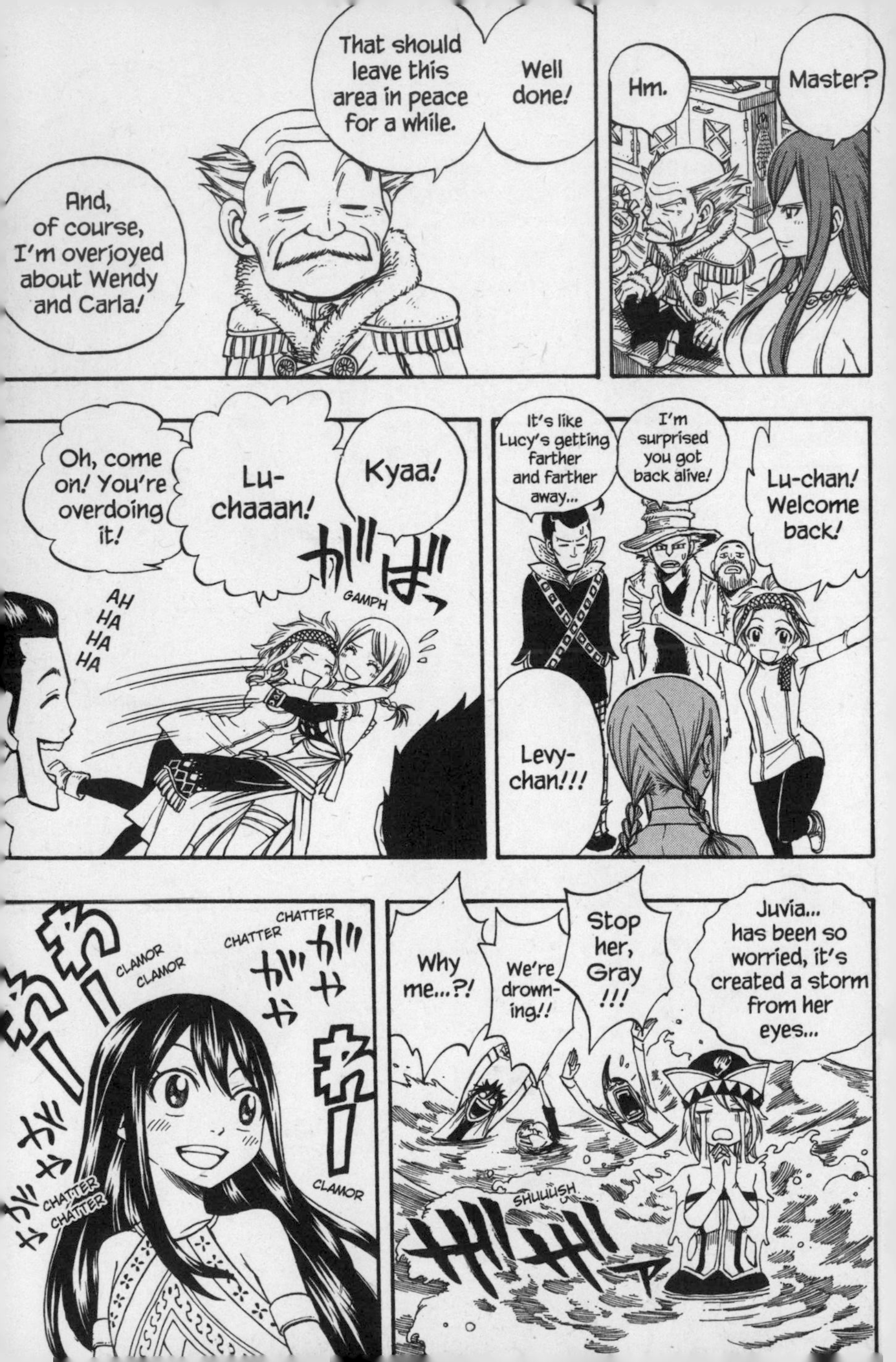
Master?
Hm.
Well done!
That should leave this area in peace for a while.
And, of course, I'm overjoyed about Wendy and Carla!
Lu-chan! Welcome back!
I'm surprised you got back alive!
It's like Lucy's getting farther and farther away...
Levy-chan!!!
Kyaa!
Lu-chaaan!
GAMPH
Oh, come on! You're overdoing it!
AH HA HA HA HA
Juvia... has been so worried, it's created a storm from her eyes...
Stop her, Gray!!!
We're drowning!!
Why me...?!
SHUUUSH
CHATTER CHATTER
CLAMOR CLAMOR
CLAMOR
CHATTER CHATTER

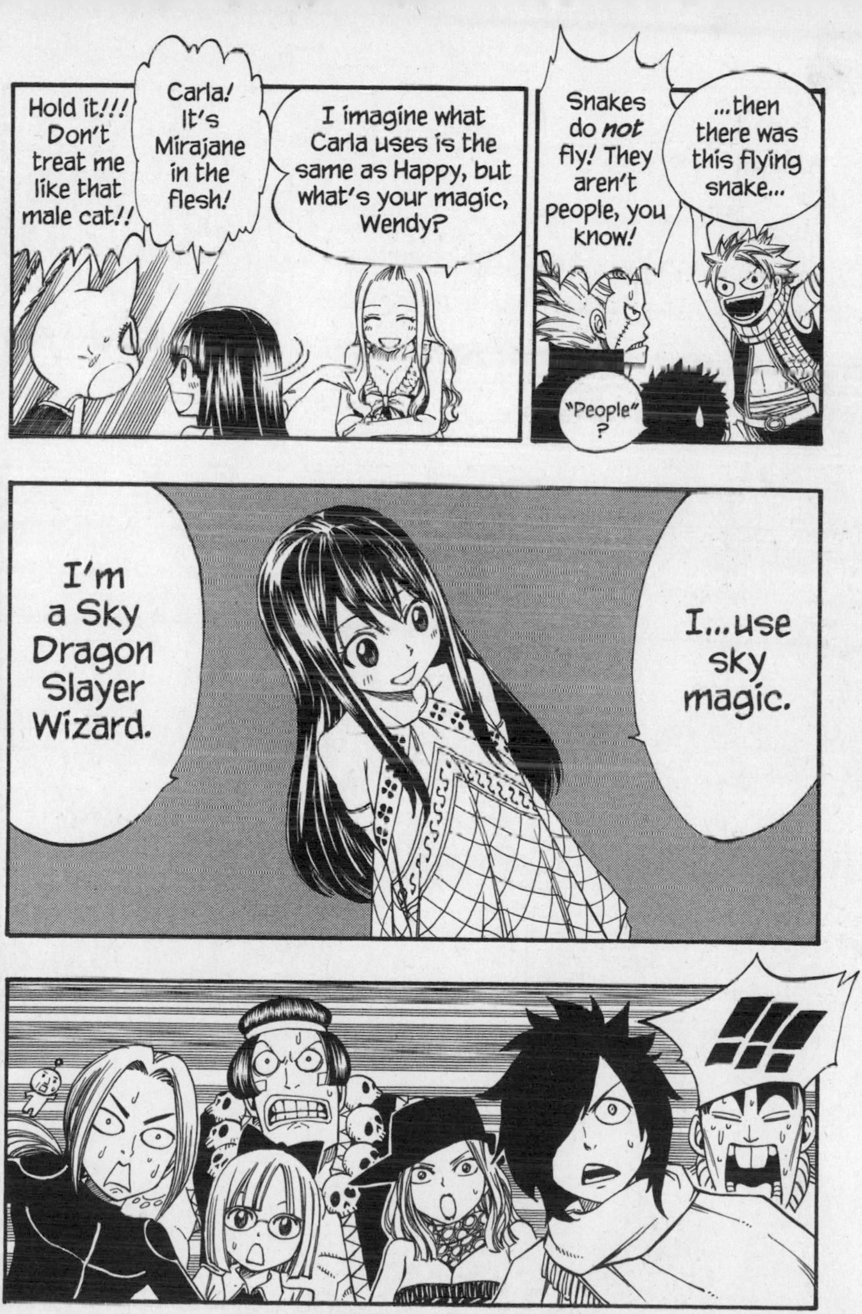
...then there was this flying snake...
Snakes do *not* fly! They aren't people, you know!
"People"?
I imagine what Carla uses is the same as Happy, but what's your magic, Wendy?
Carla! It's Mirajane in the flesh!
Hold it!!! Don't treat me like that male cat!!
I...use sky magic.
I'm a Sky Dragon Slayer Wizard.
!!!

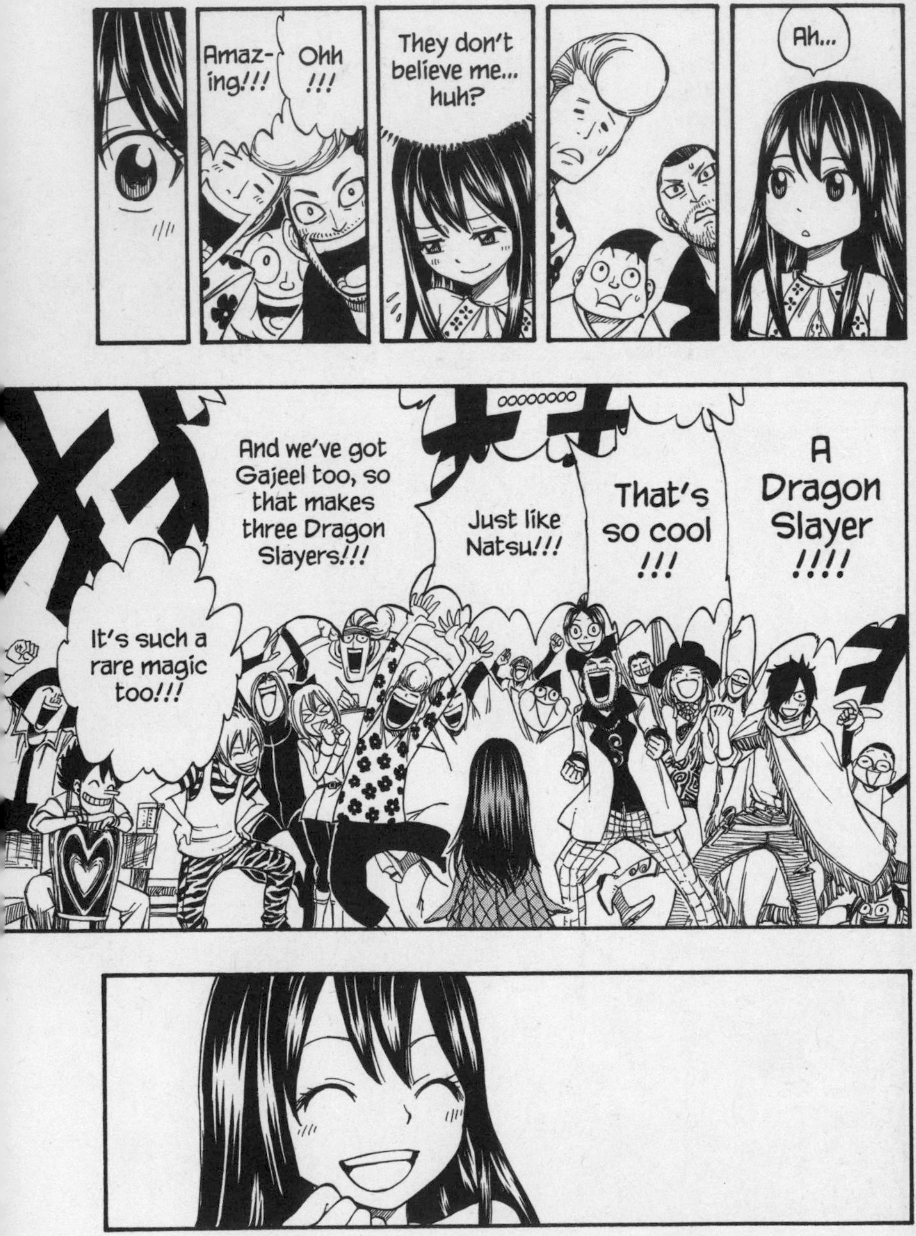
Ah...
They don't believe me... huh?
Ohh !!!
Amaz-ing!!!
A Dragon Slayer !!!!
That's so cool !!!
oooooooo
Just like Natsu!!!
And we've got Gajeel too, so that makes three Dragon Slayers!!!
It's such a rare magic too!!!

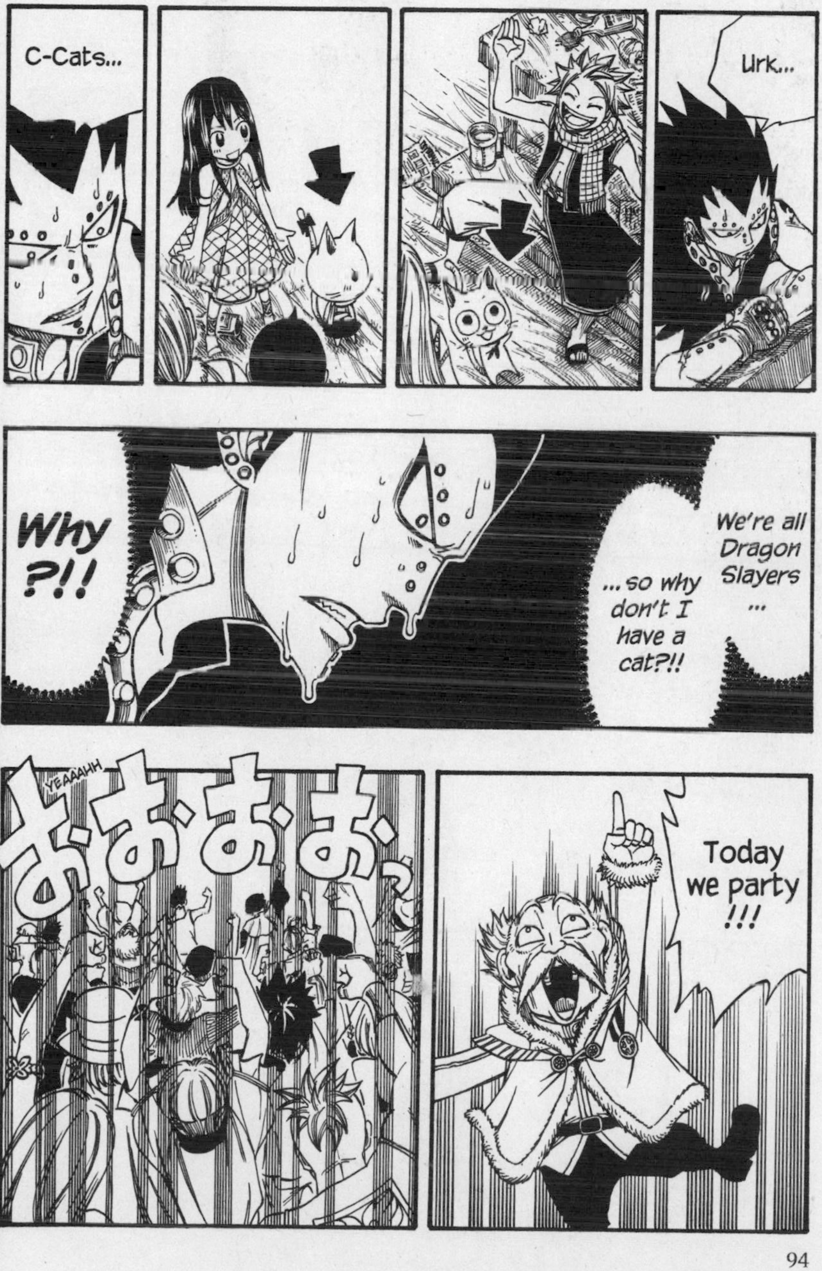
Urk...
C-Cats...
We're all Dragon Slayers ...
...so why don't I have a cat?!!
Why ?!!
Today we party !!!
YEAAAHH
おおおおっ

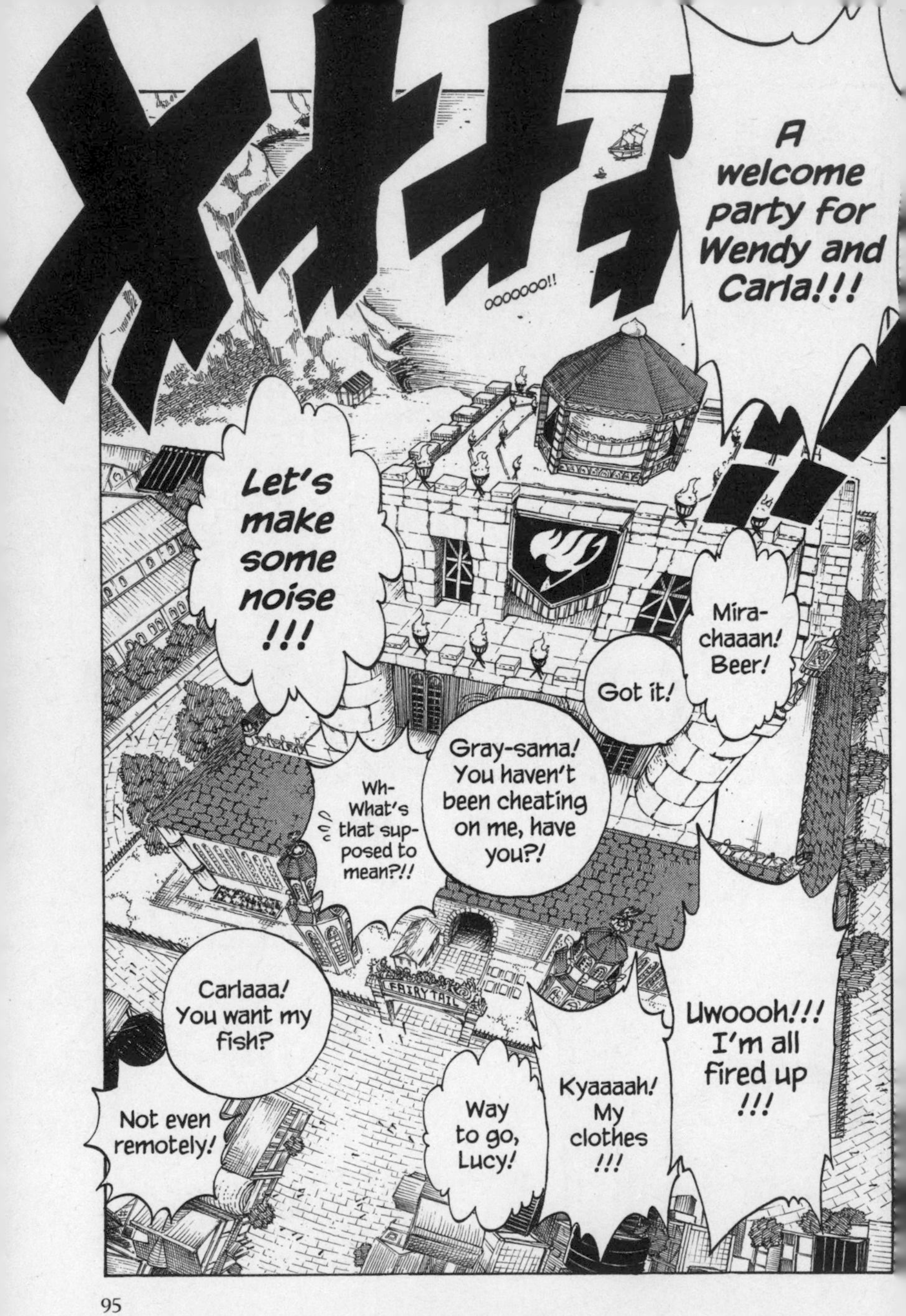
A welcome party for Wendy and Carla!!!
OOOOOOO!!
Let's make some noise!!!
Mira-chaaan! Beer!
Got it!
Gray-sama! You haven't been cheating on me, have you?!
Wh- What's that sup-posed to mean?!!
FAIRY TAIL
Uwoooh!!! I'm all fired up!!!
Kyaaaah! My clothes!!!
Way to go, Lucy!
Carlaaa! You want my fish?
Not even remotely!

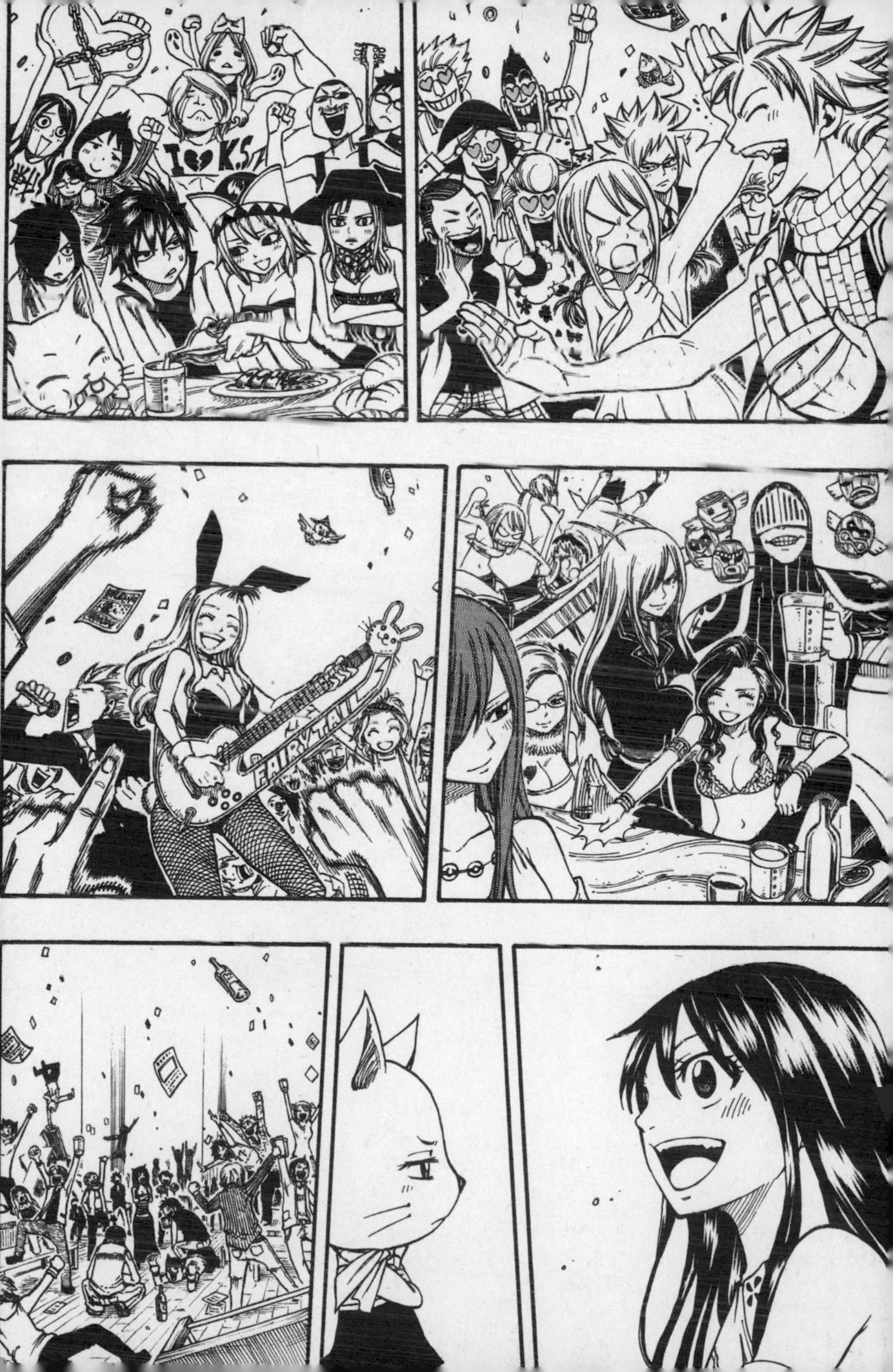
FAIRY TAIL

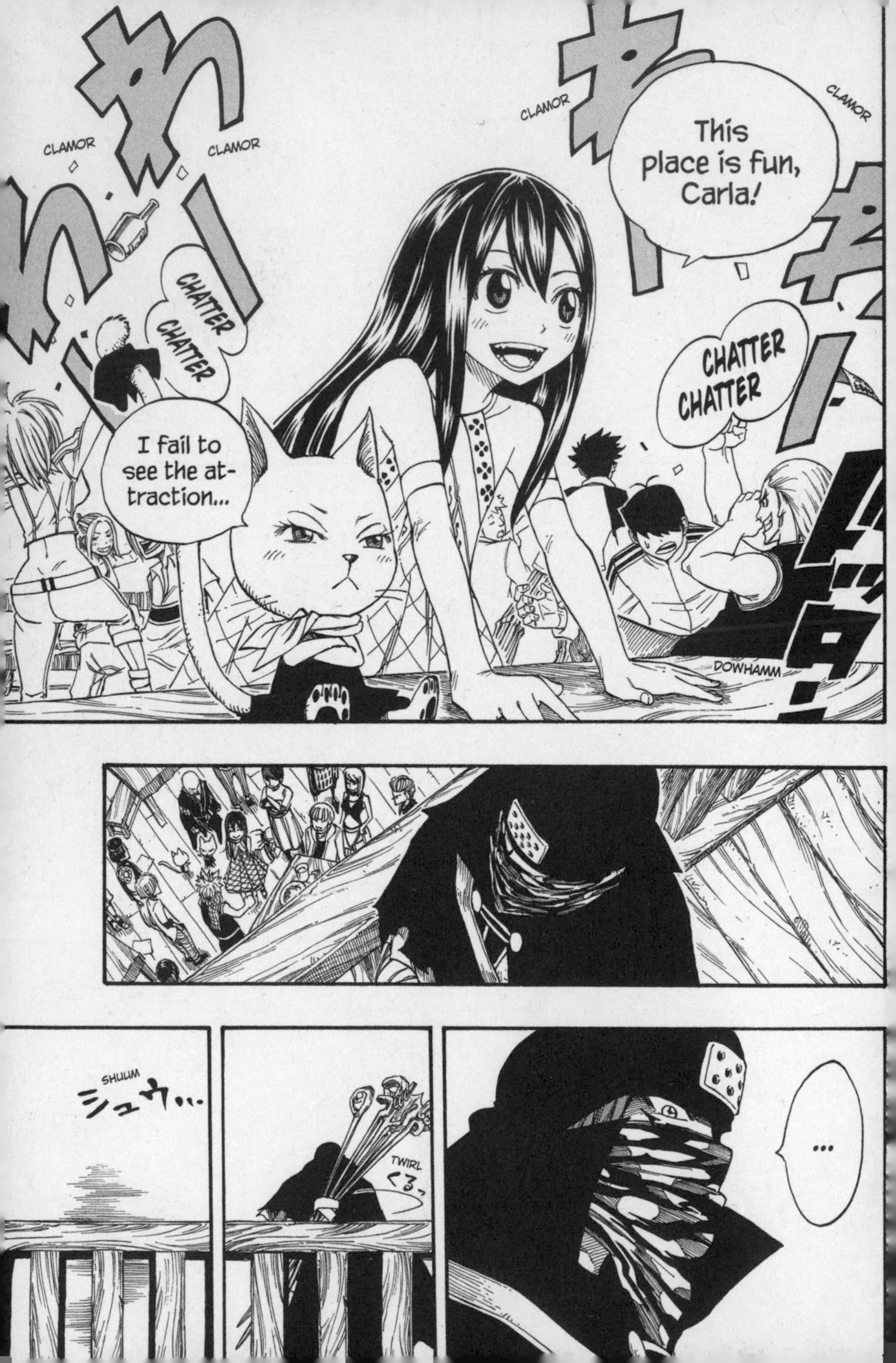
CLAMOR
This place is fun, Carla!
CLAMOR
CHATTER CHATTER
CLAMOR
CLAMOR
CHATTER CHATTER
I fail to see the attraction...
DOWHAMM
...
TWIRL
くるっ
SHUUM
シュウ…

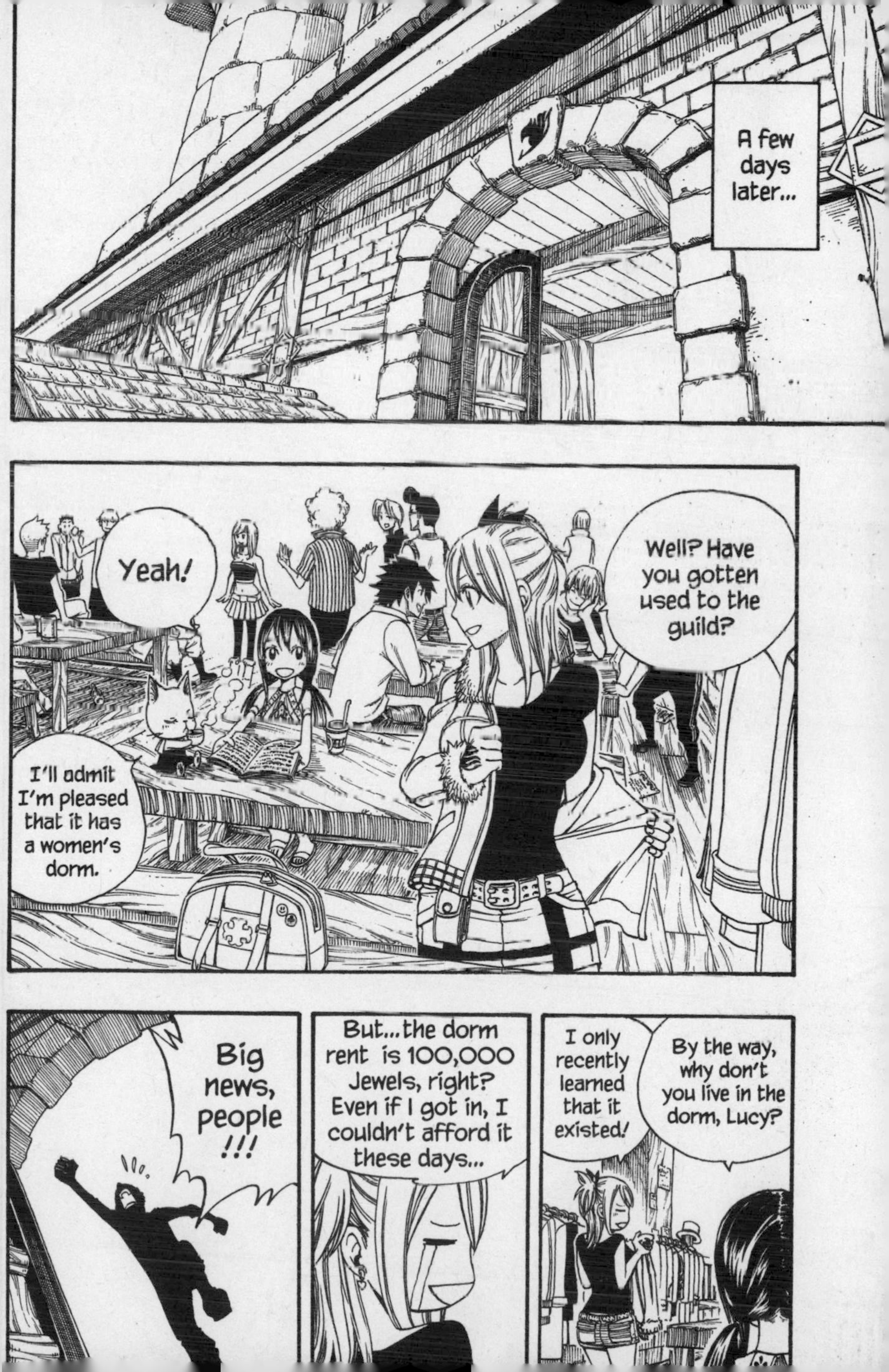
A few days later...
Well? Have you gotten used to the guild?
Yeah!
I'll admit I'm pleased that it has a women's dorm.
By the way, why don't you live in the dorm, Lucy?
I only recently learned that it existed!
But...the dorm rent is 100,000 Jewels, right? Even if I got in, I couldn't afford it these days...
Big news, people!!!

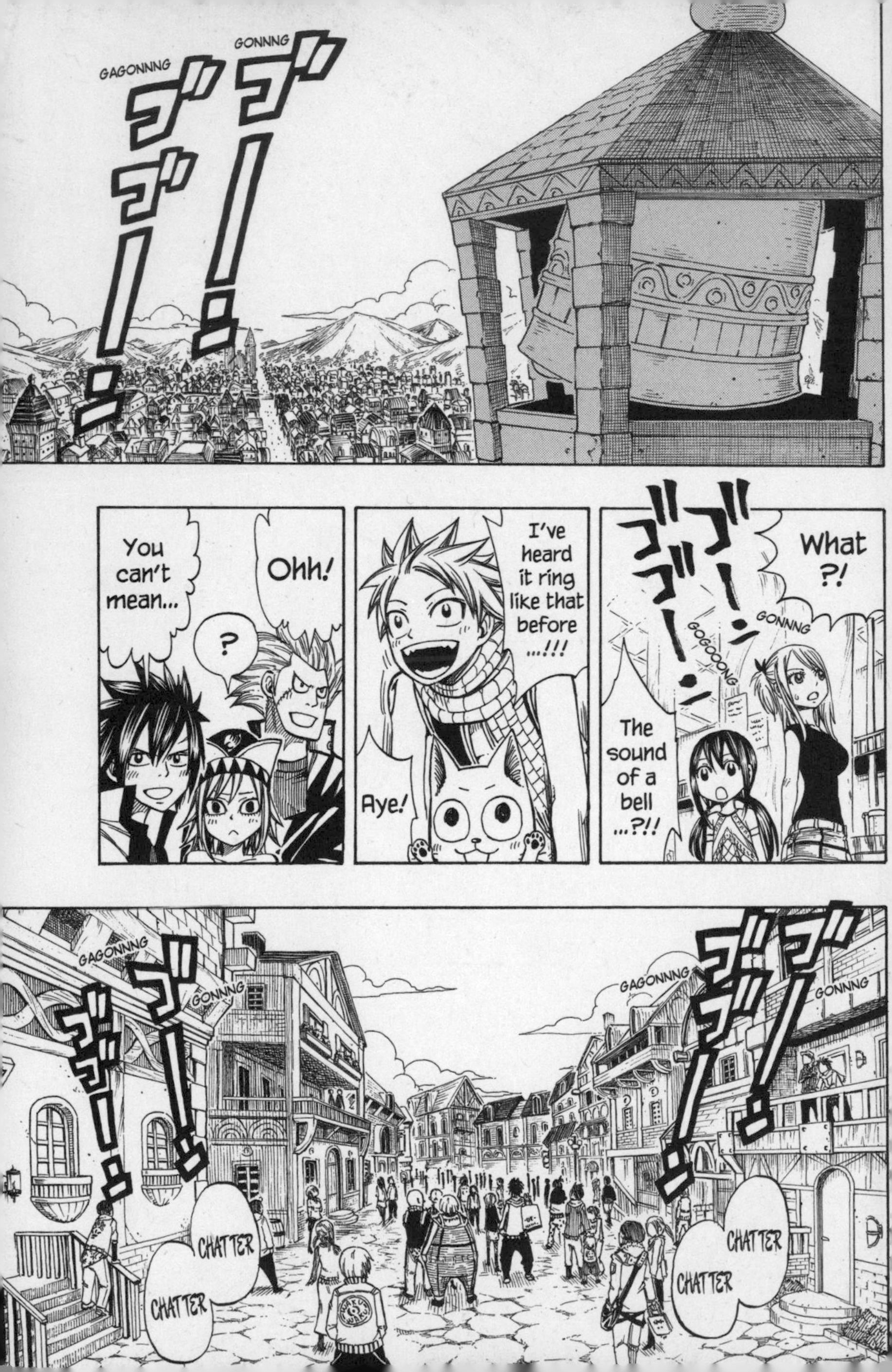
GONNNG
GAGONNNG
What?!
GONNNG
GOGOOONG
The sound of a bell ...?!!
I've heard it ring like that before ...!!!
Aye!
Ohh!
You can't mean...
?
GONNNG
GAGONNNG
CHATTER
CHATTER
GONNNG
GAGONNNG
CHATTER
CHATTER

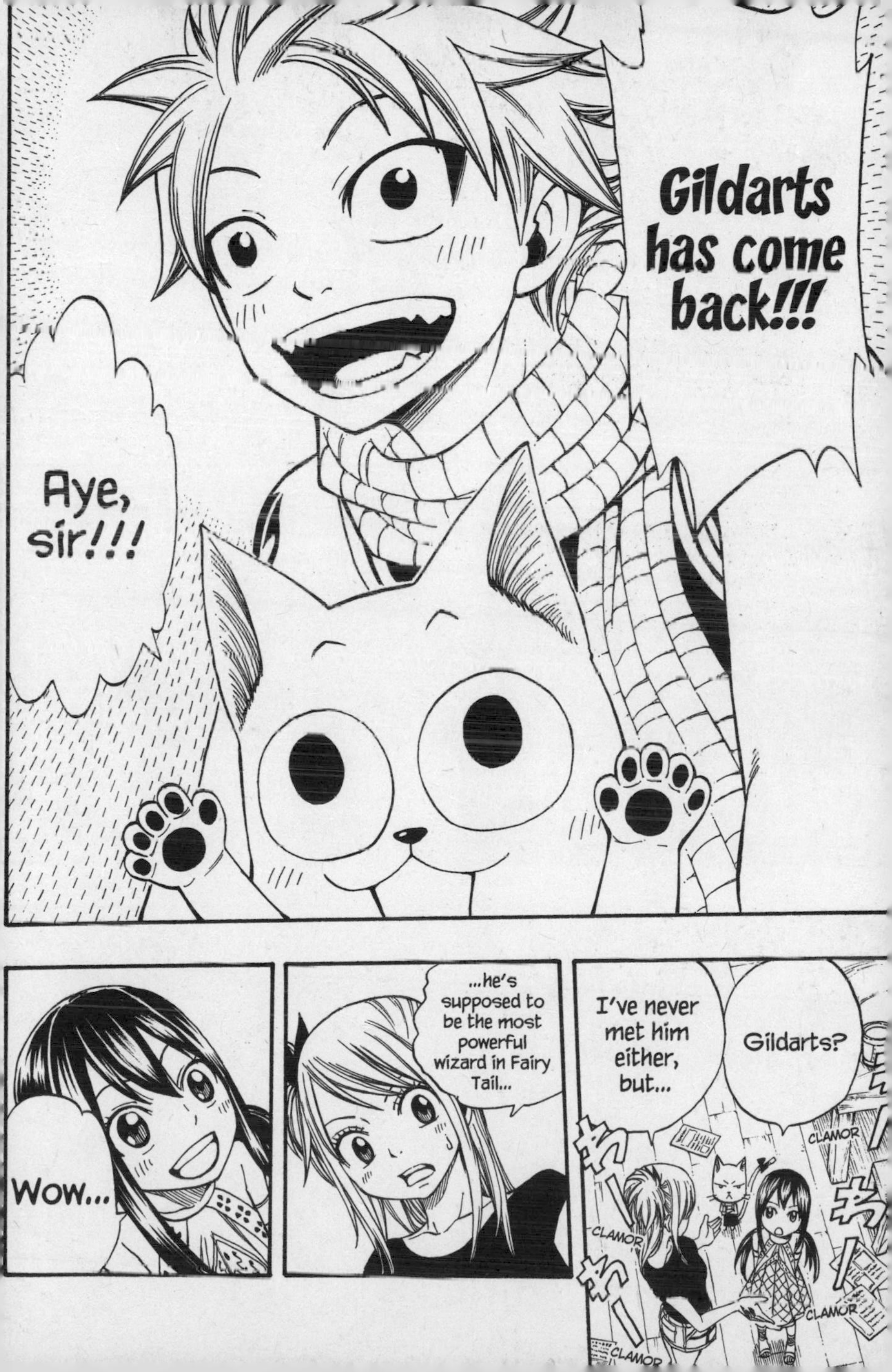

Gildarts has come back!!!
Aye, sir!!!
Gildarts?
I've never met him either, but...
CLAMOR
CLAMOR
CLAMOR
CLAMOR
...he's supposed to be the most powerful wizard in Fairy Tail...
Wow...

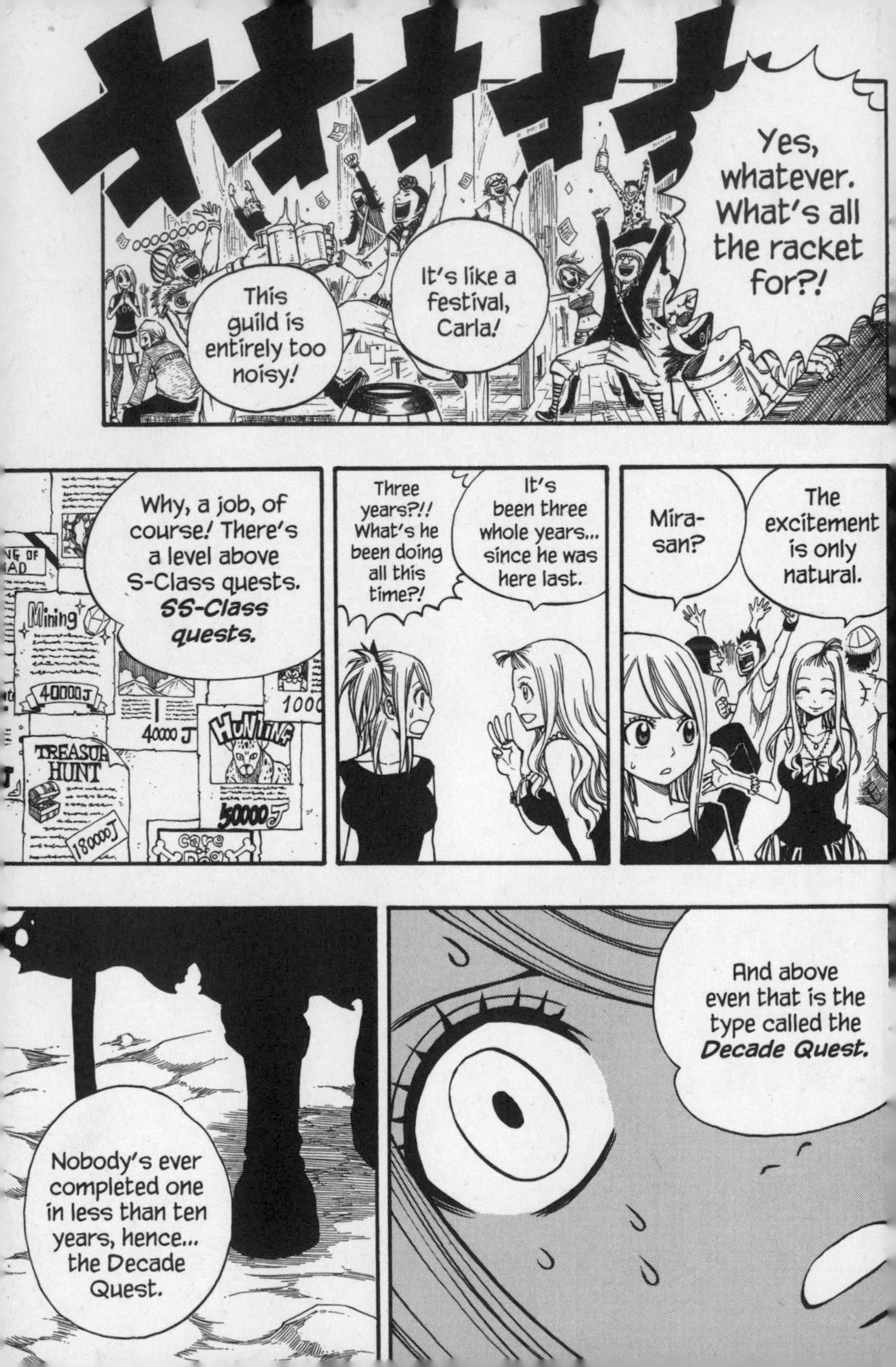
オオオオオ
Yes, whatever. What's all the racket for?!
It's like a festival, Carla!
This guild is entirely too noisy!
oooooooo
The excitement is only natural.
Mira-san?
It's been three whole years... since he was here last.
Three years?!! What's he been doing all this time?!
Why, a job, of course! There's a level above S-Class quests. ***SS-Class quests.***
Mining
40000J
40000 J
50000J
TREASUR HUNT
180000J
And above even that is the type called the ***Decade Quest.***
Nobody's ever completed one in less than ten years, hence... the Decade Quest.

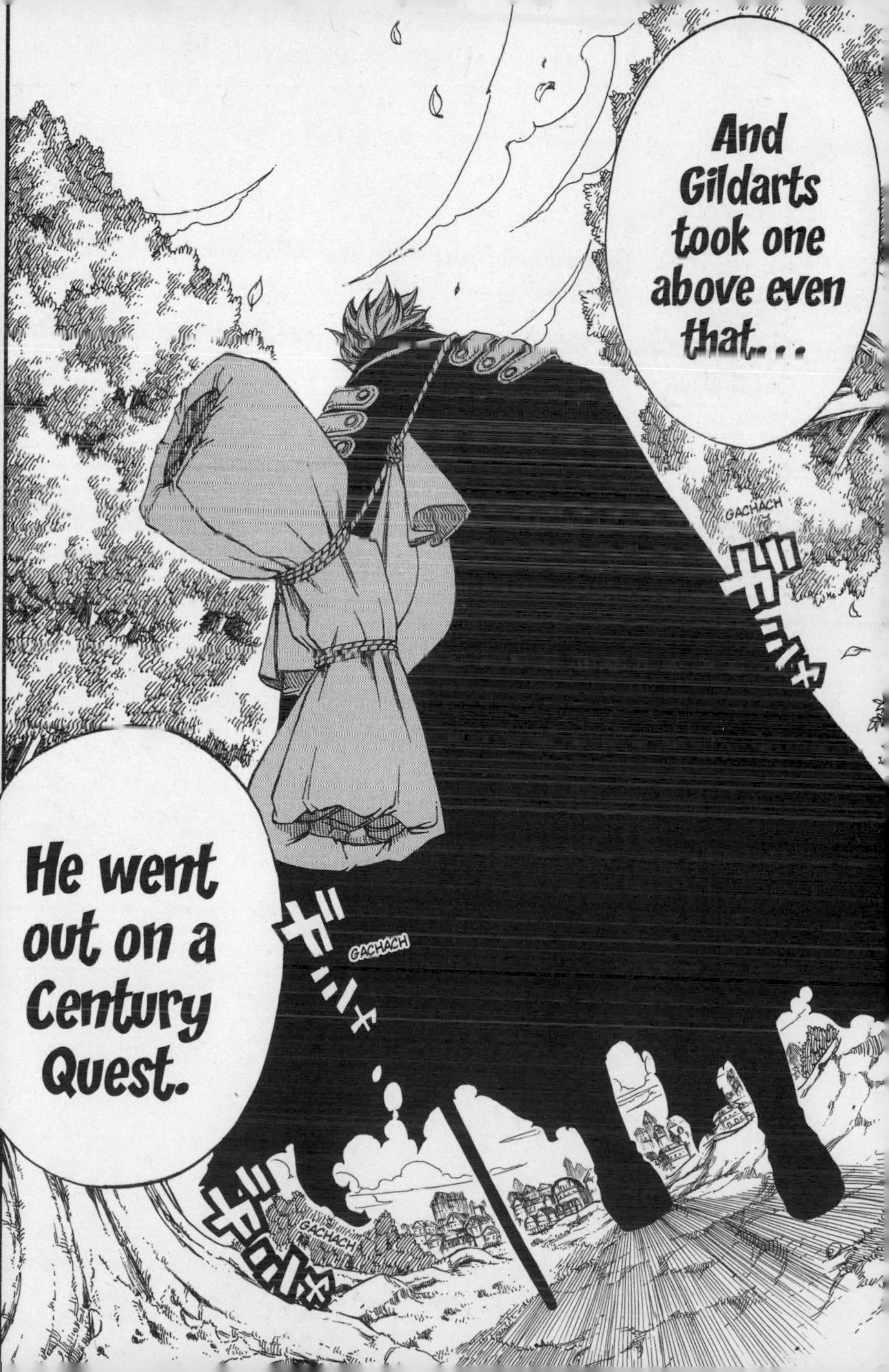
And Gildarts took one above even that...
GACHACH
He went out on a Century Quest.
GACHACH
GACHACH

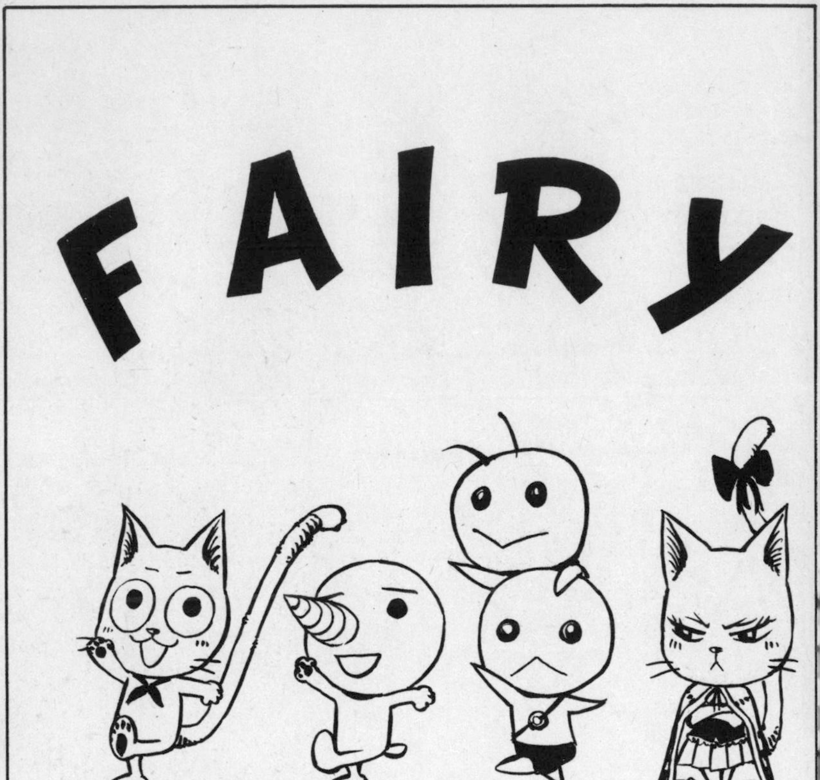
FAIRY
TAIL

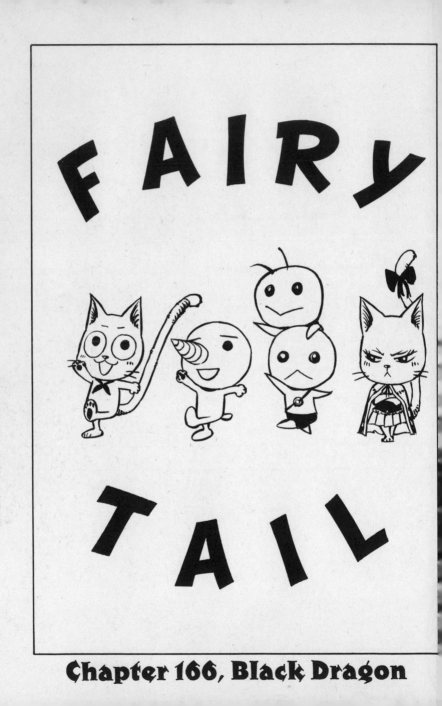

# Chapter 166, Black Dragon

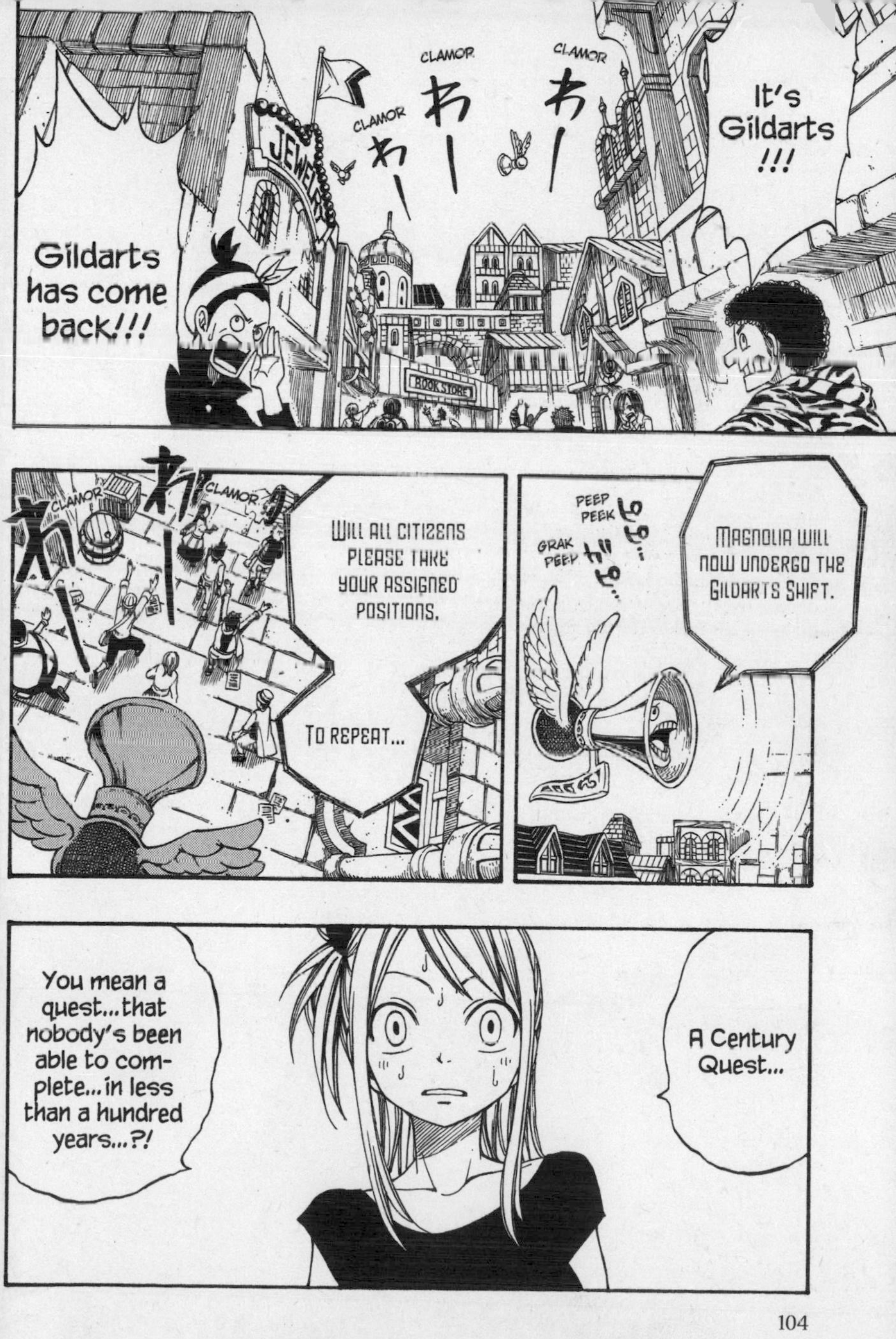
It's Gildarts!!!
CLAMOR
CLAMOR
CLAMOR
Gildarts has come back!!!
Magnolia will now undergo the Gildarts Shift.
PEEP PEEK
GRAK PEEP
Will all citizens please take your assigned positions.
To repeat...
CLAMOR
CLAMOR
A Century Quest...
You mean a quest...that nobody's been able to complete...in less than a hundred years...?!

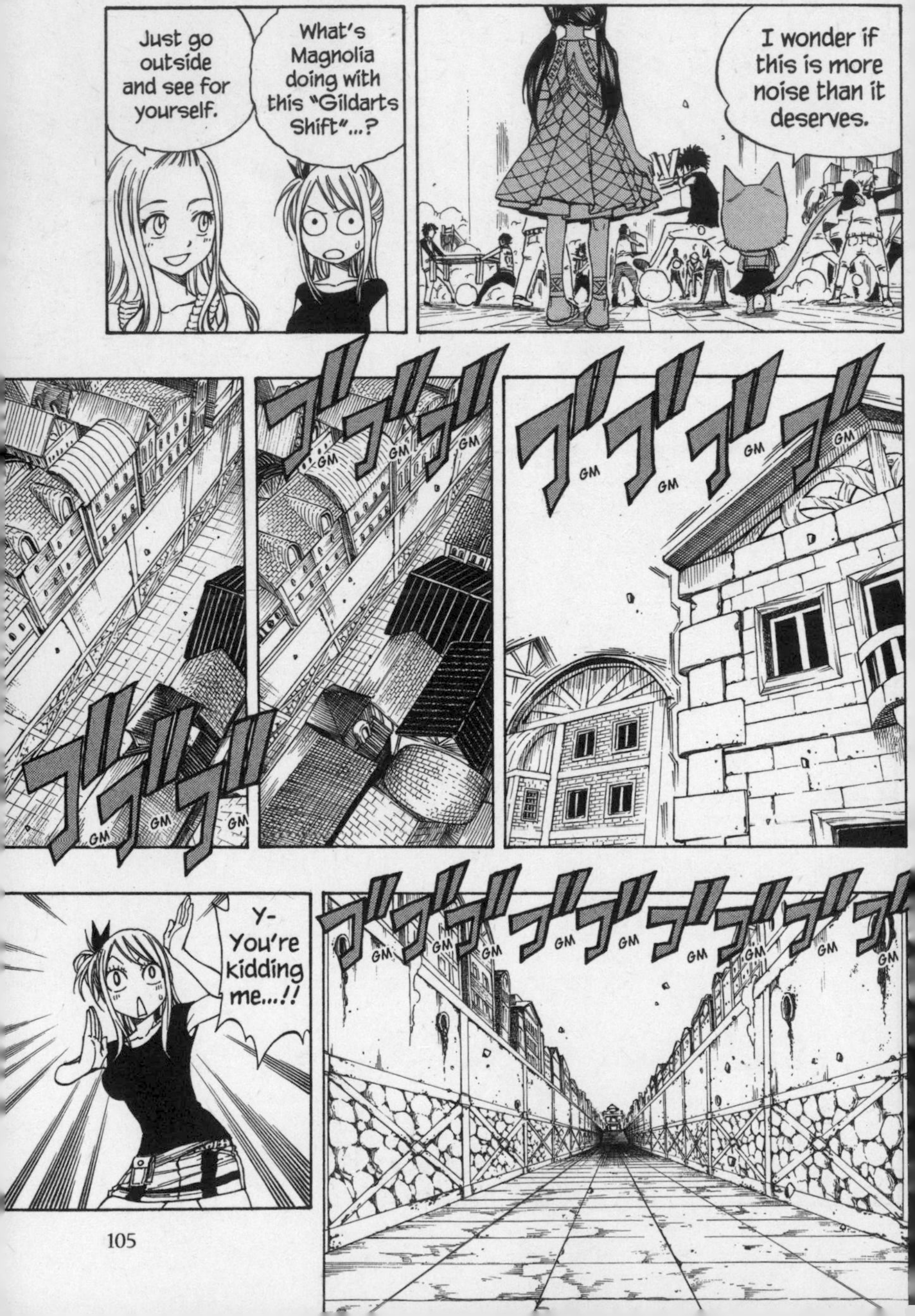
I wonder if this is more noise than it deserves.
What's Magnolia doing with this "Gildarts Shift"...?
Just go outside and see for yourself.
GM GM GM GM
GM GM GM
GM GM GM
GM GM GM GM GM GM GM GM GM
Y- You're kidding me...!!

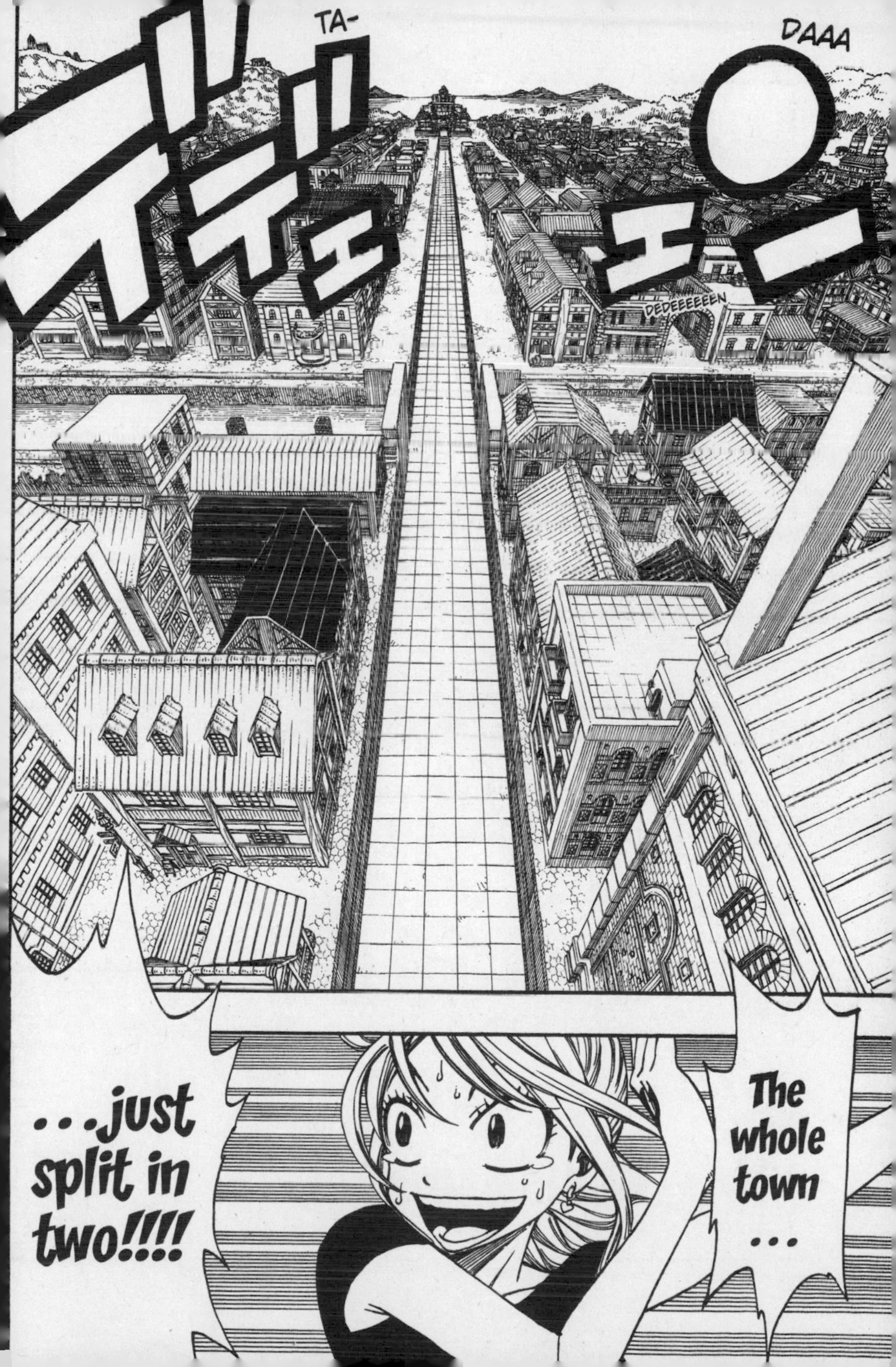
TA-
DAAA
DEDEEEEEEN
The whole town ...
...just split in two!!!!

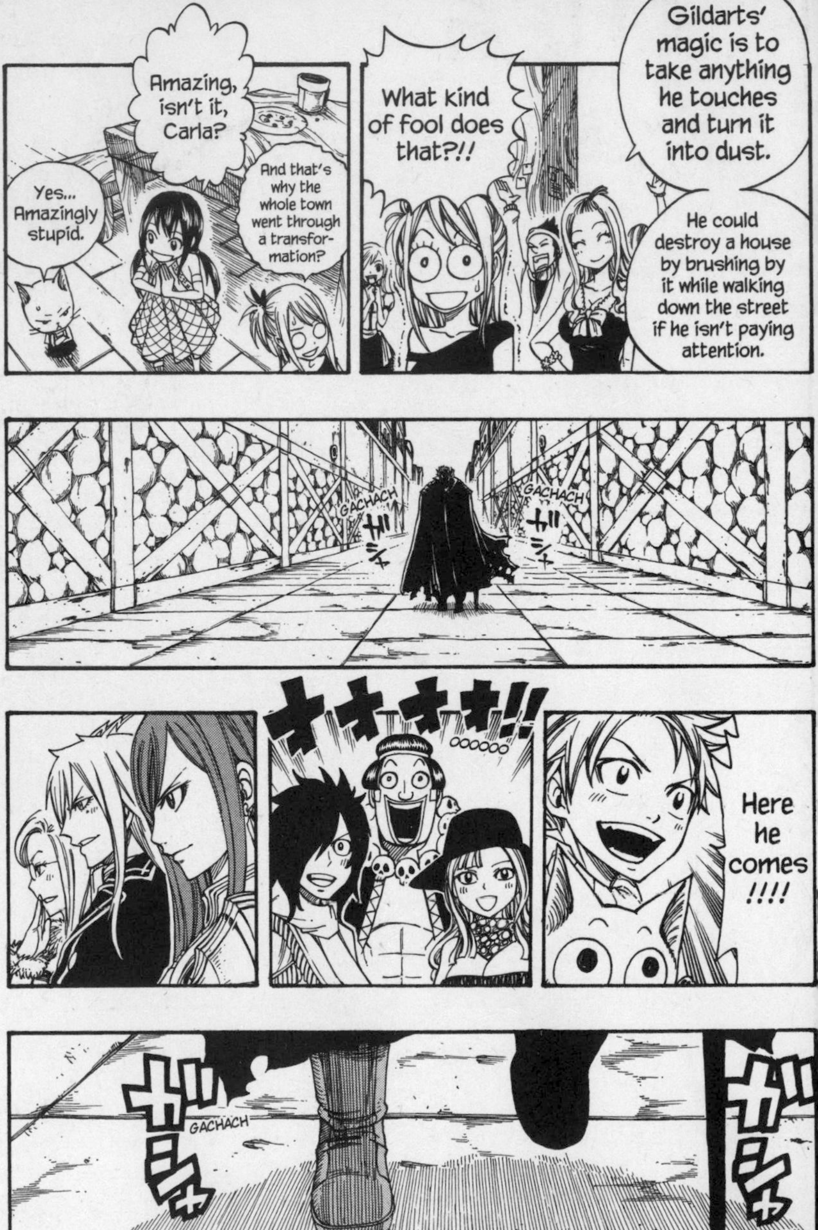

Gildarts' magic is to take anything he touches and turn it into dust.
He could destroy a house by brushing by it while walking down the street if he isn't paying attention.
What kind of fool does that?!!
Amazing, isn't it, Carla?
And that's why the whole town went through a transformation?
Yes... Amazingly stupid.
ガシャ
GACHACH
ガシャ
GACHACH
Here he comes!!!!
オオオオオ!!
OOOOOO
ガシャ
GACHACH
ガシャ
GACHACH

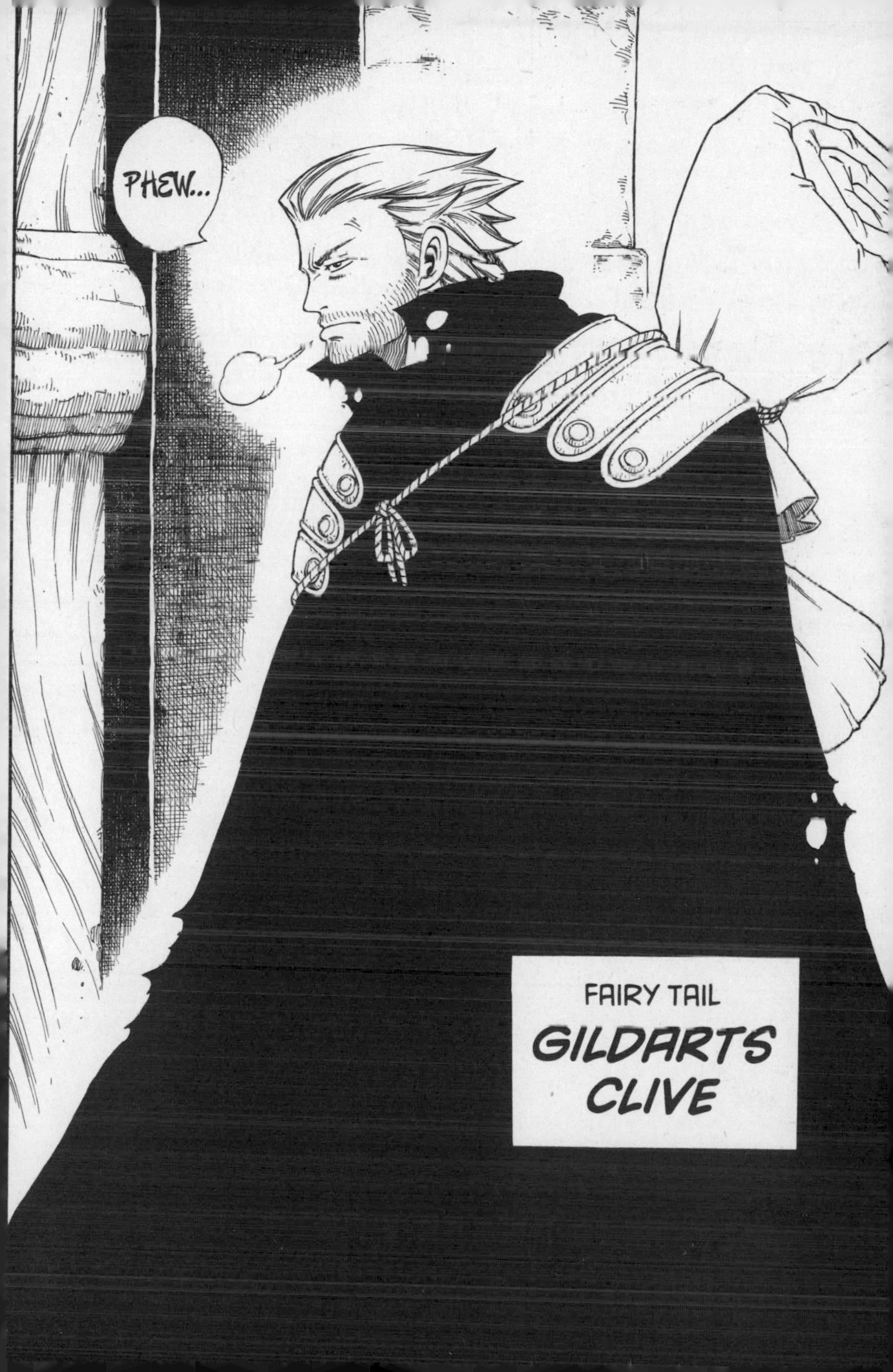
PHEW...
FAIRY TAIL
GILDARTS CLIVE

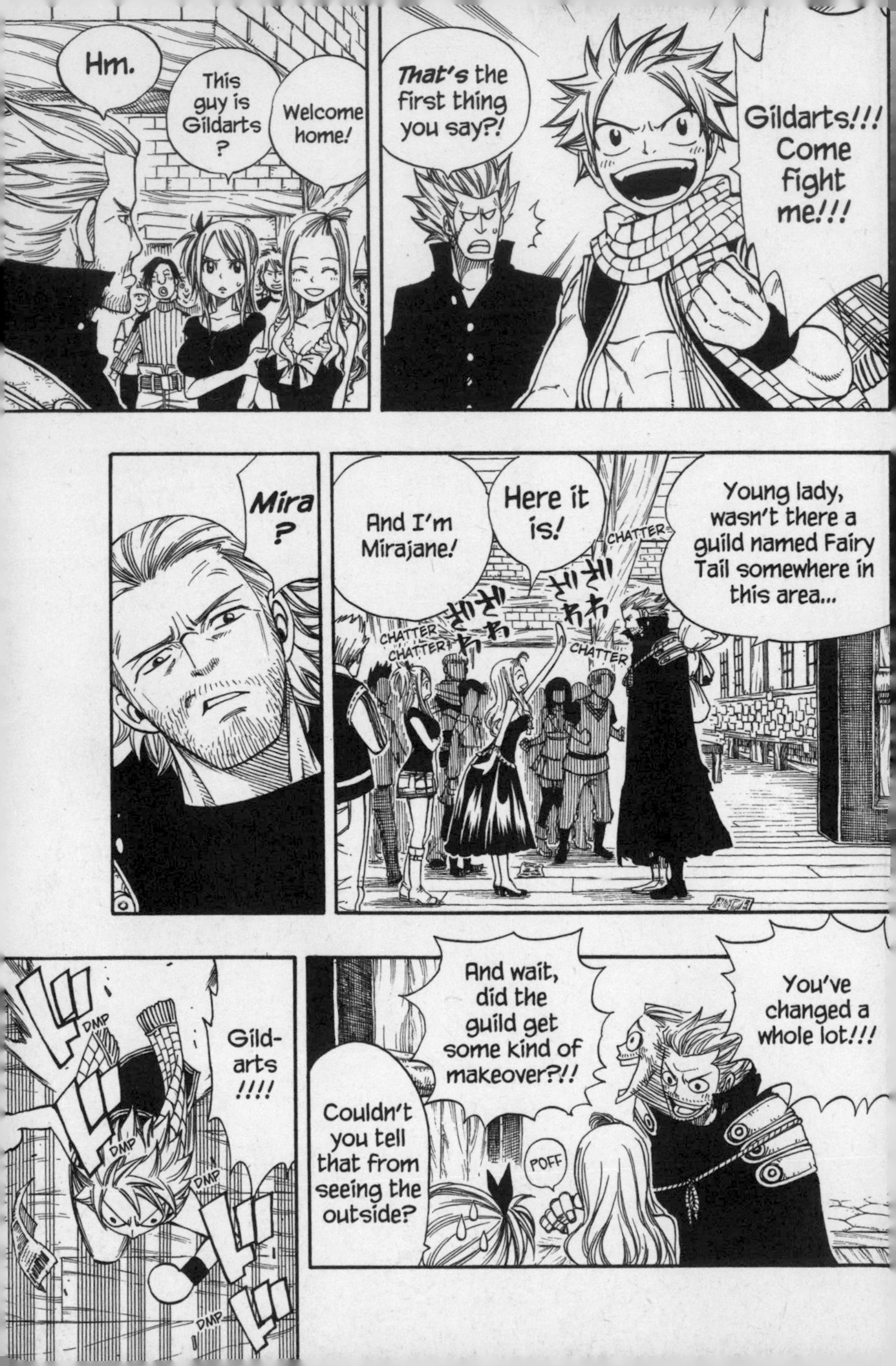
Gildarts!!! Come fight me!!!
*That's* the first thing you say?!
Welcome home!
This guy is Gildarts?
Hm.
Young lady, wasn't there a guild named Fairy Tail somewhere in this area...
CHATTER
Here it is!
And I'm Mirajane!
CHATTER
CHATTER
CHATTER
Mira?
You've changed a whole lot!!!
And wait, did the guild get some kind of makeover?!!
POFF
Couldn't you tell that from seeing the outside?
Gild-arts!!!!
DMP
DMP
DMP
DMP

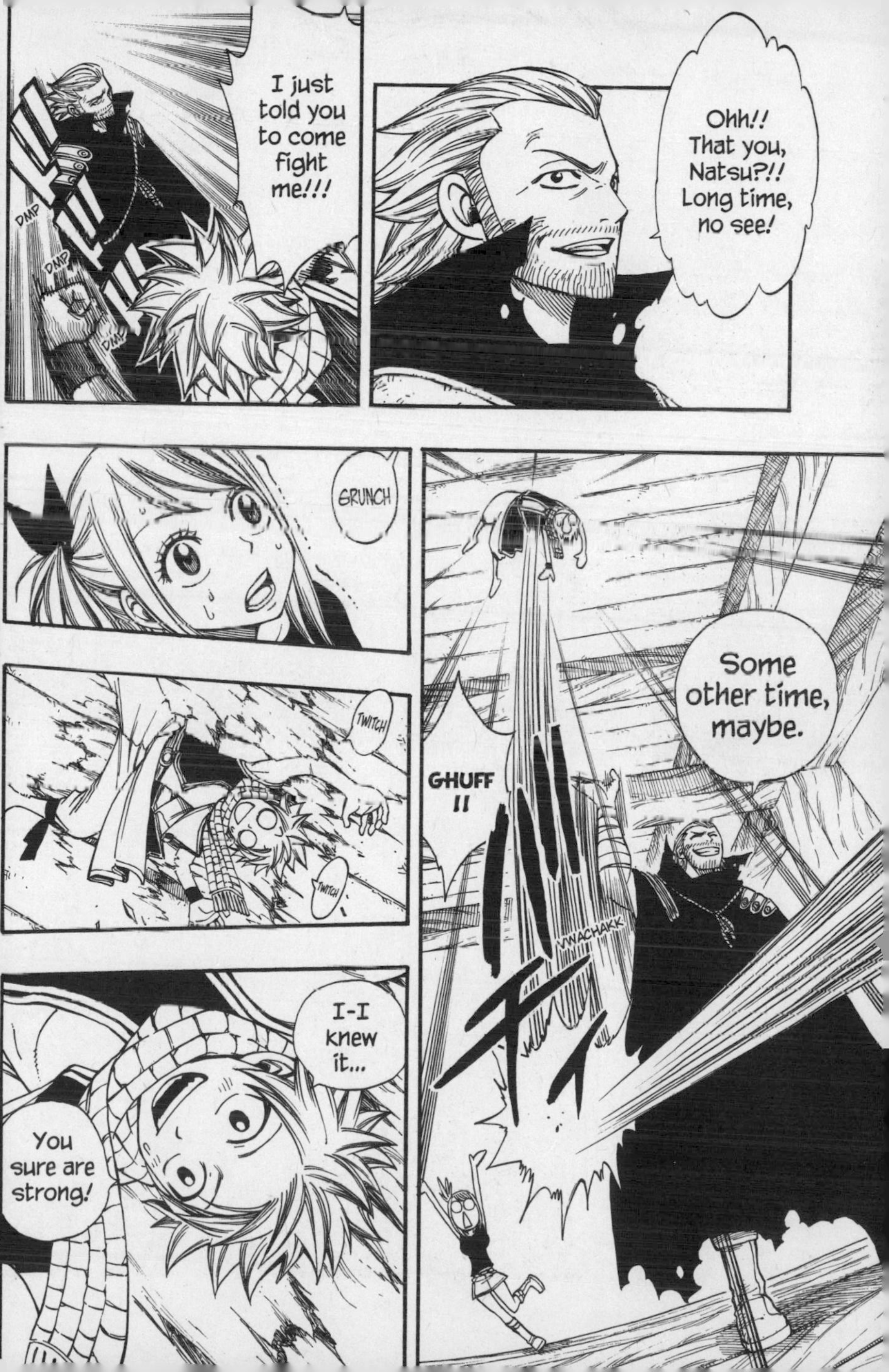

Ohh!! That you, Natsu?!! Long time, no see!
I just told you to come fight me!!!
DMP
DMP
DMP
Some other time, maybe.
GHUFF!!
VWACHAKK
GRUNCH
TWITCH
TWITCH
I-I knew it...
You sure are strong!

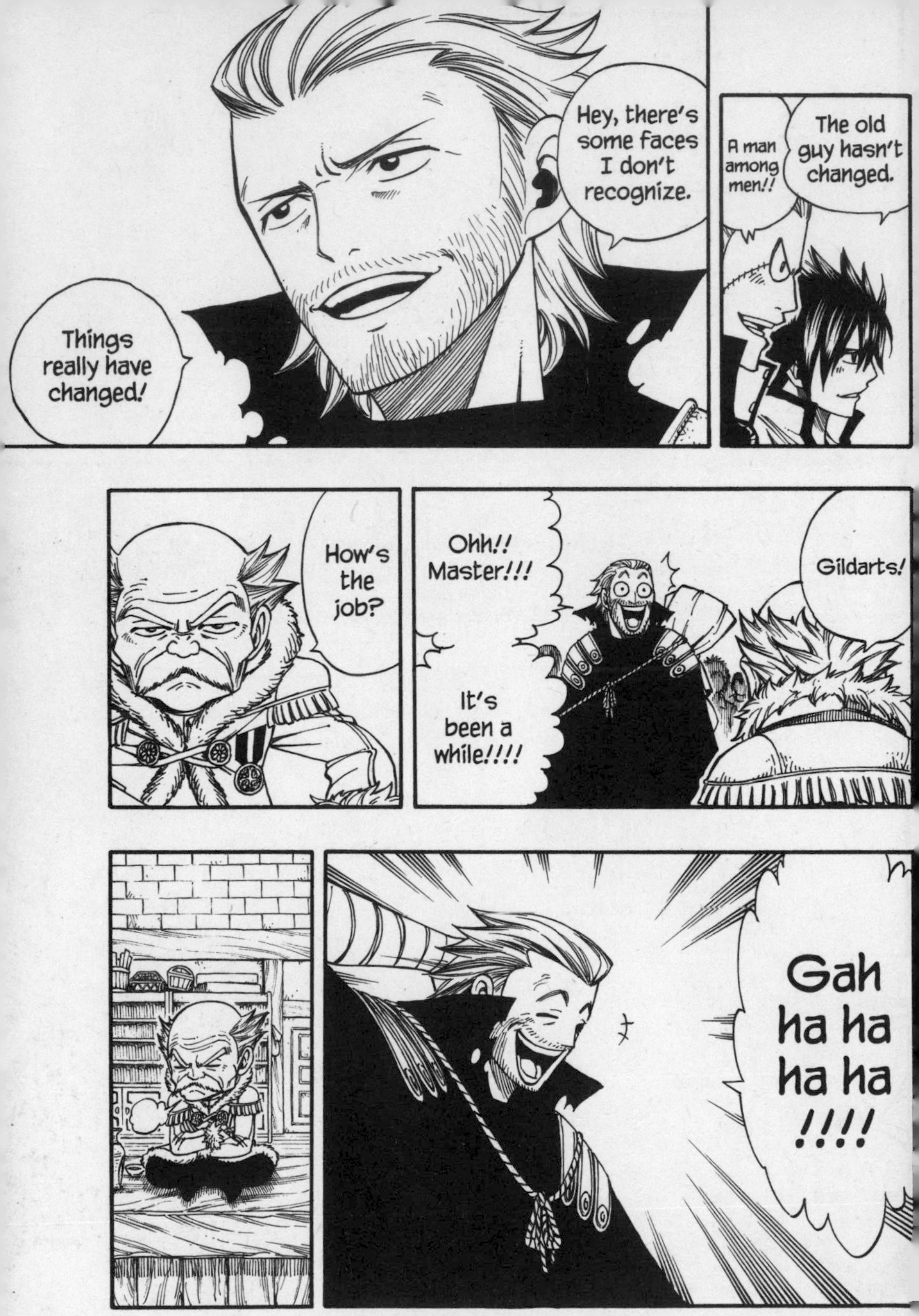
The old guy hasn't changed.
A man among men!!
Hey, there's some faces I don't recognize.
Things really have changed!
Gildarts!
Ohh!! Master!!!
It's been a while!!!!
How's the job?
Gah ha ha ha ha !!!!

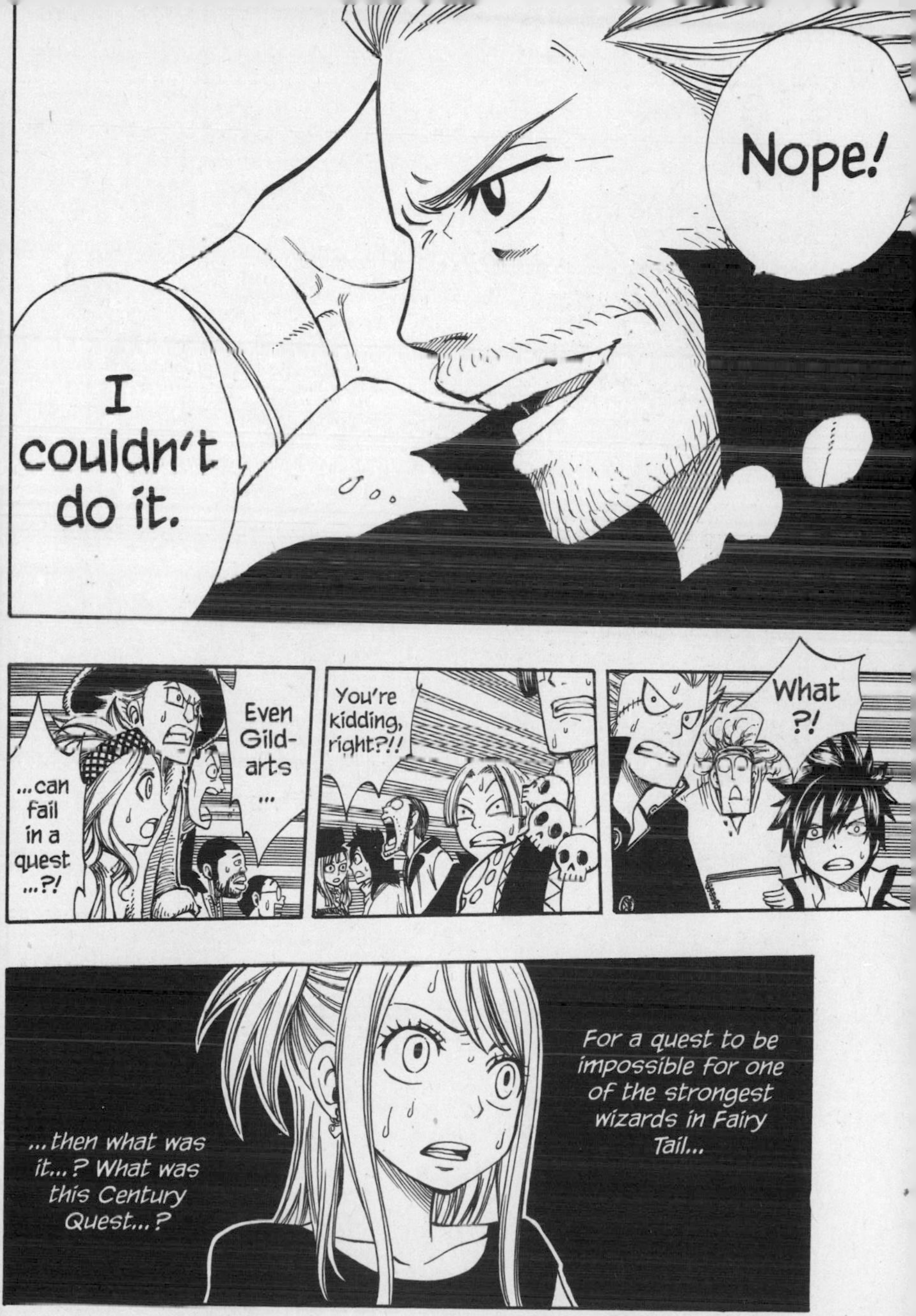

Nope!
I couldn't do it.
What ?!
You're kidding, right?!!
Even Gild-arts ...
...can fail in a quest ...?!
For a quest to be impossible for one of the strongest wizards in Fairy Tail...
...then what was it...? What was this Century Quest...?

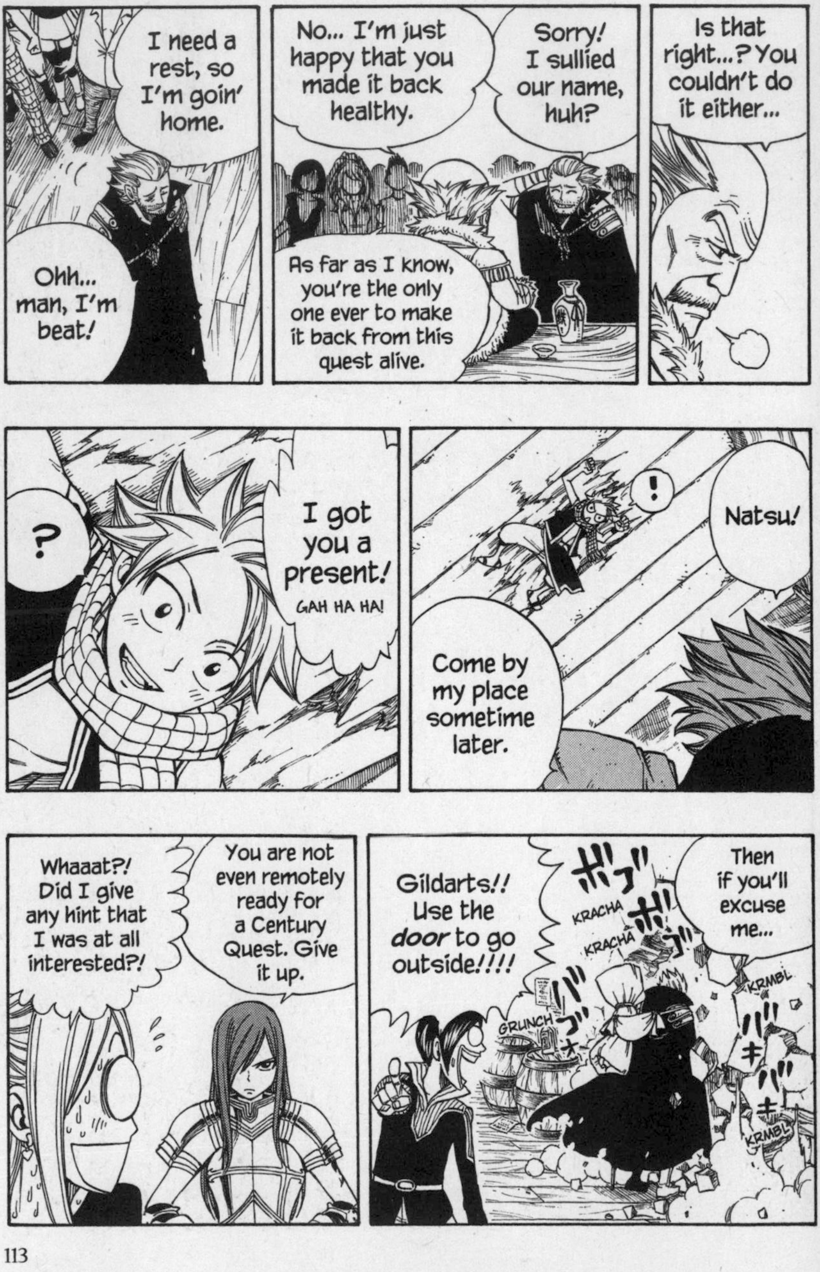
Is that right...? You couldn't do it either...
Sorry! I sullied our name, huh?
No... I'm just happy that you made it back healthy.
As far as I know, you're the only one ever to make it back from this quest alive.
I need a rest, so I'm goin' home.
Ohh... man, I'm beat!
Natsu!
!
Come by my place sometime later.
I got you a present!
GAH HA HA!
?
Then if you'll excuse me...
KRACHA
KRACHA
KRMBL
KRMBL
GRUNCH
Gildarts!! Use the *door* to go outside!!!!
You are not even remotely ready for a Century Quest. Give it up.
Whaaat?! Did I give any hint that I was at all interested?!

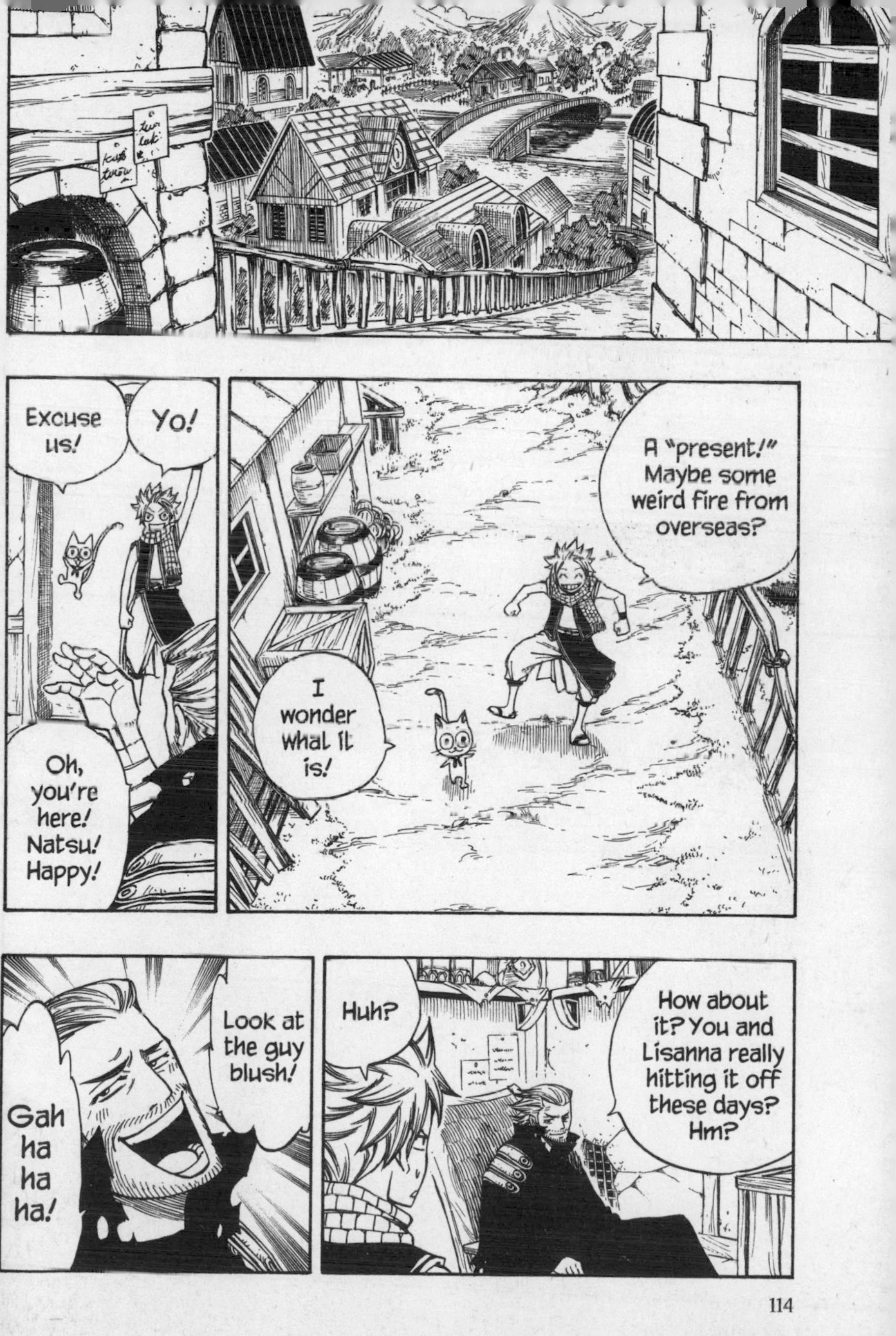
A "present!" Maybe some weird fire from overseas?
I wonder what it is!
Yo!
Excuse us!
Oh, you're here! Natsu! Happy!
How about it? You and Lisanna really hitting it off these days? Hm?
Huh?
Look at the guy blush!
Gah ha ha ha!

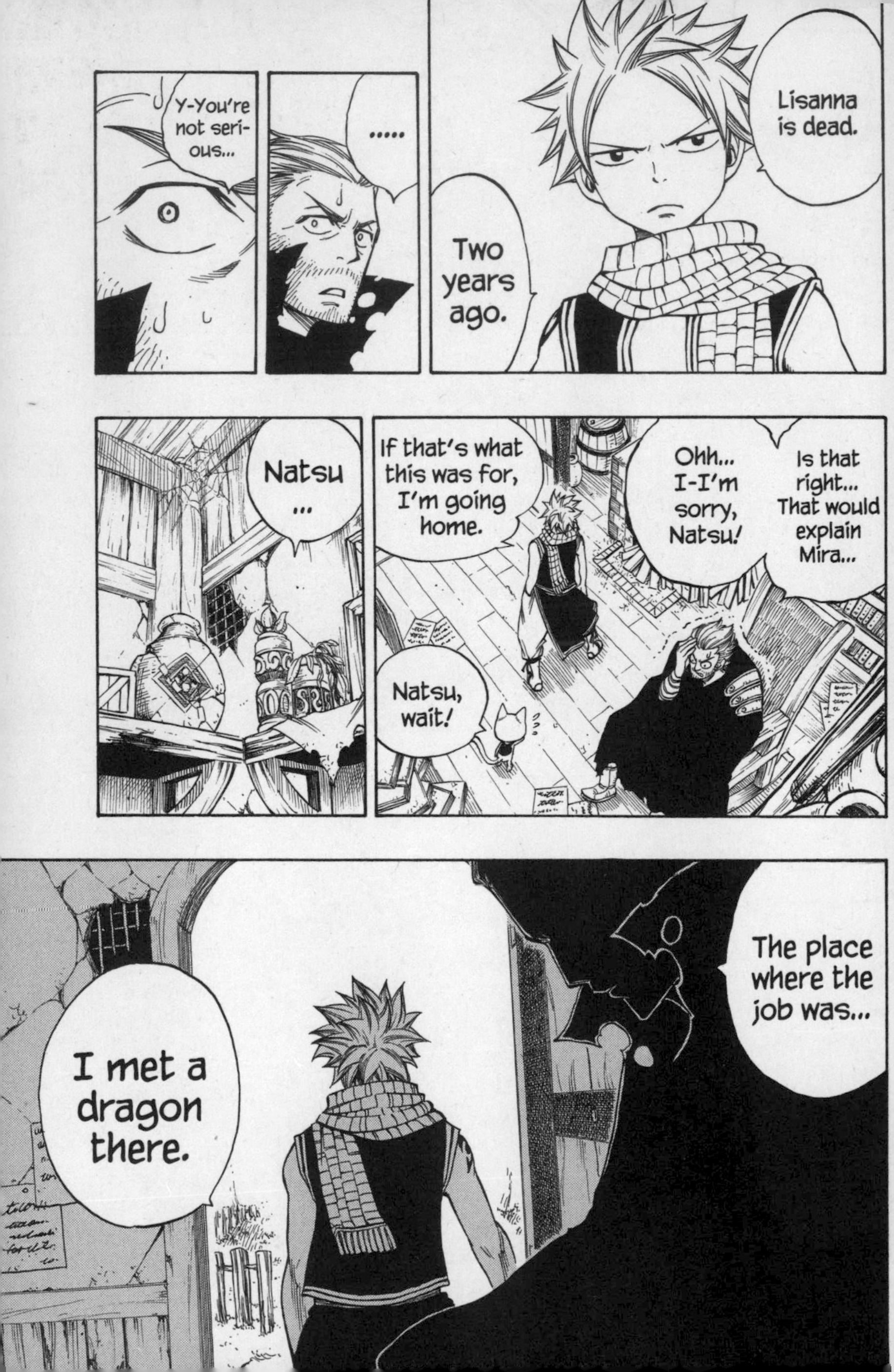

Lisanna is dead.
Two years ago.
.....
Y-You're not seri-ous...
Is that right... That would explain Mira...
Ohh... I-I'm sorry, Natsu!
If that's what this was for, I'm going home.
Natsu, wait!
Natsu ...
The place where the job was...
I met a dragon there.

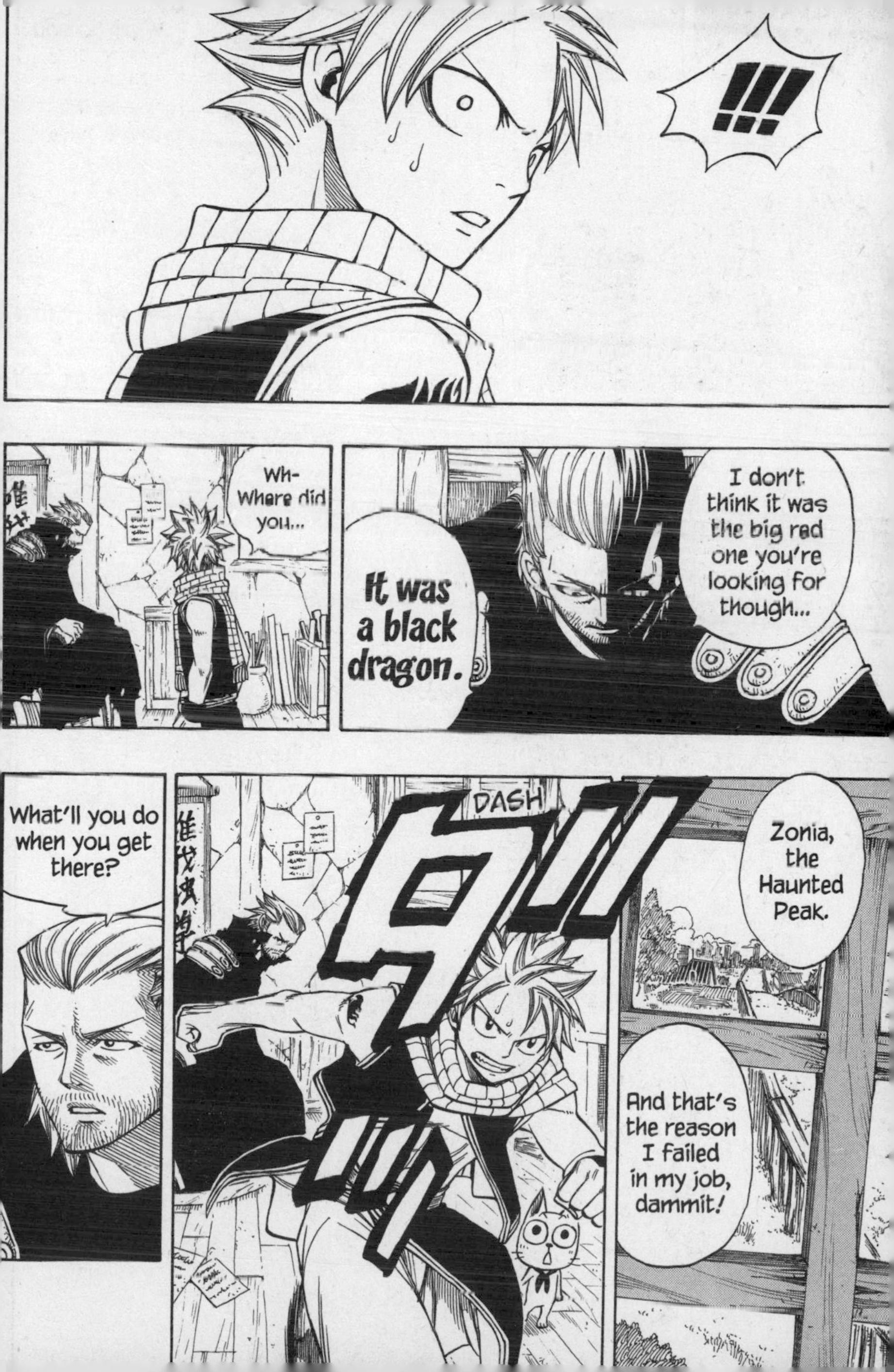
!!!
I don't think it was the big red one you're looking for though...
It was a black dragon.
Wh- Where did you...
Zonia, the Haunted Peak.
And that's the reason I failed in my job, dammit!
DASH
What'll you do when you get there?

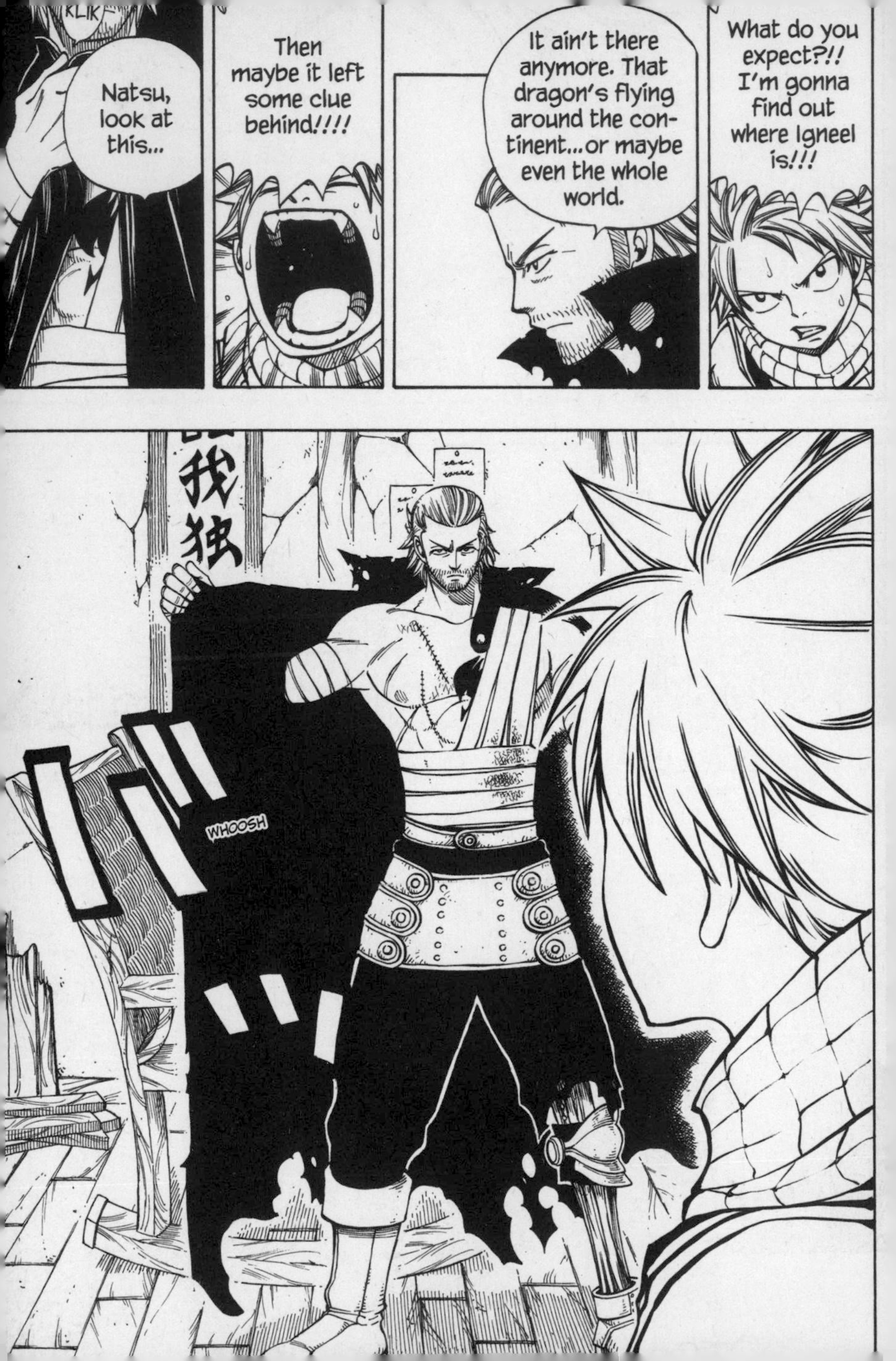
What do you expect?!! I'm gonna find out where Igneel is!!!
It ain't there anymore. That dragon's flying around the continent...or maybe even the whole world.
Then maybe it left some clue behind!!!!
KLIK
Natsu, look at this...
我独
WHOOSH

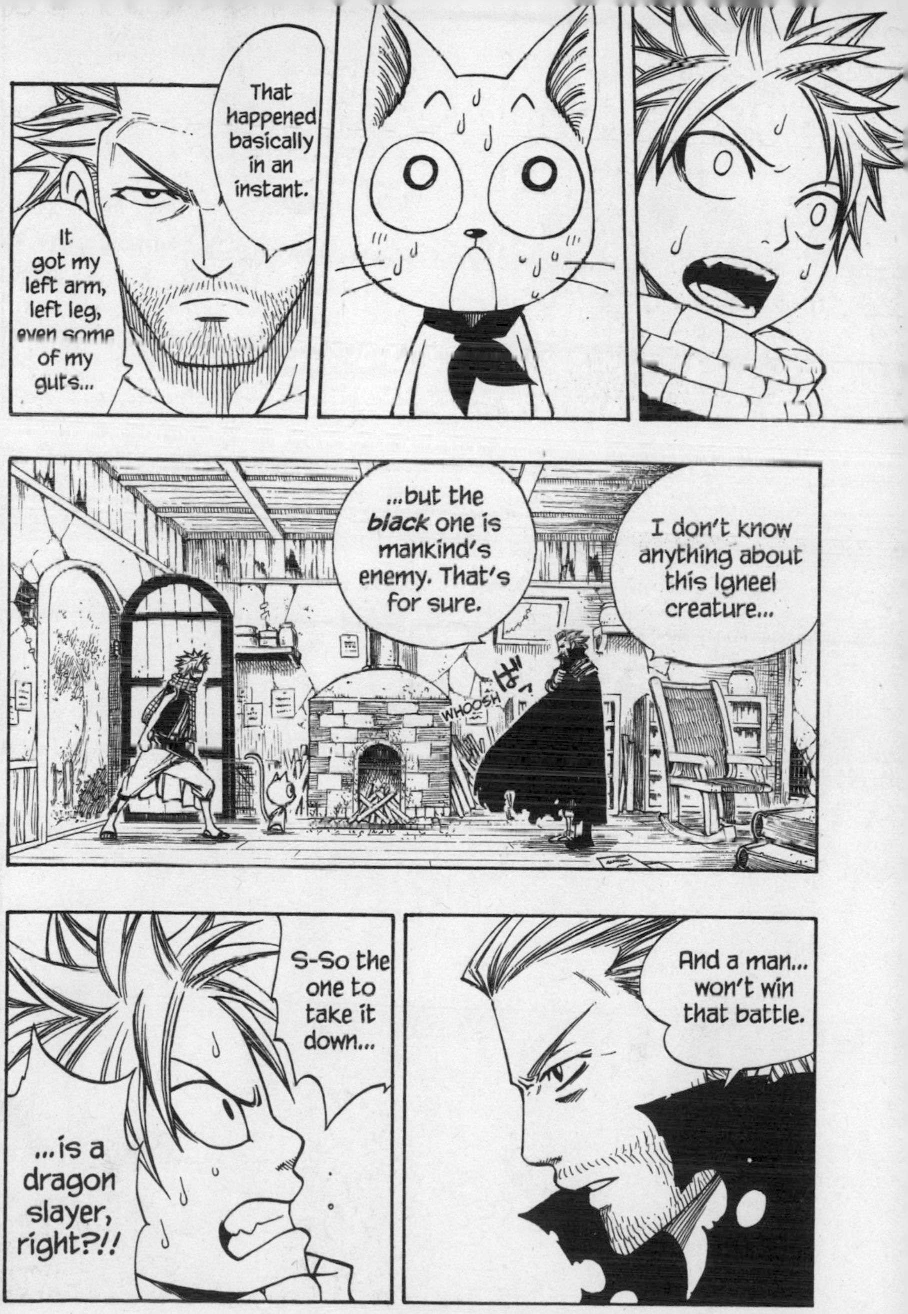
That happened basically in an instant.
It got my left arm, left leg, even some of my guts...
I don't know anything about this Igneel creature...
...but the *black* one is mankind's enemy. That's for sure.
WHOOSH
And a man... won't win that battle.
S-So the one to take it down...
...is a dragon slayer, right?!!

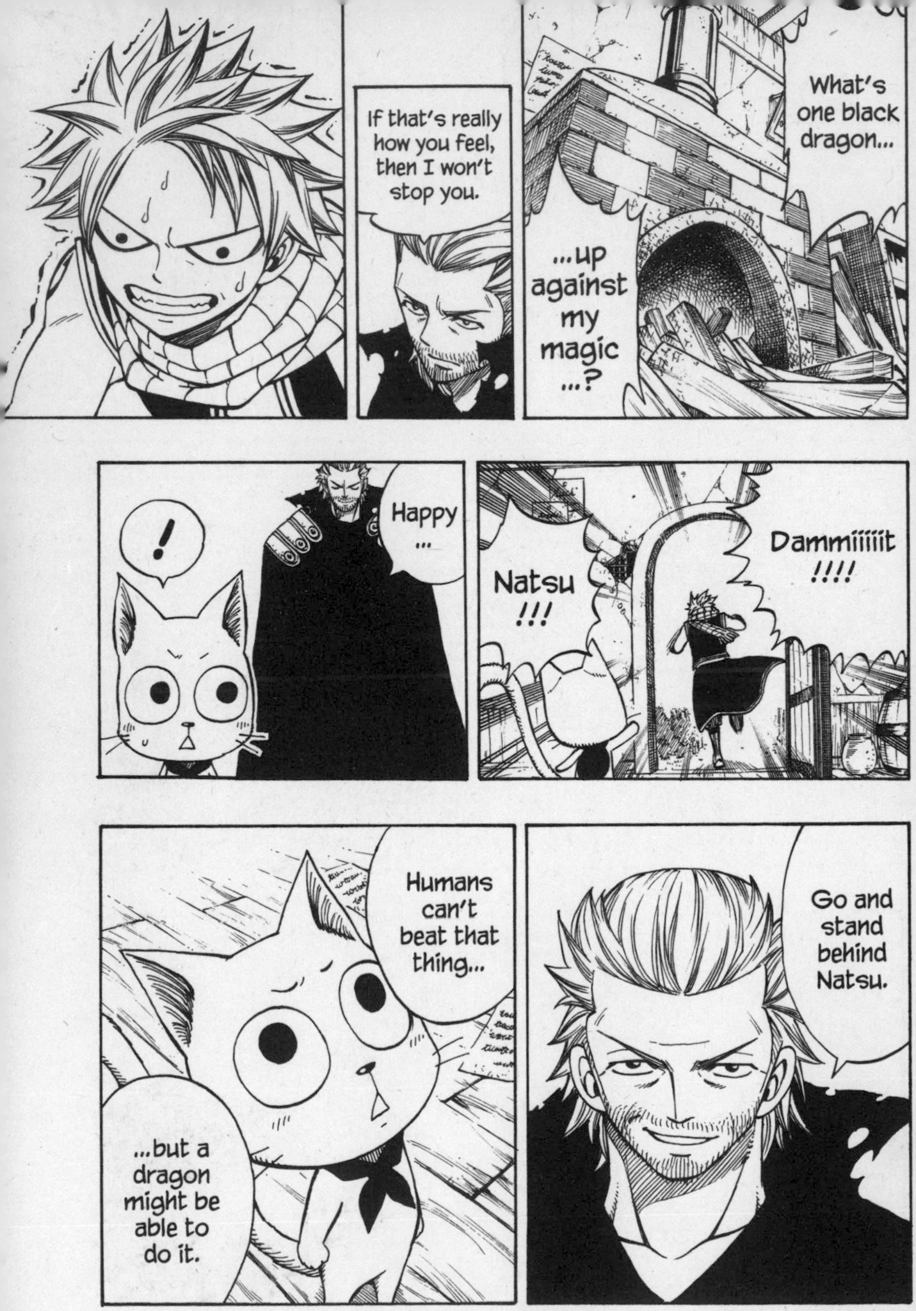

What's one black dragon...
...up against my magic ...?
If that's really how you feel, then I won't stop you.
Dammiiiiit !!!!
Natsu !!!
Happy ...
!
Go and stand behind Natsu.
Humans can't beat that thing...
...but a dragon might be able to do it.

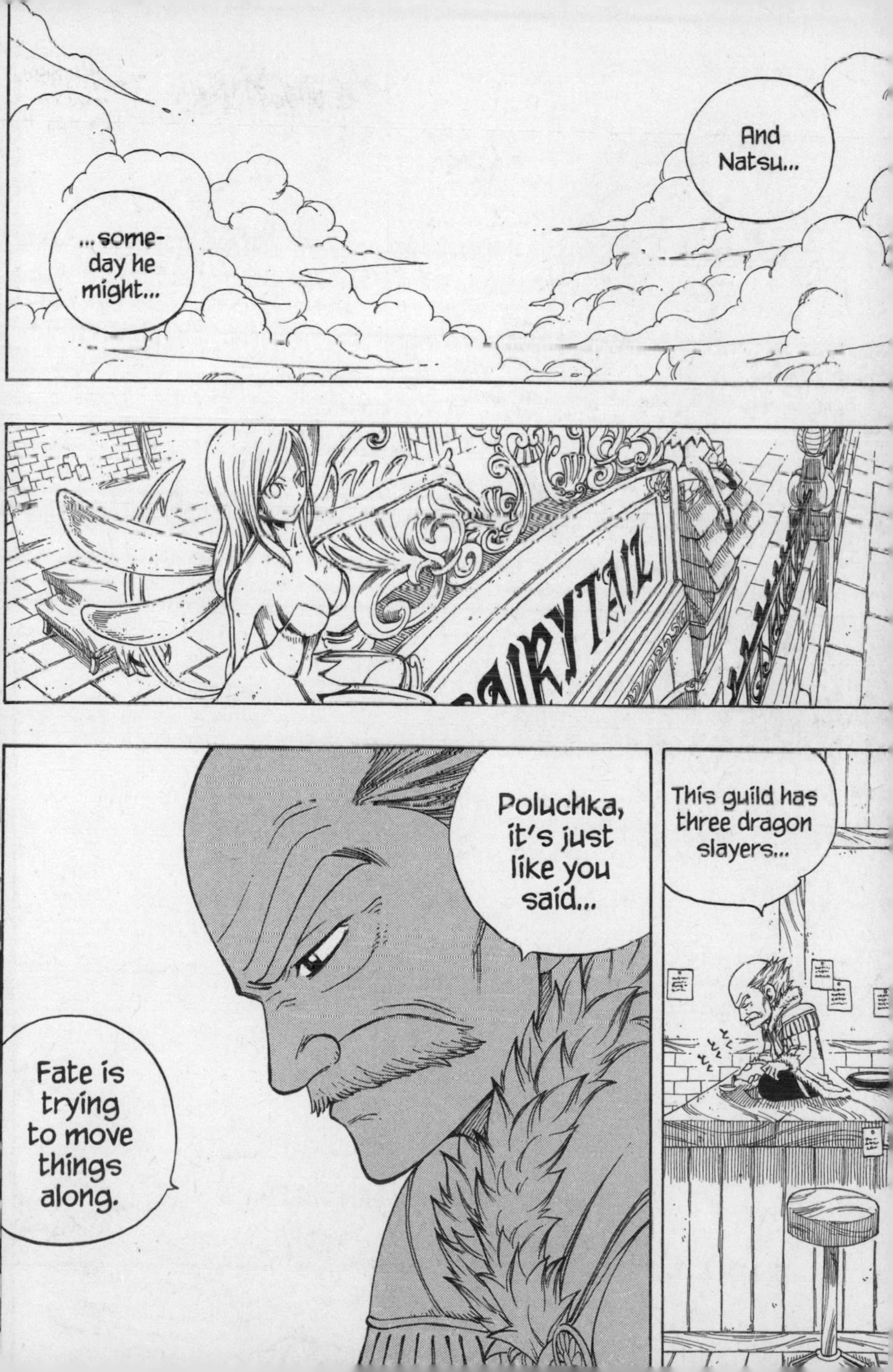
And Natsu...
...some-day he might...
This guild has three dragon slayers...
Poluchka, it's just like you said...
Fate is trying to move things along.

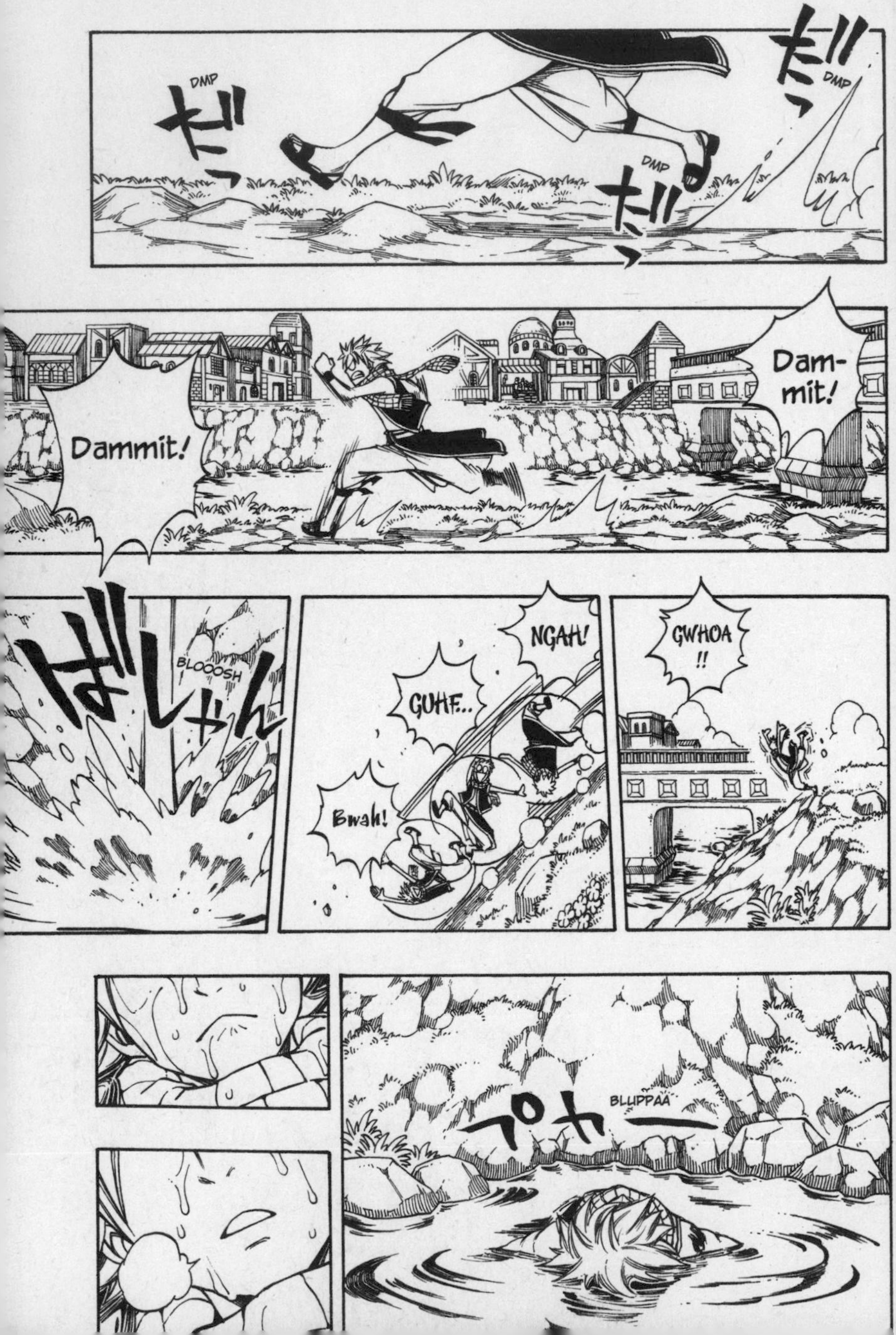
だっ!!
DMP
DMP
だっ!!
DMP
だっ
Dam-mit!
Dammit!
GWHOA !!
NGAH!
GUHF...
Bwah!
ばしゃん
BLOOOSH
BLUPPAA
プカー

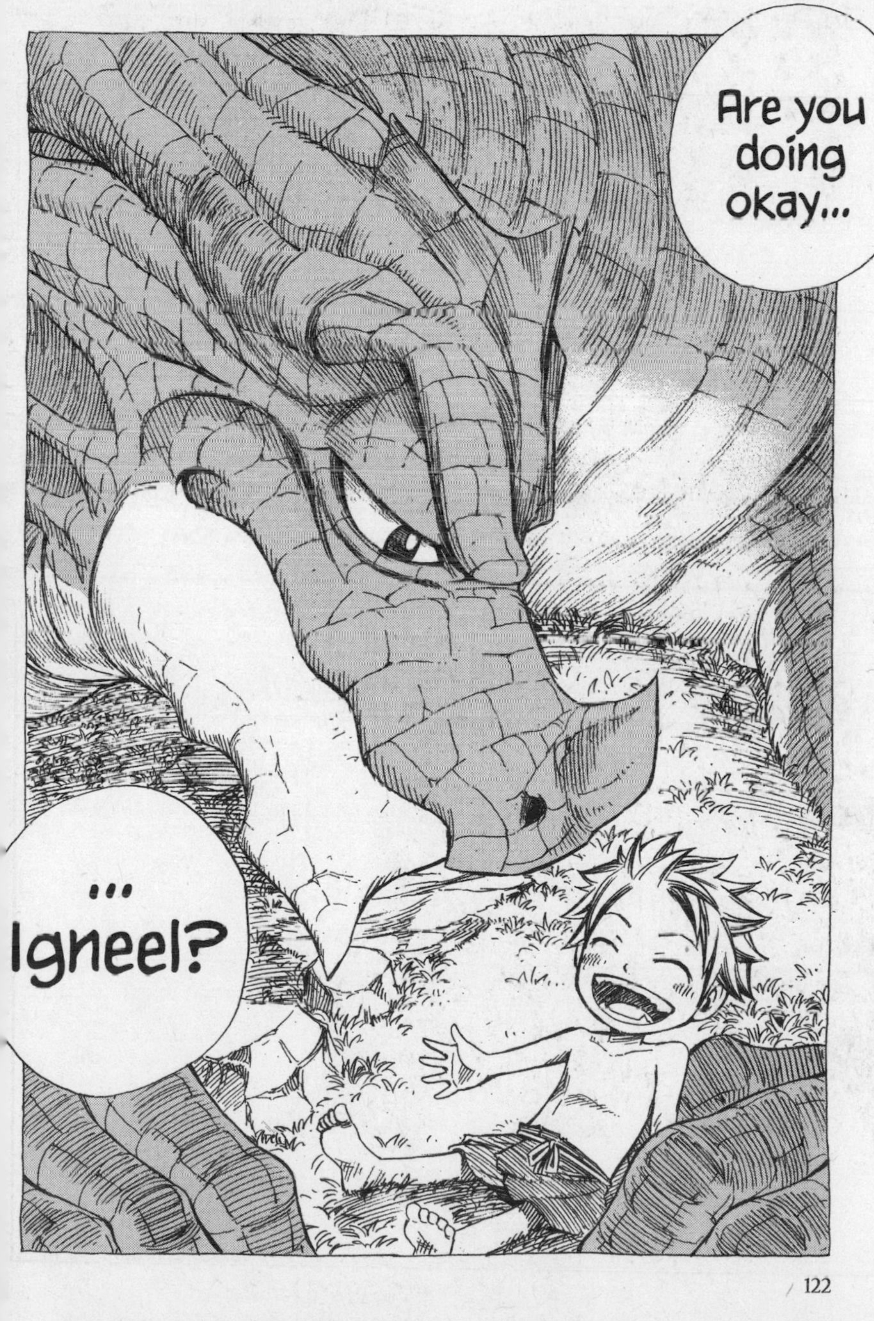
Are you doing okay...
... Igneel?

# FAIRY TAIL

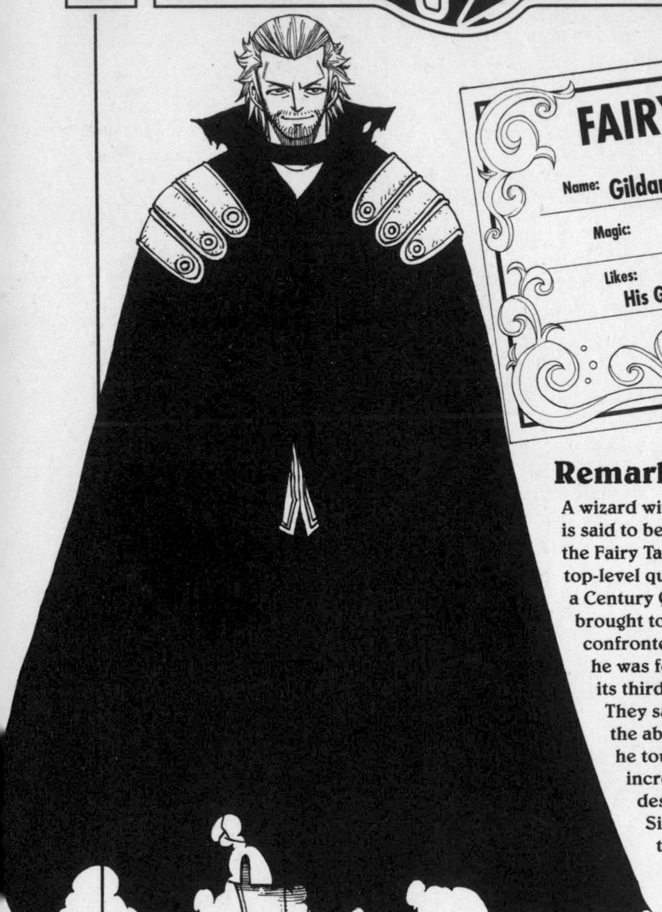

## FAIRY TAIL

**Name:** Gildarts Clive **Age:** 45

**Magic:** Crush

**Likes:** His Guild

**Dislikes:** Ivan Dreyar

WIZARD GUILD×633

### Remarks

A wizard with a high reputation who is said to be the strongest member of the Fairy Tail guild. He went on the top-level quest in the magic world, a Century Quest, but his quest was brought to an end when he was confronted by a black dragon and he was forced to quit the quest in its third year.

They say his magic, Crush, is the ability to reduce anything he touches to powder. It is an incredibly advanced kind of destruction magic.

Since he has a tendency to space out and in the process collapse buildings without realizing it, the main street of Magnolia can be transformed just for Gildarts.

## Chapter 167, The Vanishing Town

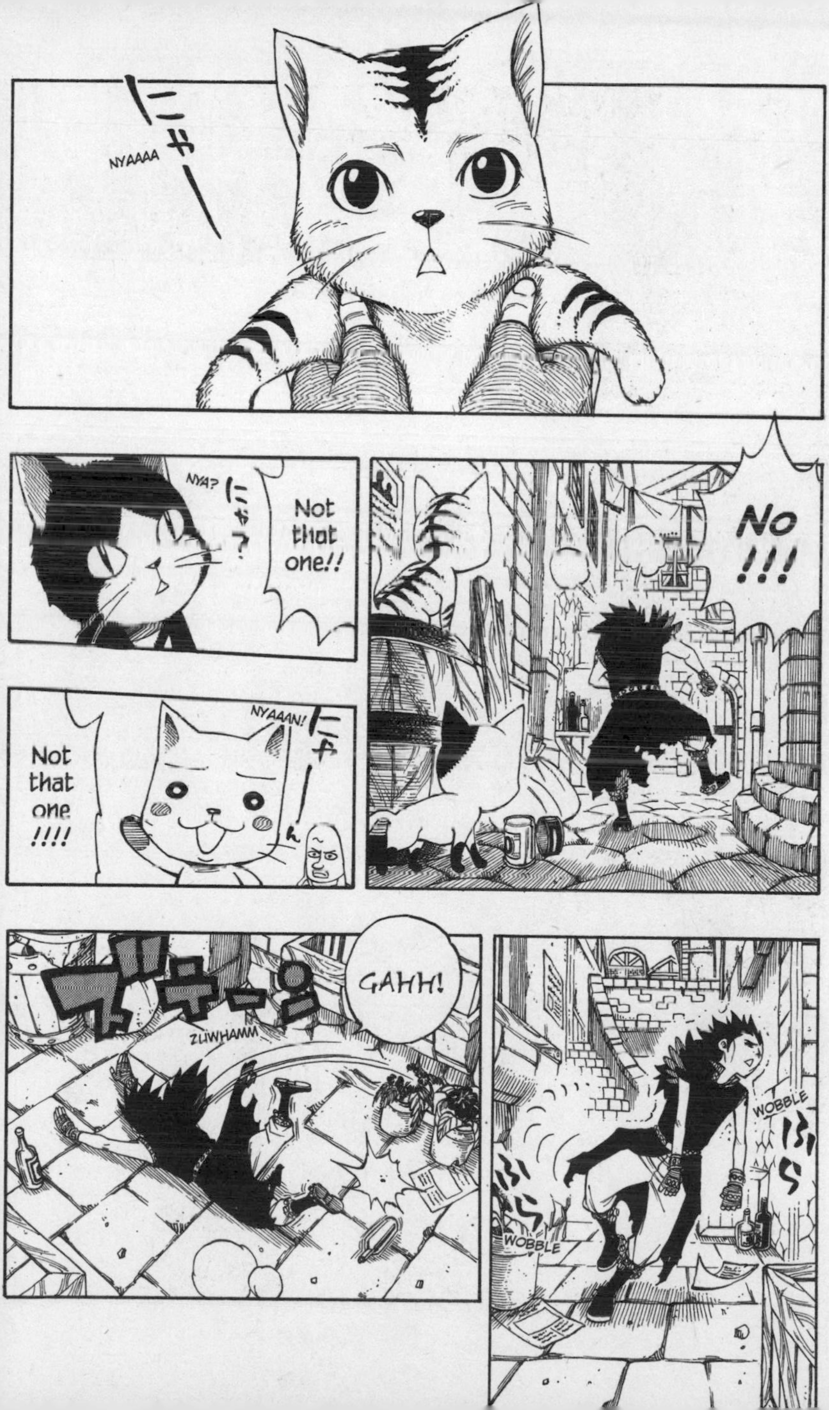
NYAAAA
にゃー
No!!!
NYA?
にゃ?
Not that one!!
Not that one!!!!
NYAAAN!
にゃーん!
WOBBLE
ふら
WOBBLE
ふら
GAHH!
ZUWHAMM

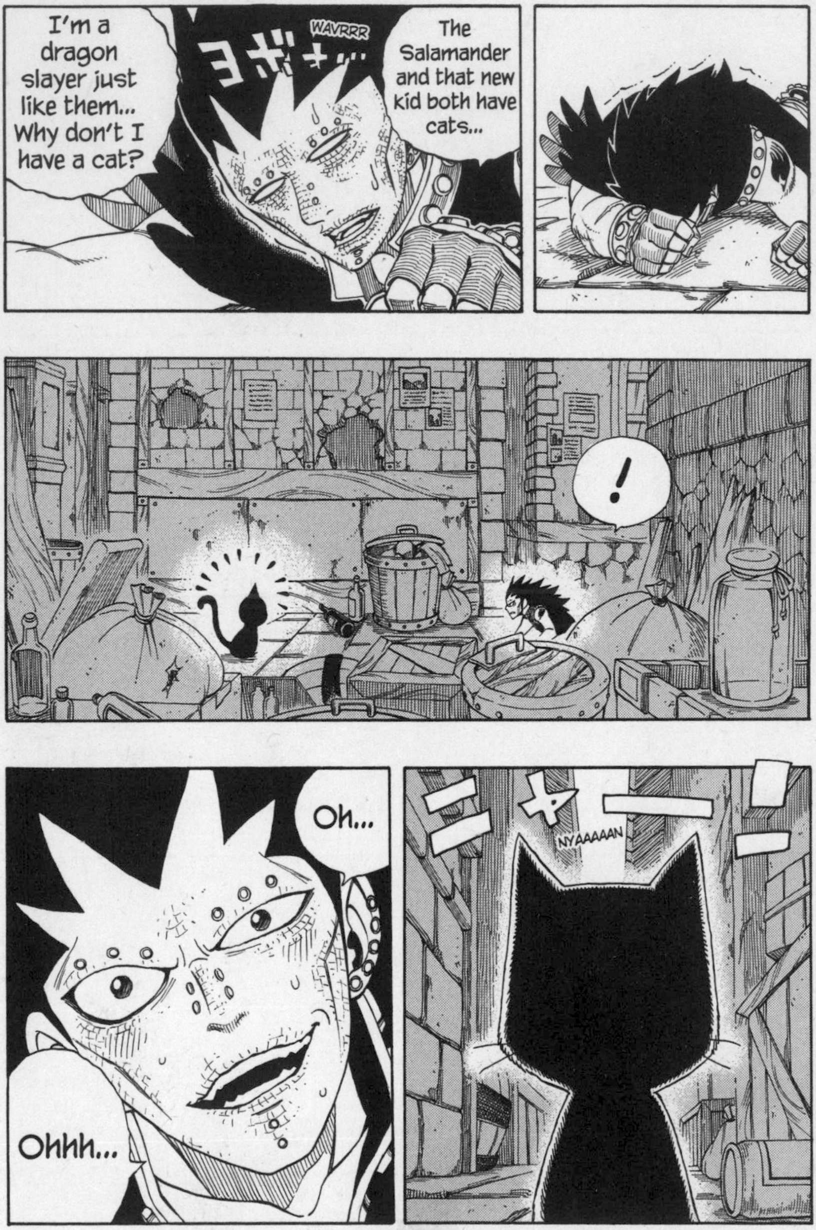
The Salamander and that new kid both have cats...
WAVRRR
I'm a dragon slayer just like them... Why don't I have a cat?
!
NYAAAAAN
Oh...
Ohhh...

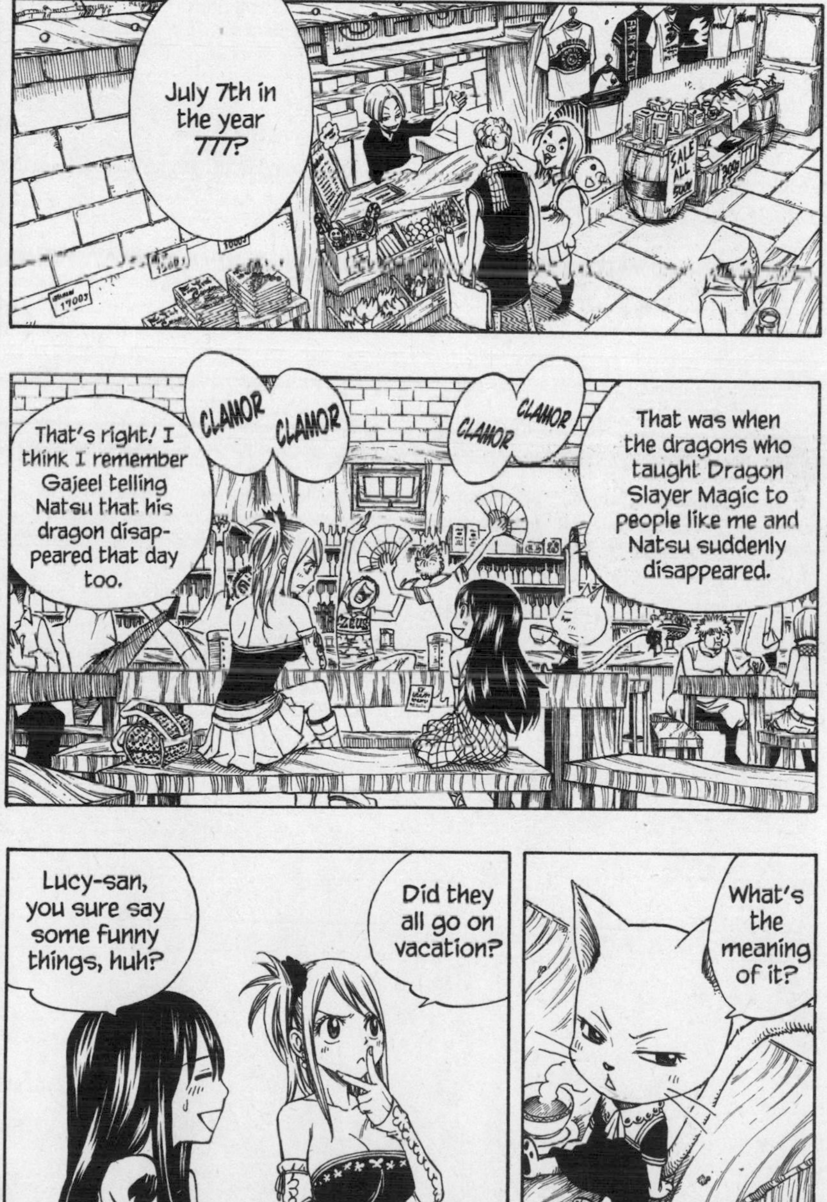
July 7th in the year 777?
That was when the dragons who taught Dragon Slayer Magic to people like me and Natsu suddenly disappeared.
CLAMOR
CLAMOR
CLAMOR
CLAMOR
That's right! I think I remember Gajeel telling Natsu that his dragon disappeared that day too.
What's the meaning of it?
Did they all go on vacation?
Lucy-san, you sure say some funny things, huh?

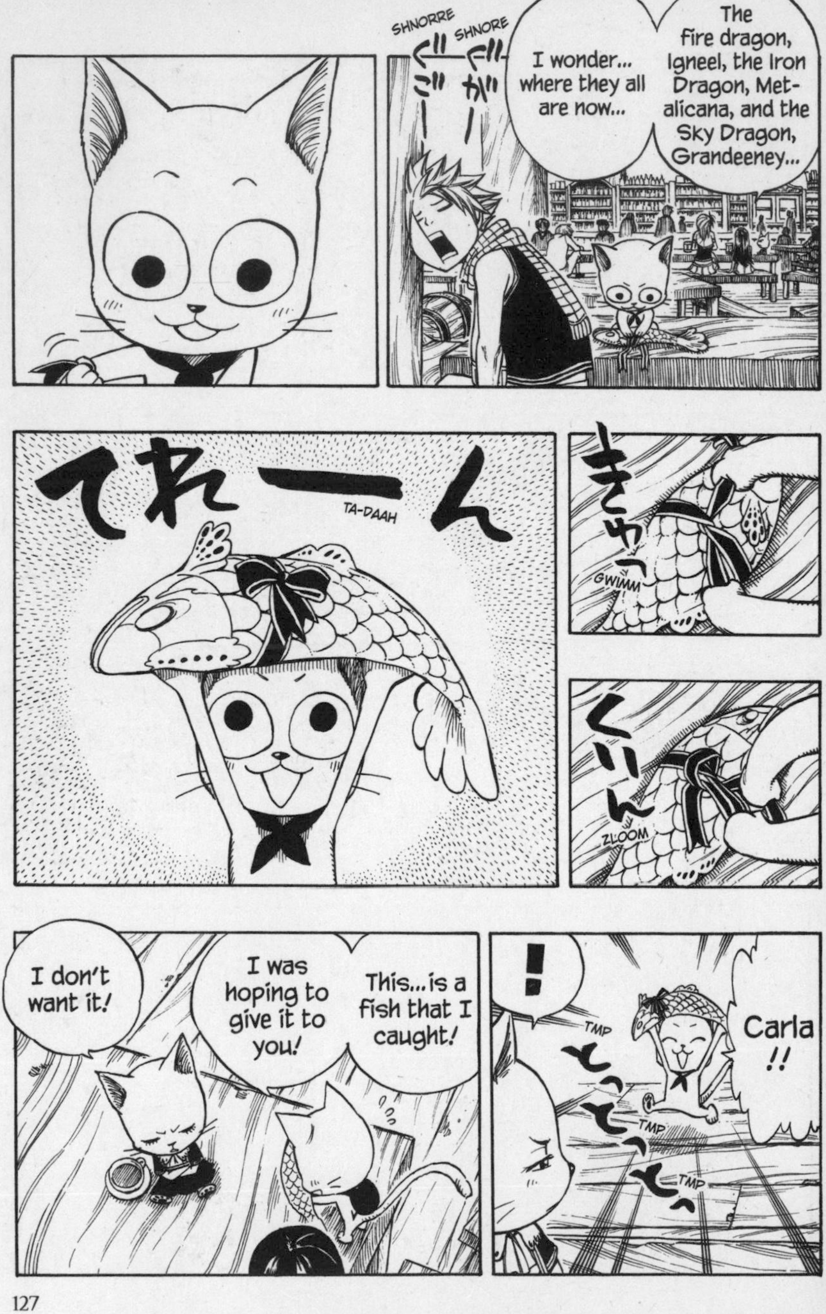

SHNORE
SHNORRE
The fire dragon, Igneel, the Iron Dragon, Metalicana, and the Sky Dragon, Grandeeney...
I wonder... where they all are now...
きゅっ
GWIMM
くりん
ZLOOM
てれーん
TA-DAAH
Carla !!
!
TMP
とてとて
TMP
TMP
This...is a fish that I caught!
I was hoping to give it to you!
I don't want it!

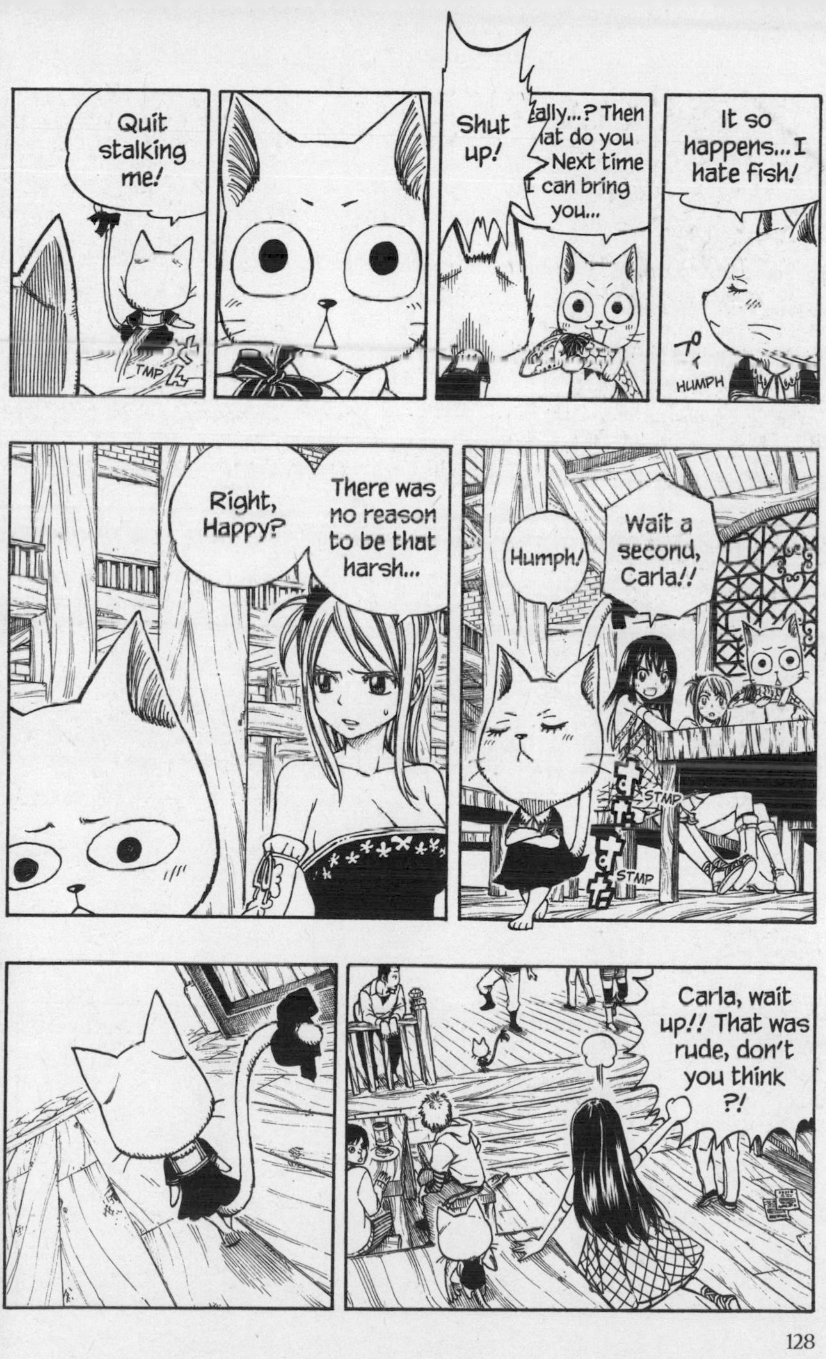
It so happens... I hate fish!
HUMPH
ally...? Then at do you Next time I can bring you...
Shut up!
Quit stalking me!
TMP
Wait a second, Carla!!
Humph!
STMP
STMP
There was no reason to be that harsh...
Right, Happy?
Carla, wait up!! That was rude, don't you think?!

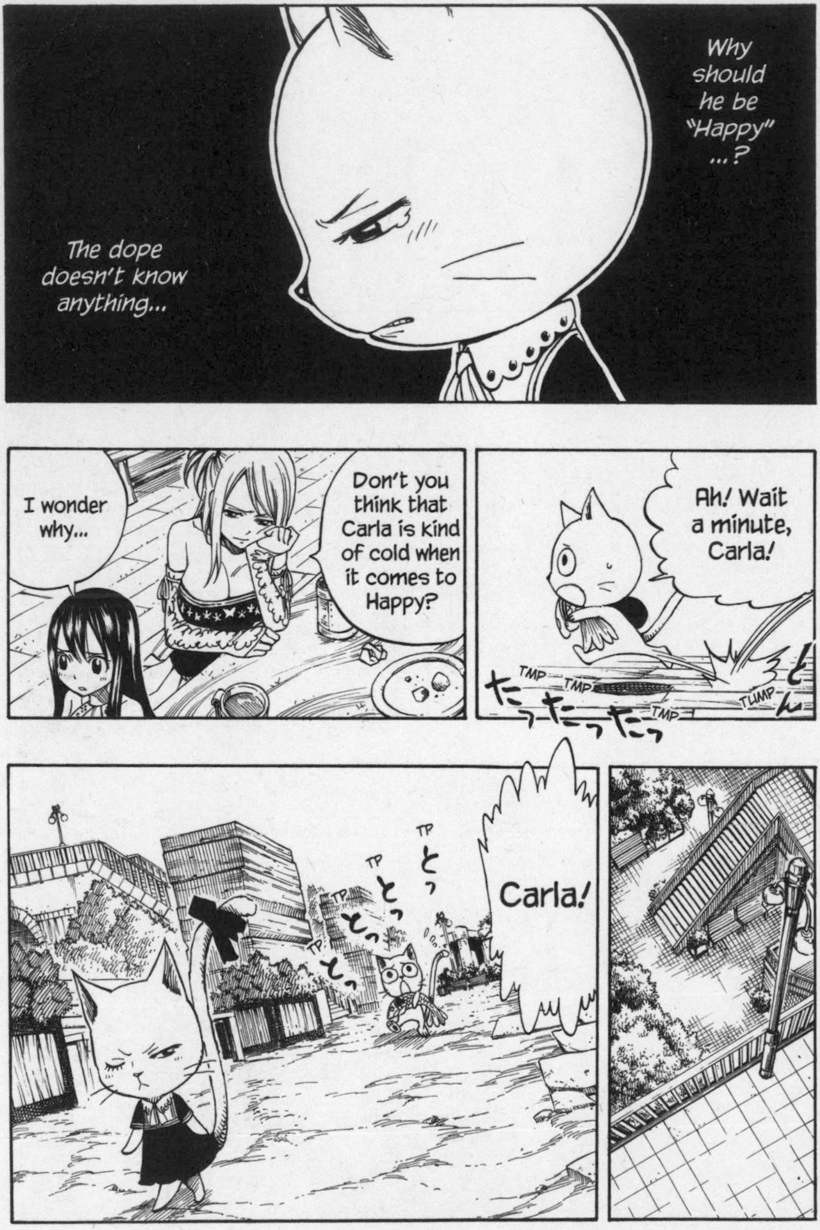
Why should he be "Happy" ...?
The dope doesn't know anything...
Ah! Wait a minute, Carla!
TMP TMP TMP
たっ たっ たっ
TUMP
とん
Don't you think that Carla is kind of cold when it comes to Happy?
I wonder why...
Carla!
TP TP TP TP
とっ とっ とっ とっ

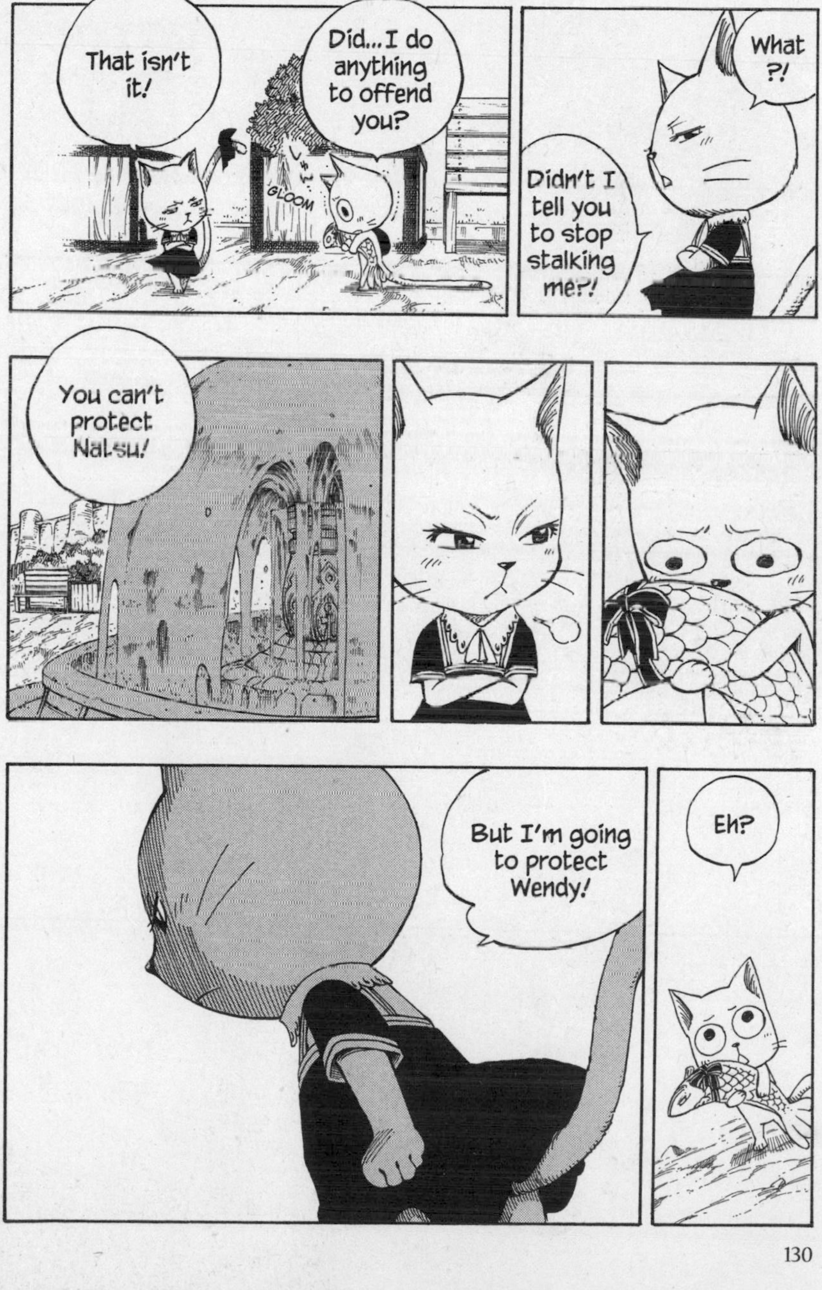
What?!
Didn't I tell you to stop stalking me?!
Did...I do anything to offend you?
That isn't it!
GLOOM
You can't protect Natsu!
Eh?
But I'm going to protect Wendy!

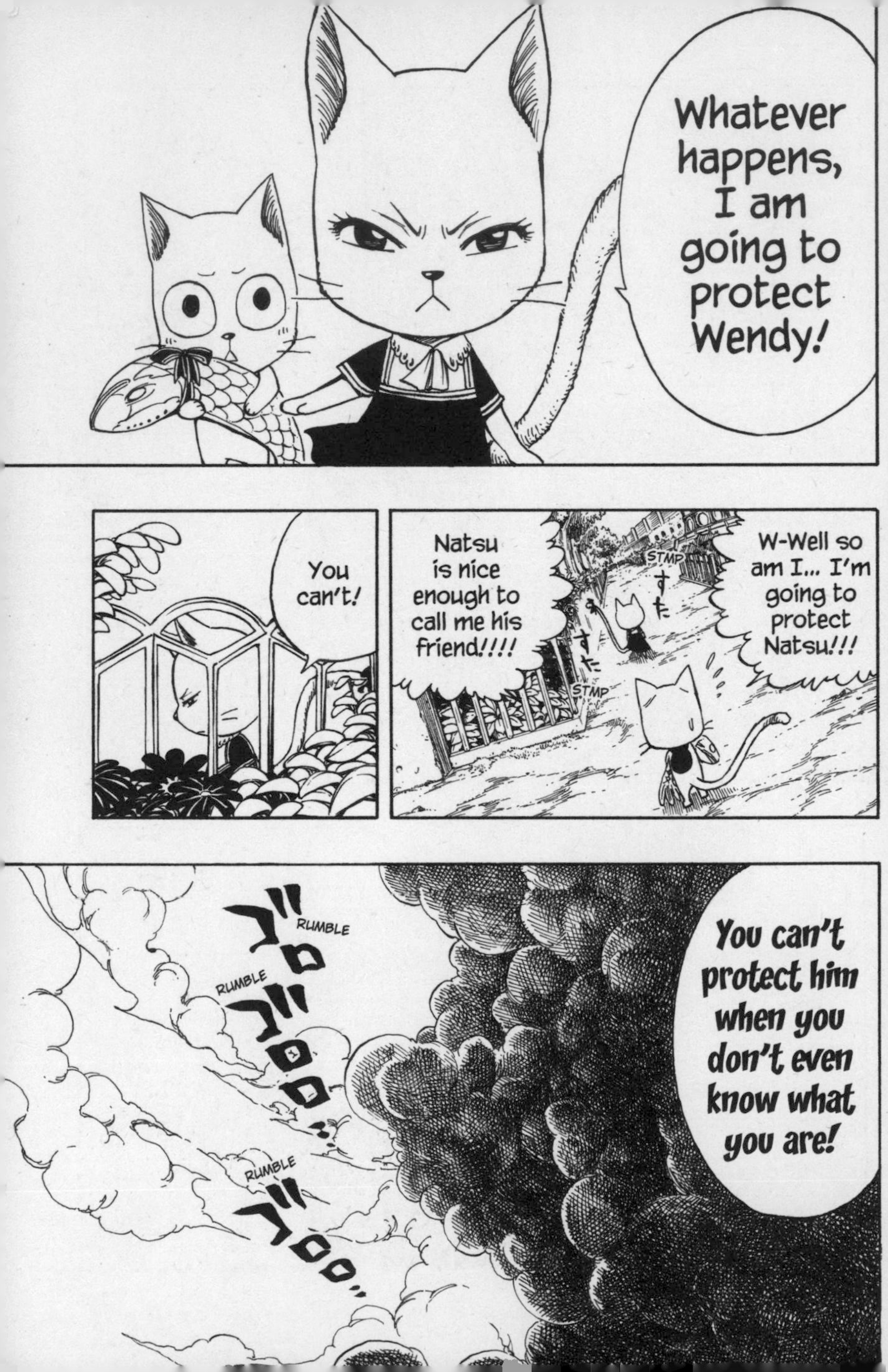
Whatever happens, I am going to protect Wendy!
W-Well so am I... I'm going to protect Natsu!!!
STMP
STMP
Natsu is nice enough to call me his friend!!!!
You can't!
You can't protect him when you don't even know what you are!
RUMBLE
RUMBLE
RUMBLE

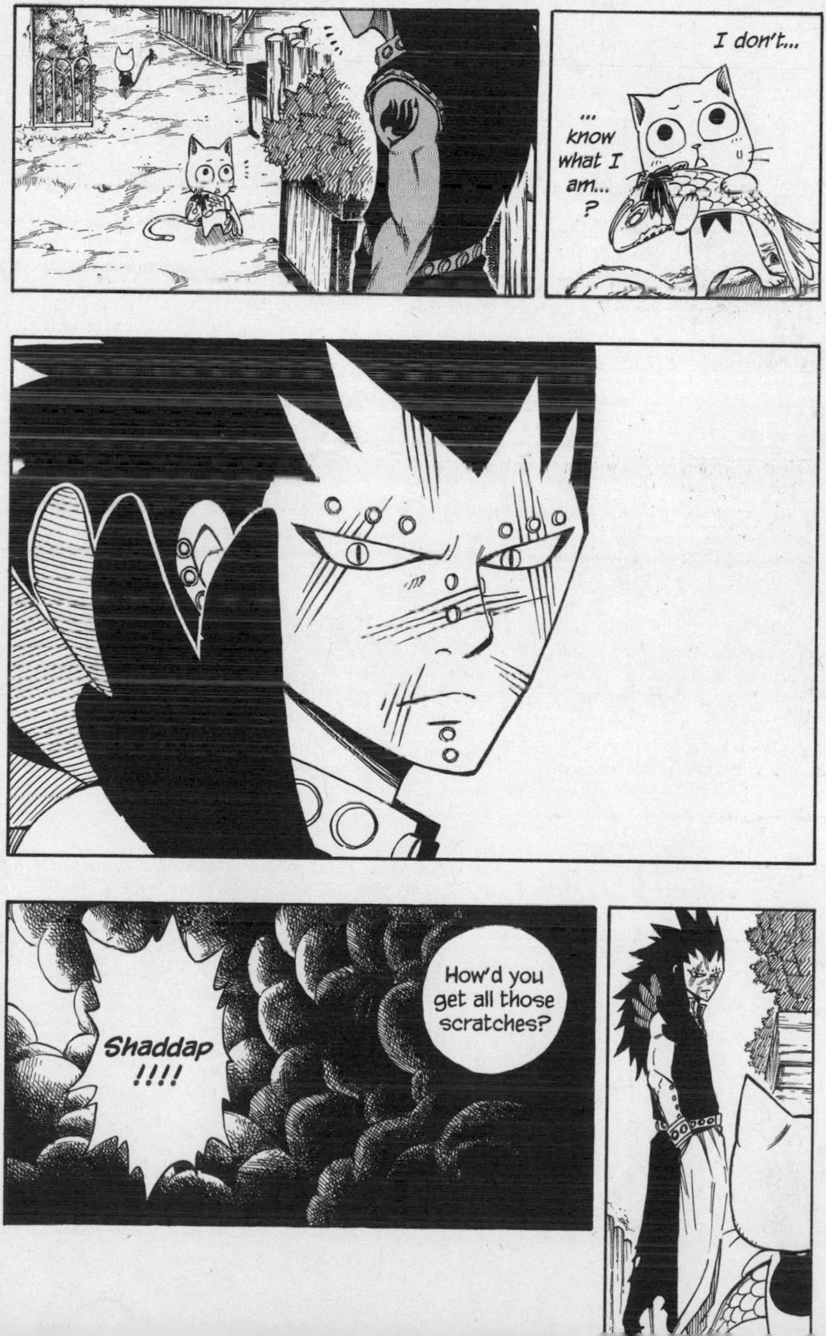
I don't...
... know what I am... ?
How'd you get all those scratches?
Shaddap !!!!

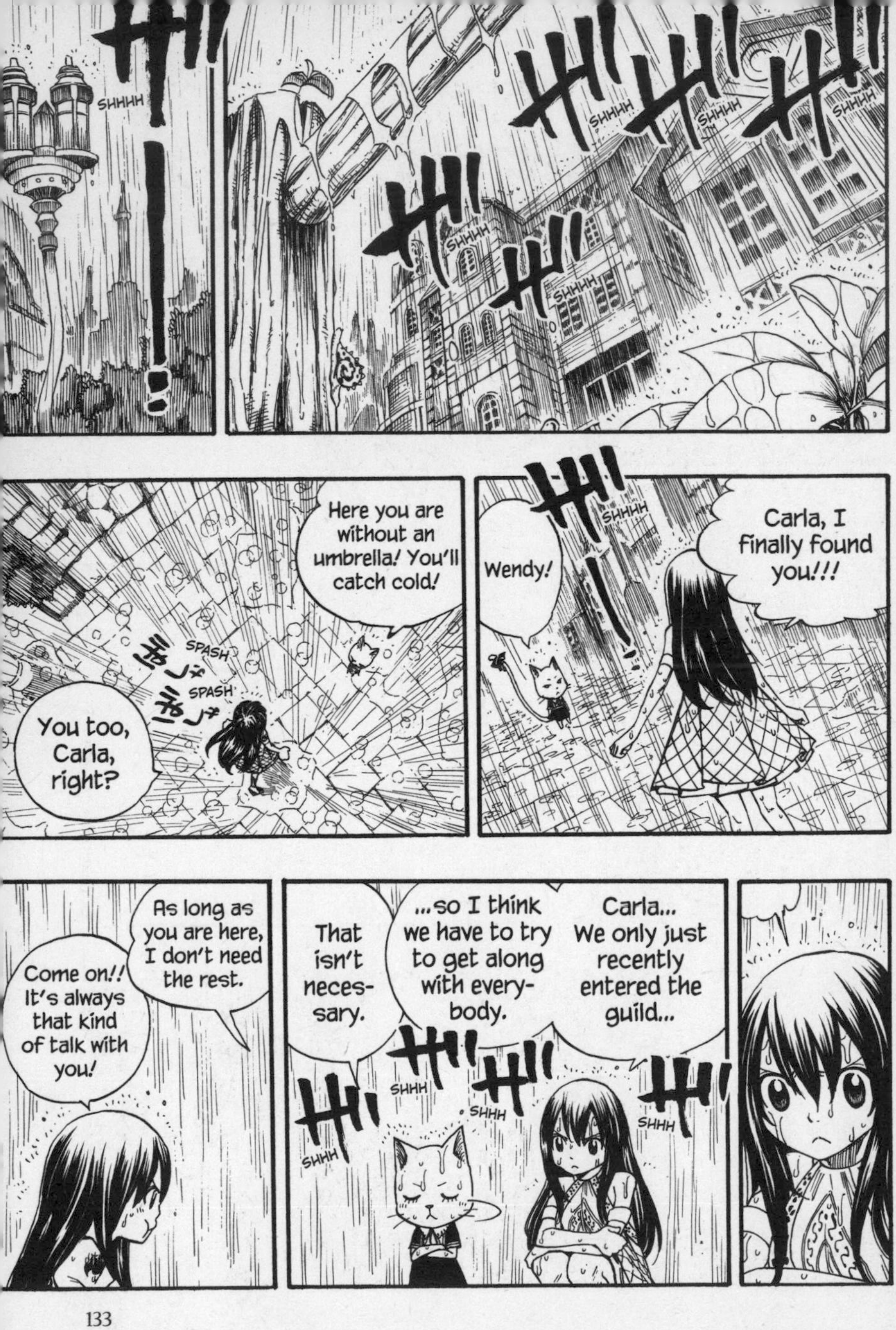
SHHHH
SHHHH
SHHHH
SHHHH
SHHHH
SHHHH
SHHHH
SHHHH
Carla, I finally found you!!!
Wendy!
Here you are without an umbrella! You'll catch cold!
SPASH
SPASH
You too, Carla, right?
Carla... We only just recently entered the guild...
...so I think we have to try to get along with every-body.
That isn't neces-sary.
SHHH
SHHH
SHHH
SHHH
As long as you are here, I don't need the rest.
Come on!! It's always that kind of talk with you!

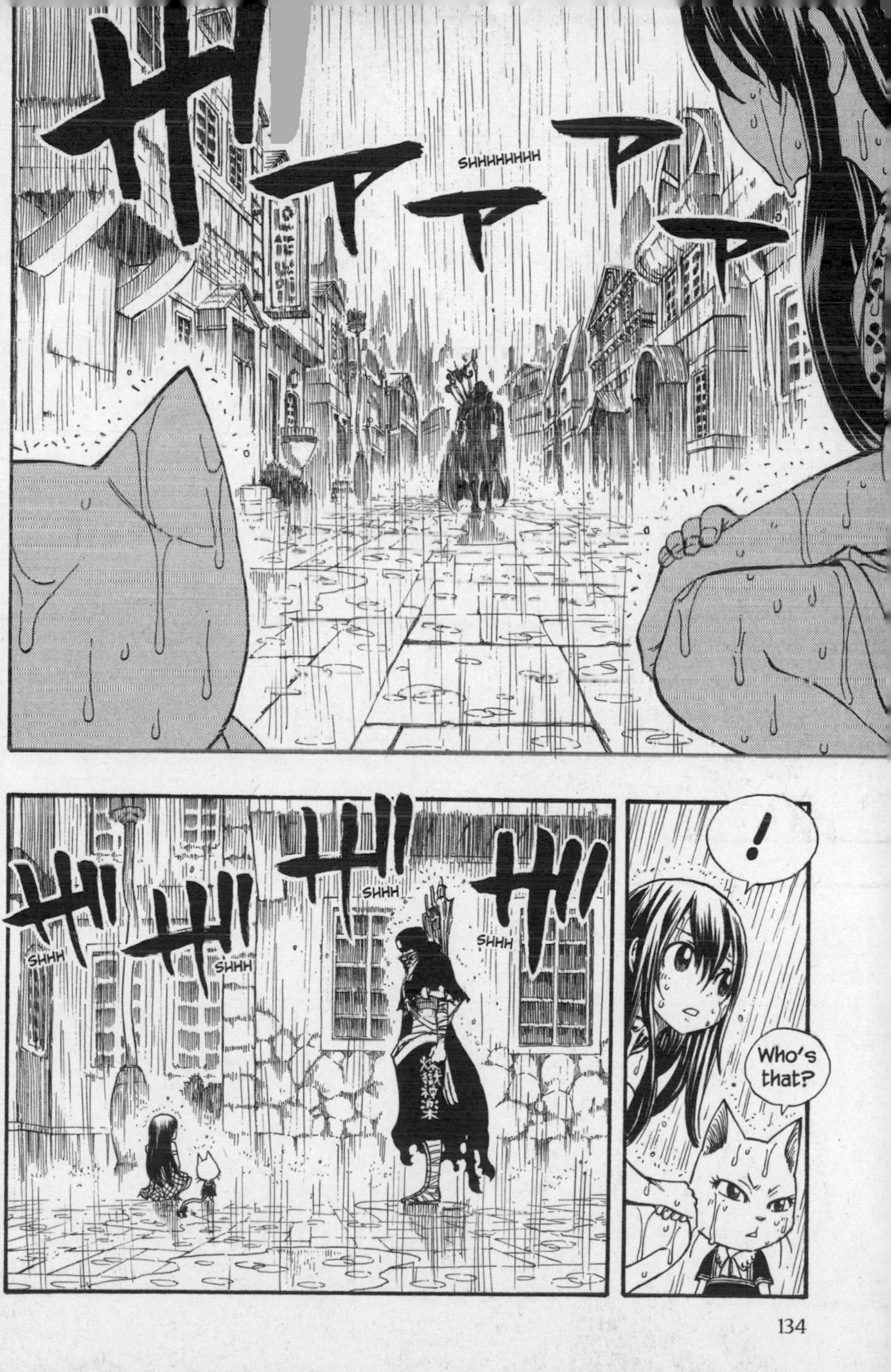
ザァァァ
SHHHHHHHH
!
Who's that?
ザザ
SHHH
ザ
SHHH
ザ
SHHH
ザ
SHHH

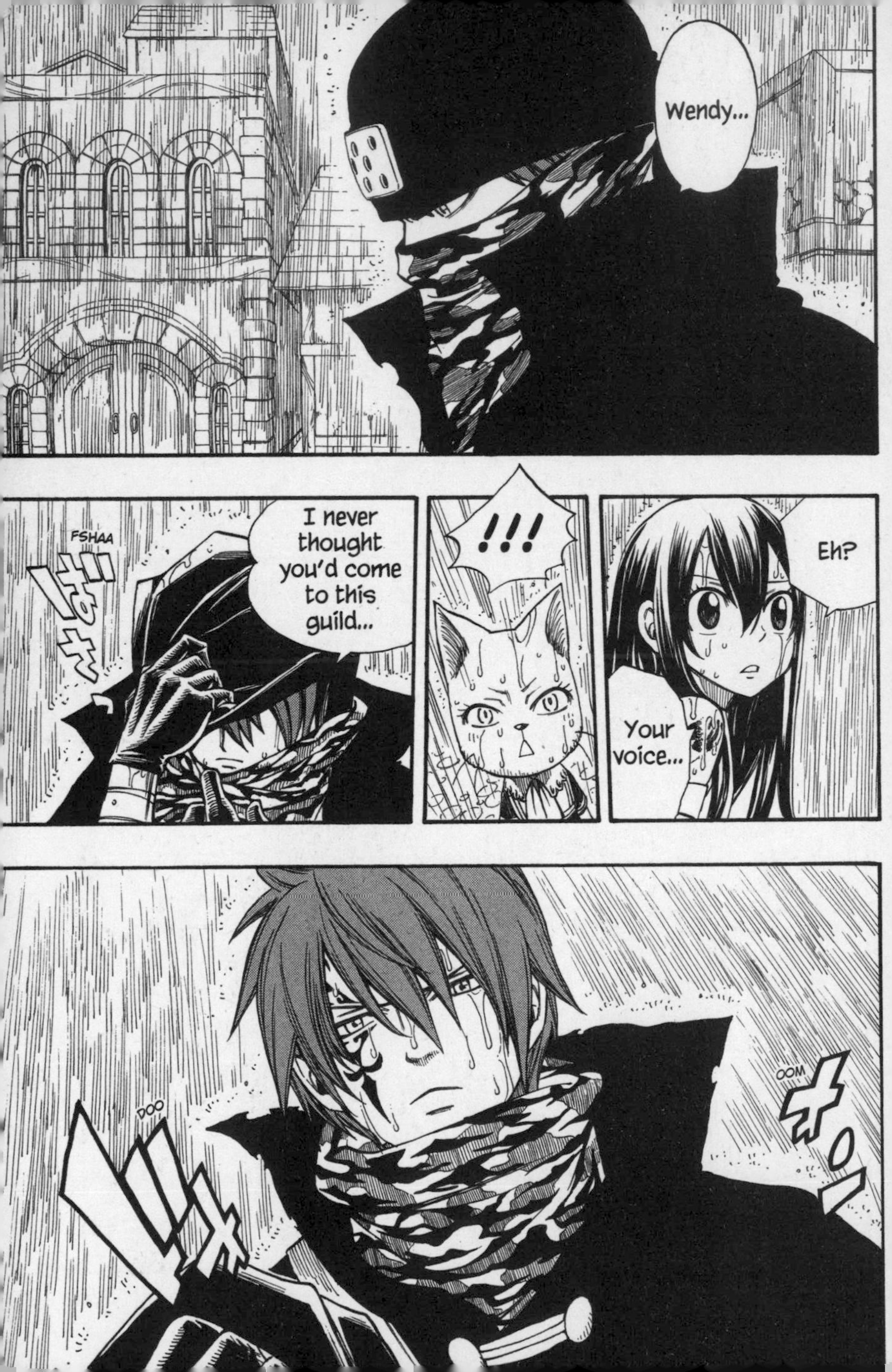
Wendy...
Eh?
Your voice...
!!!
I never thought you'd come to this guild...
FSHAA
OOM
DOO

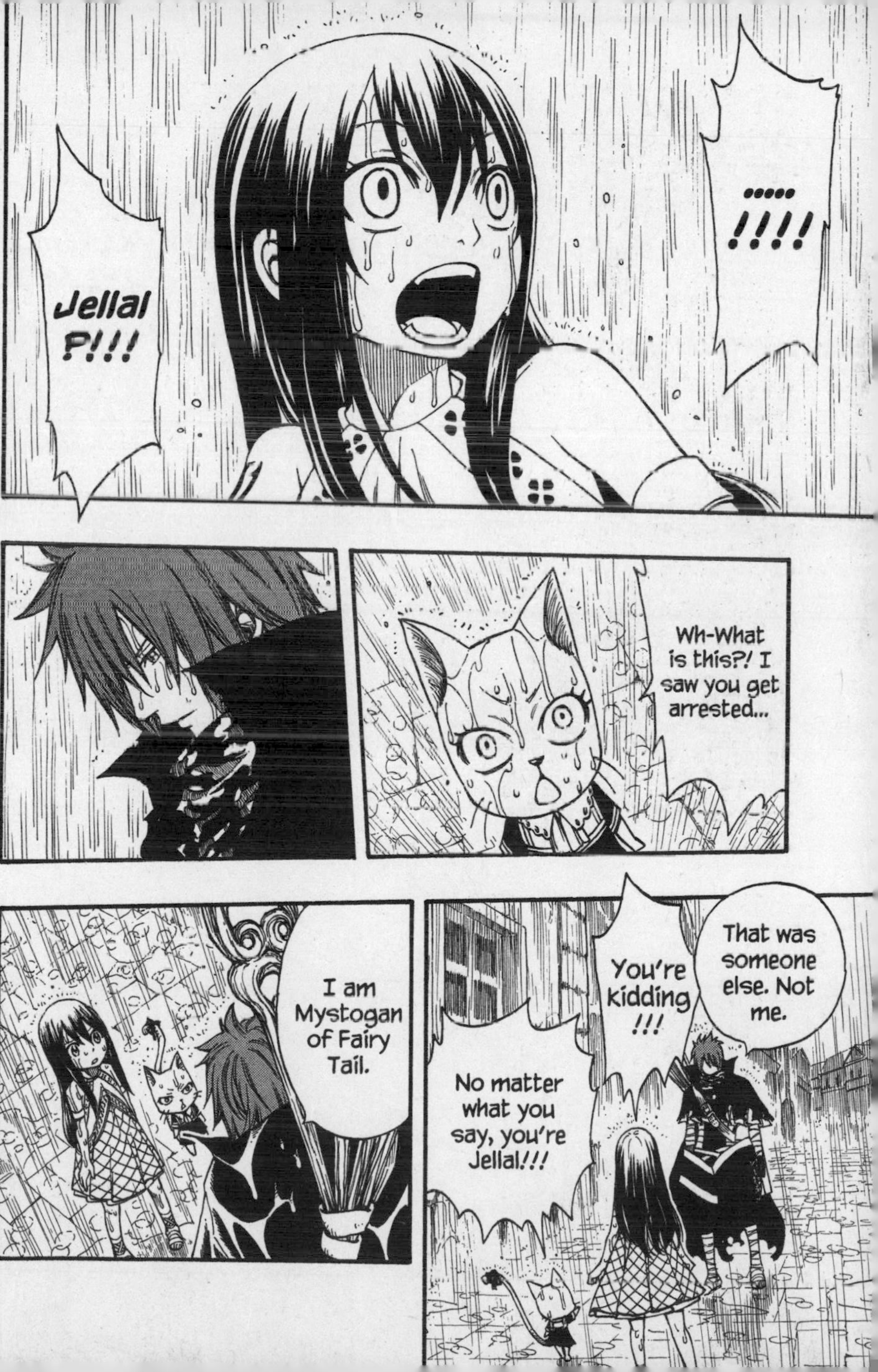
……!!!!
Jellal?!!!
Wh-What is this?! I saw you get arrested...
That was someone else. Not me.
You're kidding!!!
No matter what you say, you're Jellal!!!
I am Mystogan of Fairy Tail.

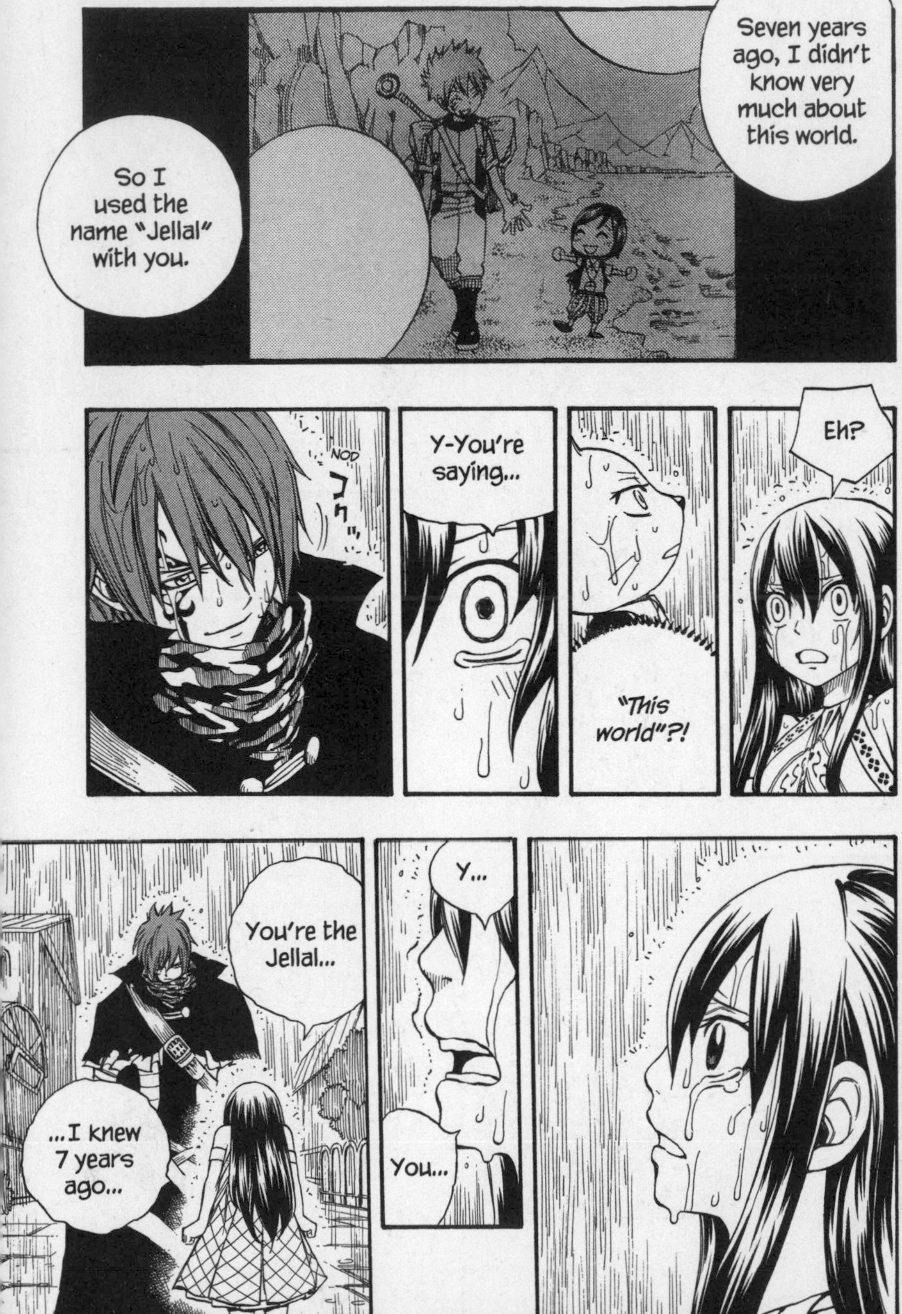
Seven years ago, I didn't know very much about this world.
So I used the name "Jellal" with you.
Eh?
"This world"?!
Y-You're saying...
NOD
Y...
You...
You're the Jellal...
...I knew 7 years ago...

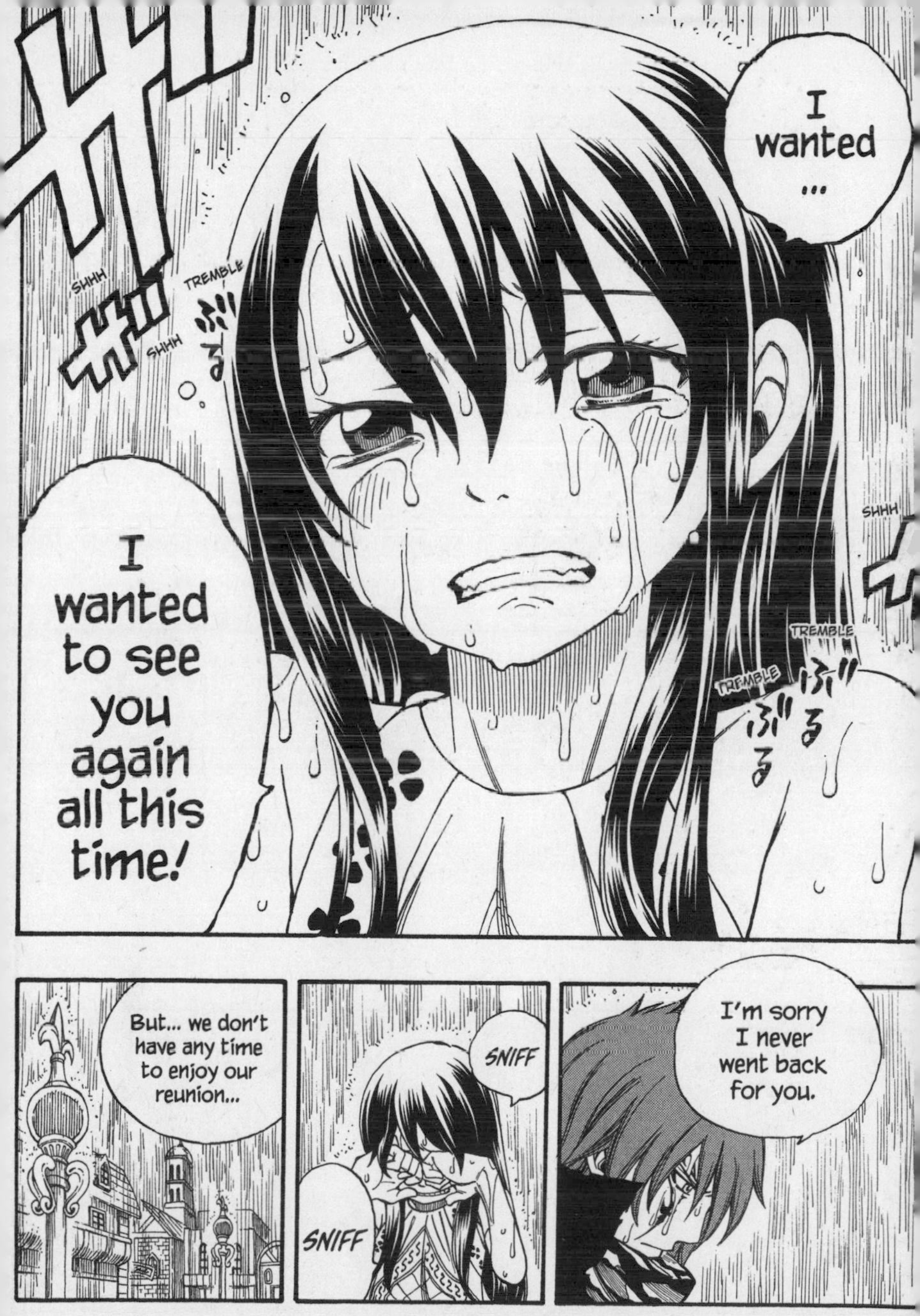
I wanted ...
SHHH
TREMBLE
SHHH
SHHH
TREMBLE
TREMBLE
I wanted to see you again all this time!
I'm sorry I never went back for you.
SNIFF
SNIFF
But... we don't have any time to enjoy our reunion...

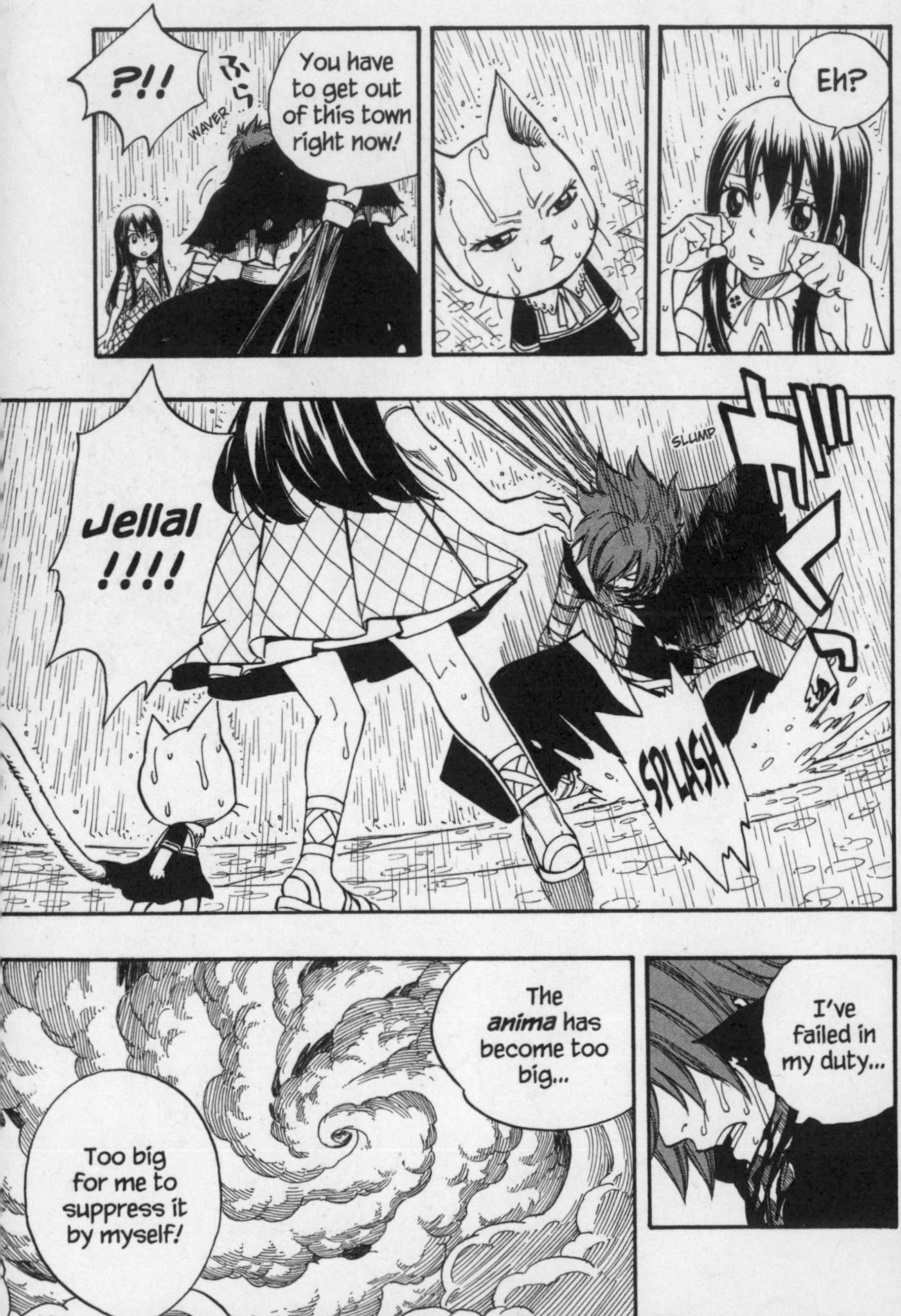
Eh?
You have to get out of this town right now!
ふら
WAVER
?!!
SLUMP
Jellal !!!!
SPLASH
I've failed in my duty...
The *anima* has become too big...
Too big for me to suppress it by myself!

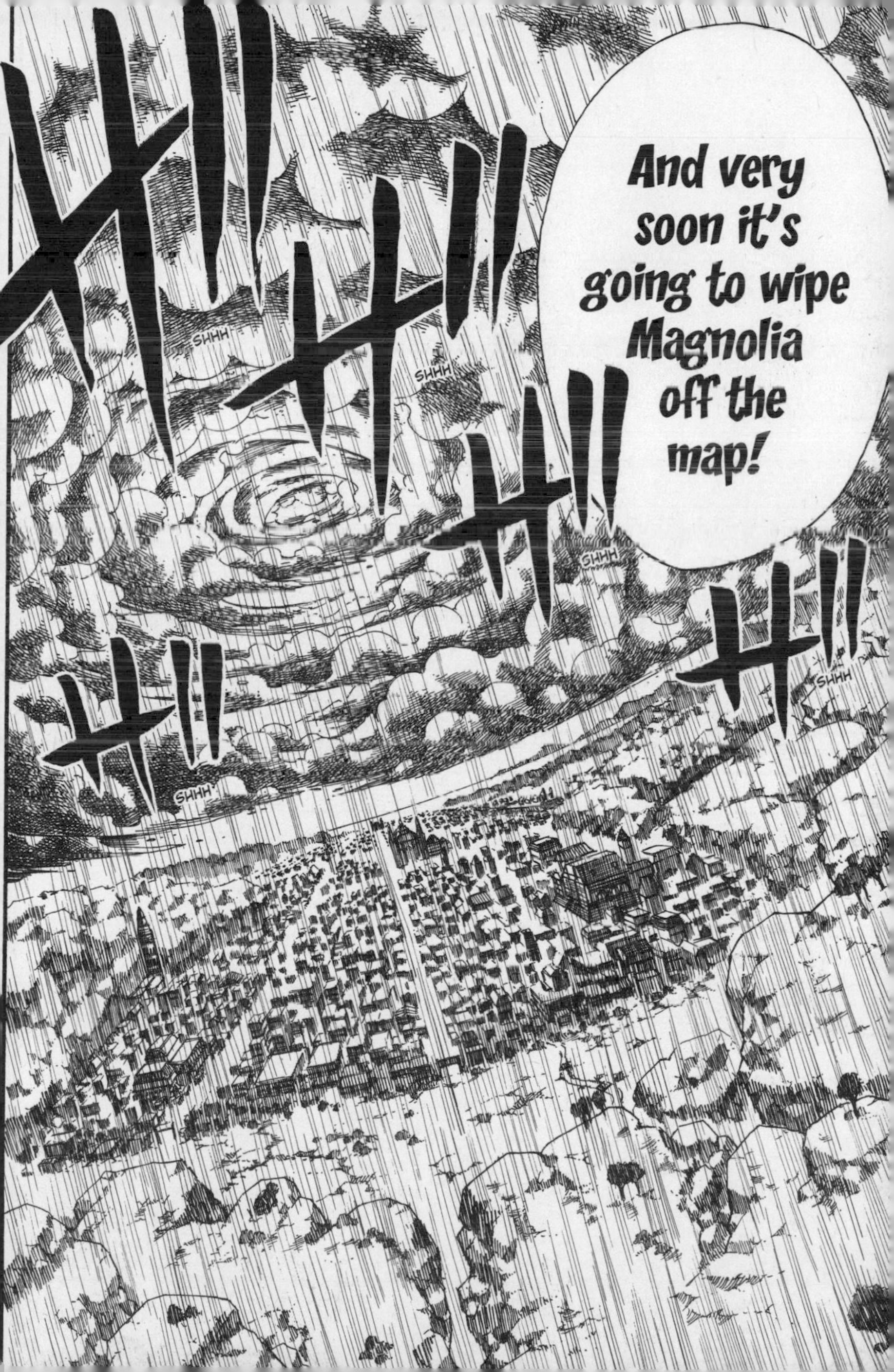
And very soon it's going to wipe Magnolia off the map!
SHHH
SHHH
SHHH
SHHH
SHHH

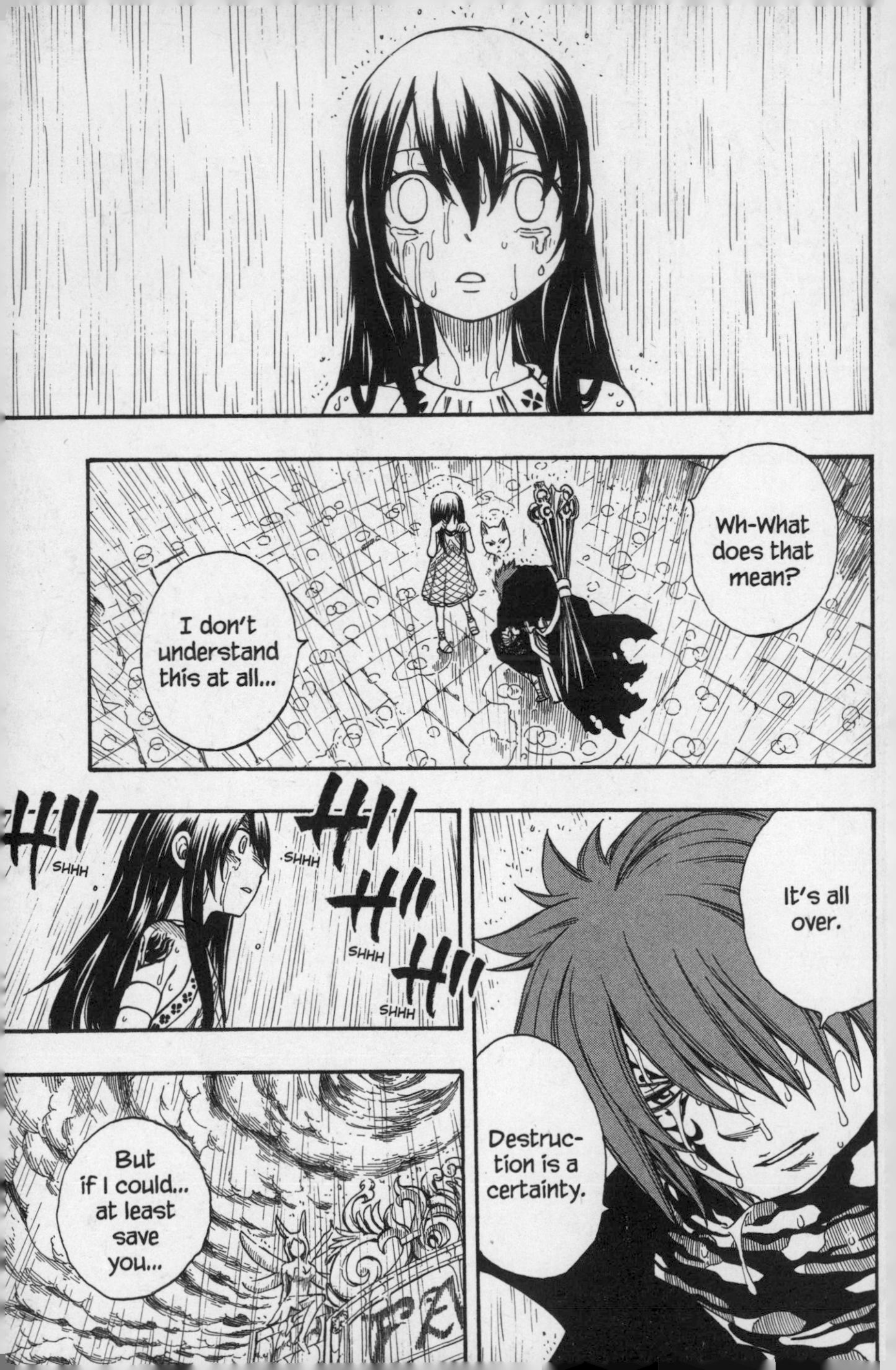
Wh-What does that mean?
I don't understand this at all...
It's all over.
Destruction is a certainty.
SHHH
SHHH
SHHH
SHHH
But if I could... at least save you...

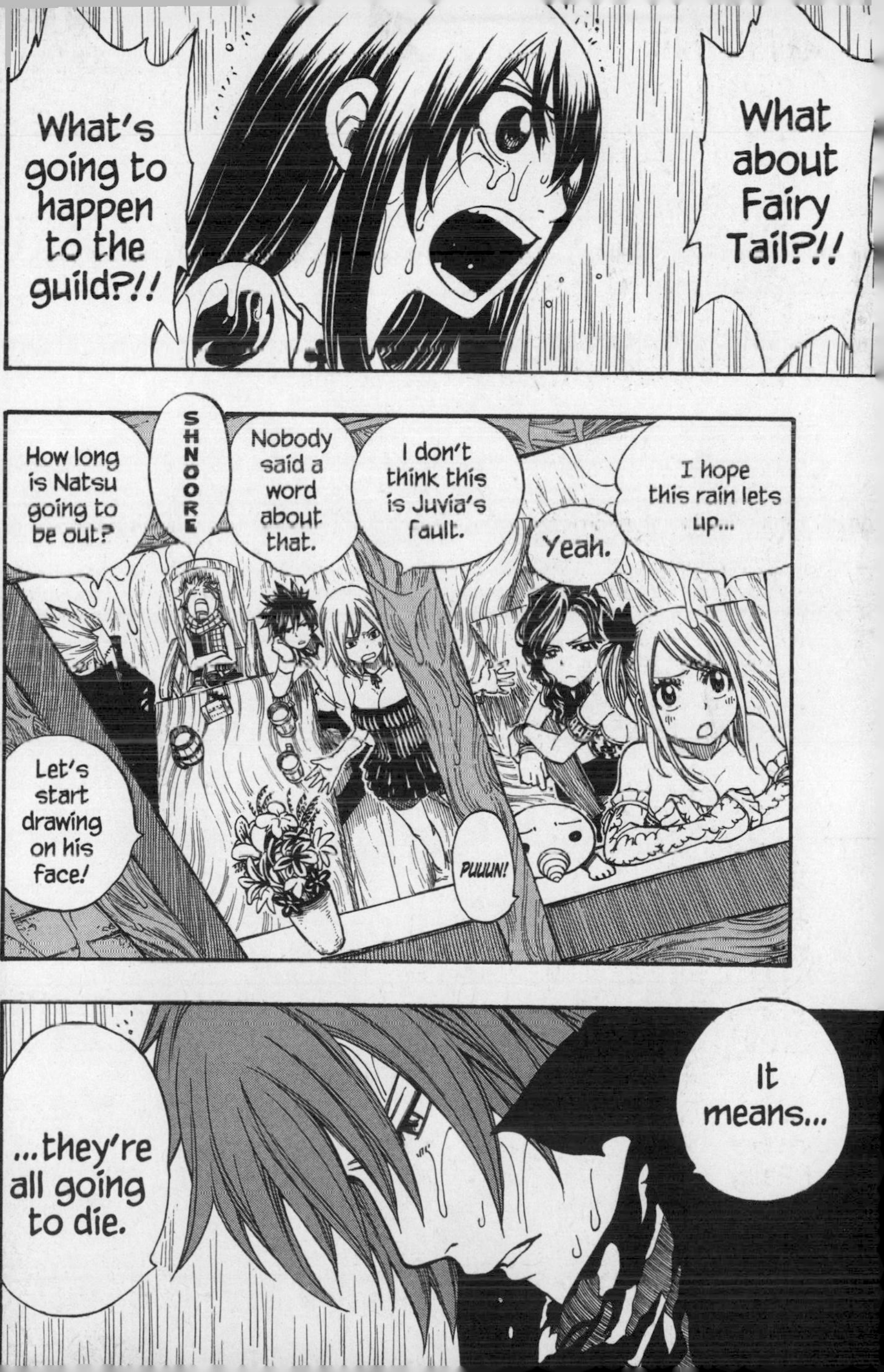
What about Fairy Tail?!!
What's going to happen to the guild?!!
I hope this rain lets up...
Yeah.
I don't think this is Juvia's fault.
Nobody said a word about that.
SHNOORE
How long is Natsu going to be out?
PUUUN!
Let's start drawing on his face!
It means...
...they're all going to die.

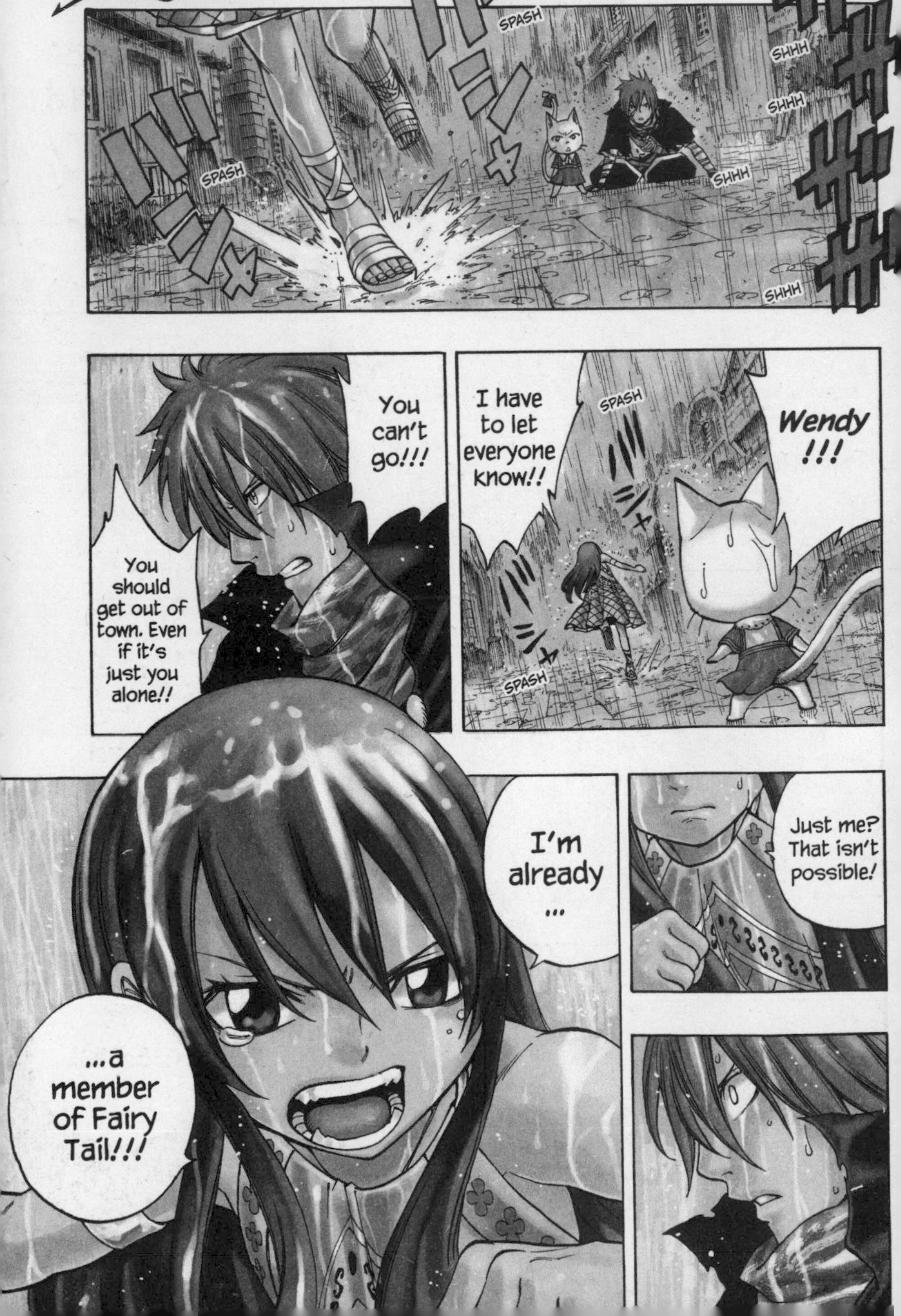
SHHH
SHHH
SHHH
SHHH
SPASH
SPASH
Wendy!!!
I have to let everyone know!!
SPASH
SPASH
You can't go!!!
You should get out of town. Even if it's just you alone!!
Just me? That isn't possible!
I'm already ...
...a member of Fairy Tail!!!

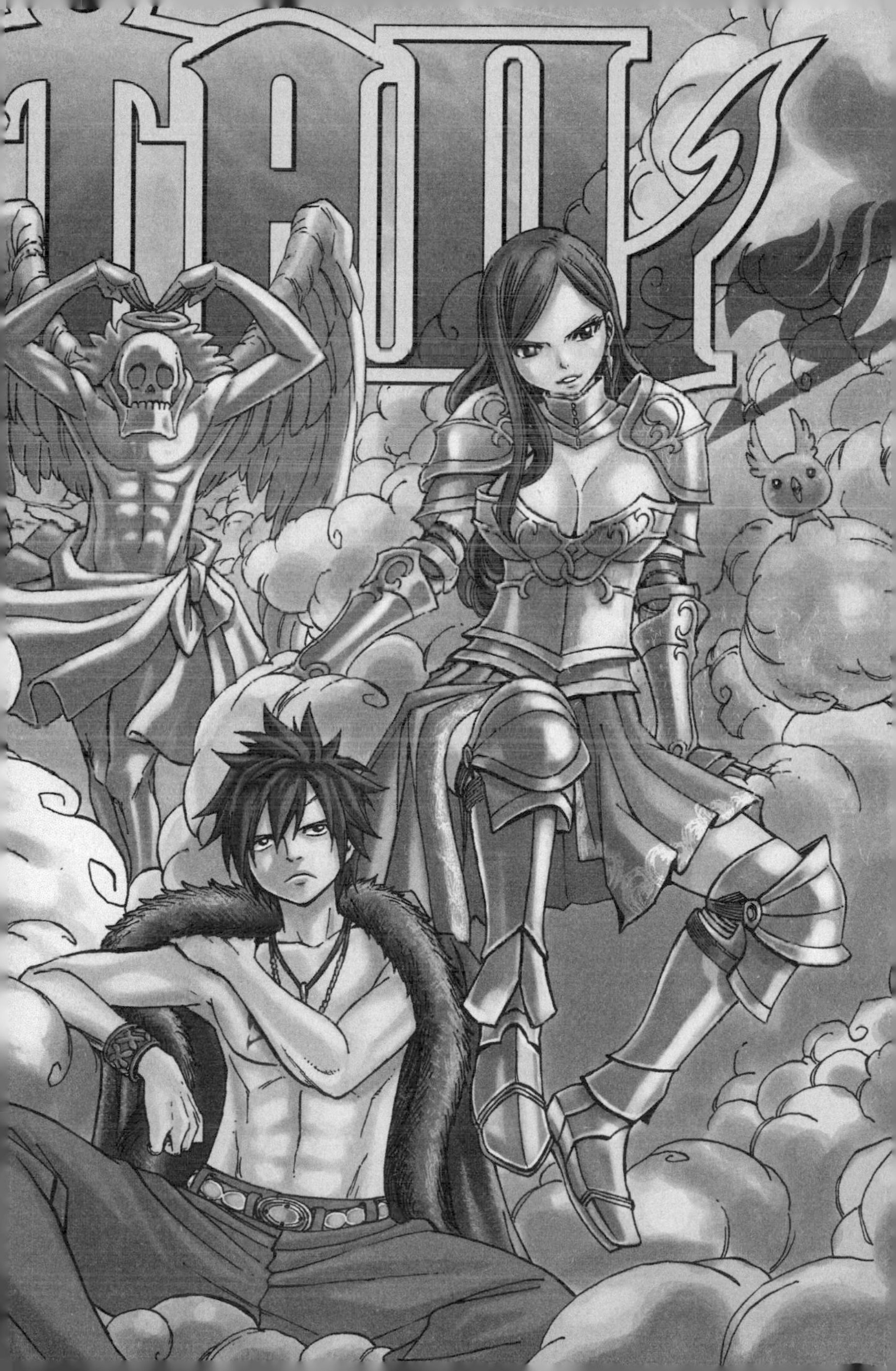

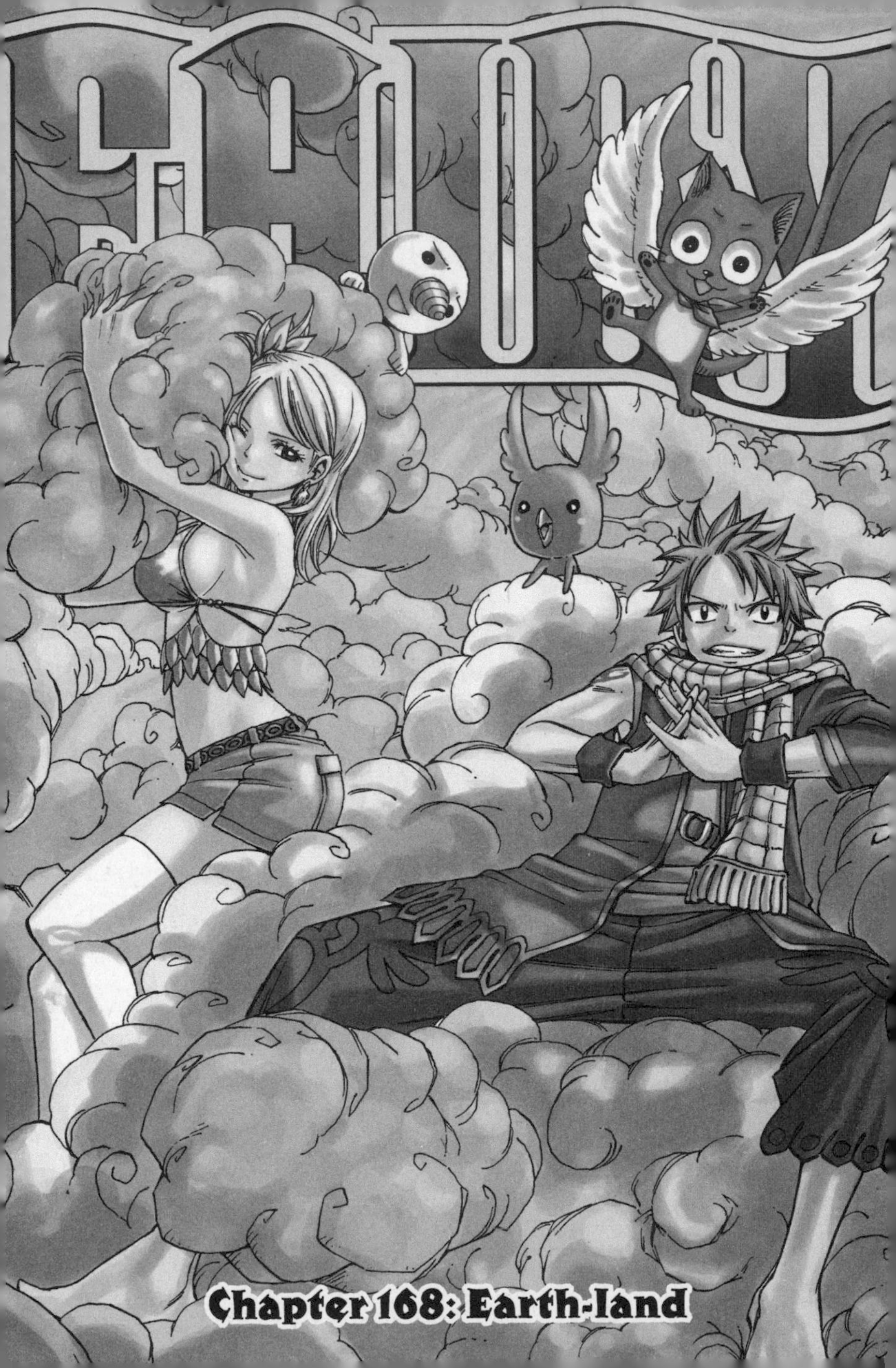

# Chapter 168: Earth-land

# Search for the Differences

Compare this to the splash page of Chapter 162! There are a total of ten difference to find.

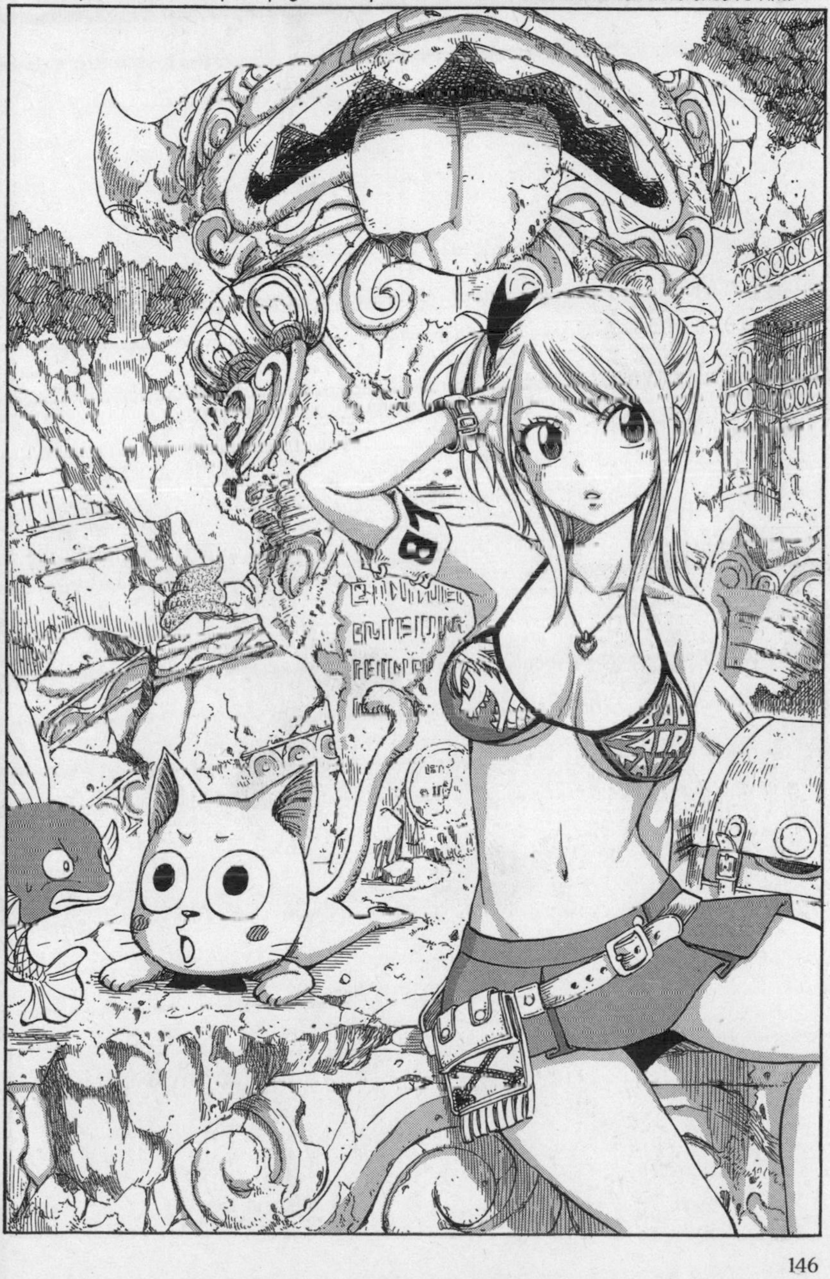

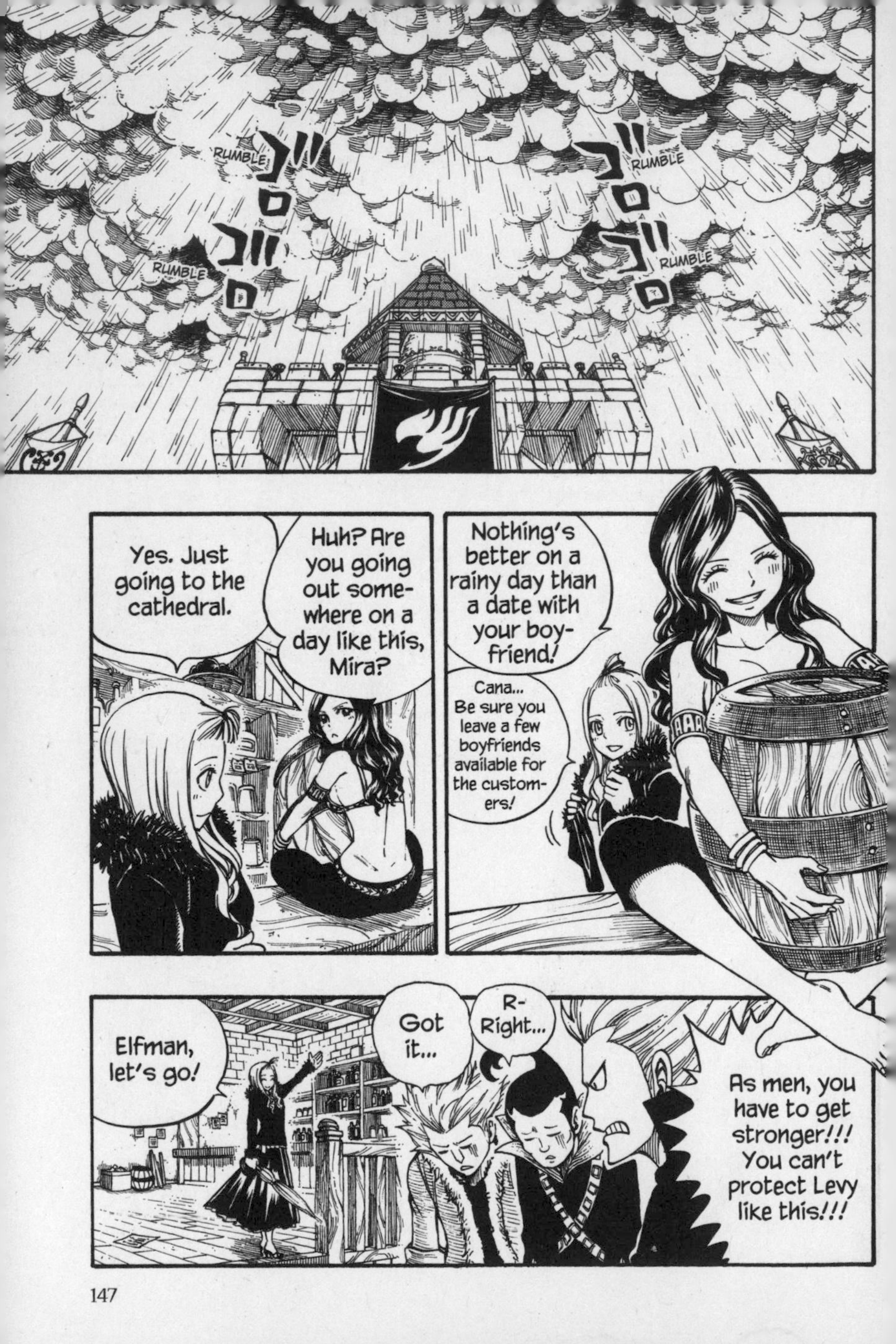
RUMBLE
RUMBLE
RUMBLE
RUMBLE
Nothing's better on a rainy day than a date with your boyfriend!
Cana... Be sure you leave a few boyfriends available for the customers!
Huh? Are you going out somewhere on a day like this, Mira?
Yes. Just going to the cathedral.
As men, you have to get stronger!!! You can't protect Levy like this!!!
R-Right...
Got it...
Elfman, let's go!

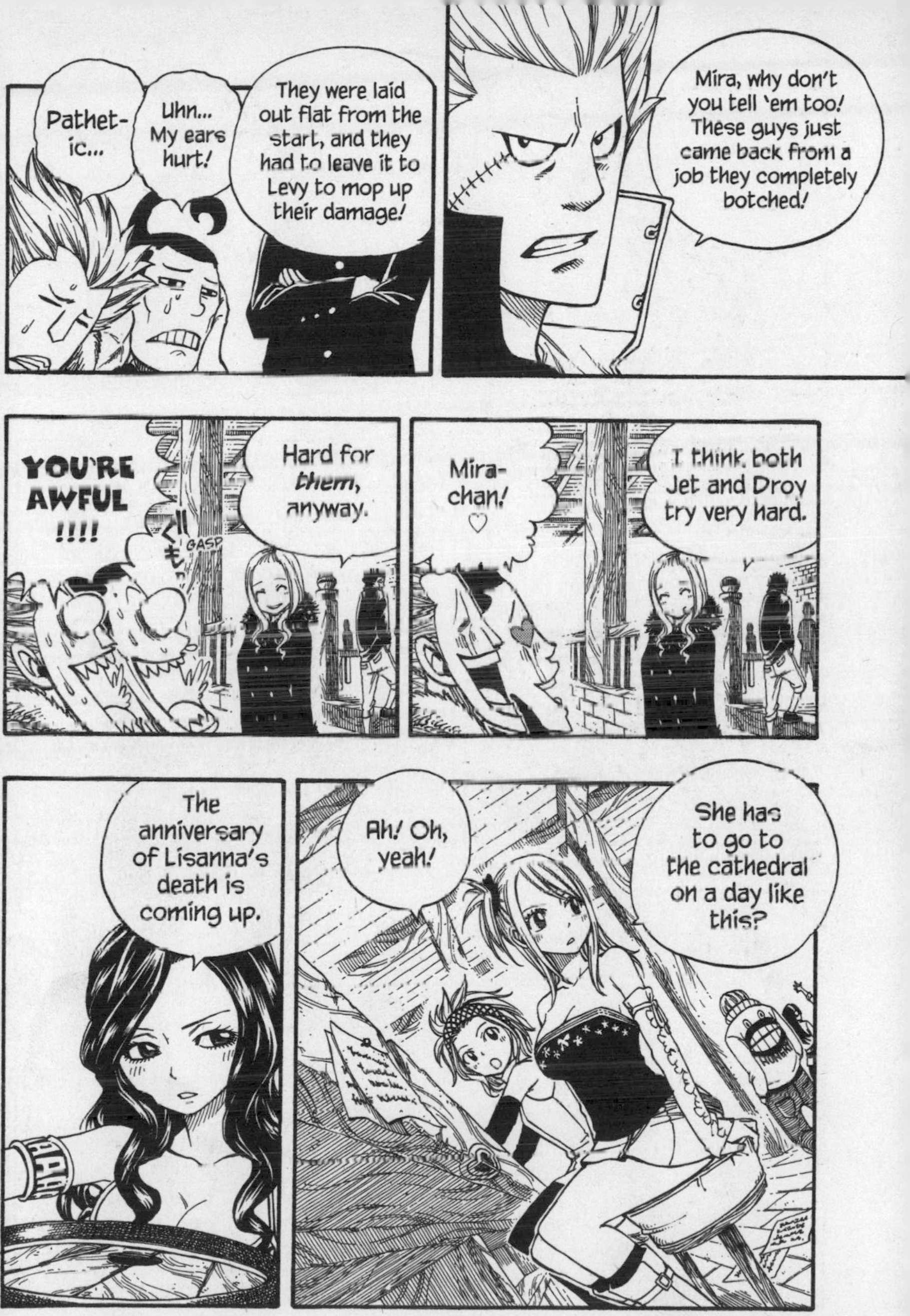
Mira, why don't you tell 'em too! These guys just came back from a job they completely botched!
They were laid out flat from the start, and they had to leave it to Levy to mop up their damage!
Uhn... My ears hurt!
Pathet-ic...
I think both Jet and Droy try very hard.
Mira-chan! ♡
Hard for *them*, anyway.
GASP
YOU'RE AWFUL !!!!
She has to go to the cathedral on a day like this?
Ah! Oh, yeah!
The anniversary of Lisanna's death is coming up.

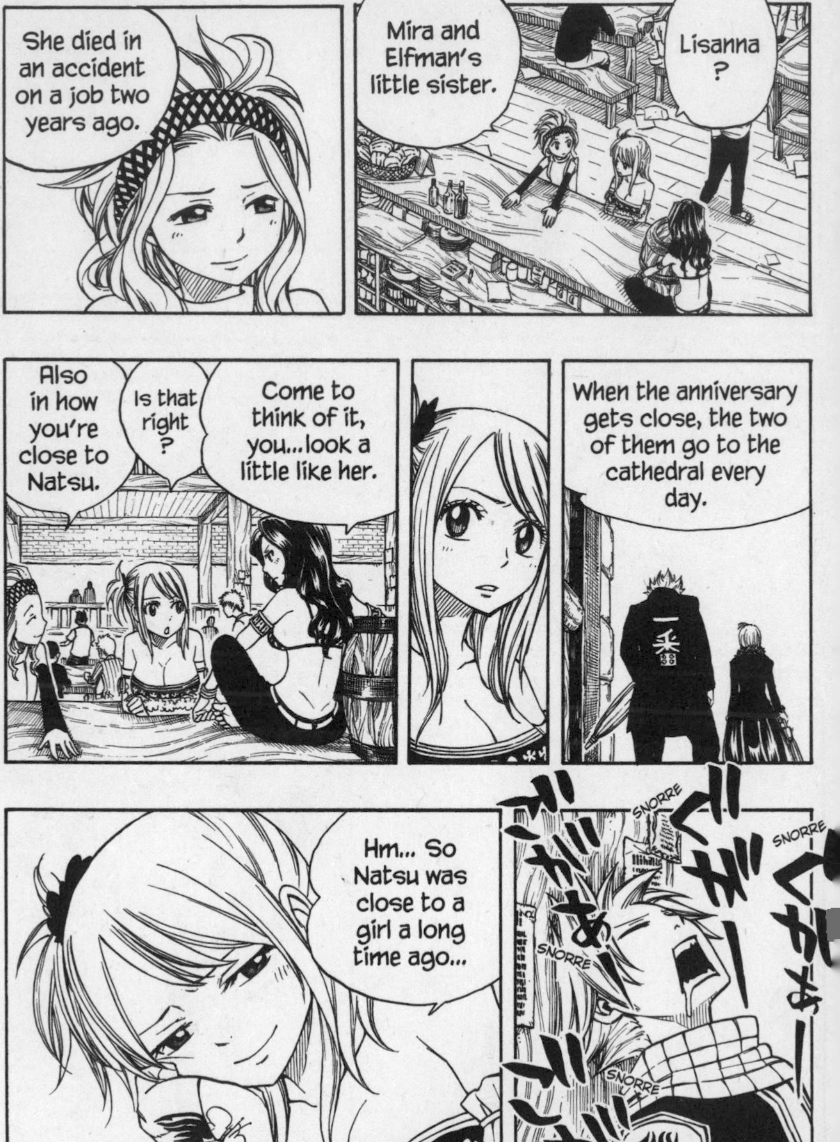
Lisanna?
Mira and Elfman's little sister.
She died in an accident on a job two years ago.
When the anniversary gets close, the two of them go to the cathedral every day.
Come to think of it, you...look a little like her.
Is that right?
Also in how you're close to Natsu.
SNORRE
SNORRE
SNORRE
SNORRE
Hm... So Natsu was close to a girl a long time ago...

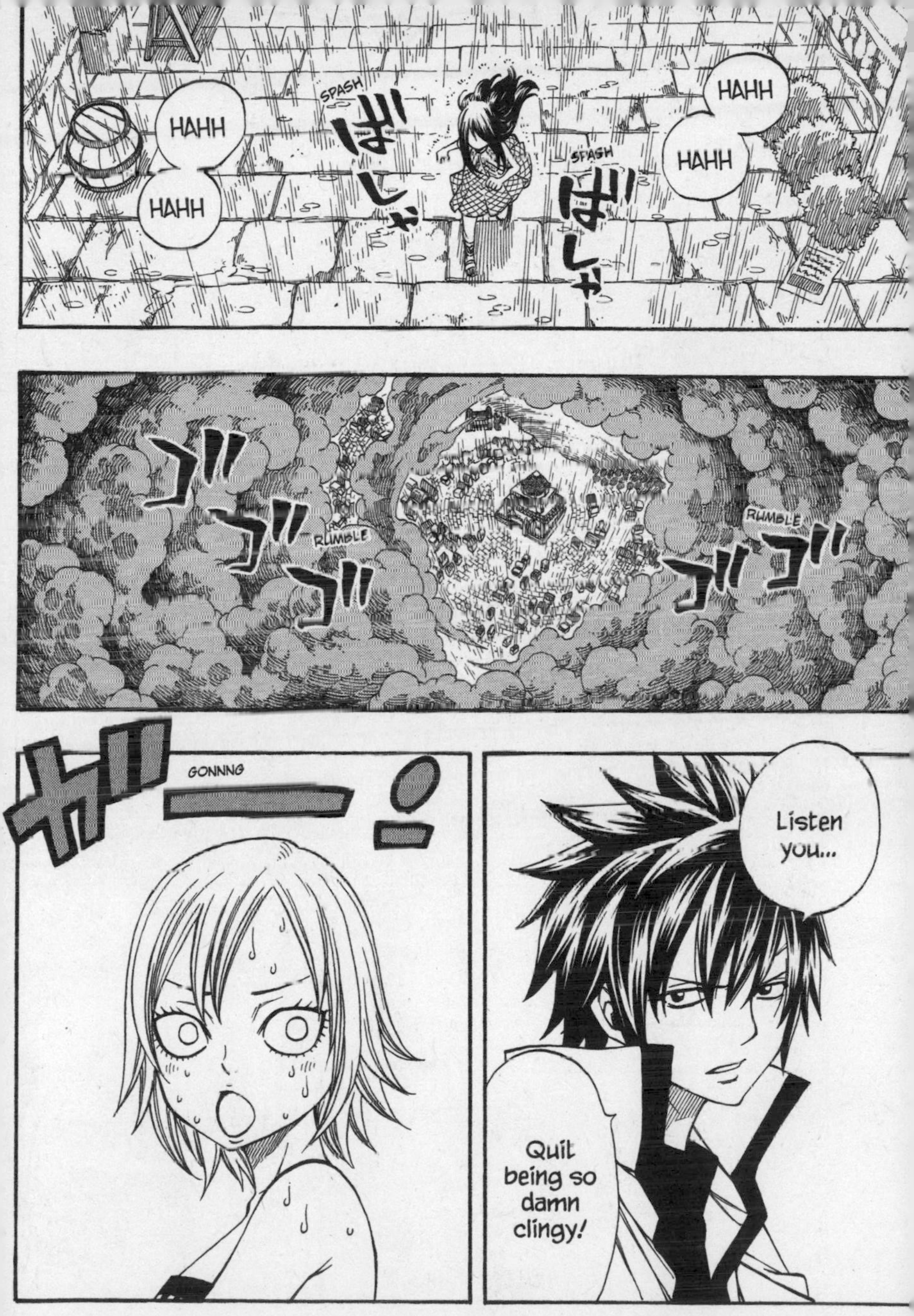
HAHH
HAHH
SPASH
ばしゃ
SPASH
ばしゃ
HAHH
HAHH
RUMBLE
ゴゴ
RUMBLE
ゴゴゴ
Listen you...
Quit being so damn clingy!
GONNNG
ガーン

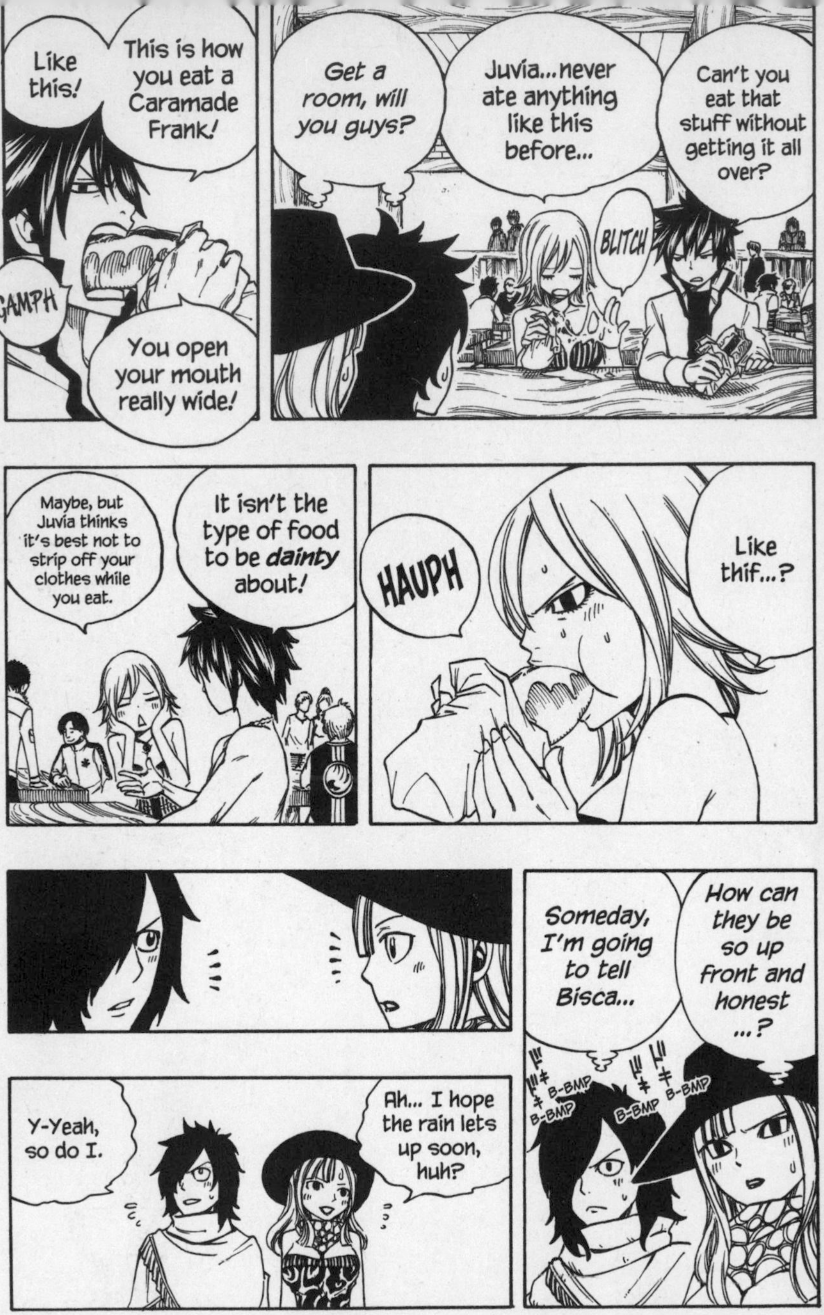
Can't you eat that stuff without getting it all over?
Juvia...never ate anything like this before...
BLITCH
Get a room, will you guys?
This is how you eat a Caramade Frank!
Like this!
You open your mouth really wide!
GAMPH
Like thif...?
HAUPH
It isn't the type of food to be dainty about!
Maybe, but Juvia thinks it's best not to strip off your clothes while you eat.
How can they be so up front and honest ...?
Someday, I'm going to tell Bisca...
B-BMP B-BMP
B-BMP B-BMP
Ah... I hope the rain lets up soon, huh?
Y-Yeah, so do I.

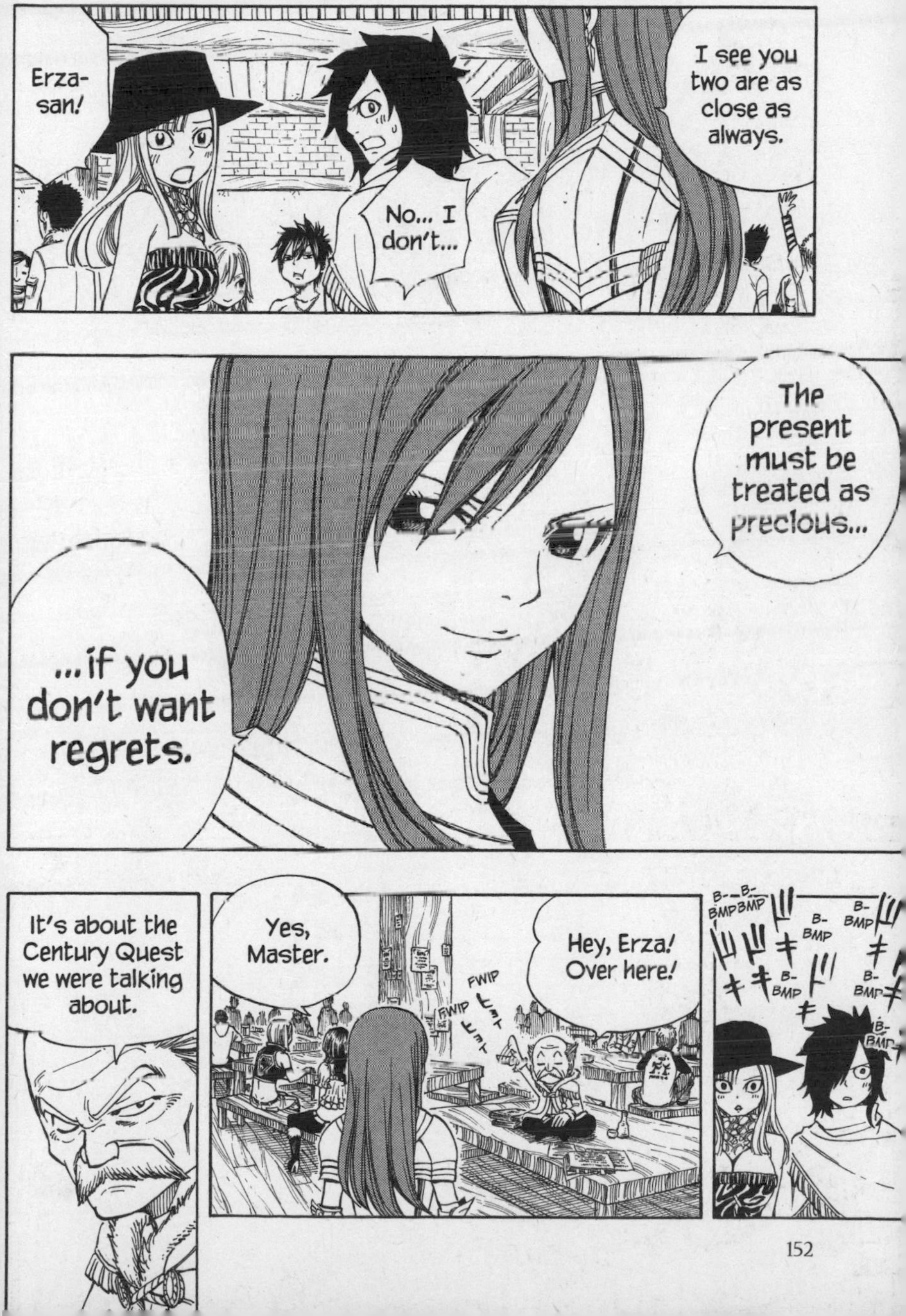
I see you two are as close as always.
Erza-san!
No... I don't...
The present must be treated as precious...
...if you don't want regrets.
B-BMP B-BMP
B-BMP
B-BMP
B-BMP
B-BMP
B-BMP
Hey, Erza! Over here!
FWIP
FWIP
Yes, Master.
It's about the Century Quest we were talking about.

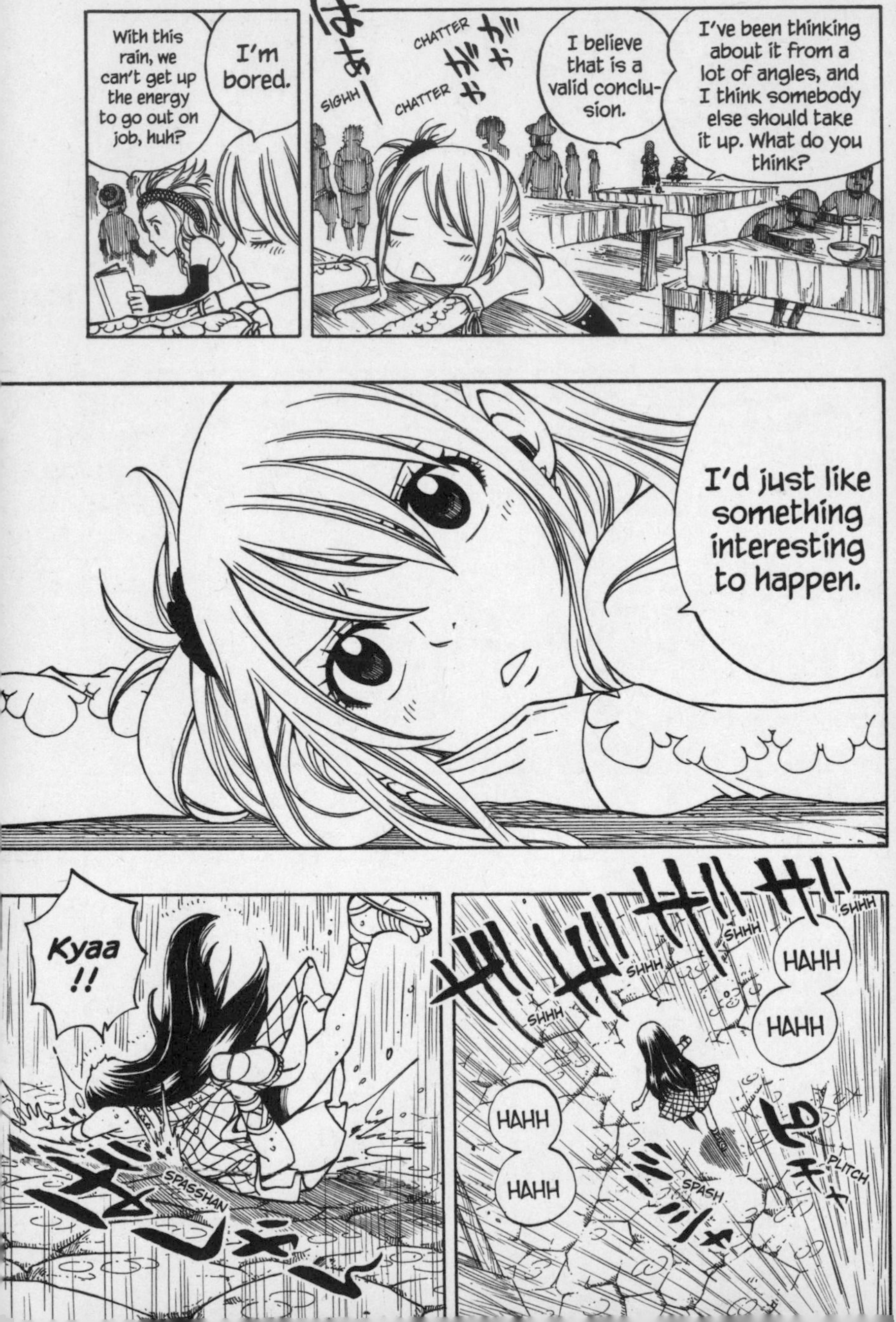

I've been thinking about it from a lot of angles, and I think somebody else should take it up. What do you think?
I believe that is a valid conclusion.
CHATTER
CHATTER
SIGHH
I'm bored.
With this rain, we can't get up the energy to go out on job, huh?
I'd just like something interesting to happen.
SHHH
SHHH
SHHH
SHHH
HAHH
HAHH
PLITCH
SPASH
HAHH
HAHH
Kyaa!!
SPASSHAN

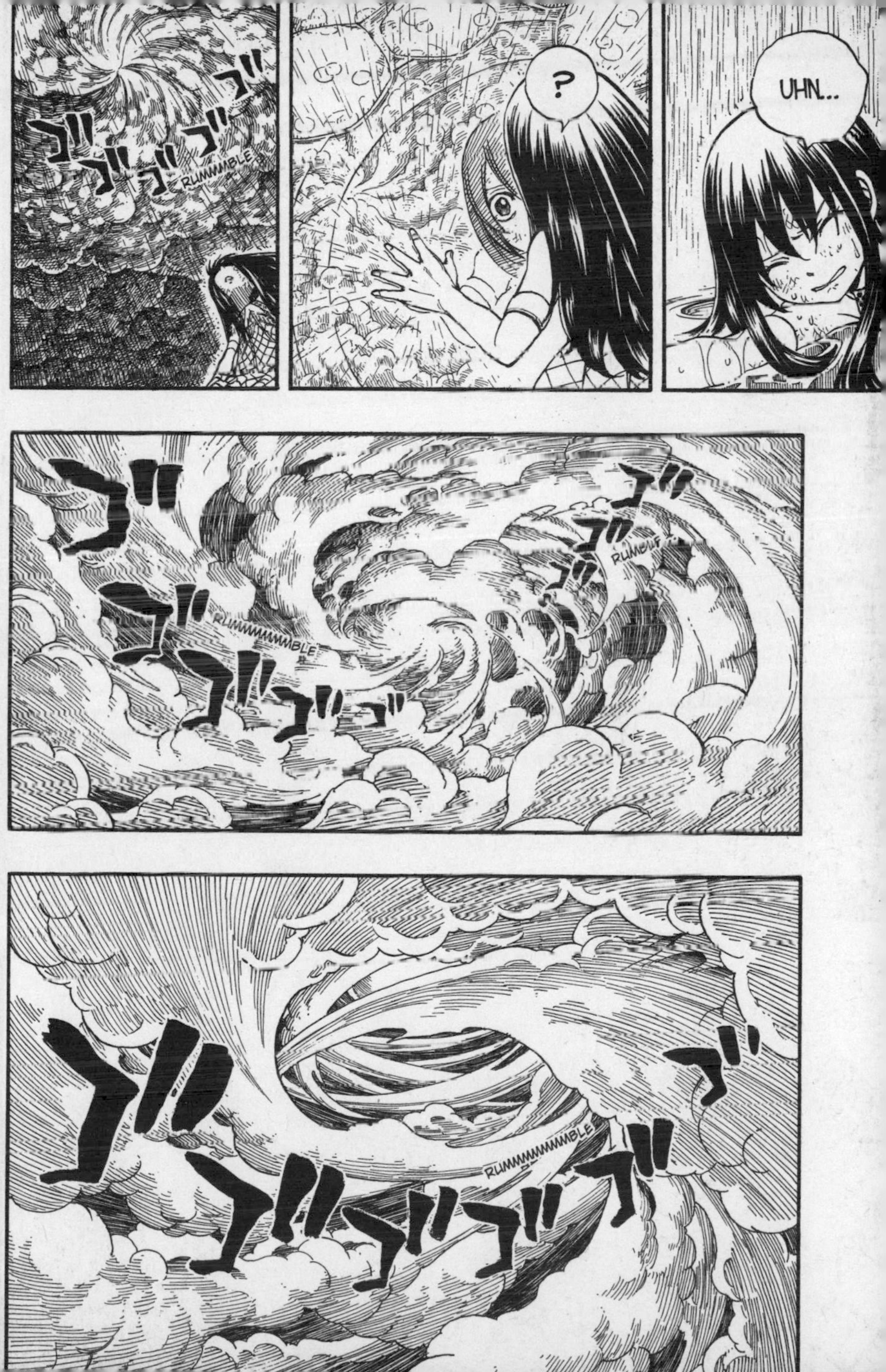
UHN...
?
RUMMMBLE
RUMBLE
RUMMMMMMMBLE
RUMMMMMMMMBLE

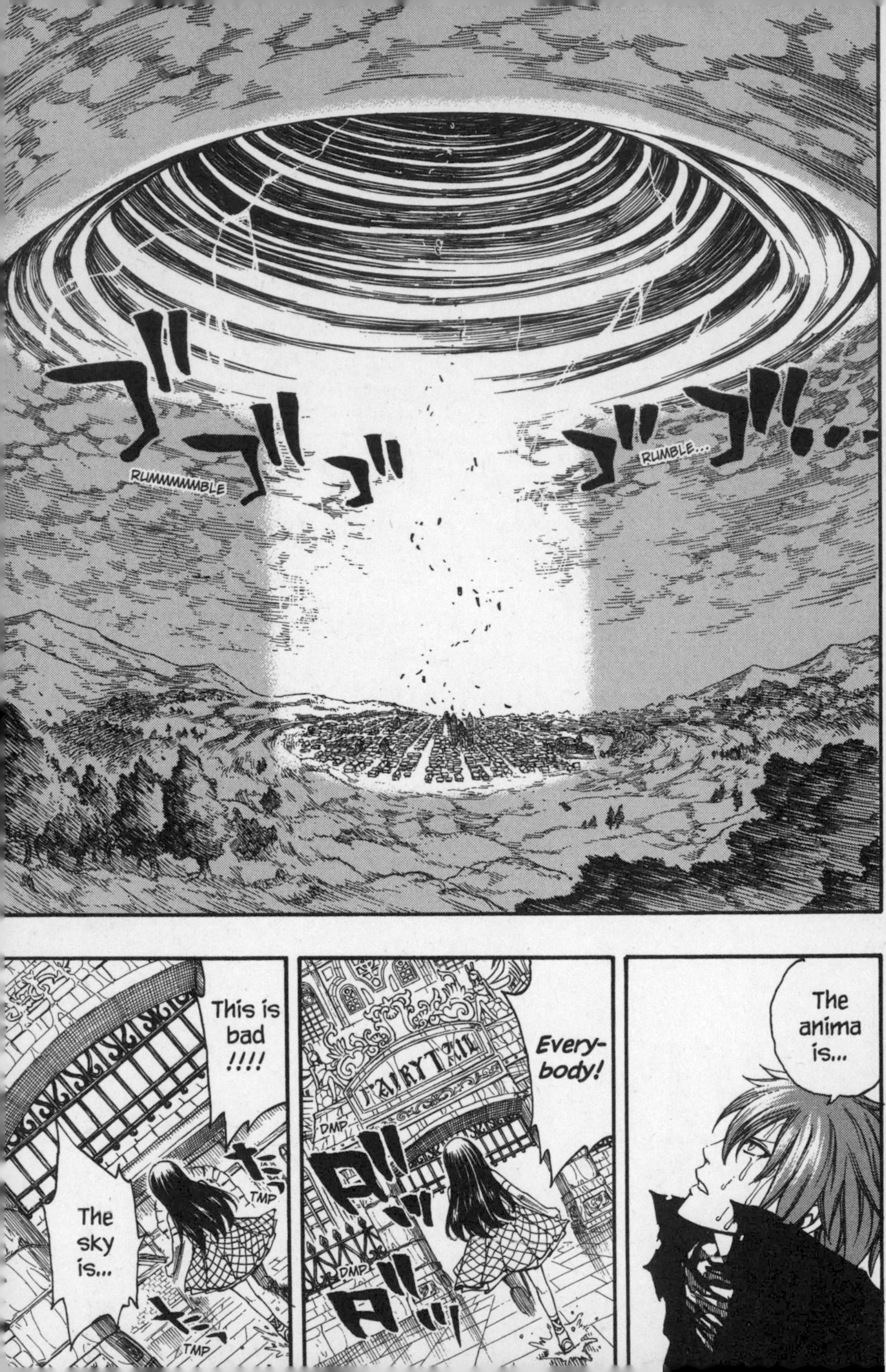
RUMBLE...
RUMMMMMMBLE
The anima is...
Every-body!
DMP
DMP
This is bad!!!!
The sky is...
TMP
TMP

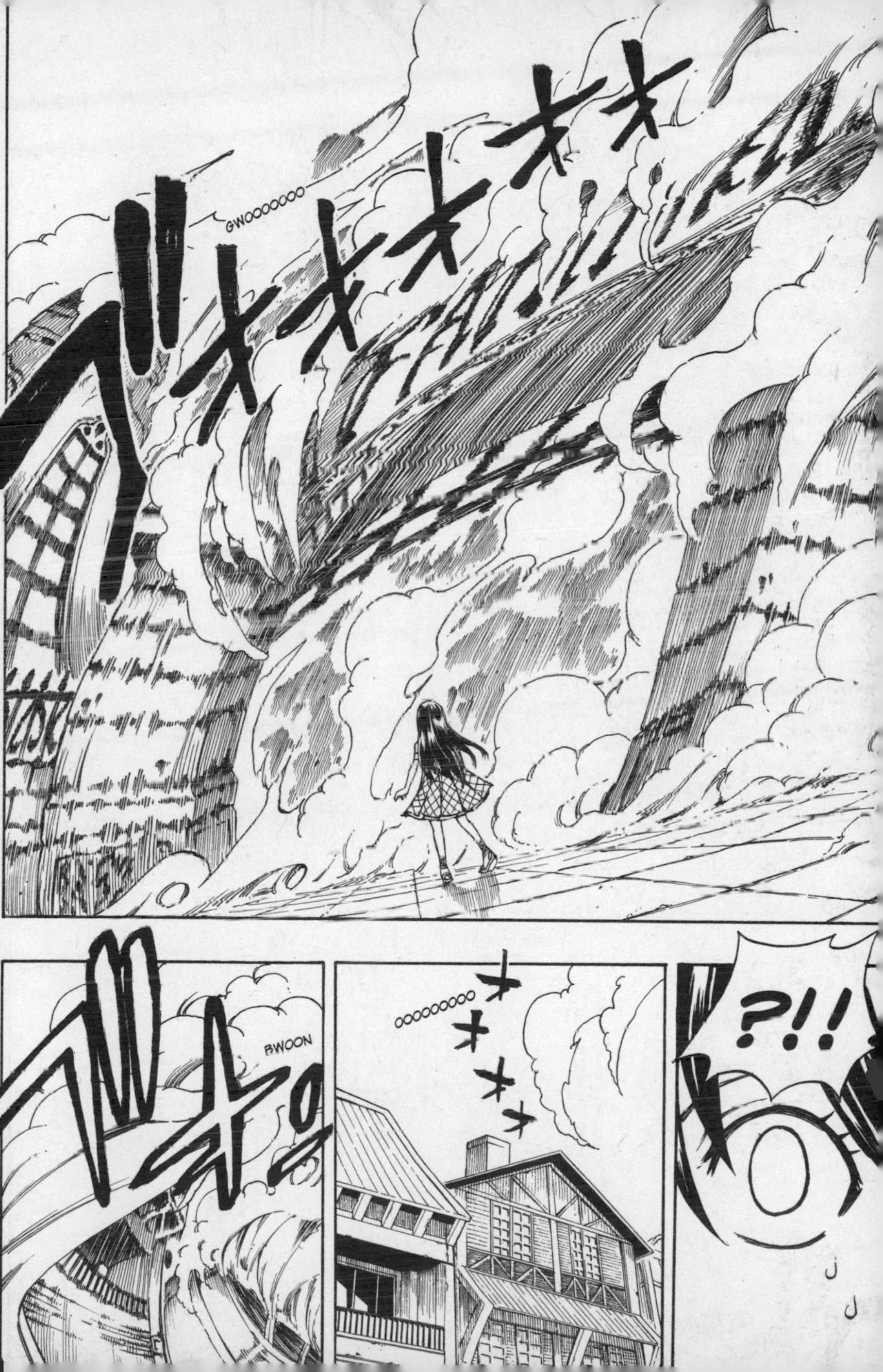
GWOOOOOOOO
?!!
OOOOOOOOO
BWOON

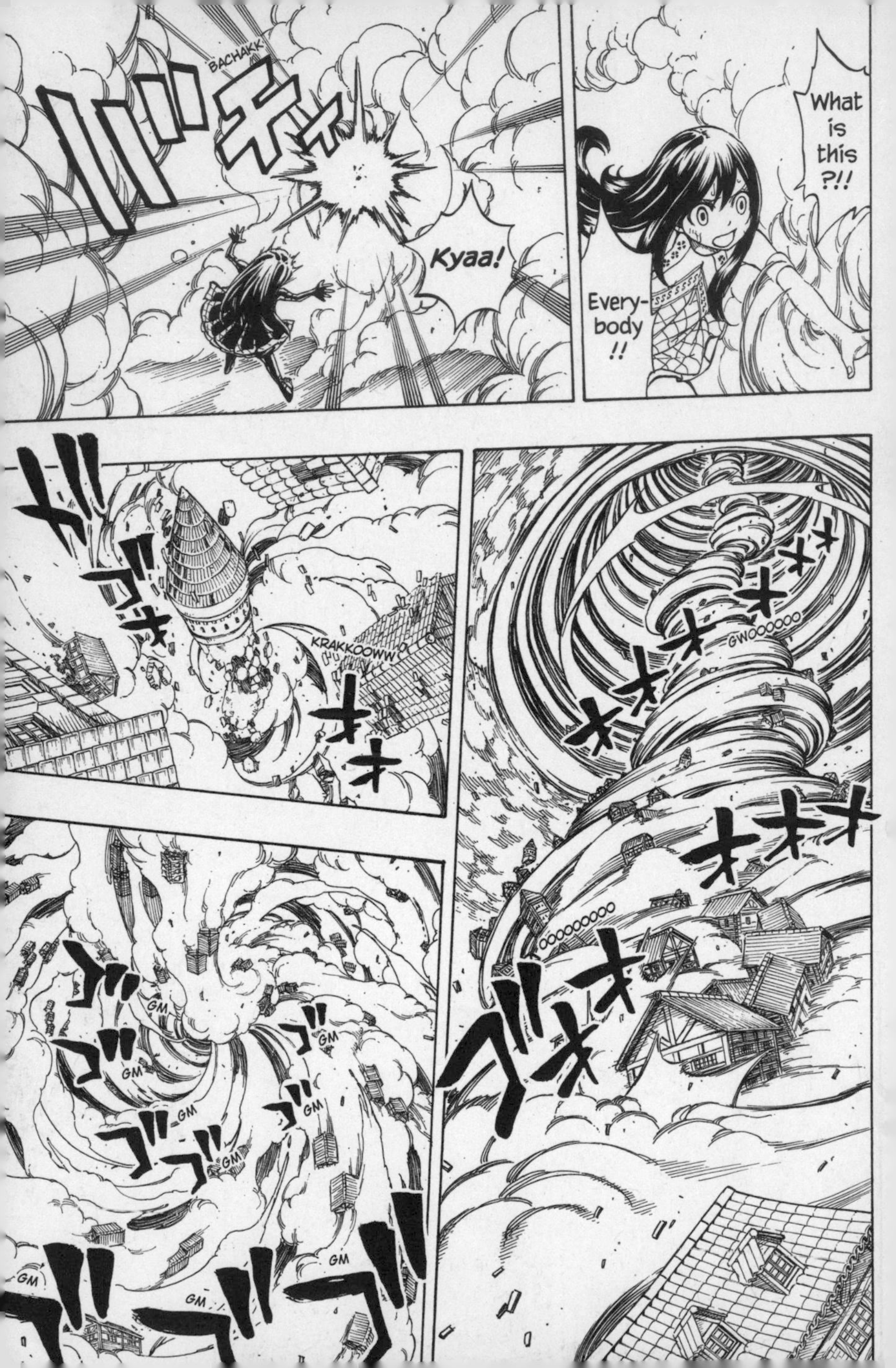
What is this ?!!
Every-body !!
BACHAKK
Kyaa!
GWOOOOOO
OOOOOOOOO
KRAKKOOWW
GM
GM
GM
GM
GM
GM
GM
GM
GM

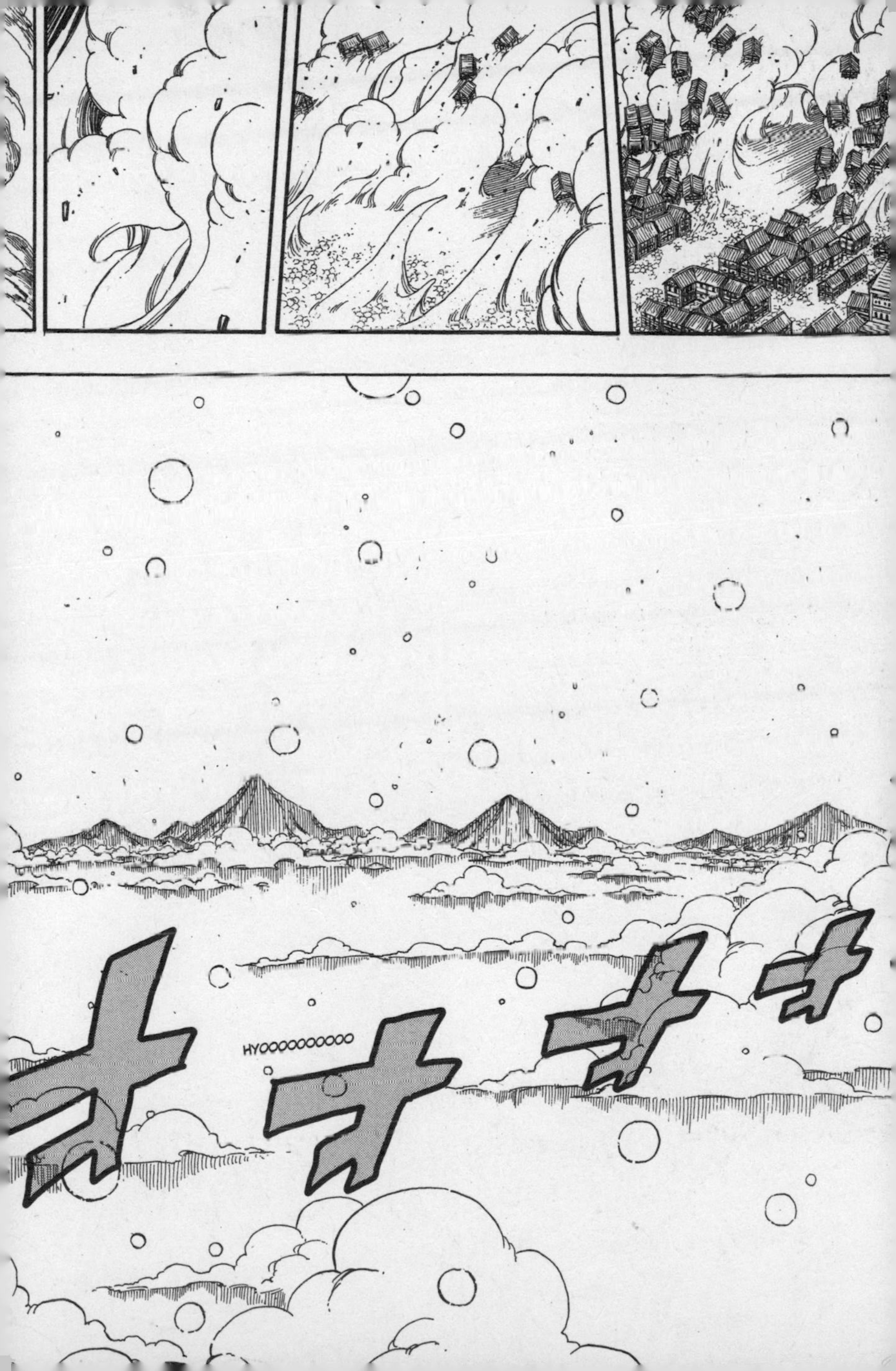
HYOOOOOOOOOO

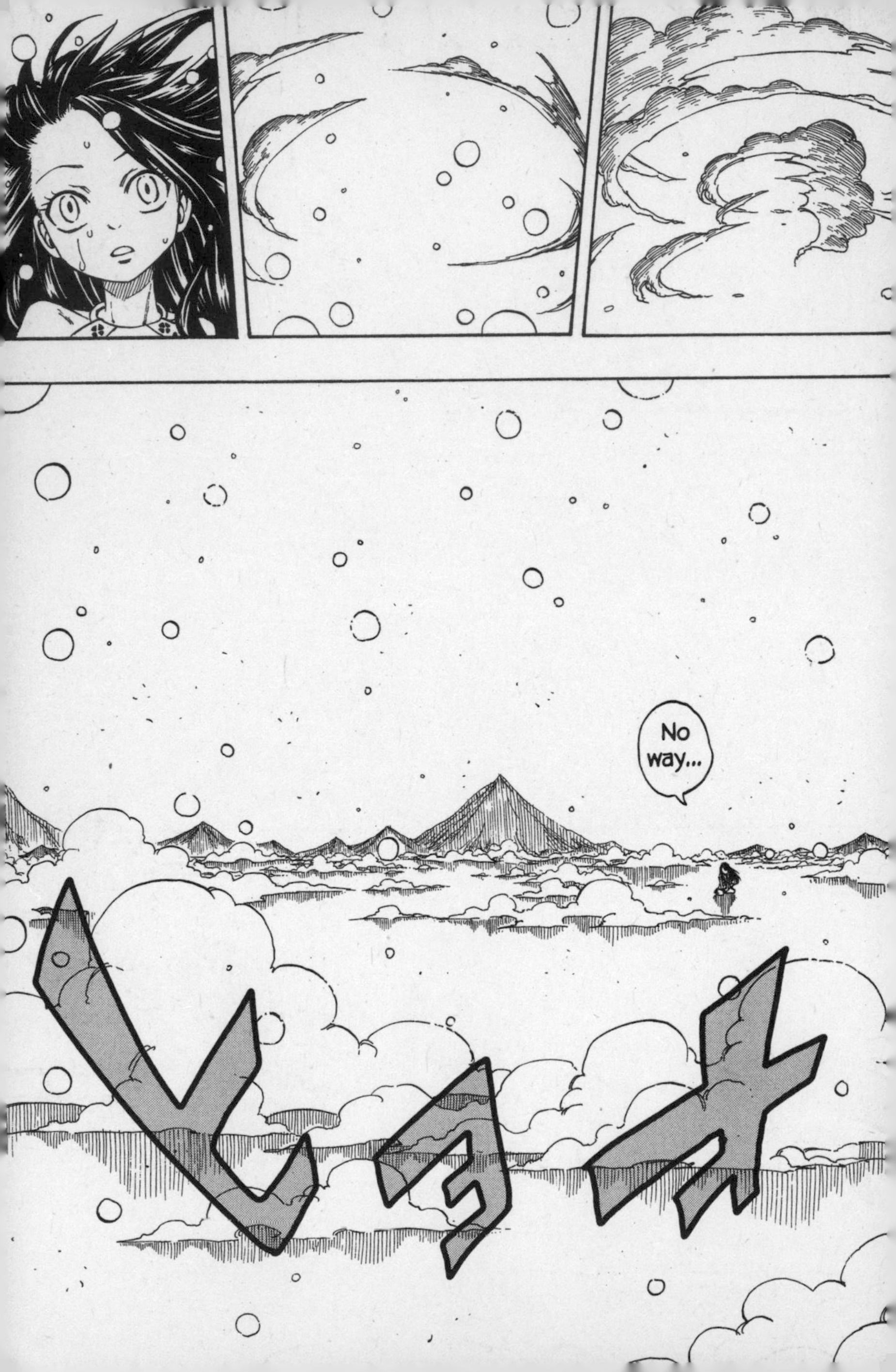
No way...

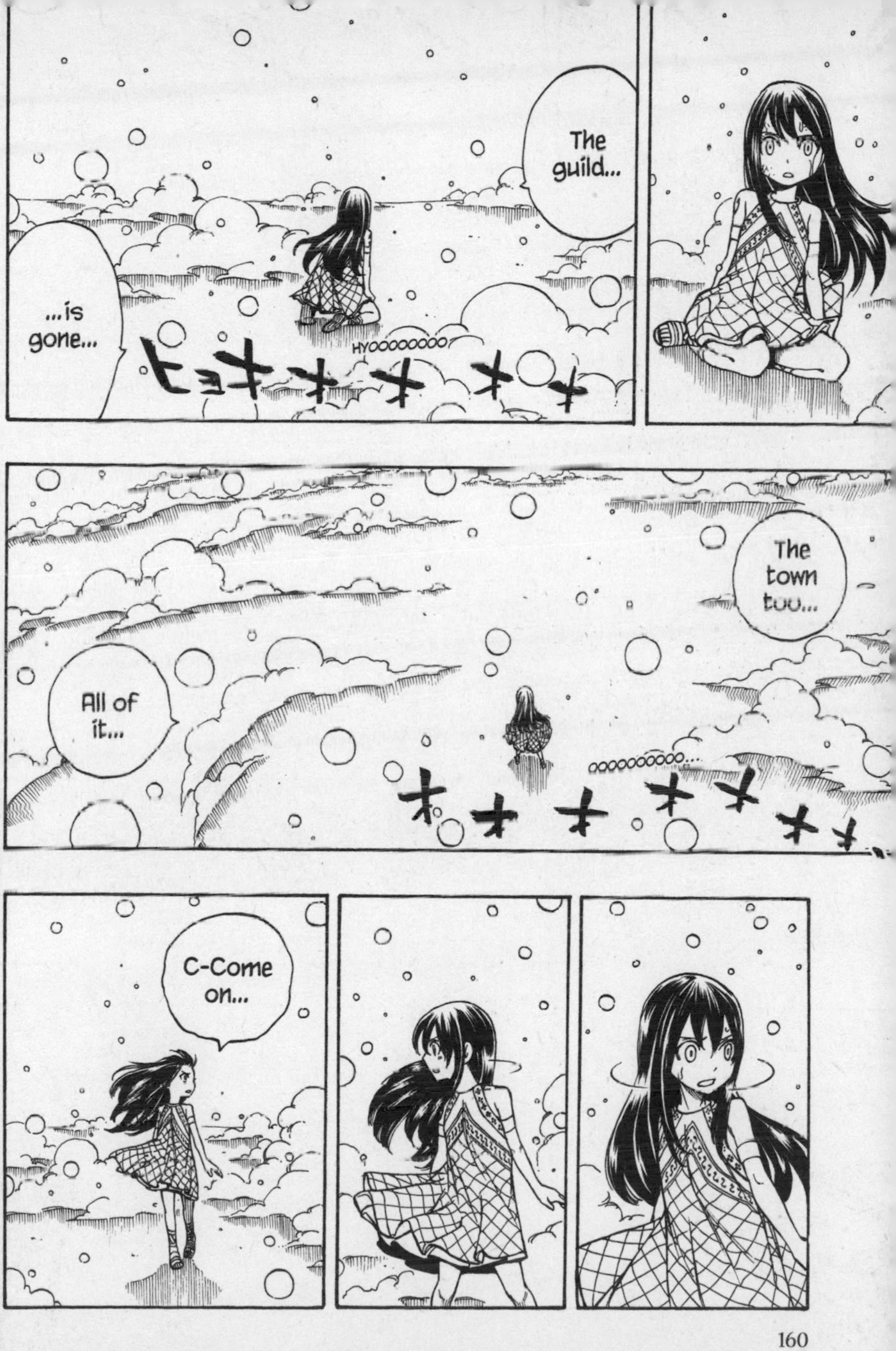
The guild...
...is gone...
HYOOOOOOOO
The town too...
All of it...
OOOOOOOOOO...
C-Come on...

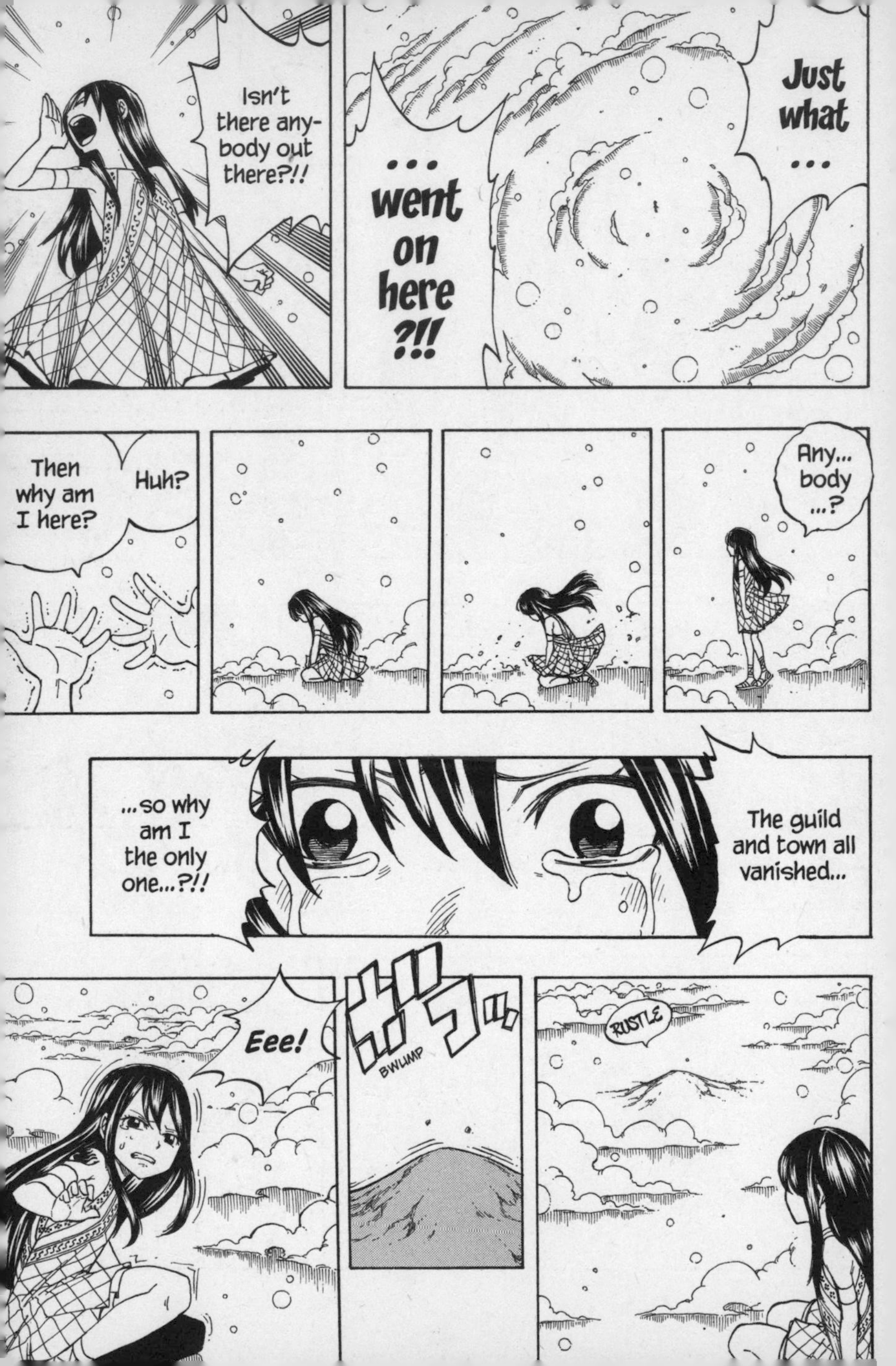
Just what...
...went on here?!!
Isn't there anybody out there?!!
Any... body ...?
Huh?
Then why am I here?
The guild and town all vanished...
...so why am I the only one...?!!
RUSTLE
BWUMP
Eee!

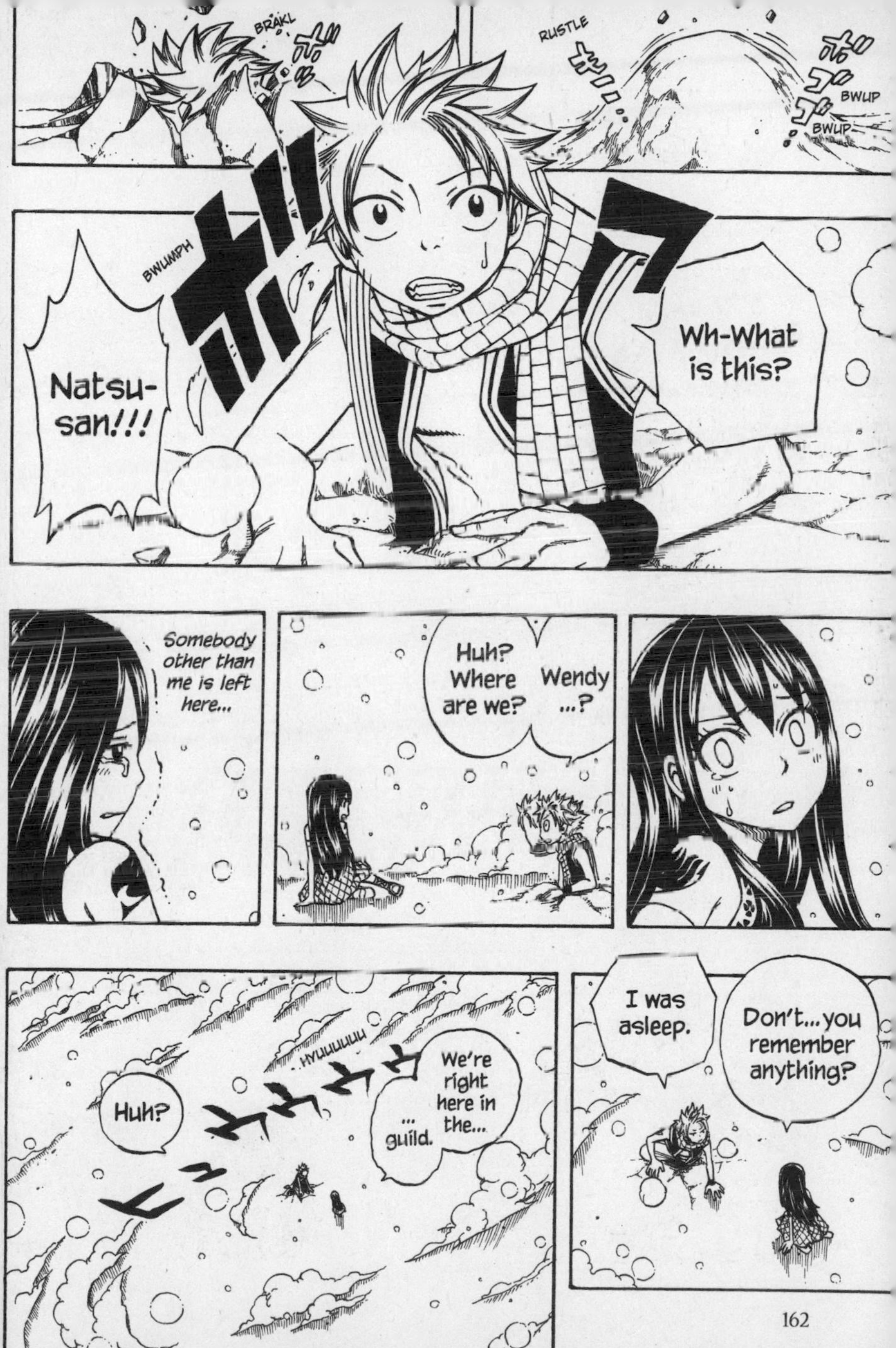
BWUP
BWUP
RUSTLE
BRAKL
Wh-What is this?
BWUMPH
Natsu-san!!!
Wendy ...?
Huh? Where are we?
Somebody other than me is left here...
Don't...you remember anything?
I was asleep.
We're right here in the...
... guild.
HYUUUUUU
Huh?

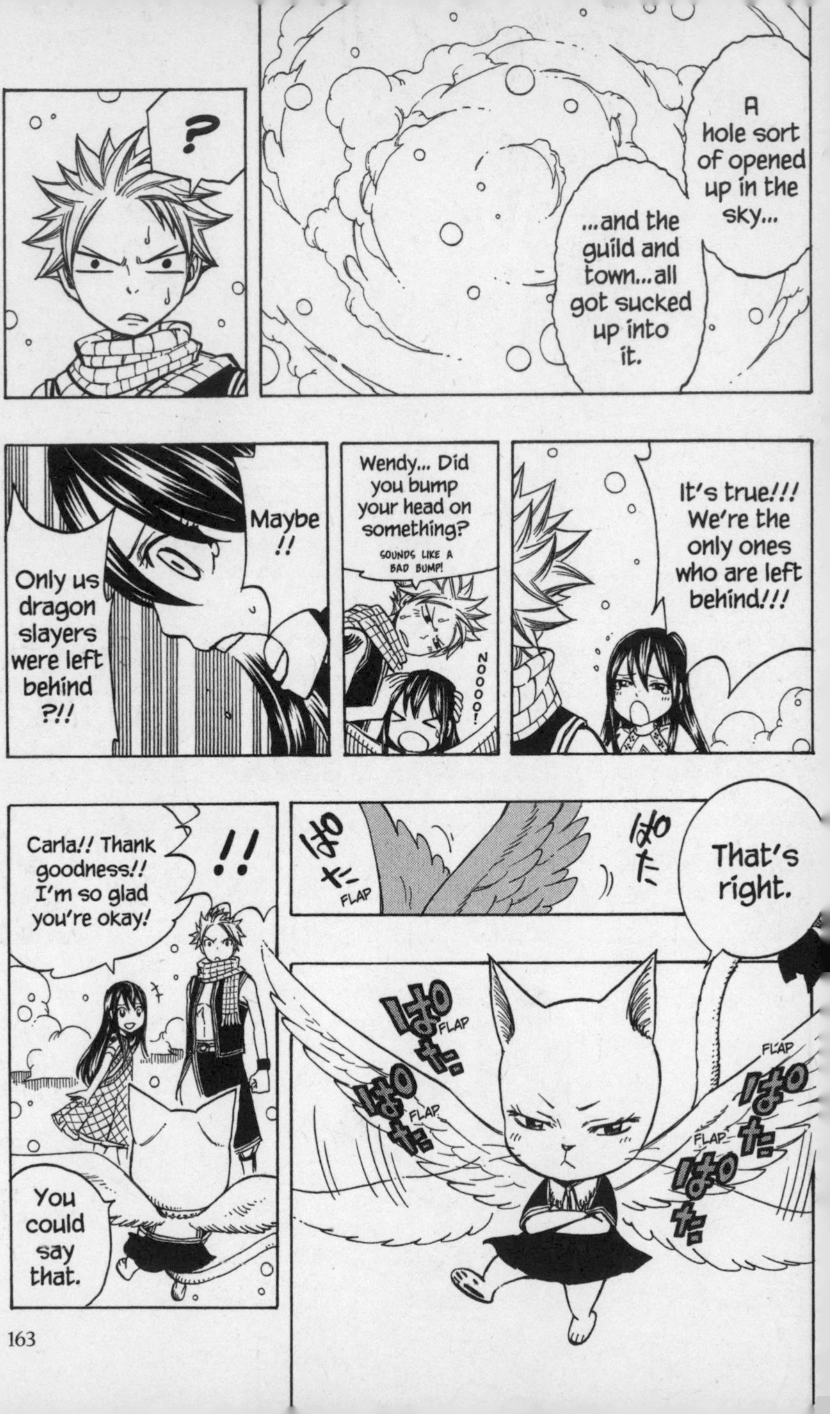
A hole sort of opened up in the sky...
...and the guild and town...all got sucked up into it.
?
It's true!!! We're the only ones who are left behind!!!
Wendy... Did you bump your head on something?
SOUNDS LIKE A BAD BUMP!
NOOOOO!
Maybe!!
Only us dragon slayers were left behind?!!
ぱた
ぱた FLAP
That's right.
ぱた FLAP
ぱた FLAP
ぱた FLAP
ぱた FLAP
!!
Carla!! Thank goodness!! I'm so glad you're okay!
You could say that.

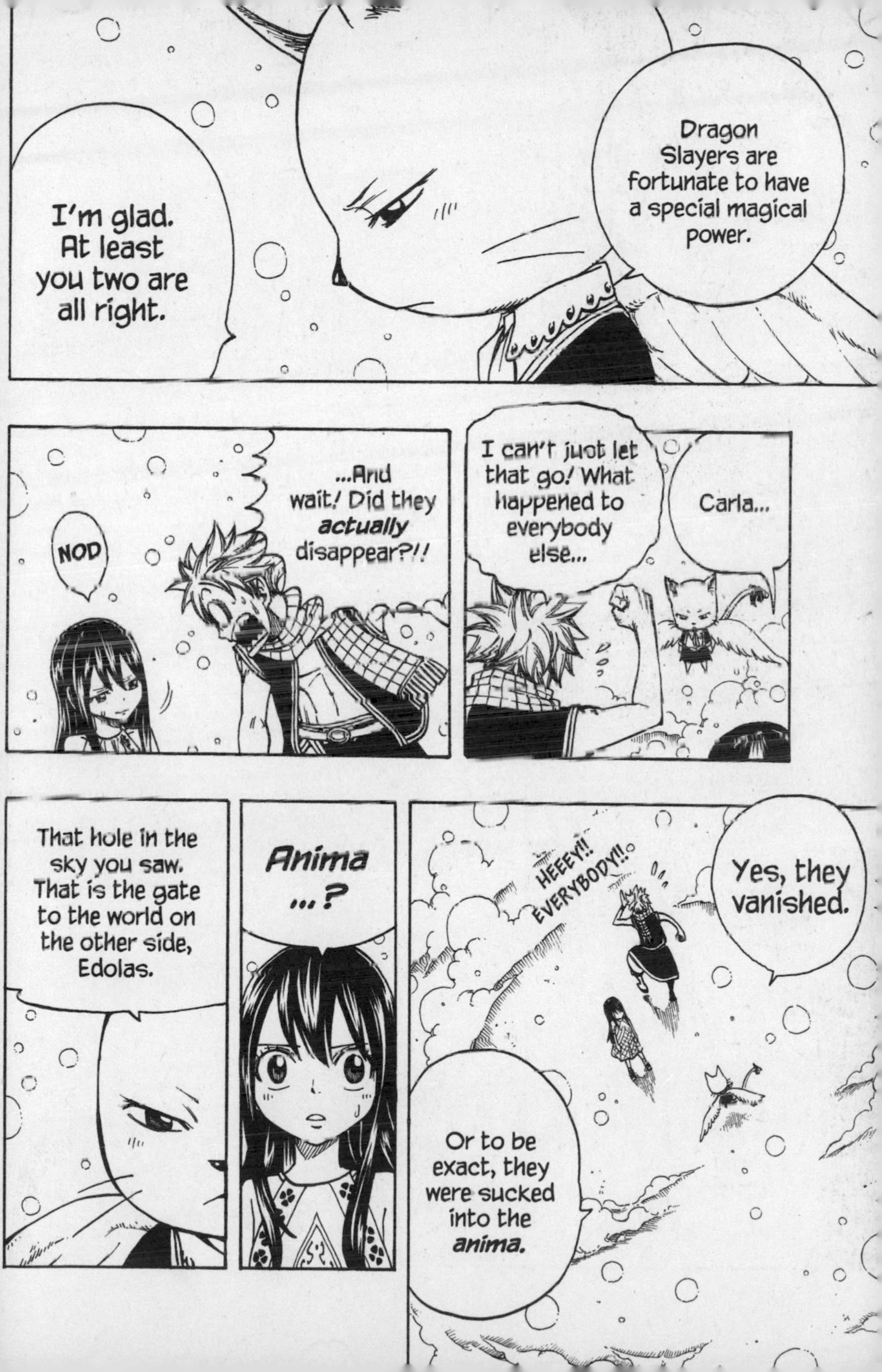
Dragon Slayers are fortunate to have a special magical power.
I'm glad. At least you two are all right.
Carla...
I can't just let that go! What happened to everybody else...
...And wait! Did they *actually* disappear?!!
NOD
Yes, they vanished.
HEEEY!! EVERYBODY!!
Or to be exact, they were sucked into the *anima.*
*Anima* ...?
That hole in the sky you saw. That is the gate to the world on the other side, Edolas.

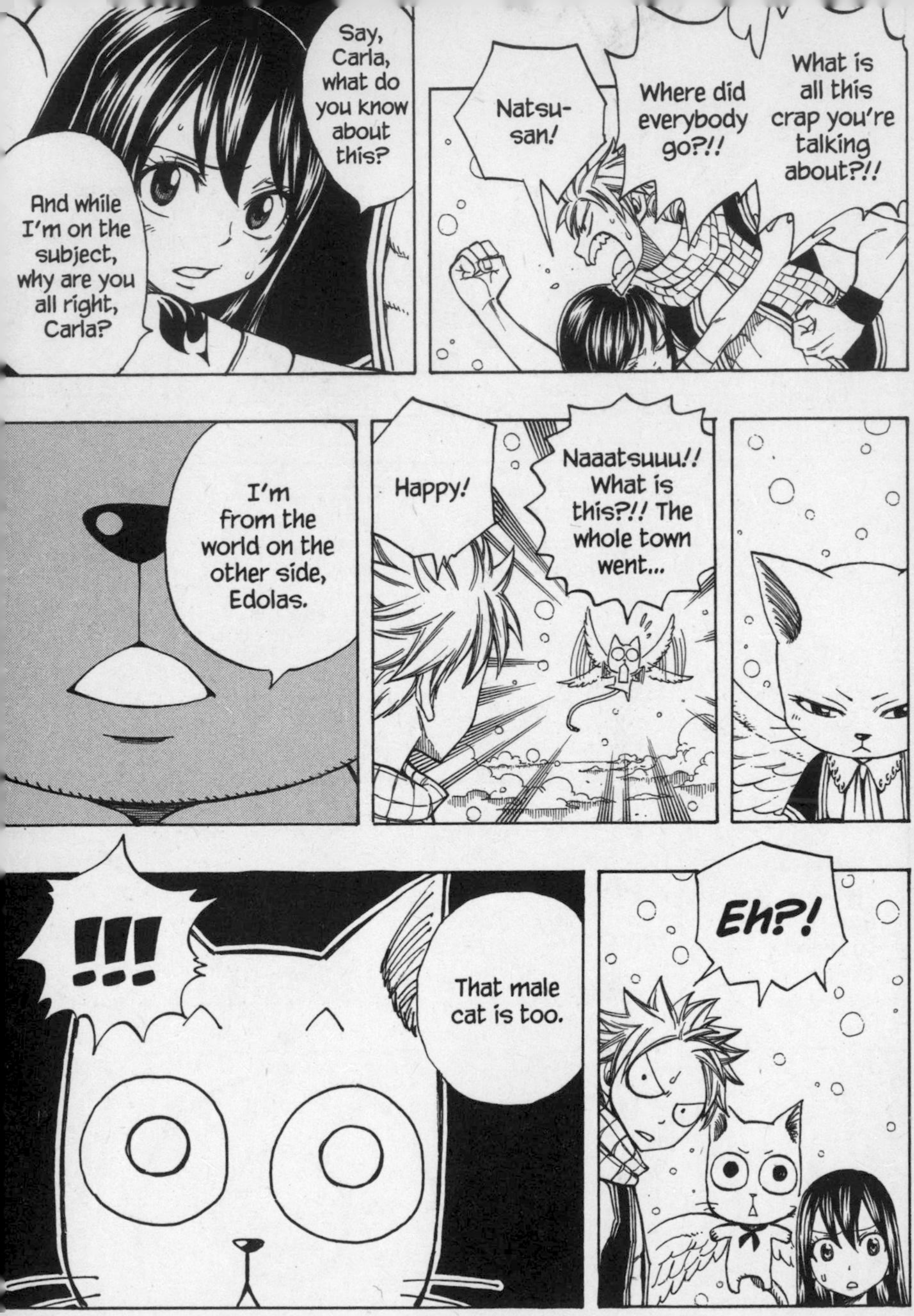
What is all this crap you're talking about?!!
Where did everybody go?!!
Natsu-san!
Say, Carla, what do you know about this?
And while I'm on the subject, why are you all right, Carla?
Naaatsuuu!! What is this?!! The whole town went...
Happy!
I'm from the world on the other side, Edolas.
Eh?!
That male cat is too.
!!!

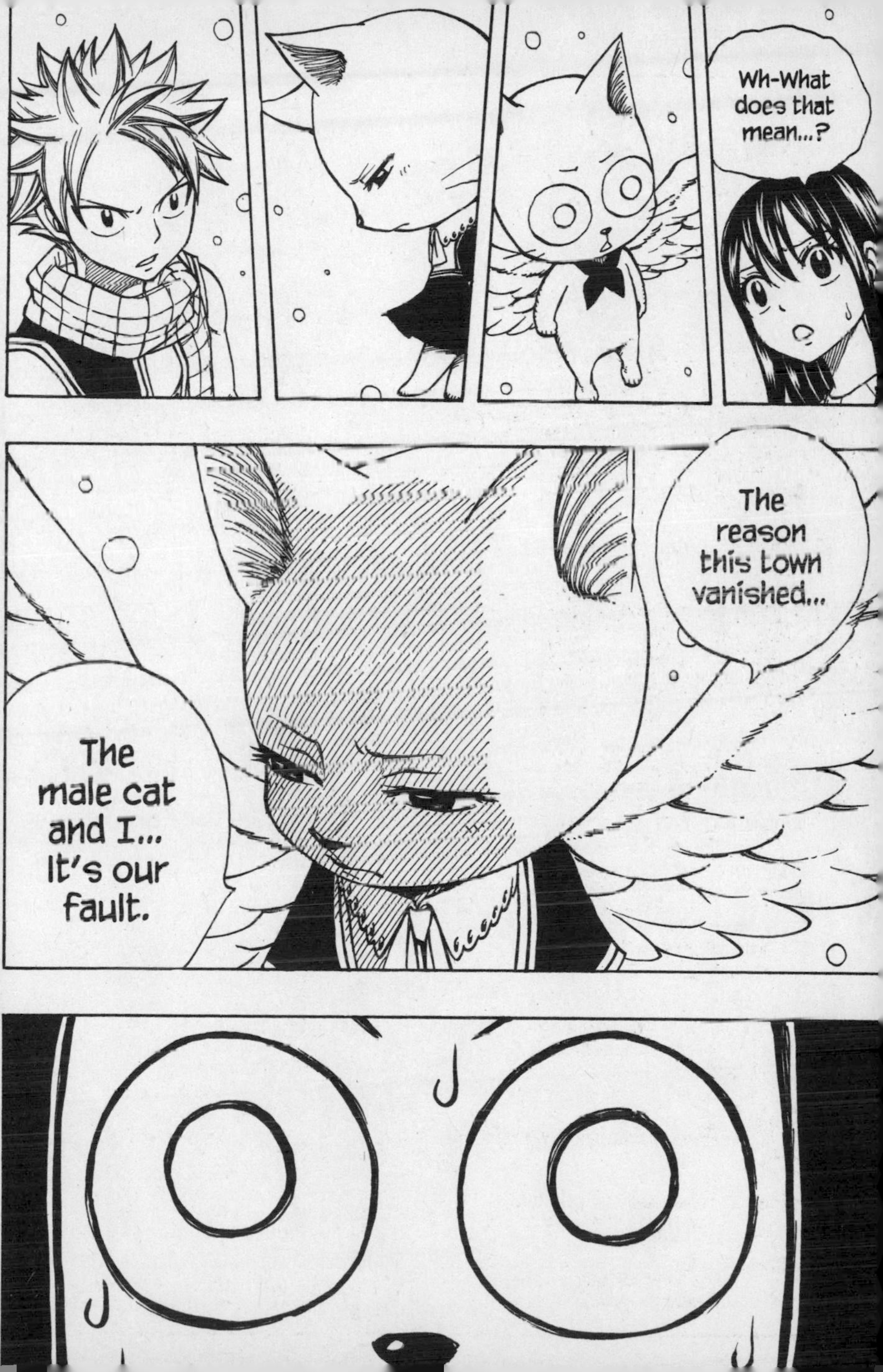
Wh-What does that mean...?
The reason this town vanished...
The male cat and I... It's our fault.

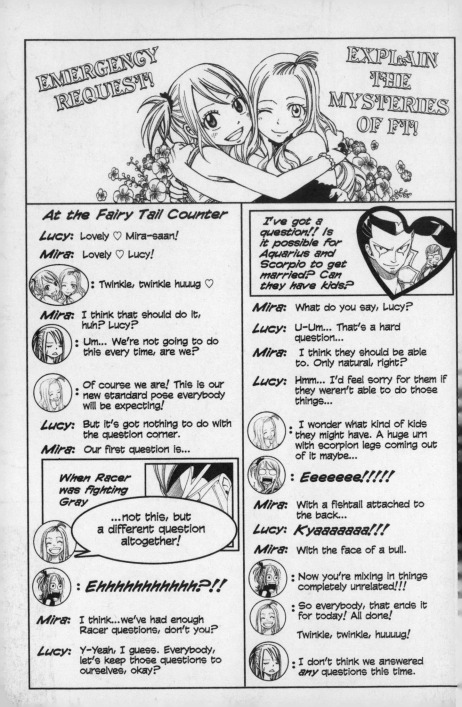

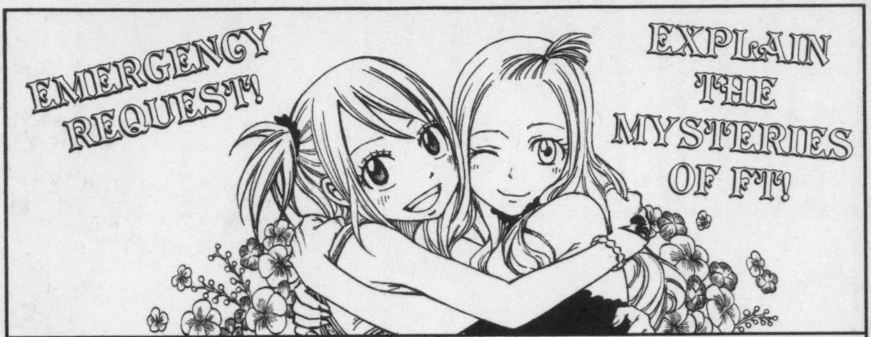
EMERGENCY REQUEST!
EXPLAIN THE MYSTERIES OF FT!

***At the Fairy Tail Counter***

***Lucy:*** Lovely ♡ Mira-saan!

***Mira:*** Lovely ♡ Lucy!

: Twinkle, twinkle huuug ♡

***Mira:*** I think that should do it, huh? Lucy?

: Um... We're not going to do this every time, are we?

: Of course we are! This is our new standard pose everybody will be expecting!

***Lucy:*** But it's got nothing to do with the question corner.

***Mira:*** Our first question is...

*When Racer was fighting Gray*

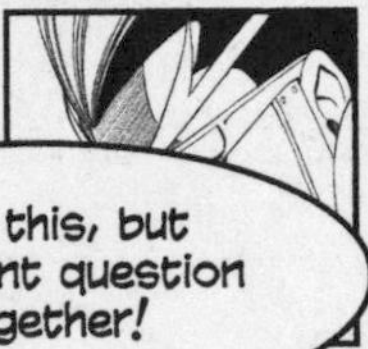

...not this, but a different question altogether!

: ***Ehhhhhhhhhhh?!!***

***Mira:*** I think...we've had enough Racer questions, don't you?

***Lucy:*** Y-Yeah, I guess. Everybody, let's keep those questions to ourselves, okay?

*I've got a question!! Is it possible for Aquarius and Scorpio to get married? Can they have kids?*

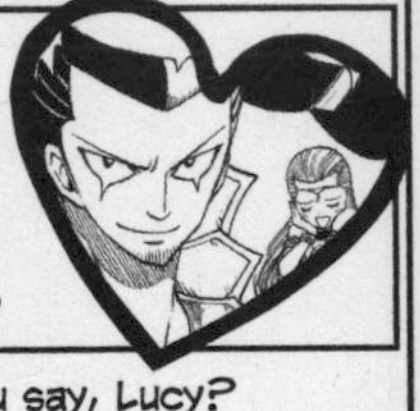

***Mira:*** What do you say, Lucy?

***Lucy:*** U-Um... That's a hard question...

***Mira:*** I think they should be able to. Only natural, right?

***Lucy:*** Hmm... I'd feel sorry for them if they weren't able to do those things...

: I wonder what kind of kids they might have. A huge urn with scorpion legs coming out of it maybe...

: ***Eeeeeee!!!!!***

***Mira:*** With a fishtail attached to the back...

***Lucy:*** ***Kyaaaaaaa!!!***

***Mira:*** With the face of a bull.

: Now you're mixing in things completely unrelated!!!

: So everybody, that ends it for today! All done!

Twinkle, twinkle, huuuug!

: I don't think we answered ***any*** questions this time.

# FAIRY TAIL

フェアリーテイル

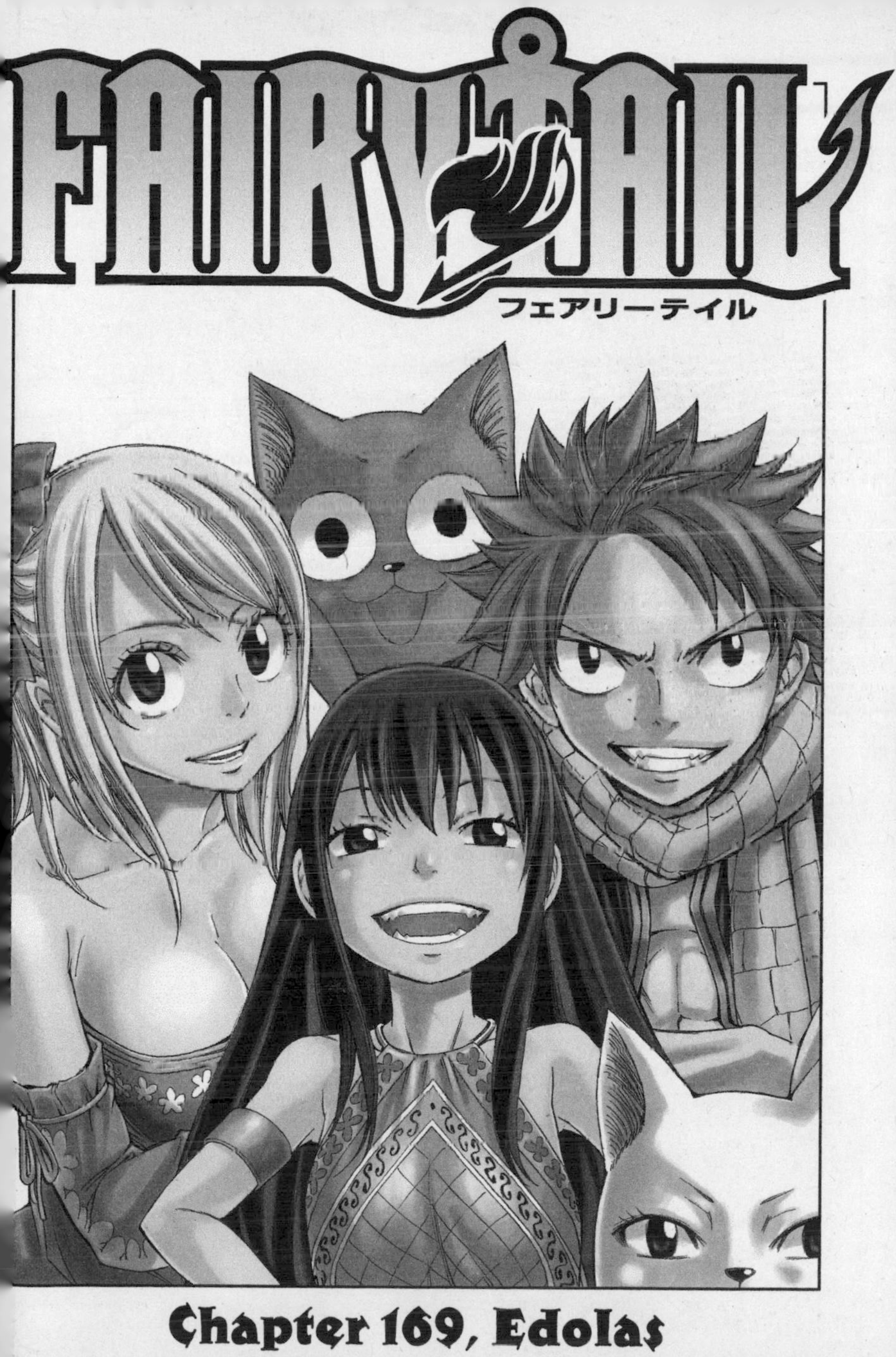

## Chapter 169, Edolas

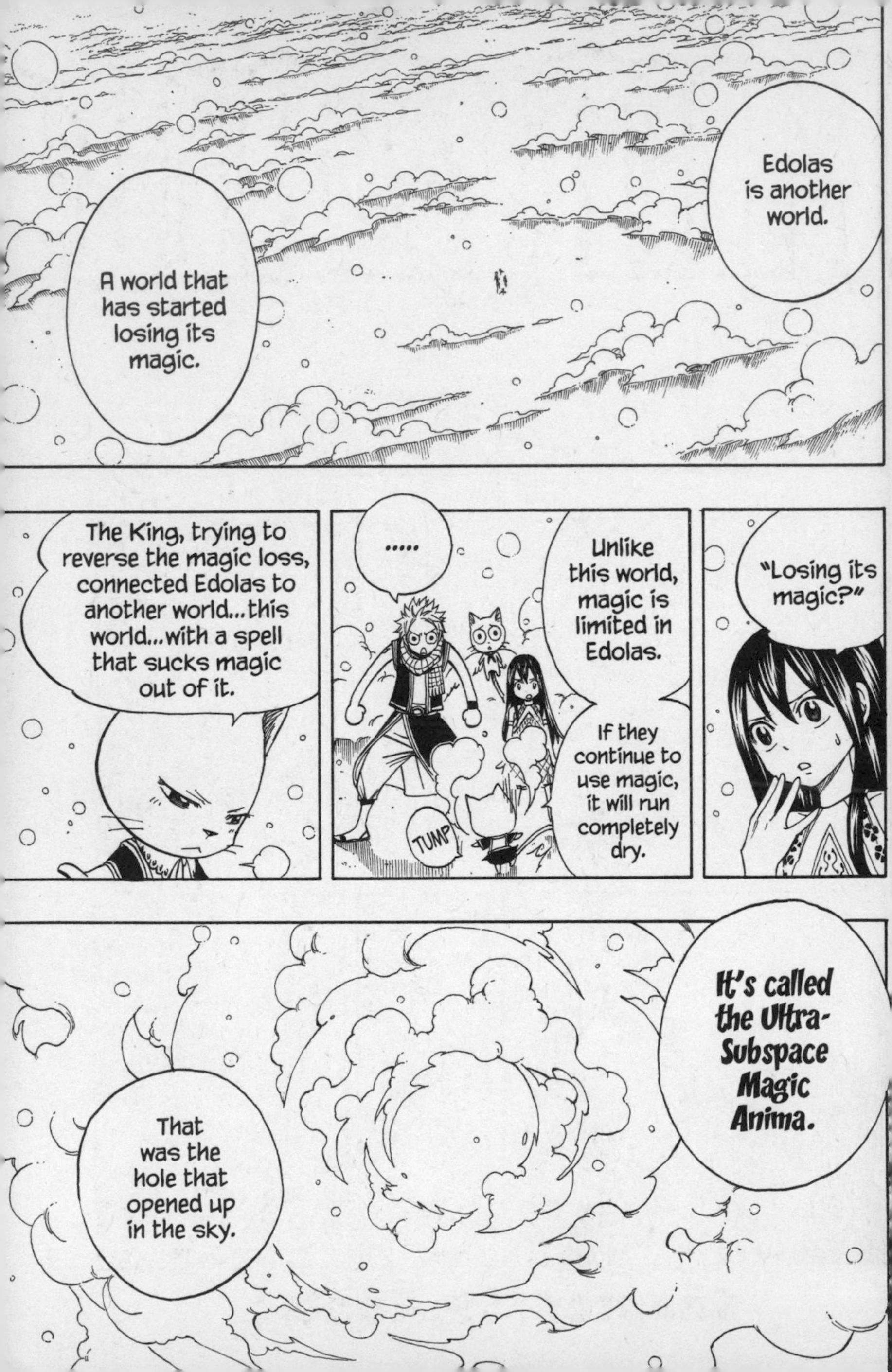
Edolas is another world.
A world that has started losing its magic.
"Losing its magic?"
Unlike this world, magic is limited in Edolas.
.....
If they continue to use magic, it will run completely dry.
TUMP
The King, trying to reverse the magic loss, connected Edolas to another world...this world...with a spell that sucks magic out of it.
It's called the Ultra-Subspace Magic Anima.
That was the hole that opened up in the sky.

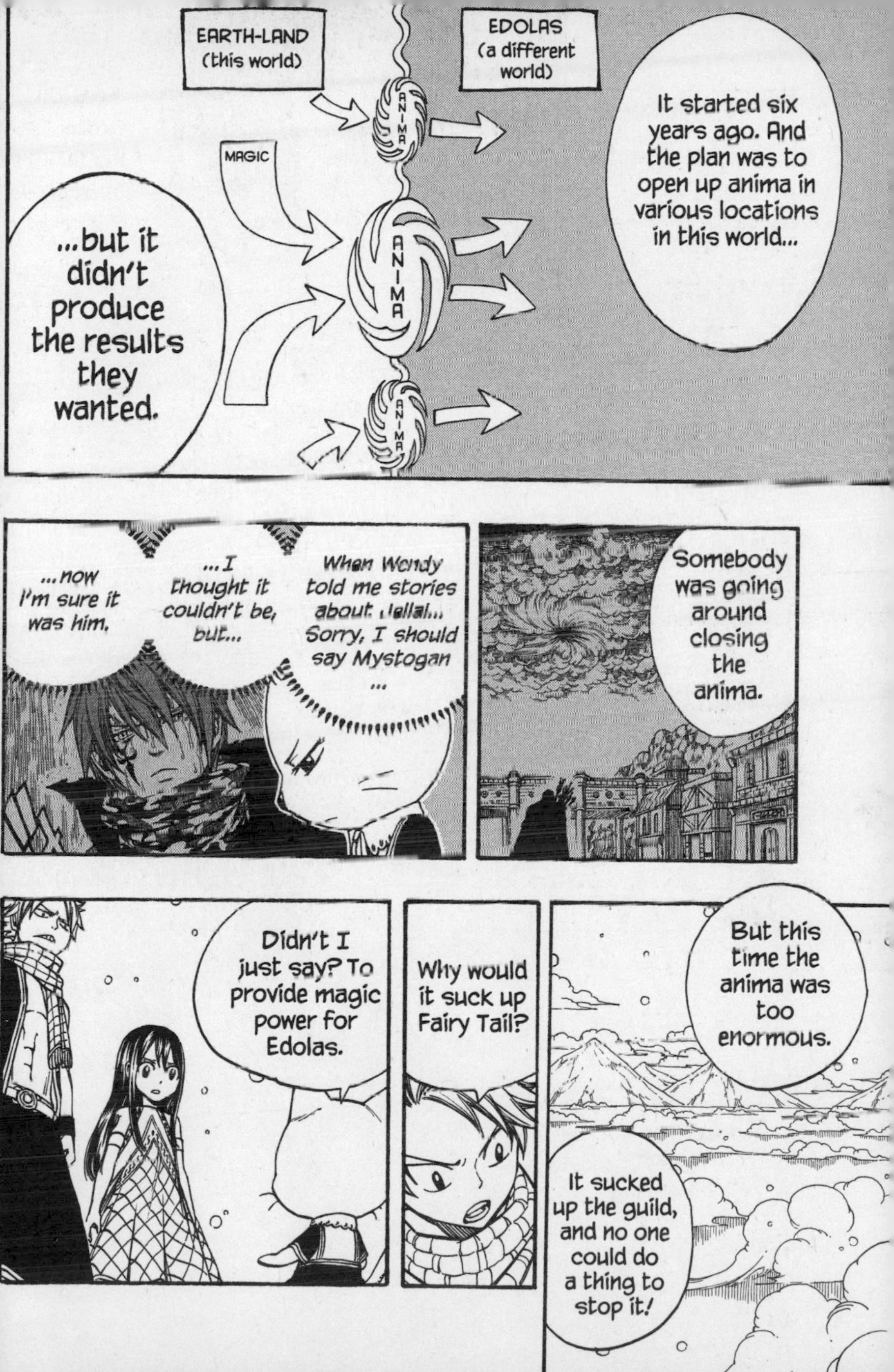
EDOLAS (a different world)
EARTH-LAND (this world)
It started six years ago. And the plan was to open up anima in various locations in this world...
ANIMA
MAGIC
ANIMA
ANIMA
...but it didn't produce the results they wanted.
Somebody was going around closing the anima.
When Wendy told me stories about Jellal... Sorry, I should say Mystogan ...
...I thought it couldn't be, but...
...now I'm sure it was him.
But this time the anima was too enormous.
It sucked up the guild, and no one could do a thing to stop it!
Why would it suck up Fairy Tail?
Didn't I just say? To provide magic power for Edolas.

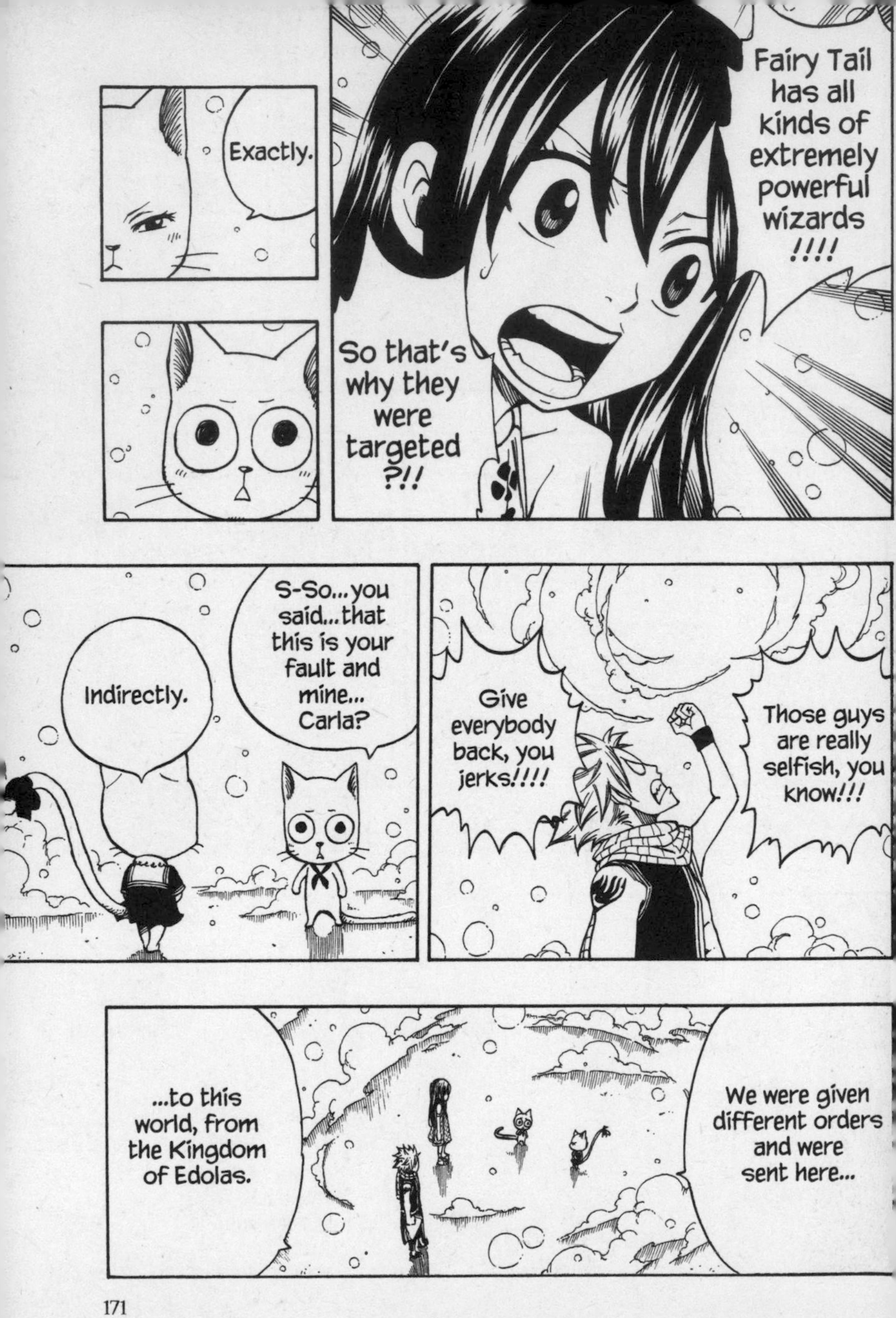
Fairy Tail has all kinds of extremely powerful wizards!!!!
So that's why they were targeted?!!
Exactly.
Those guys are really selfish, you know!!!
Give everybody back, you jerks!!!!
S-So...you said...that this is your fault and mine... Carla?
Indirectly.
We were given different orders and were sent here...
...to this world, from the Kingdom of Edolas.

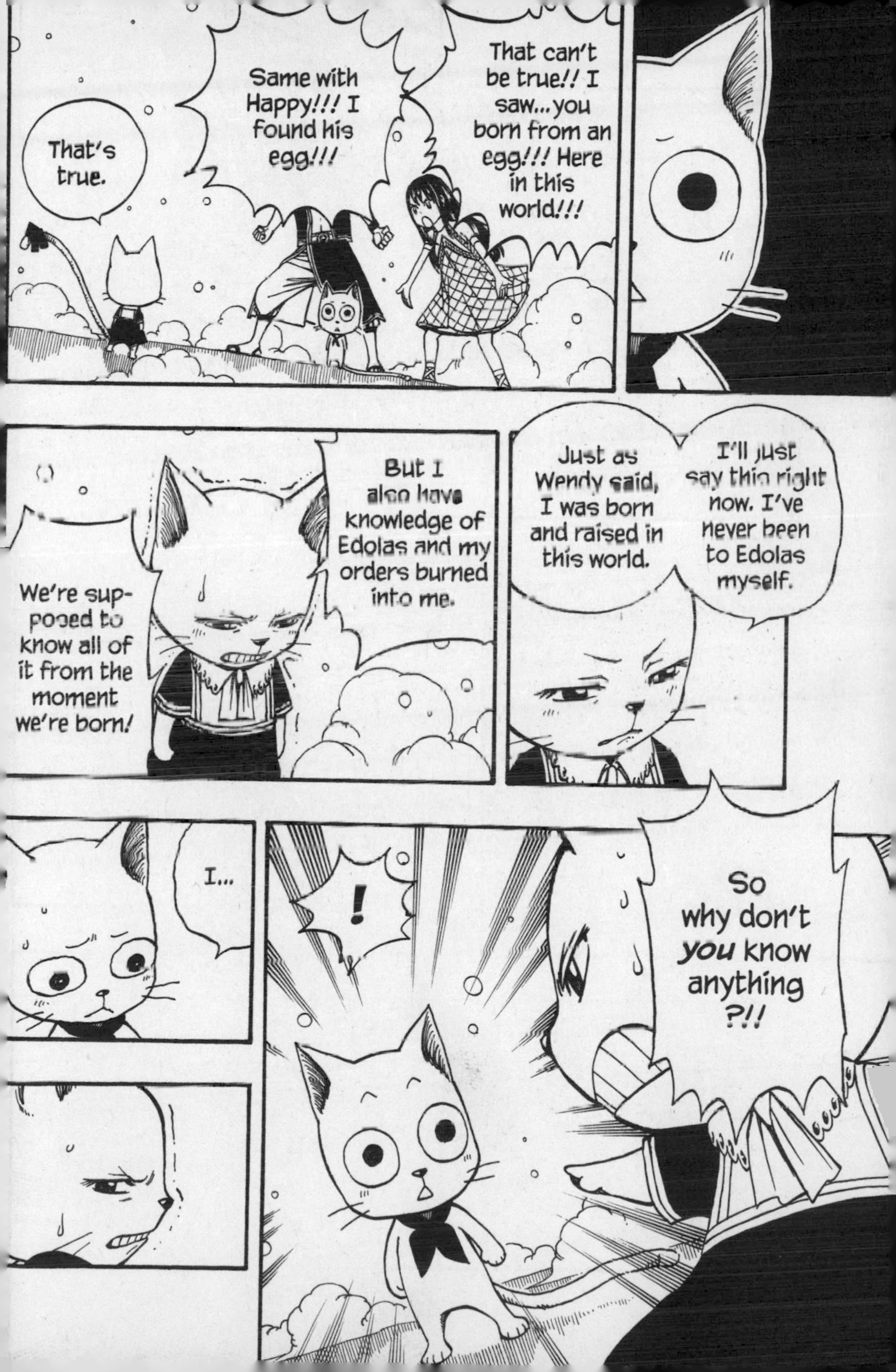
That can't be true!! I saw...you born from an egg!!! Here in this world!!!
Same with Happy!!! I found his egg!!!
That's true.
I'll just say this right now. I've never been to Edolas myself.
Just as Wendy said, I was born and raised in this world.
But I also have knowledge of Edolas and my orders burned into me.
We're sup-posed to know all of it from the moment we're born!
So why don't *you* know anything?!!
!
I...

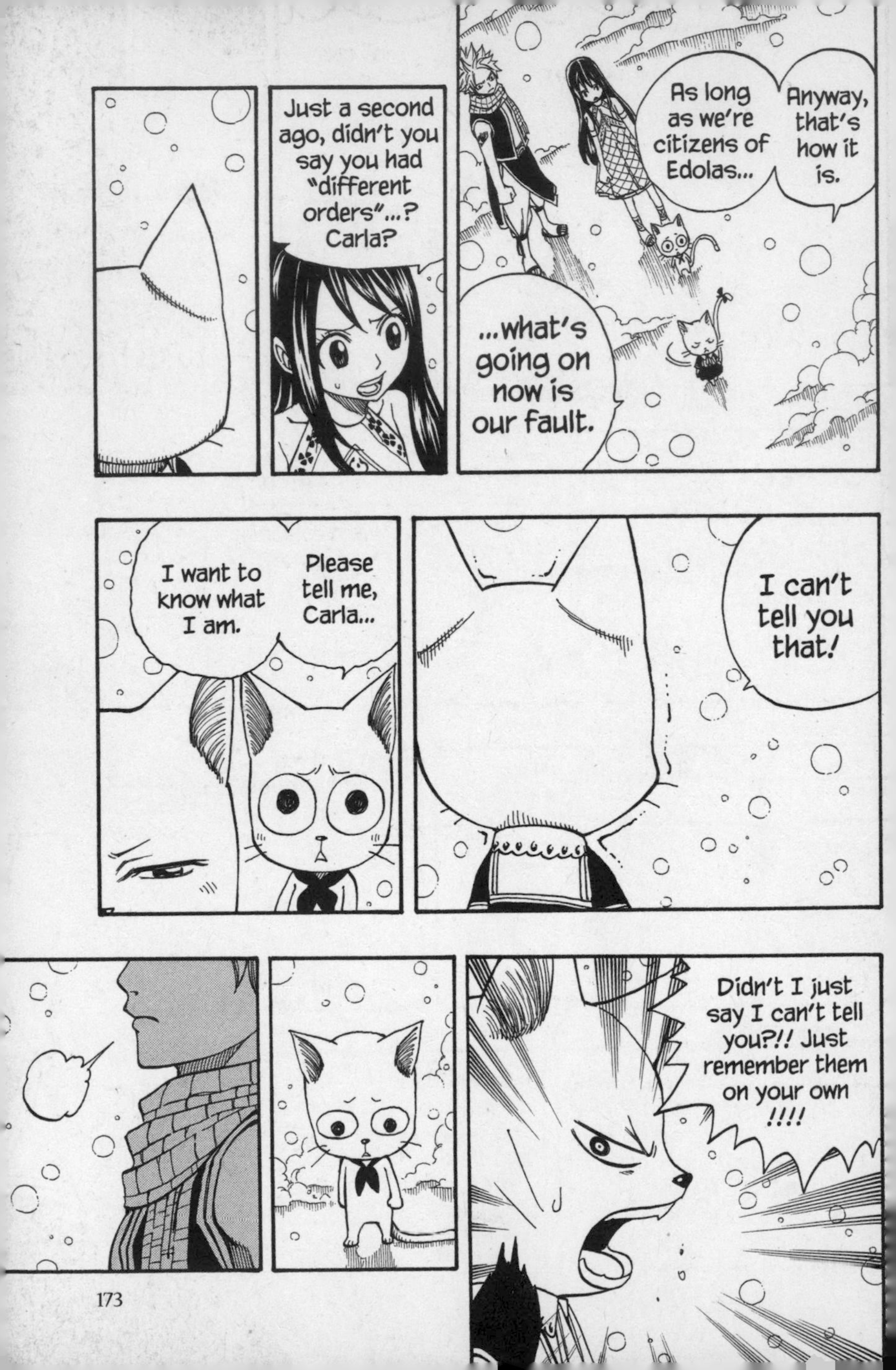
Anyway, that's how it is.
As long as we're citizens of Edolas...
...what's going on now is our fault.
Just a second ago, didn't you say you had "different orders"...? Carla?
I can't tell you that!
Please tell me, Carla...
I want to know what I am.
Didn't I just say I can't tell you?!! Just remember them on your own !!!!

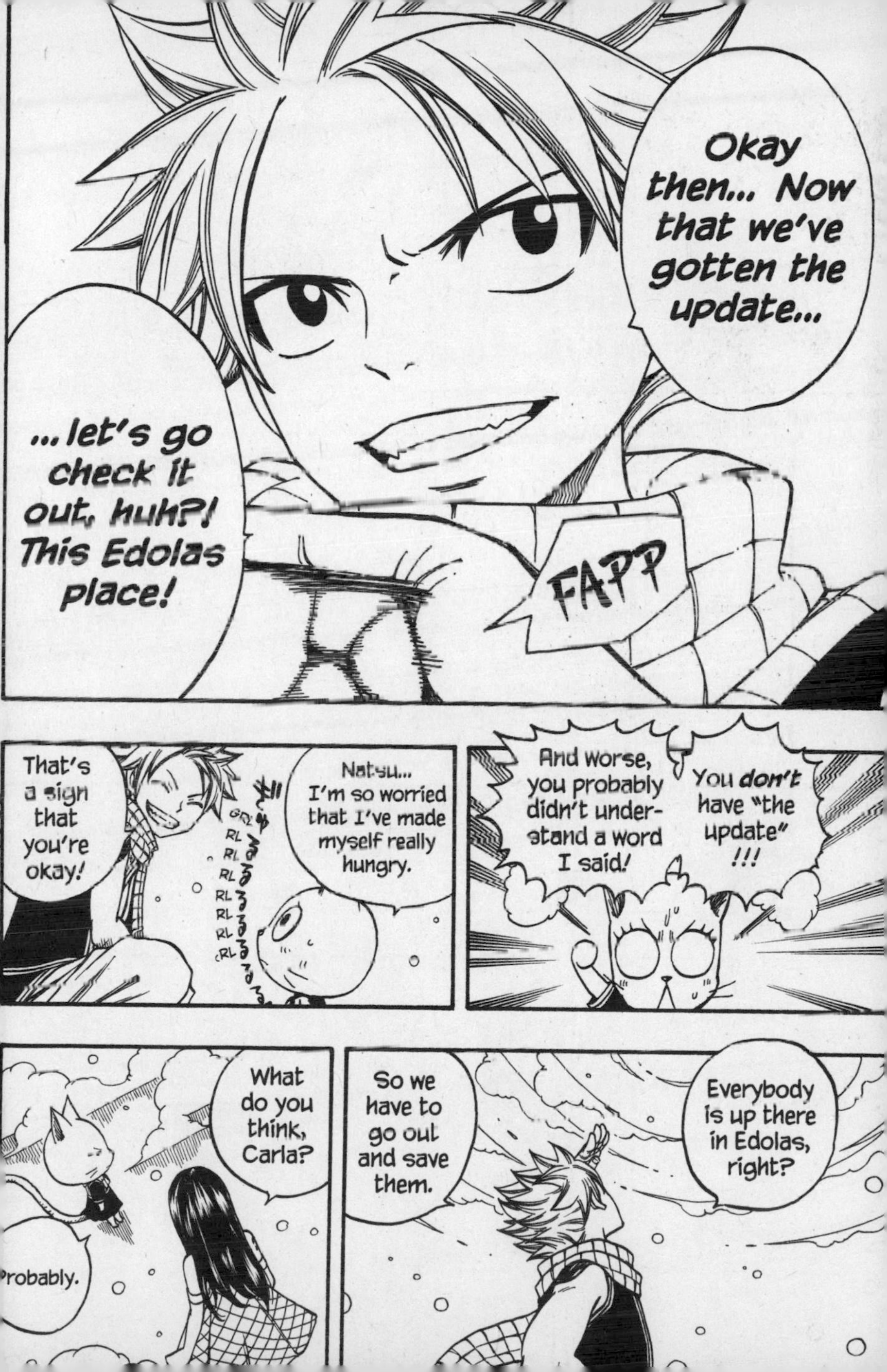
Okay then... Now that we've gotten the update...
FAPP
...let's go check it out, huh?! This Edolas place!
You don't have "the update" !!!
And worse, you probably didn't understand a word I said!
Natsu... I'm so worried that I've made myself really hungry.
GRRL RL RL RL RL RL RL CRL
That's a sign that you're okay!
Everybody is up there in Edolas, right?
So we have to go out and save them.
What do you think, Carla?
Probably.

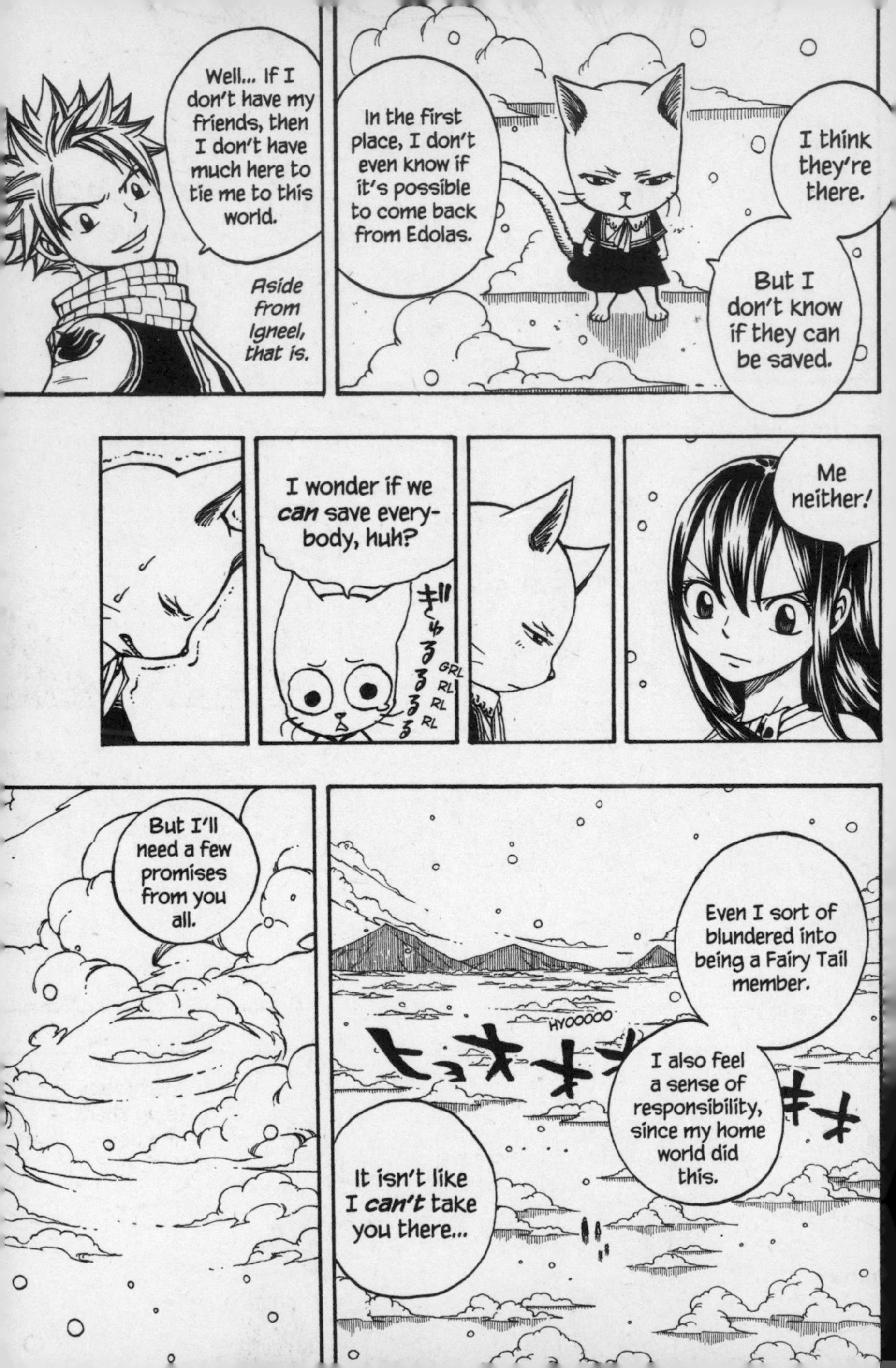
I think they're there.
But I don't know if they can be saved.
In the first place, I don't even know if it's possible to come back from Edolas.
Well... If I don't have my friends, then I don't have much here to tie me to this world.
Aside from Igneel, that is.
Me neither!
I wonder if we *can* save every-body, huh?
ぎゅるるるる
GRL RL RL RL
Even I sort of blundered into being a Fairy Tail member.
I also feel a sense of responsibility, since my home world did this.
HYOOOOO
It isn't like I *can't* take you there...
But I'll need a few promises from you all.

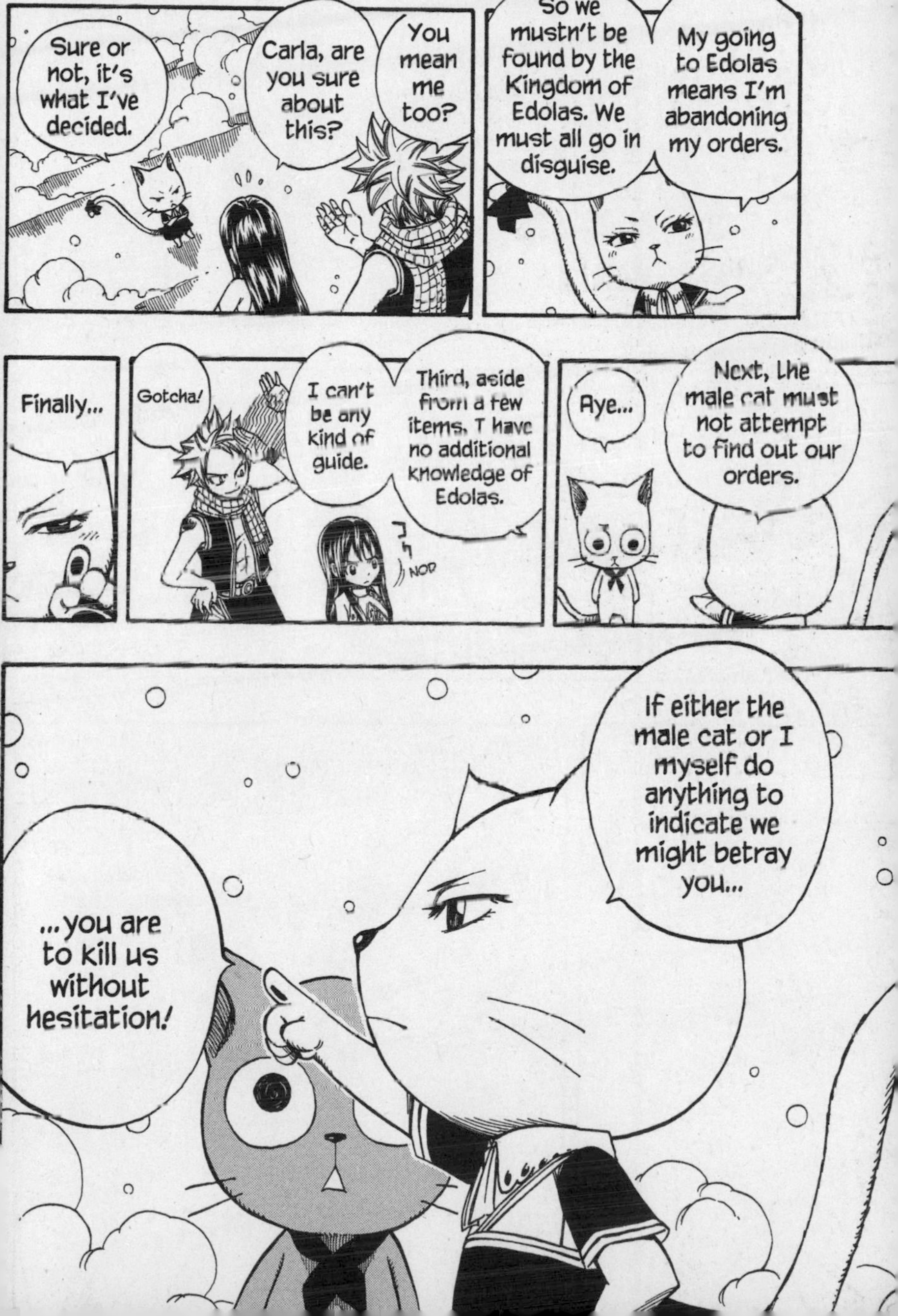
My going to Edolas means I'm abandoning my orders.
So we mustn't be found by the Kingdom of Edolas. We must all go in disguise.
You mean me too?
Carla, are you sure about this?
Sure or not, it's what I've decided.
Next, the male cat must not attempt to find out our orders.
Aye...
Third, aside from a few items, I have no additional knowledge of Edolas.
I can't be any kind of guide.
Gotcha!
NOD
Finally...
If either the male cat or I myself do anything to indicate we might betray you...
...you are to kill us without hesitation!

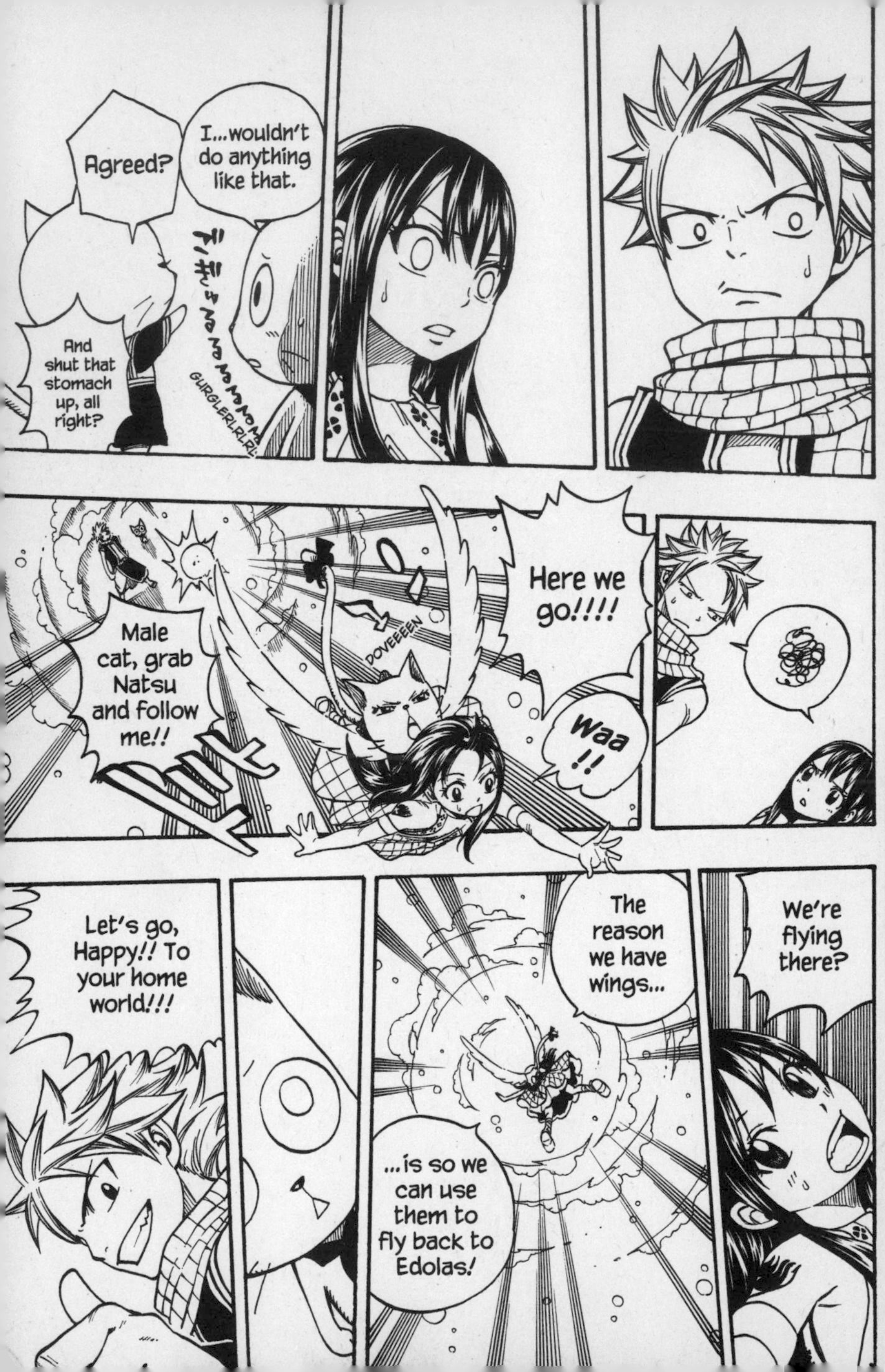
I...wouldn't do anything like that.
Agreed?
GURGLERLRLRL
And shut that stomach up, all right?
Here we go!!!!
Waa!!
DOVEEEEN
Male cat, grab Natsu and follow me!!
We're flying there?
The reason we have wings...
...is so we can use them to fly back to Edolas!
Let's go, Happy!! To your home world!!!

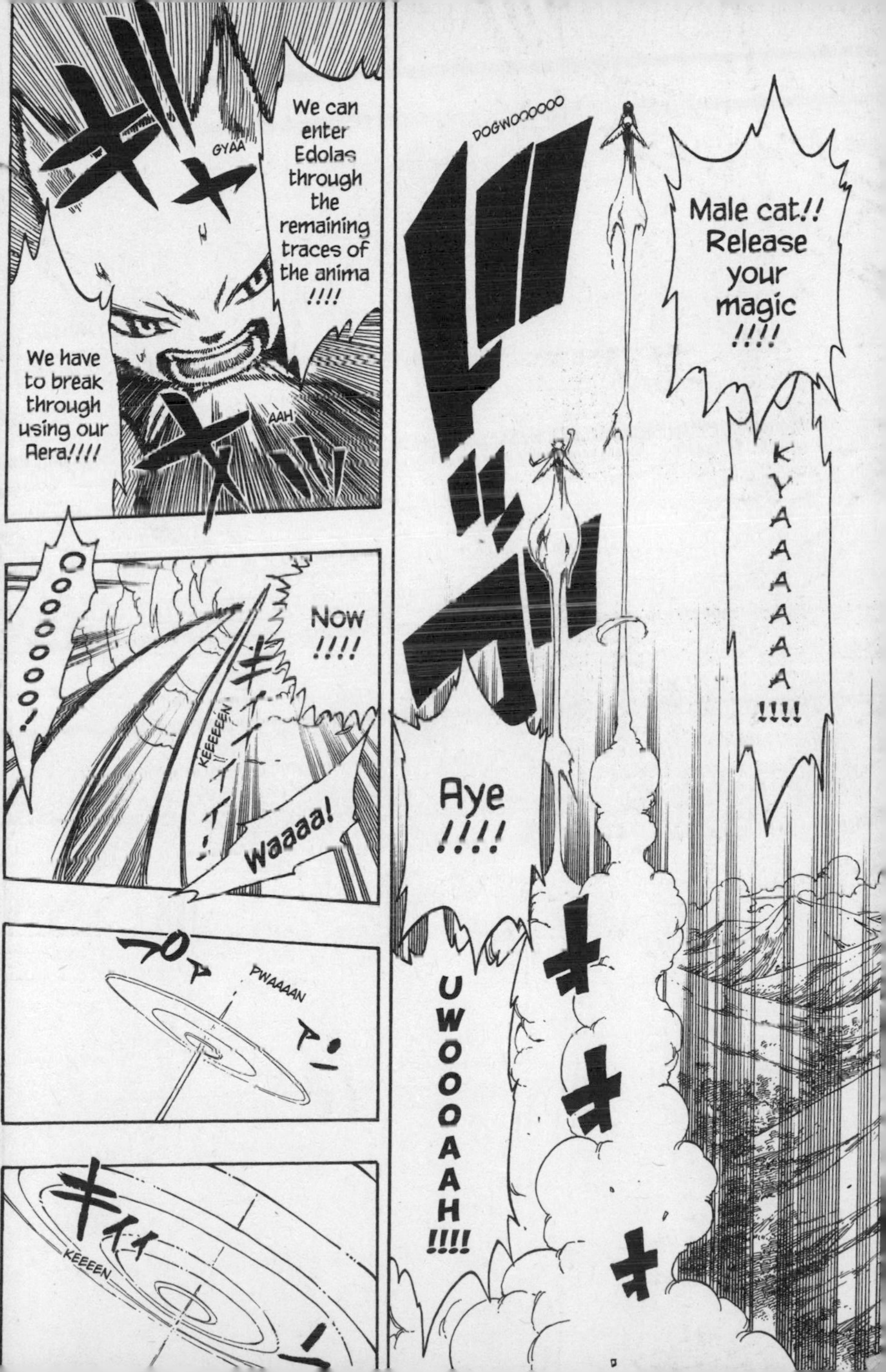
Male cat!! Release your magic!!!!
KYAAAAAAAA!!!!
DOGWOOOOOO
Aye!!!!
UWOOOAAAH!!!!
We can enter Edolas through the remaining traces of the anima!!!!
GYAA
We have to break through using our Aera!!!!
AAH
Now!!!!
KEEEEEEN
Waaaa!
Ooooooooo!
PWAAAAN
KEEEEN

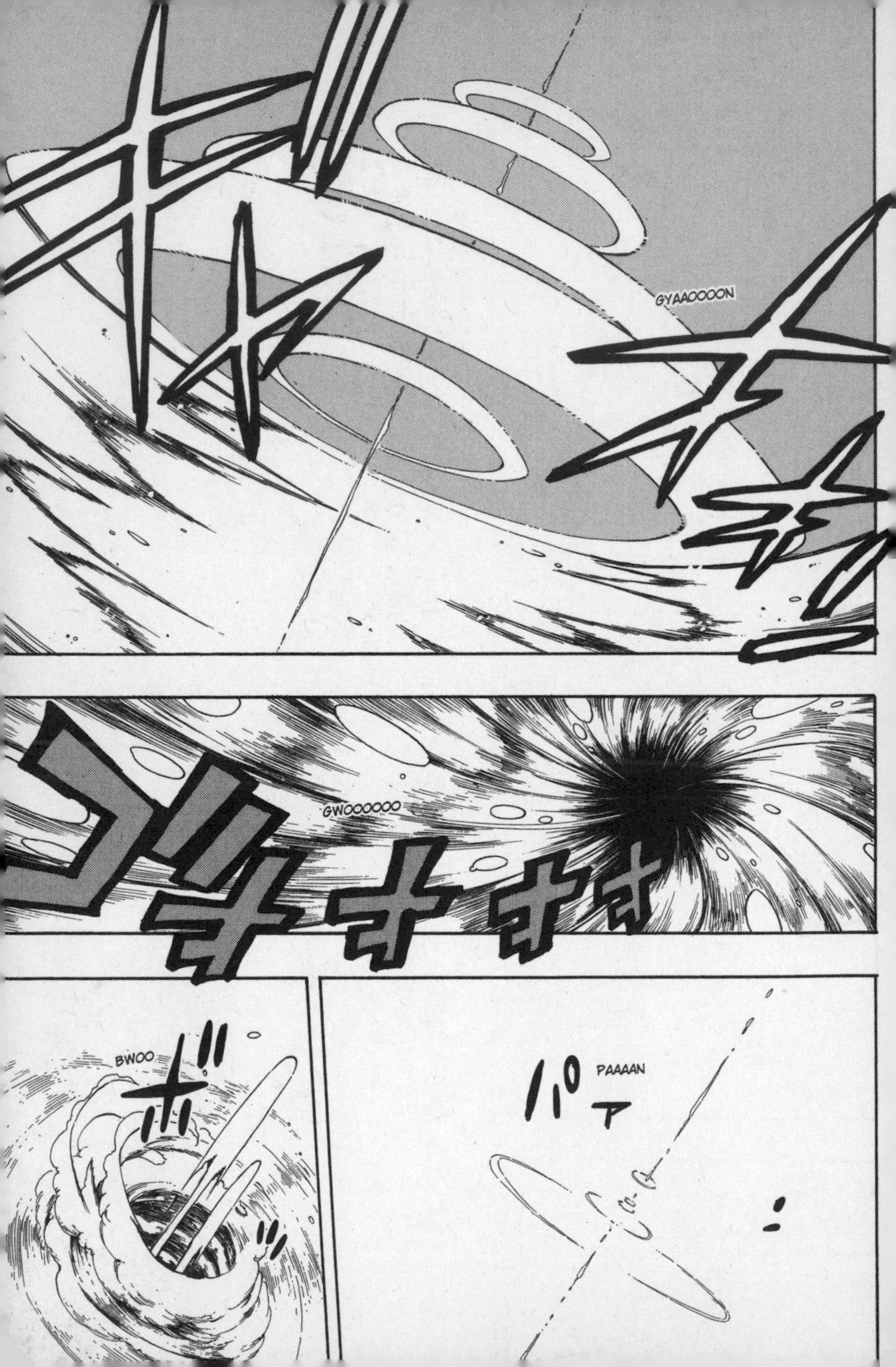
GYAAOOOON
GWOOOOOO
PAAAAN
BWOO

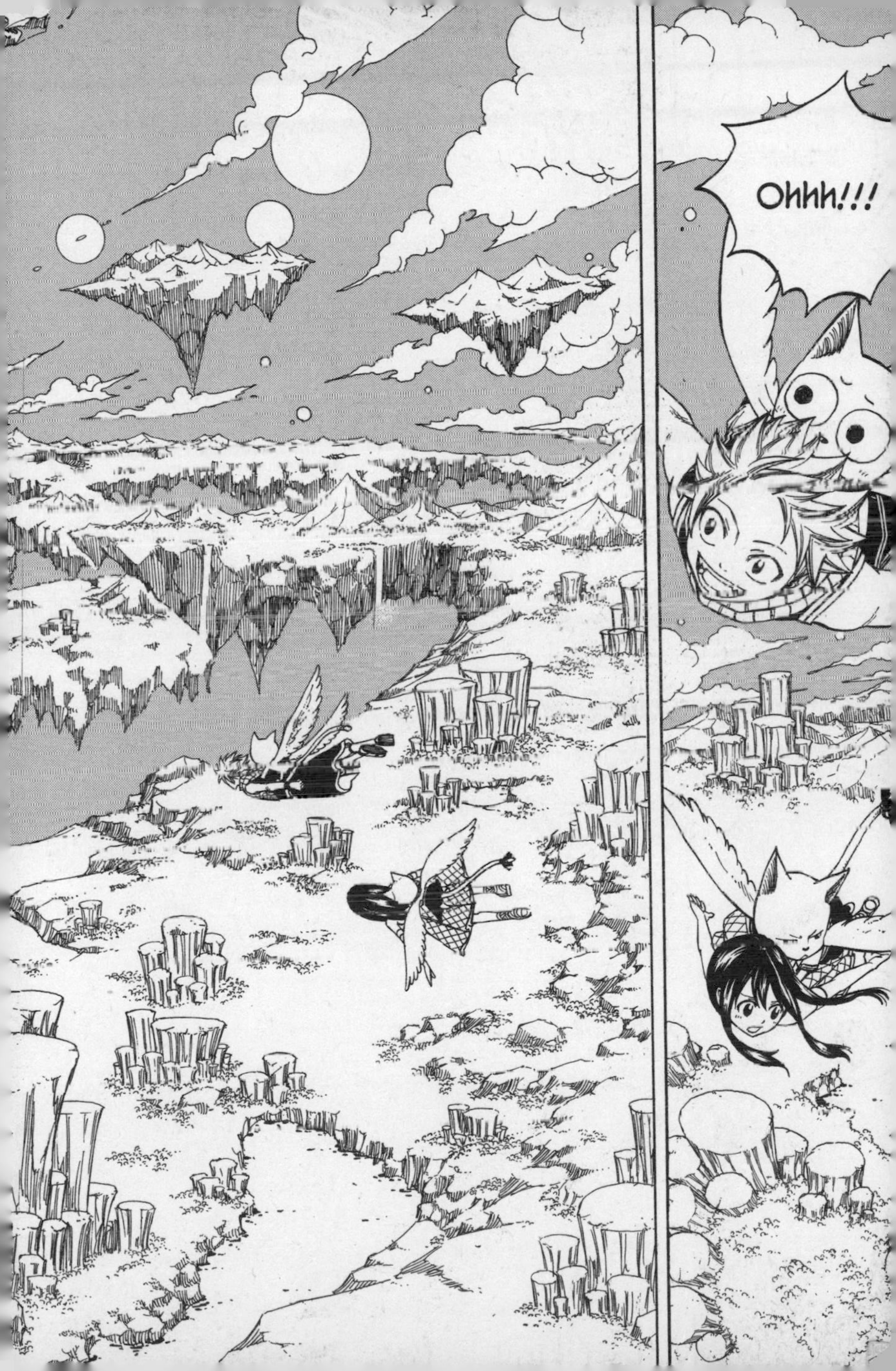
Ohhh!!!

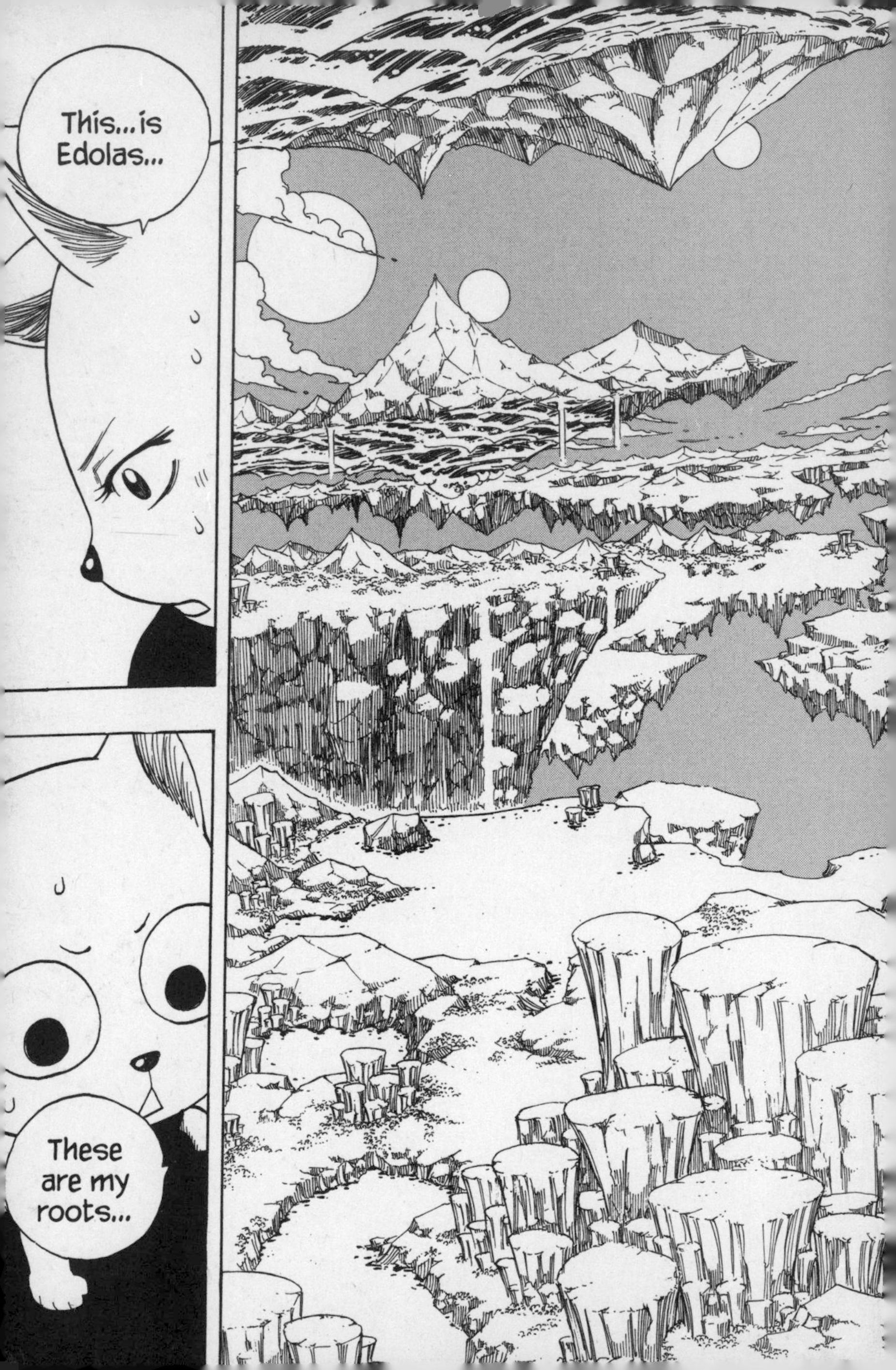
This...is Edolas...
These are my roots...

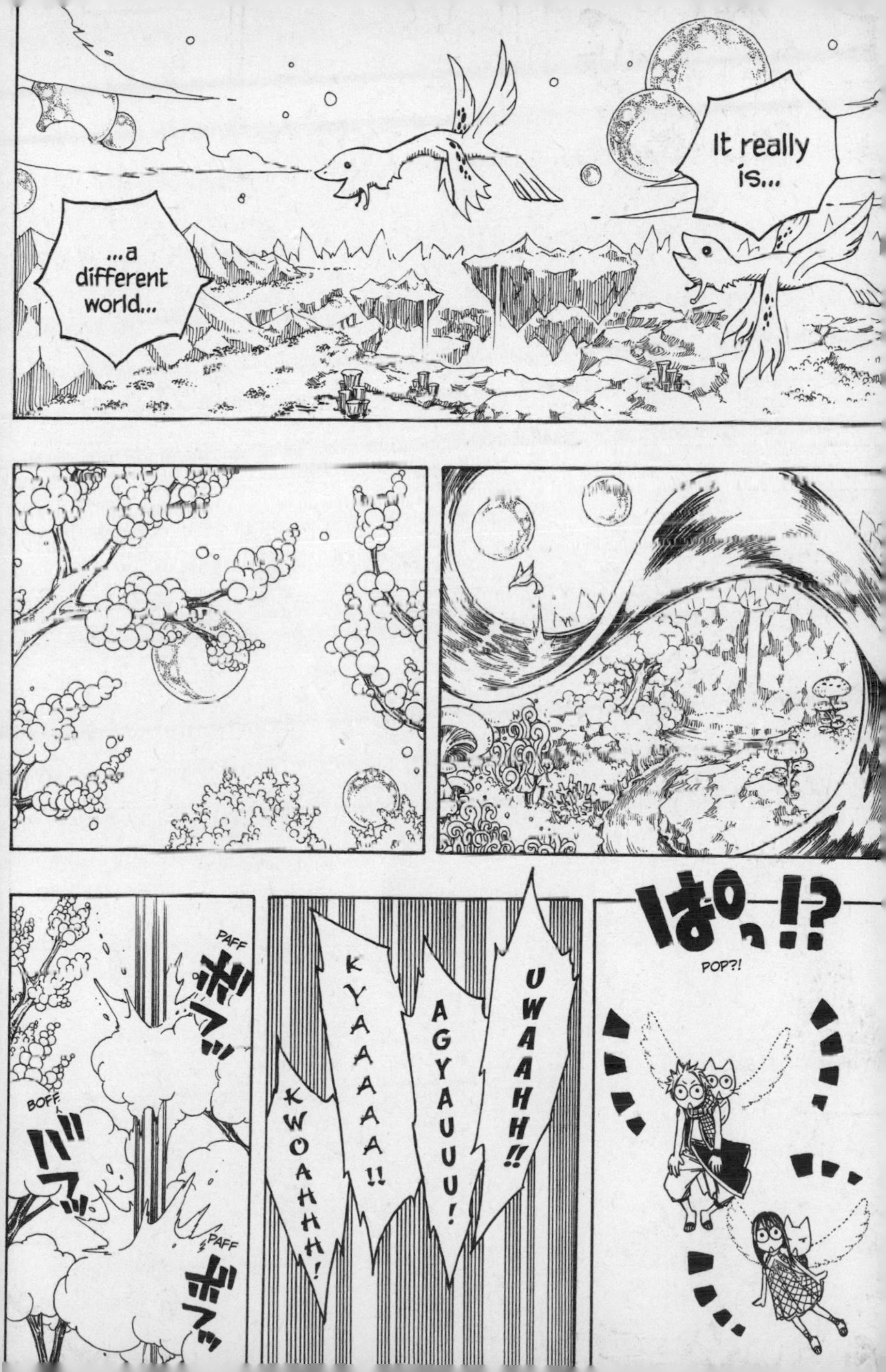

It really is...
...a different world...
ぱっ!?
POP?!
UWAAHH!!
AGYAUUU!
KYAAAAA!!
KWOAHHHH!
PAFF
BOFF
PAFF

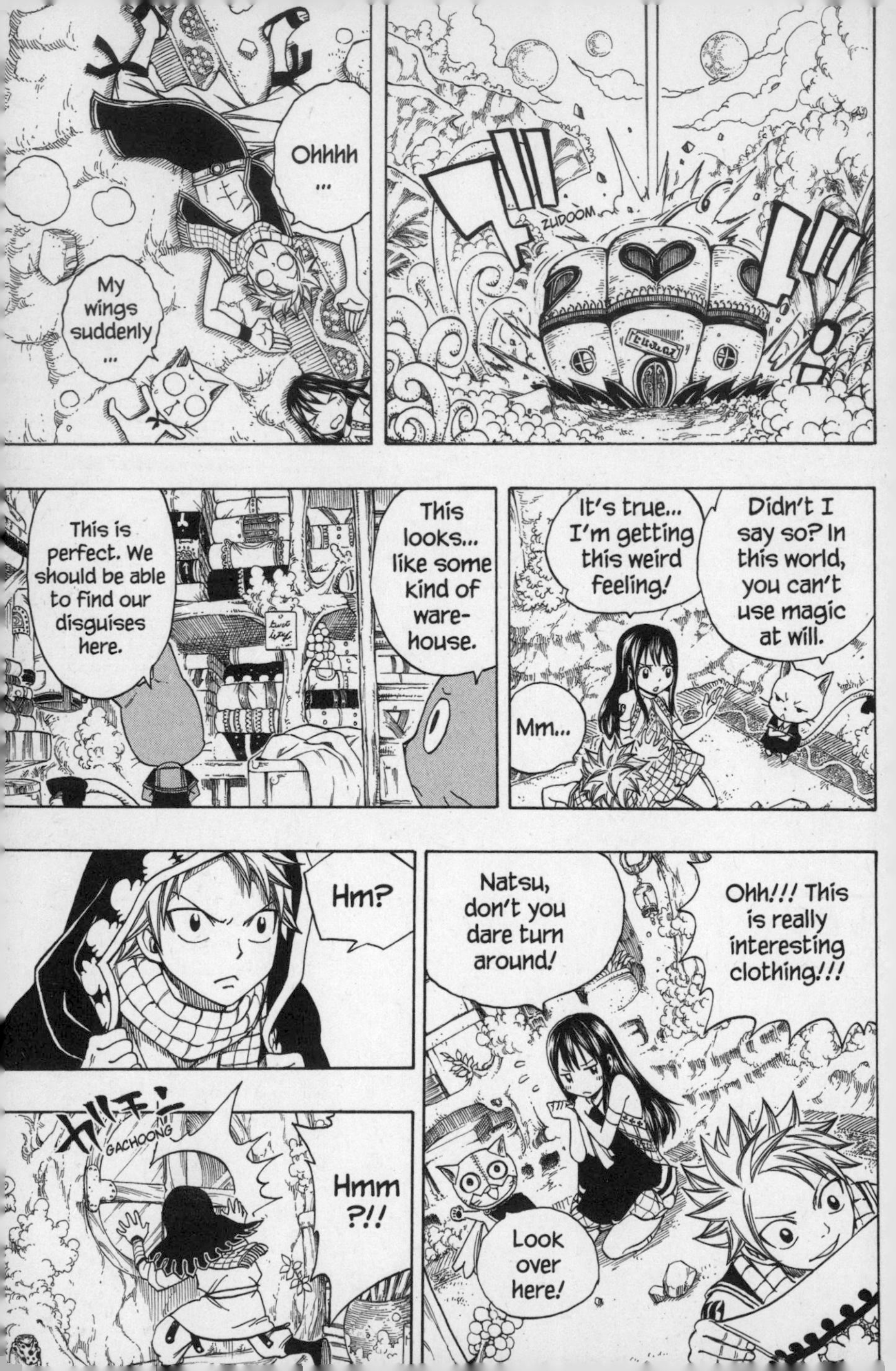
ZUDOOM
Ohhhh ...
My wings suddenly ...
Didn't I say so? In this world, you can't use magic at will.
It's true... I'm getting this weird feeling!
Mm...
This looks... like some kind of ware-house.
This is perfect. We should be able to find our disguises here.
Ohh!!! This is really interesting clothing!!!
Natsu, don't you dare turn around!
Look over here!
Hm?
GACHOONG
Hmm ?!!

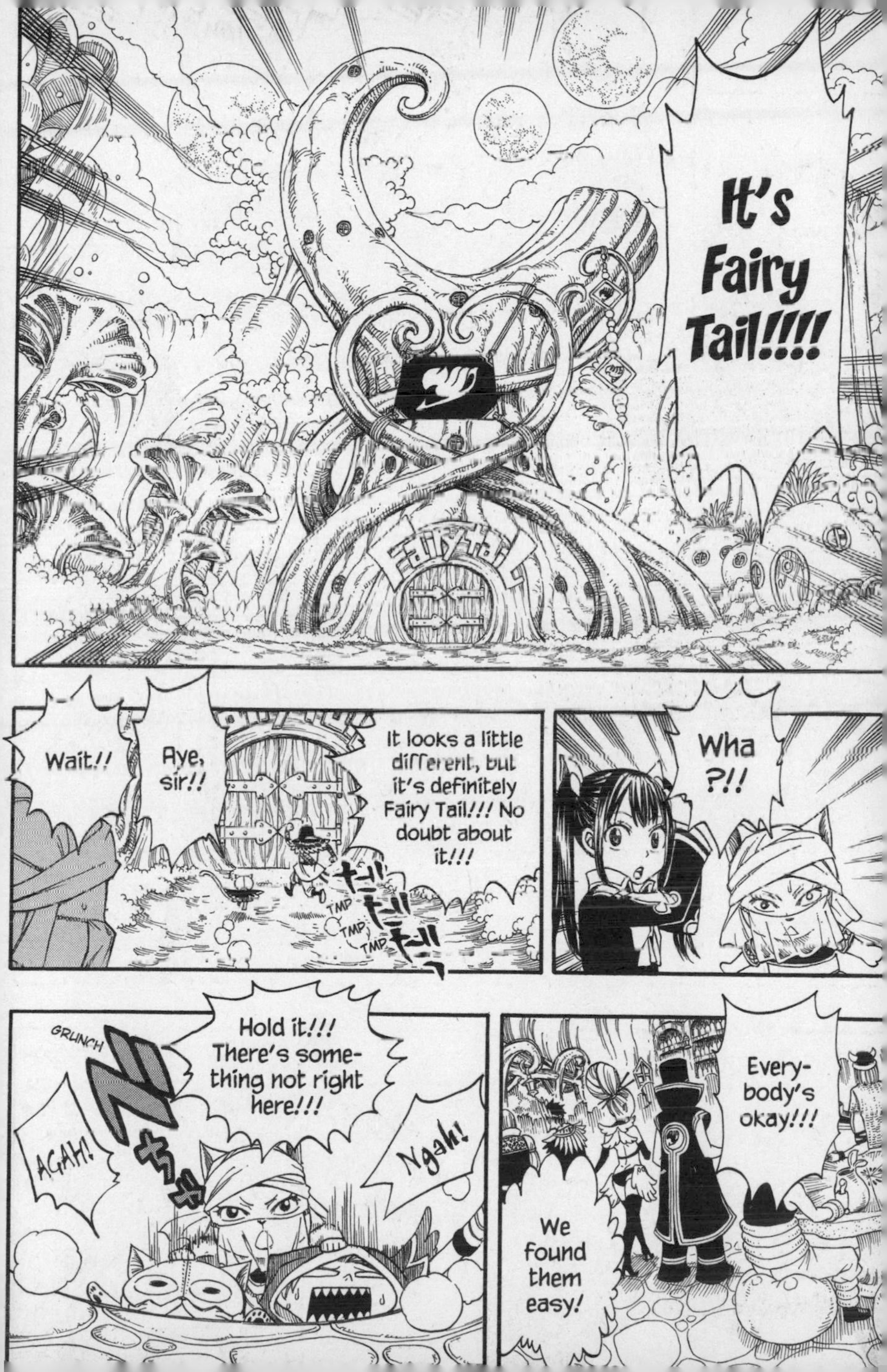
It's Fairy Tail!!!!
Wha ?!!
It looks a little different, but it's definitely Fairy Tail!!! No doubt about it!!!
Aye, sir!!
Wait!!
TMP
TMP
TMP
Every-body's okay!!!
We found them easy!
Hold it!!! There's some-thing not right here!!!
GRUNCH
Ngah!
AGAH!

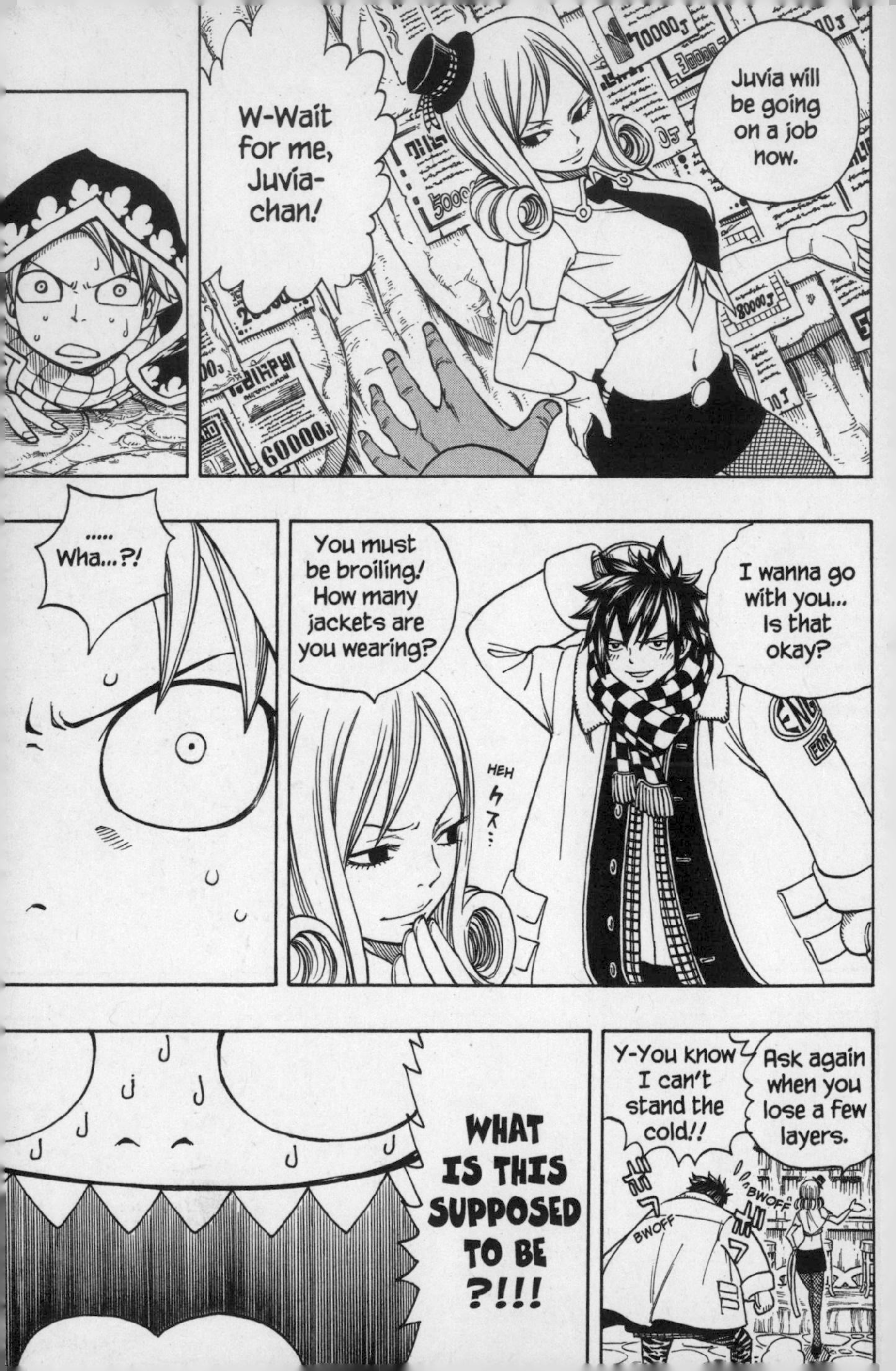
Juvia will be going on a job now.
W-Wait for me, Juvia-chan!
I wanna go with you... Is that okay?
You must be broiling! How many jackets are you wearing?
HEH
..... Wha...?!
Ask again when you lose a few layers.
Y-You know I can't stand the cold!!
BWOFF
BWOFF
WHAT IS THIS SUPPOSED TO BE ?!!!

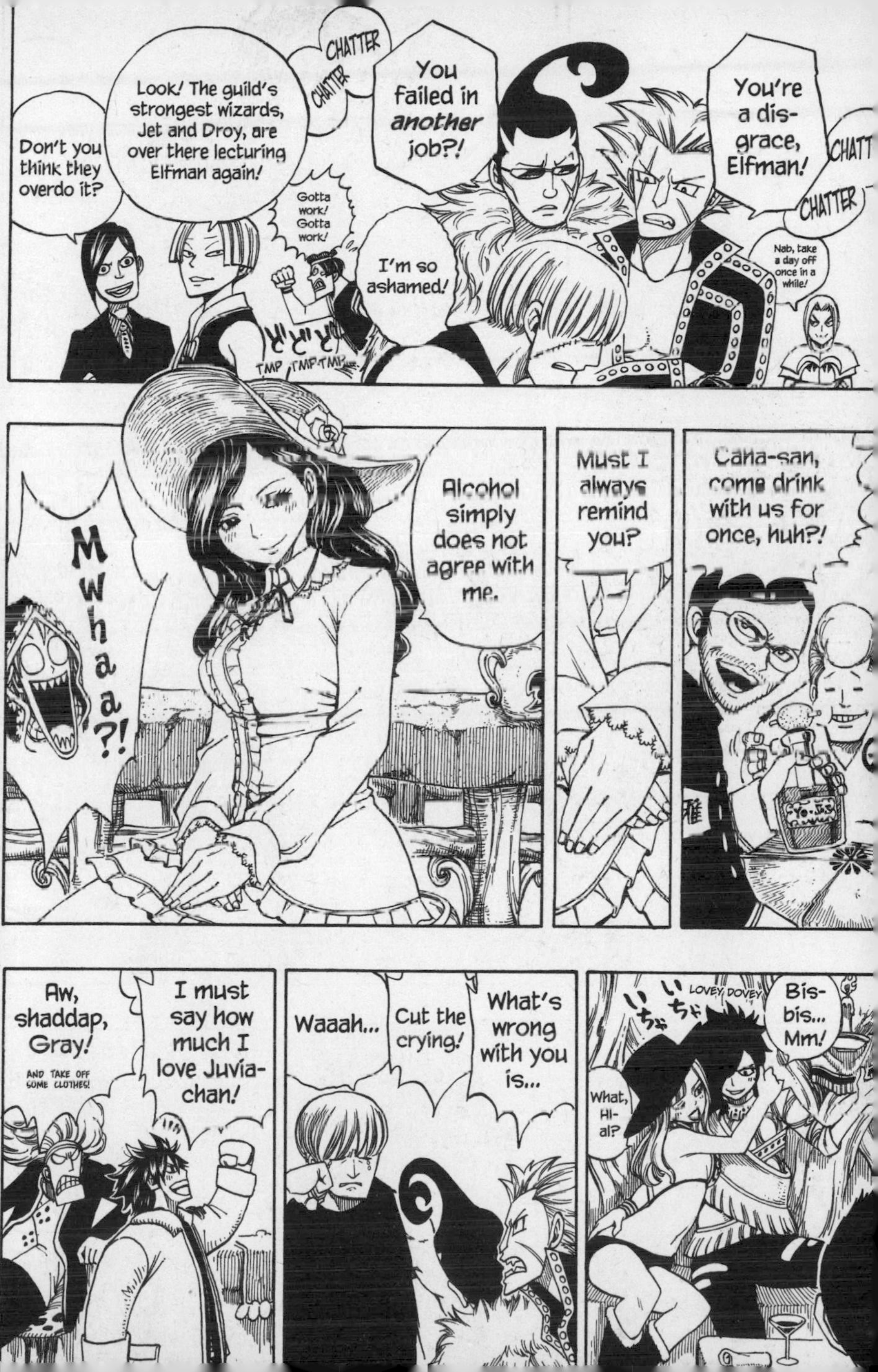
You're a disgrace, Elfman!
CHATTER
Nab, take a day off once in a while!
You failed in *another* job?!
I'm so ashamed!
CHATTER CHATTER
Gotta work! Gotta work!
TMP TMP TMP
Look! The guild's strongest wizards, Jet and Droy, are over there lecturing Elfman again!
Don't you think they overdo it?
Cana-san, come drink with us for once, huh?!
Must I always remind you?
Alcohol simply does not agree with me.
Mwhaa?!
LOVEY DOVEY
Bis-bis... Mm!
What, Hi-al?
What's wrong with you is...
Cut the crying!
Waaah...
I must say how much I love Juvia-chan!
Aw, shaddap, Gray!
AND TAKE OFF SOME CLOTHES!

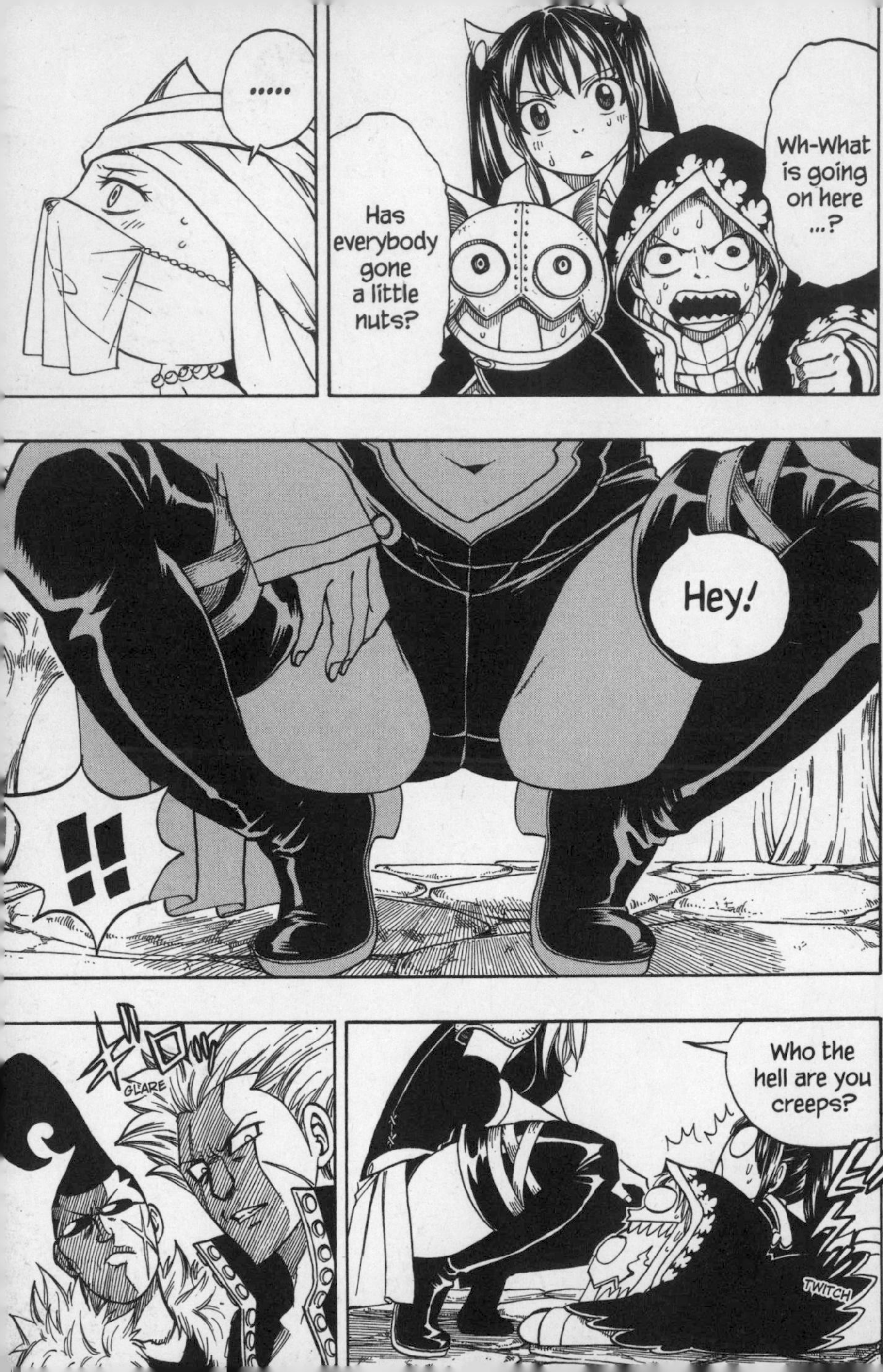
Wh-What is going on here ...?
Has everybody gone a little nuts?
......
Hey!
!!
Who the hell are you creeps?
TWITCH
GLARE

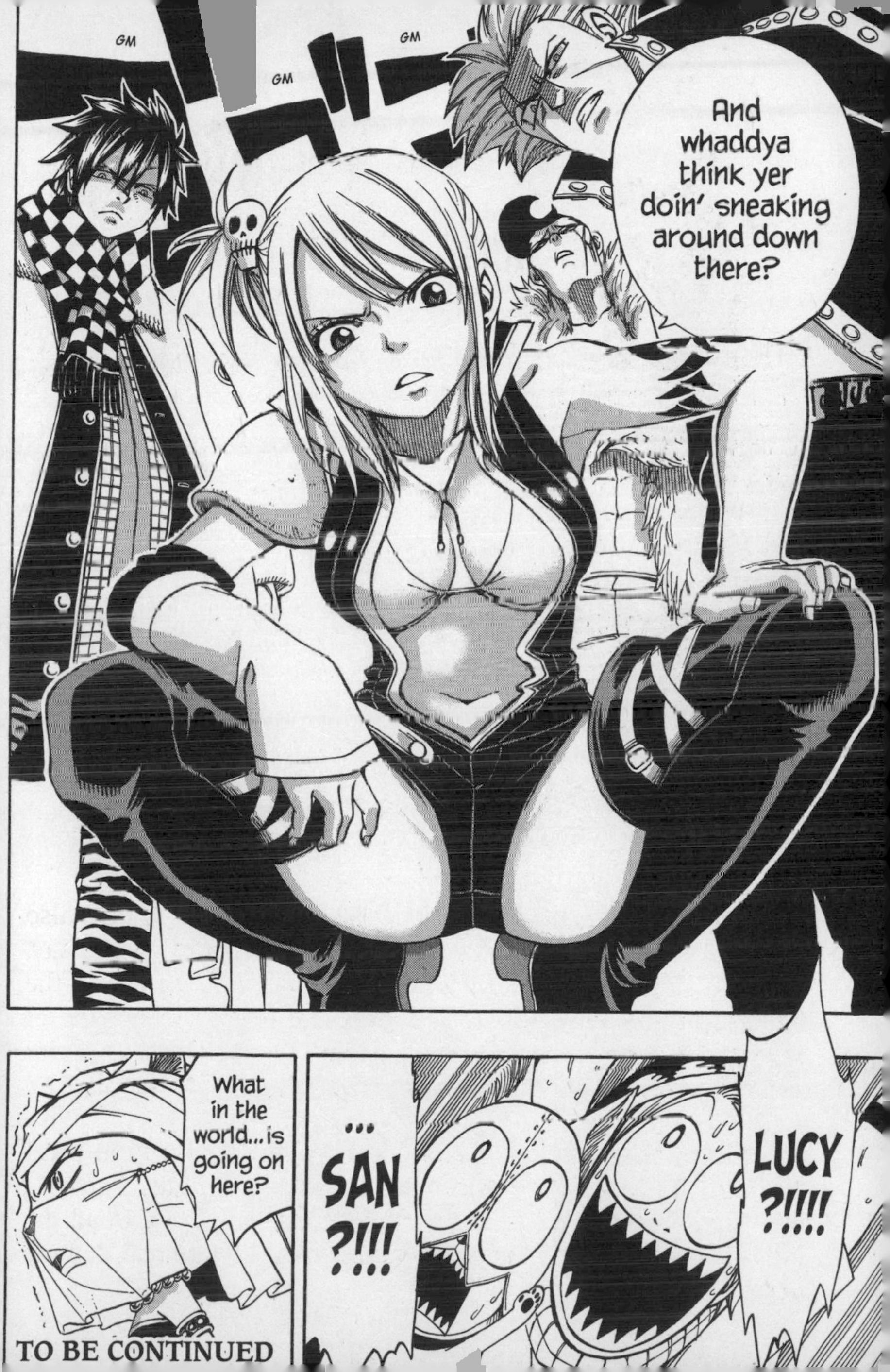
GM
GM
GM
And whaddya think yer doin' sneaking around down there?
LUCY ?!!!!
...SAN ?!!!
What in the world...is going on here?
TO BE CONTINUED

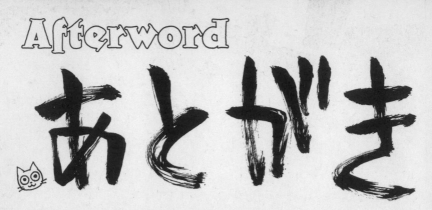

# Afterword

あとがき

Made it to 20 volumes!! Everybody, thank you so much for always being there!! This time, I'm going to take this opportunity to thank everyone who has supported this effort! I could never have kept this up this long alone, so I want to show my gratitude to everyone connected with Fairy Tail! Of course that includes you readers. You don't know how much your letters of support keep me going... Really! My appreciation knows no bounds!

By the way, counting my other series and short story collections, this makes my 66th graphic novel volume. That's a pretty impressive number too, huh? There sure are a huge number of drawings... But I'm determined to try even harder from here on out! Probably.

Now this volume marks the start of the Edolas story, but it's also the Happy story that I mentioned a little while ago. I go and say, "Someday I want to do that!" and then I go and do it right off the bat. That's so like me! I can't tell for sure exactly what kind of story it'll turn out to be, but I predict that there will be tons of plot twists like you've never seen before! What's going to happen?

Come to think of it, there was one more really big event in here! The arrival of Gildarts! What a dumb-looking old guy, huh? He was kind of dumb in his early concepts too, but when I had the idea of the town split in two, I thought, "Ah! I'm the real dummy here!"

# TAIL de ART

The Fairy Tail Guild de Art is looking for illustrations! Please send in your art on a postcard or at postcard size, and do it in black pen, okay? Those chosen to be published will get a signed mini poster! ♪ Make sure you write your real name and address on the back of your illustration!

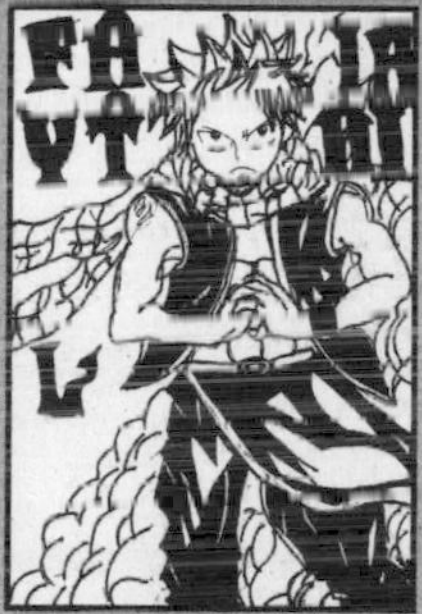

Hyogo Prefecture, Kisshi

▼ Bold Natsu striking a brave pose! The moment before his fire comes roaring out!!

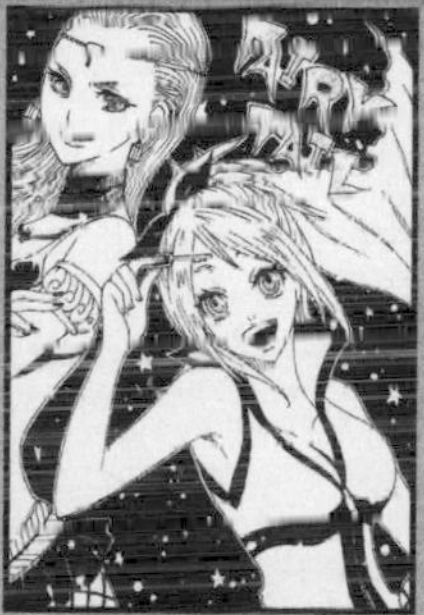

Kanagawa Prefecture, Hikaru Shiina

▼ Lucy and Aquarius!! Very well done!

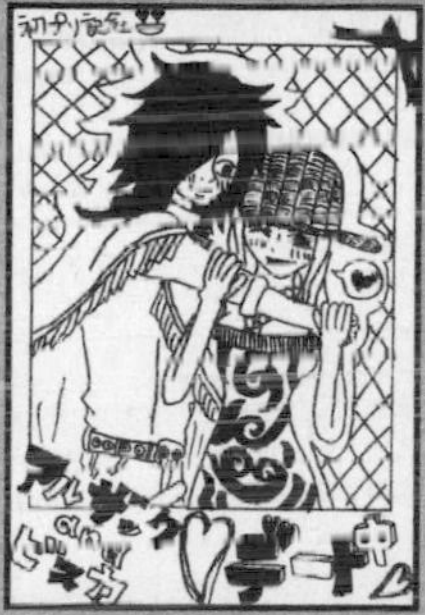

Hokkaido, I Want to Be in Fairy Tail!!

▼ If you say Fairy Tail's best couple(?), it's probably these two, maybe.

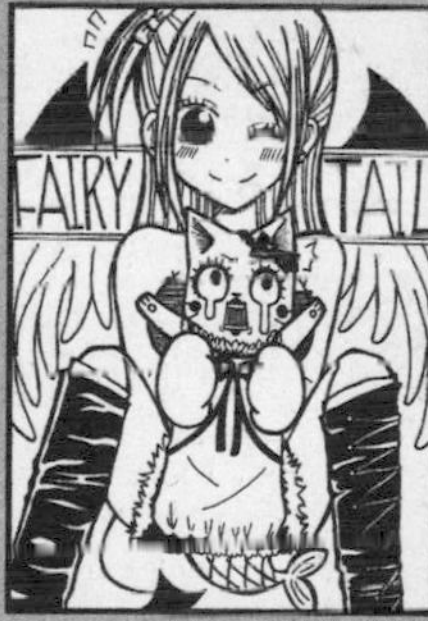
FAIRY TAIL

Taiwan, Xiaoxi

▼ Every now and then I get a card from Taiwan! Xie xie!

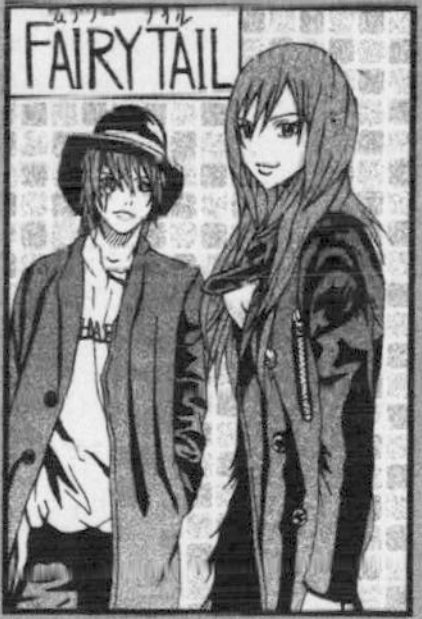
FAIRY TAIL

Hyogo Prefecture, Takanari Yamamoto

▼ That final scene with Jellal...was just too sad, huh...?

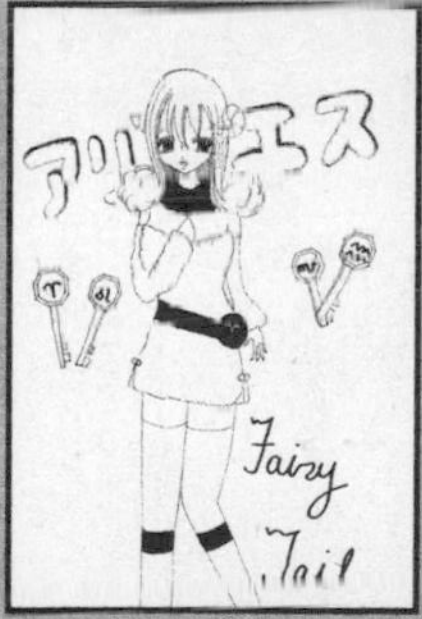
アリエス
Fairy Tail

Osaka, Girls☆

▼ Wooly-wooly Aries! Finally she's joined Lucy's group!

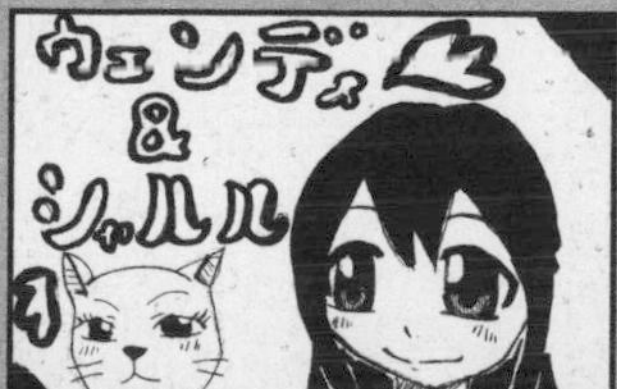
ウェンディ
&
シャルル

Aichi Prefecture, Rasshii ☆

▼ They had so many fans that they actually made it into Fairy Tail.

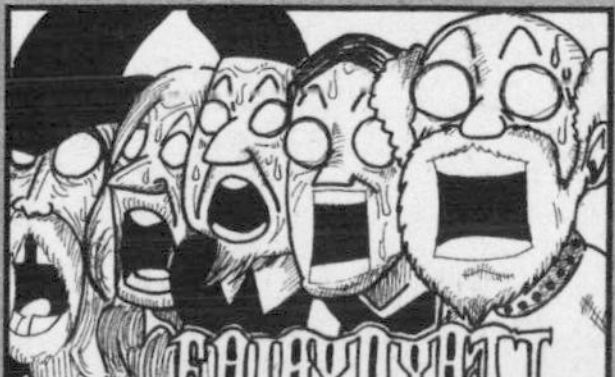

Hokkaido, Reina Saitō

▼ Look at all the guild masters lined up! Gah!

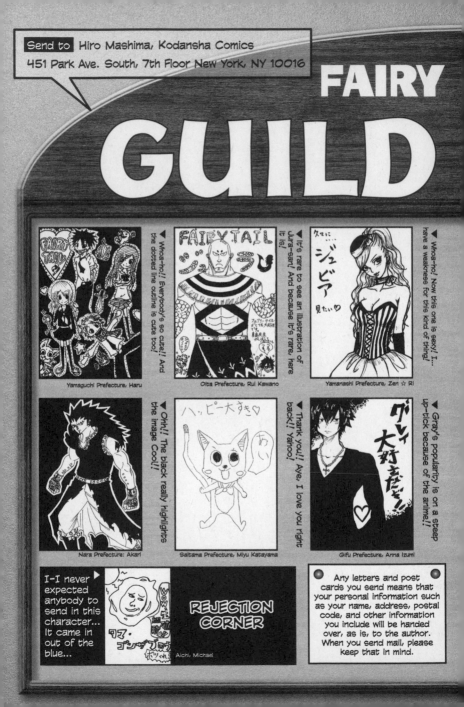

**Send to** Hiro Mashima, Kodansha Comics
451 Park Ave. South, 7th Floor New York, NY 10016

# FAIRY GUILD

▼ Whoa-ho! Now this one is sexy! I... have a weakness for this kind of thing!

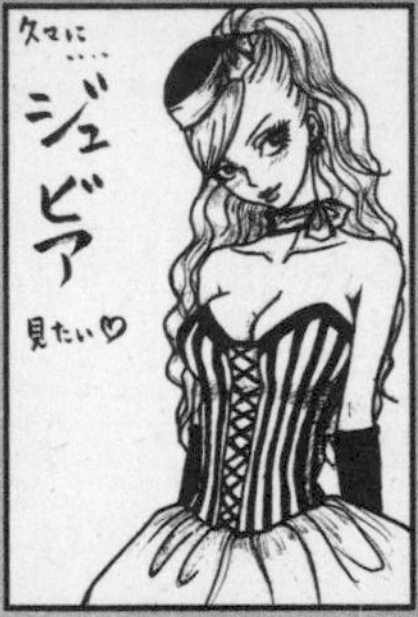
久々に……
ジュビア
見たい♡

Yamanashi Prefecture, Zen ☆ Ri

▼ It's rare to see an illustration of Jura-san! And because it's rare, here it is!

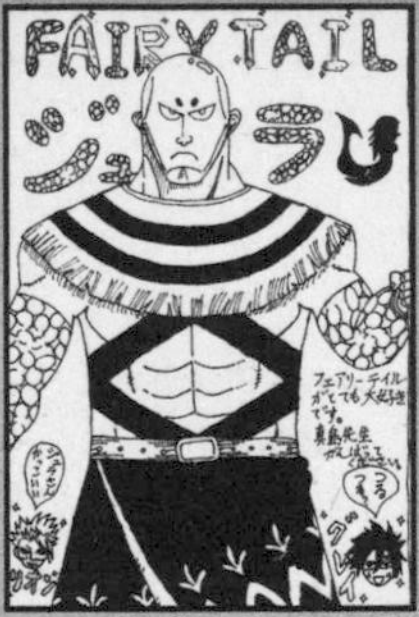
FAIRY TAIL
ジュラ

Oita Prefecture, Rui Kawano

▼ Whoa-ho!! Everybody's so cute!! And the dotted line outline is cute too!

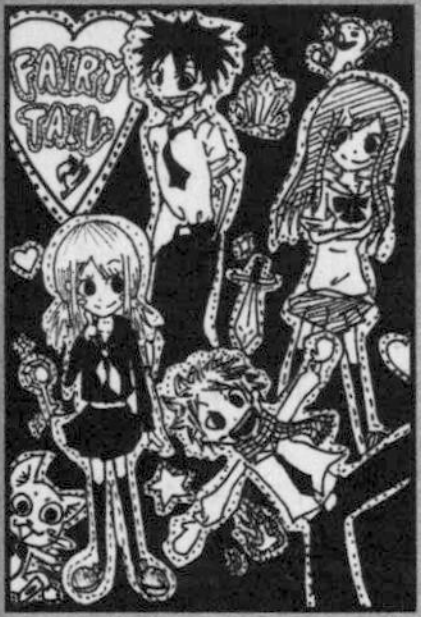
FAIRY TAIL

Yamaguchi Prefecture, Haru

▼ Gray's popularity is on a steep up-tick because of the anime!!

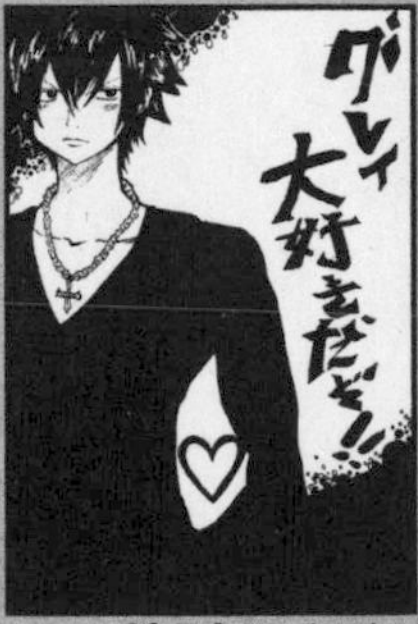
グレイ
大好きだぞ!!

Gifu Prefecture, Anna Izumi

▼ Thank you!! Aye, I love you right back!! Yahoo!

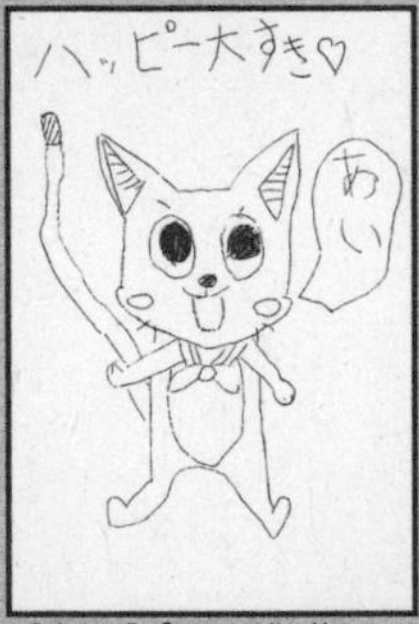
ハッピー大すき♡
あい

Saitama Prefecture, Miyu Katayama

▼ Ohh!! The black really highlights the image Cool!!

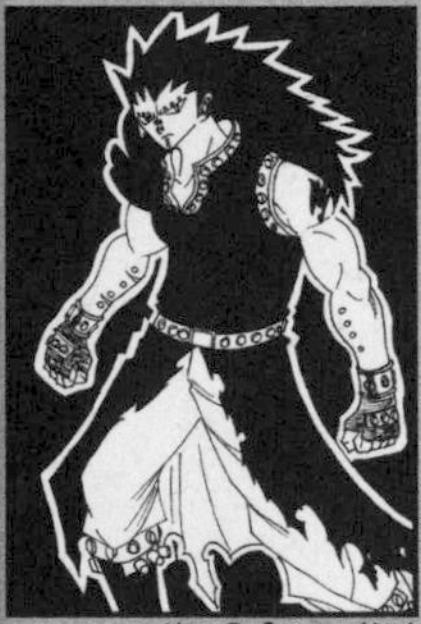

Nara Prefecture: Akari

**REJECTION CORNER**

I-I never expected anybody to send in this character... It came in out of the blue... ▶

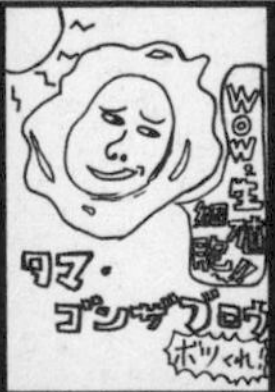
WOW
タマ・ゴンザブロウ

Aichi, Michael

Any letters and post cards you send means that your personal information such as your name, address, postal code, and other information you include will be handed over, as is, to the author. When you send mail, please keep that in mind.

**FROM HIRO MASHIMA**

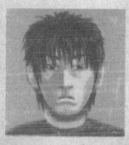

That was quick! We're already at Volume 20!

At first, this was just a story of Natsu going off on a search for Igneel, but that story has been put on the shelf. And while I've been fooling around with other things, before I know it, it's Volume 20!

Maybe I should get started on that Igneel story... And while I'm saying that, there's been another plot twist... What's going to happen...? What's going on in my brain...?

Original Jacket Design: Hisao Ogawa

# Translation Notes:

Japanese is a tricky language for most Westerners, and translation is often more art than science. For your edification and reading pleasure, here are notes on some of the places where we could have gone in a different direction with our translation of the work, or where a Japanese cultural reference is used.

## Page 4, Fight for Right

In Japanese this was a phrase that meant both "fighting evil," and "walking the narrow path of righteousness." It is also something that comes out a bit like a slogan, so it seemed that "Fight for Right" would be a close translation.

## Page 15, Shiranui-gata

*Shiranui* literally means "unknown fire," and it can be used to describe the mysterious lights you see on the ocean, or bioluminescence. Natsu's probably using it because he doesn't know where the fire Jellal fed him came from.

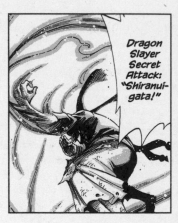

Dragon Slayer Secret Attack: "Shiranui-gata!"

## Page 32, Host

As people familiar with Japanese culture would know, the "host" is taken from the word "hostess," which has taken on the meaning in Japan of a woman who works in a bar making conversation and drinking with the male customers. The host here is the male version of that: A generally good-looking young adult man who drinks with female patrons and amuses them with conversation and flattery.

## Page 67, Nabura

As listed in the notes for the previous volume, *nabura* is a word of unknown meaning that the master of Cait Shelter, Robaul, says often. Not even his guild members know what it means, so the reader is left to guess.

## Page 68, "Now Ichiya…" "Now Ichiya?"

This is a kind of song that is often heard in Japanese festivals where a master-of-ceremonies-like person calls out a word or phrase and the crowd is supposed to repeat it. However they can repeat it as a question or a statement, so the song can be thought of as a sort of limited conversation between the caller and the crowd.

**Page 68, Wa-hoo**

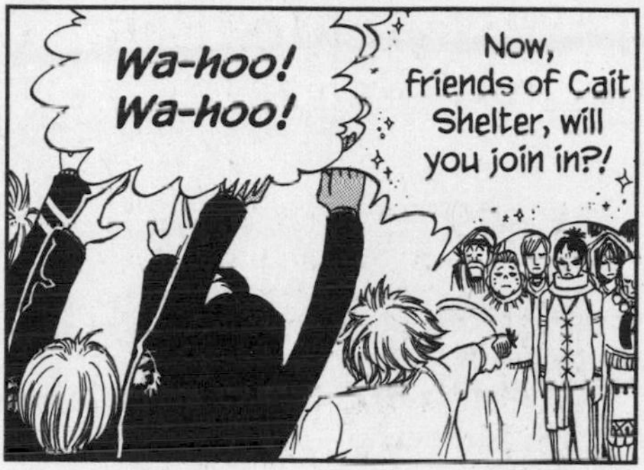
Now, friends of Cait Shelter, will you join in?!
Wa-hoo! Wa-hoo!

In Japanese, this was *Wa-shoi*, which is a common response from a crowd during festival songs and activities. It's most commonly found when groups in festivals are bearing Shinto shrine or Buddhist altar floats on their shoulders and carry ing the portable shrines in a parade-like fashion. Unfortunately this nuance was difficult to put in the English, so I substituted a similar sounding happy shout instead.

**Page 87, Forms**

This was a way that Lucy referred to her Celestial Spirits back in Volume 1. See the notes in Volume 1 for more information on "counter" words and why I chose "forms" as my translation for it in the first place.

**Page 148, My Ears Hurt**

He doesn't mean physically, of course. This is a standard idiom meaning that the listener is hearing something that they really don't want to hear. I could have translated it more culturally, but I think the meaning still comes through with a literal translation of the Japanese.

**Page 188, ...san**

Sometimes having Japanese honorifics left in the translation makes a passage easier to translate. In this case, Happy realizes that Lucy is a lot tougher and worthy of respect than the Lucy he knows. So whereas with the regular Lucy, they're close enough that he doesn't have to use honorifics, he adds the honorific to this Lucy so as not to offend her.

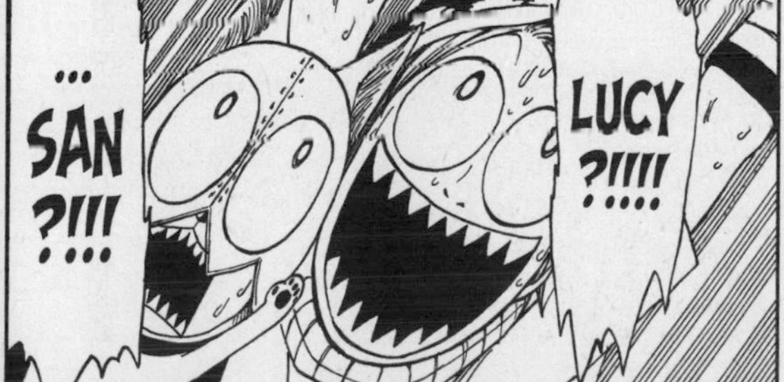
LUCY ?!!!!....
...SAN ?!!!....

# Preview of Fairy Tail, volume 21

We're pleased to present a preview of Fairy Tail Volume 21, now available from Kodansha Comics.

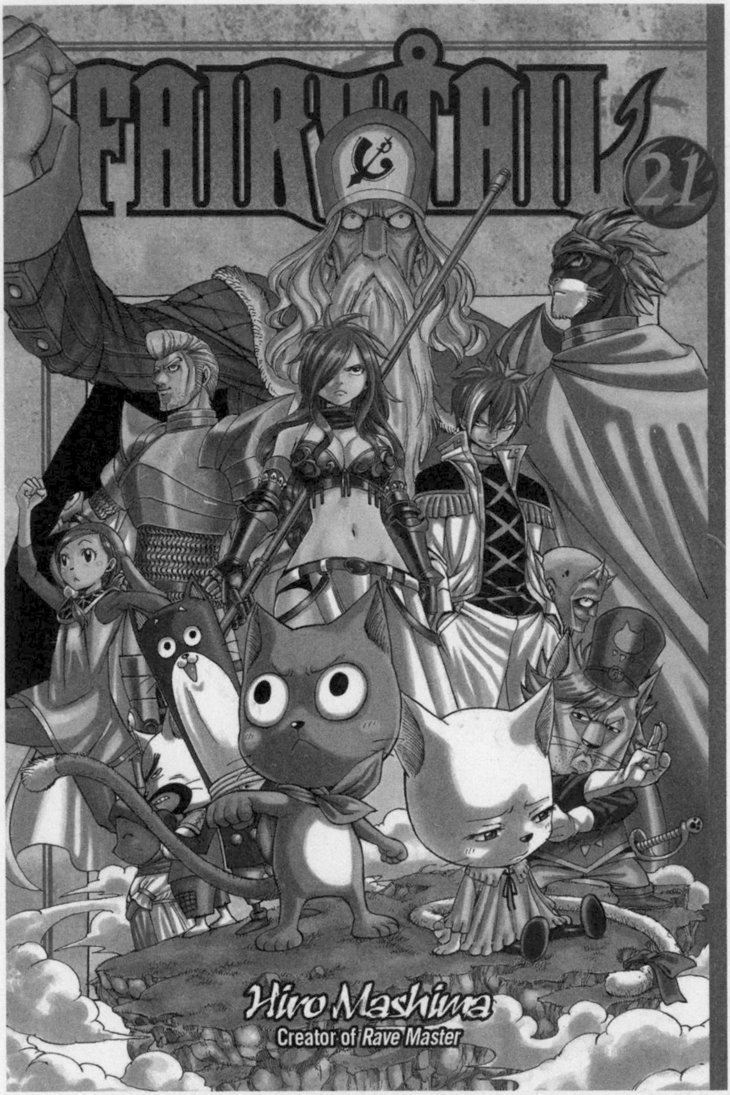
FAIRY TAIL
21
Hiro Mashima
Creator of Rave Master

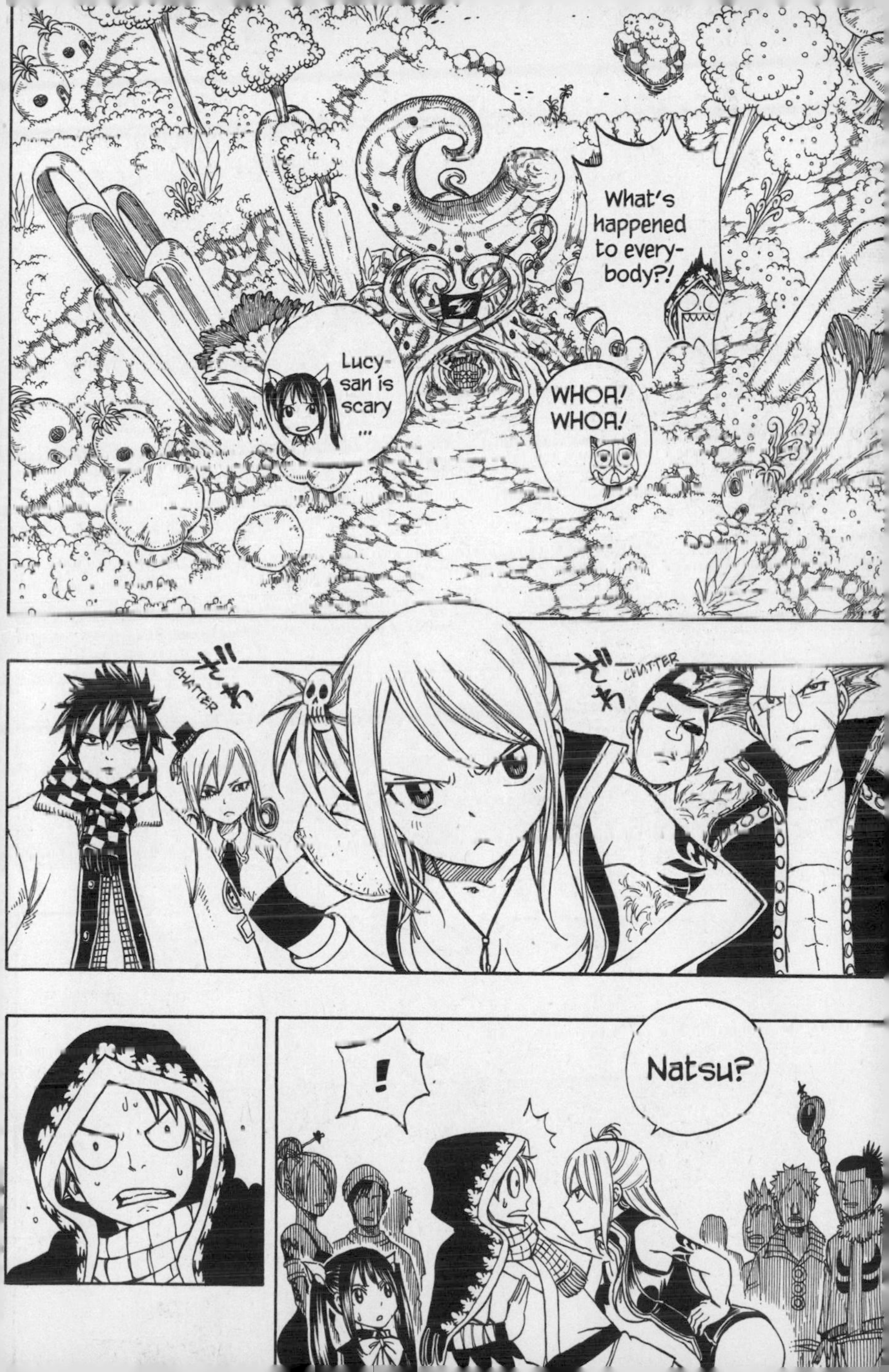
What's happened to every-body?!
WHOA! WHOA!
Lucy-san is scary ...
ざわ CHATTER
ざわ CHATTER
Natsu?
!

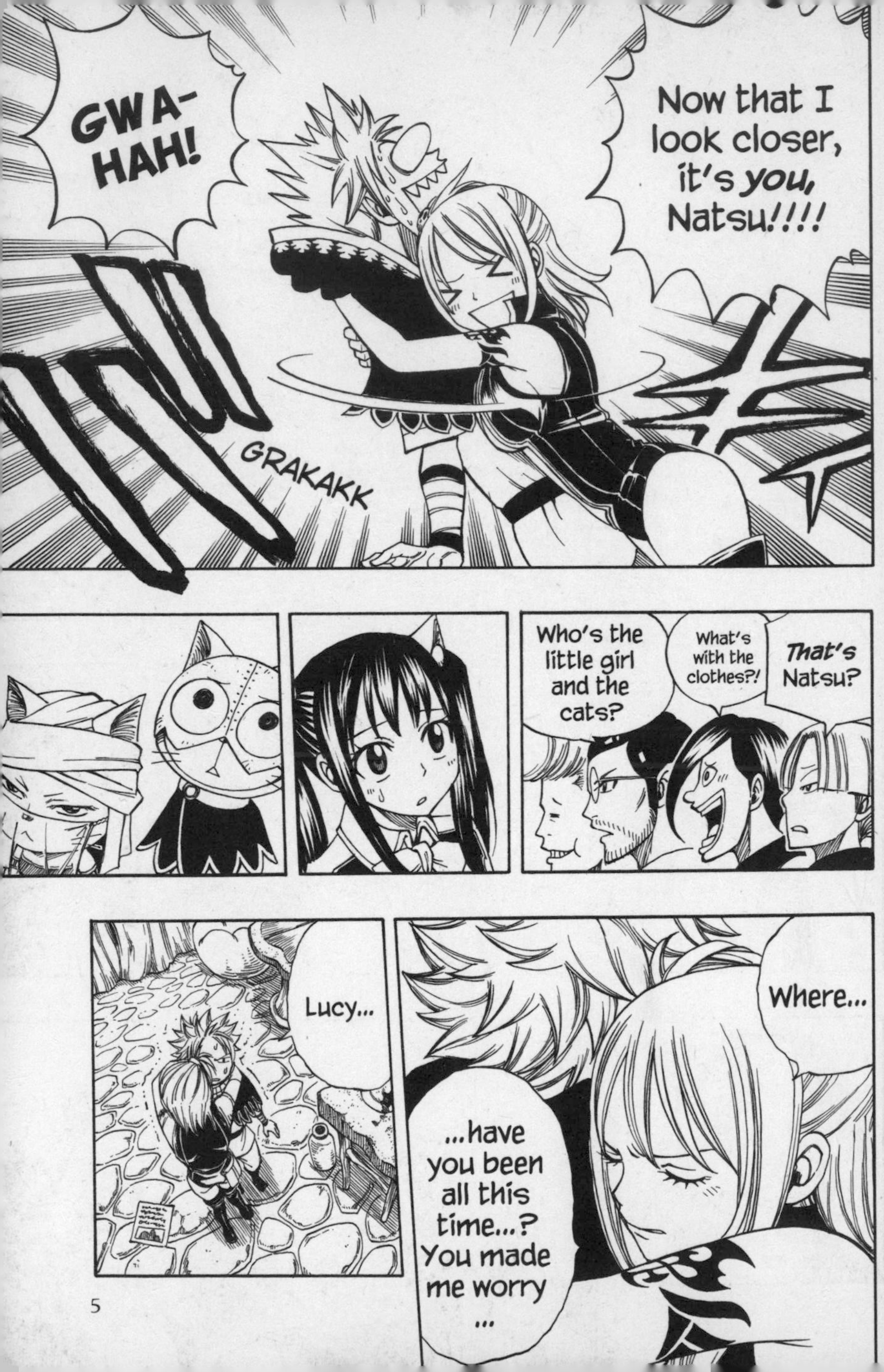
Now that I look closer, it's *you*, Natsu!!!!
GWA-HAH!
GRAKAKK
*That's* Natsu?
What's with the clothes?!
Who's the little girl and the cats?
Where...
...have you been all this time...? You made me worry ...
Lucy...

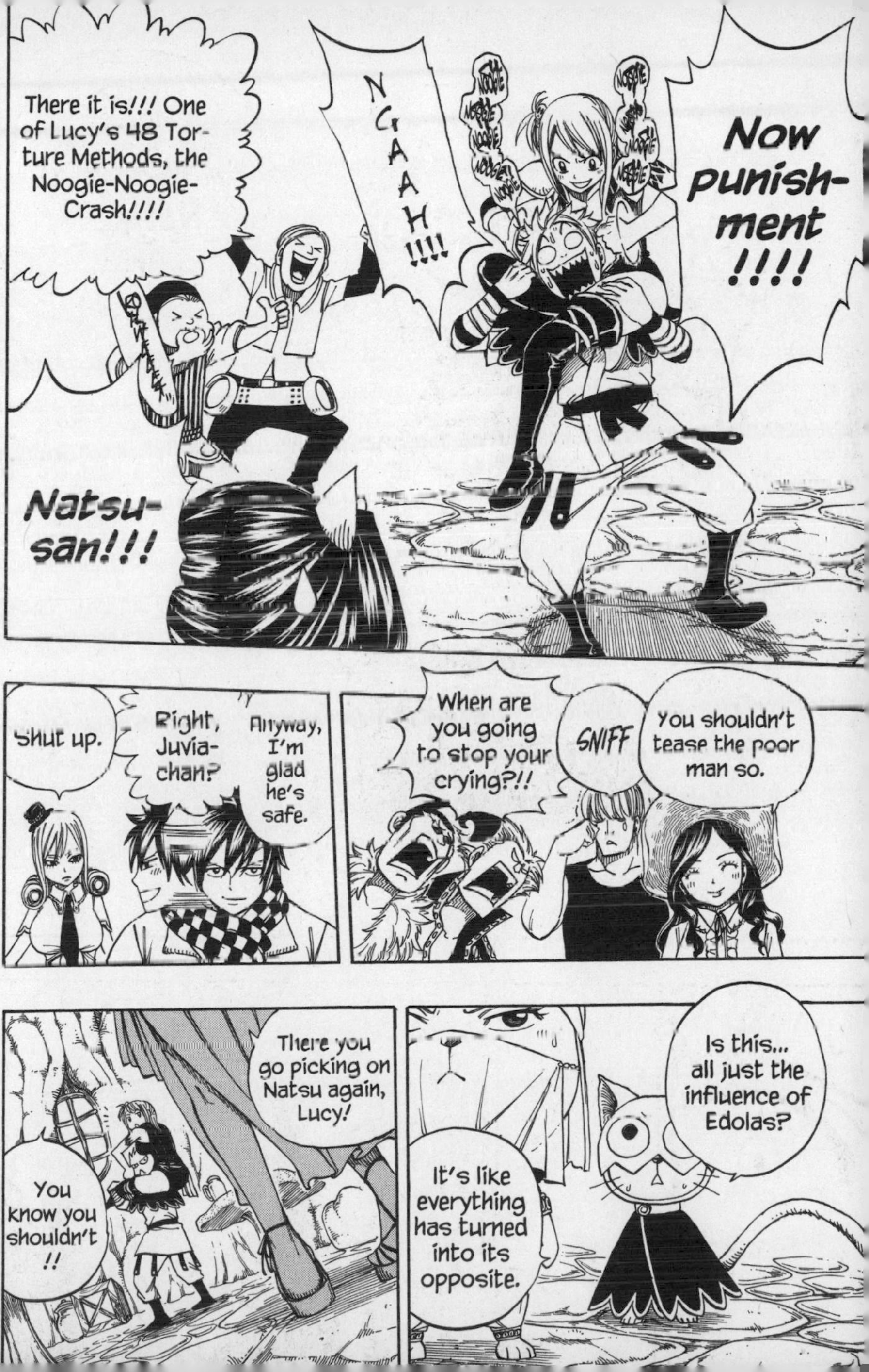

Now punishment!!!!
NGAAH!!!!
There it is!!! One of Lucy's 48 Torture Methods, the Noogie-Noogie-Crash!!!!
Natsu-san!!!
You shouldn't tease the poor man so.
SNIFF
When are you going to stop your crying?!!
Anyway, I'm glad he's safe.
Right, Juvia-chan?
Shut up.
Is this... all just the influence of Edolas?
It's like everything has turned into its opposite.
There you go picking on Natsu again, Lucy!
You know you shouldn't!!

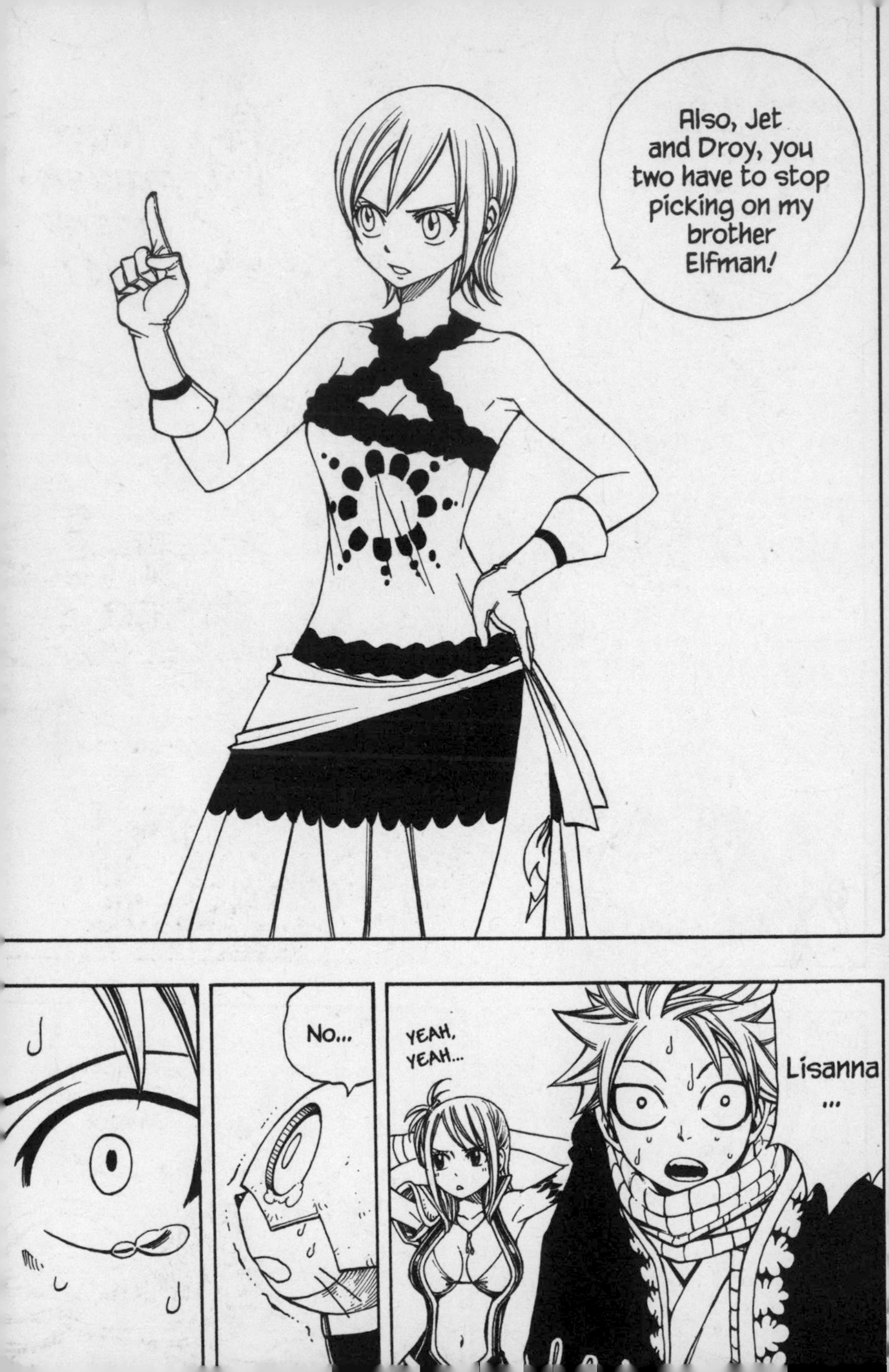
Also, Jet and Droy, you two have to stop picking on my brother Elfman!
Lisanna ...
YEAH, YEAH...
No...

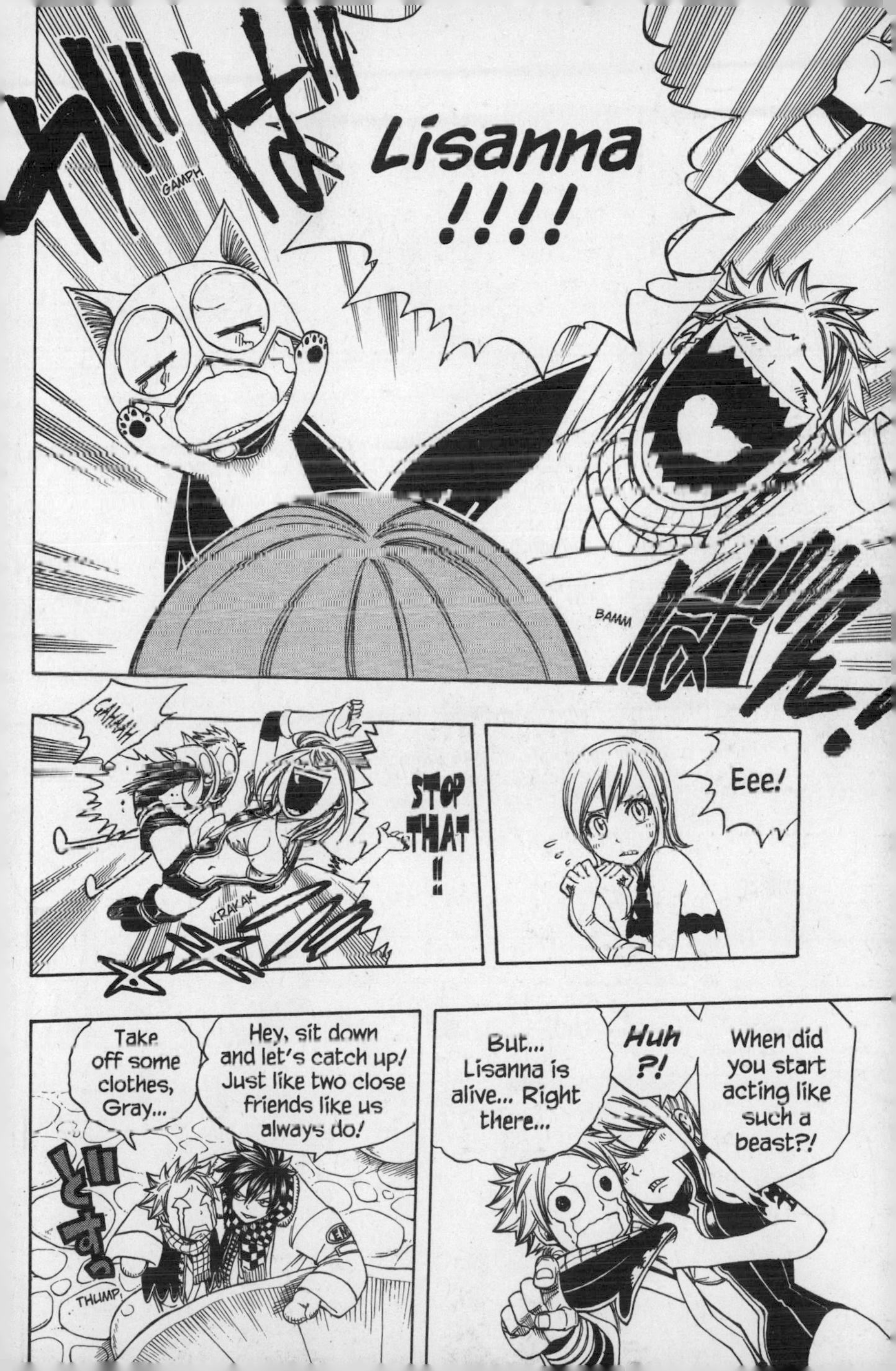

Lisanna !!!!
GAMPH
BAMM
Eee!
GAHAH
STOP THAT !!
KRAKAK
When did you start acting like such a beast?!
Huh ?!
But... Lisanna is alive... Right there...
Hey, sit down and let's catch up! Just like two close friends like us always do!
Take off some clothes, Gray...
THUMP

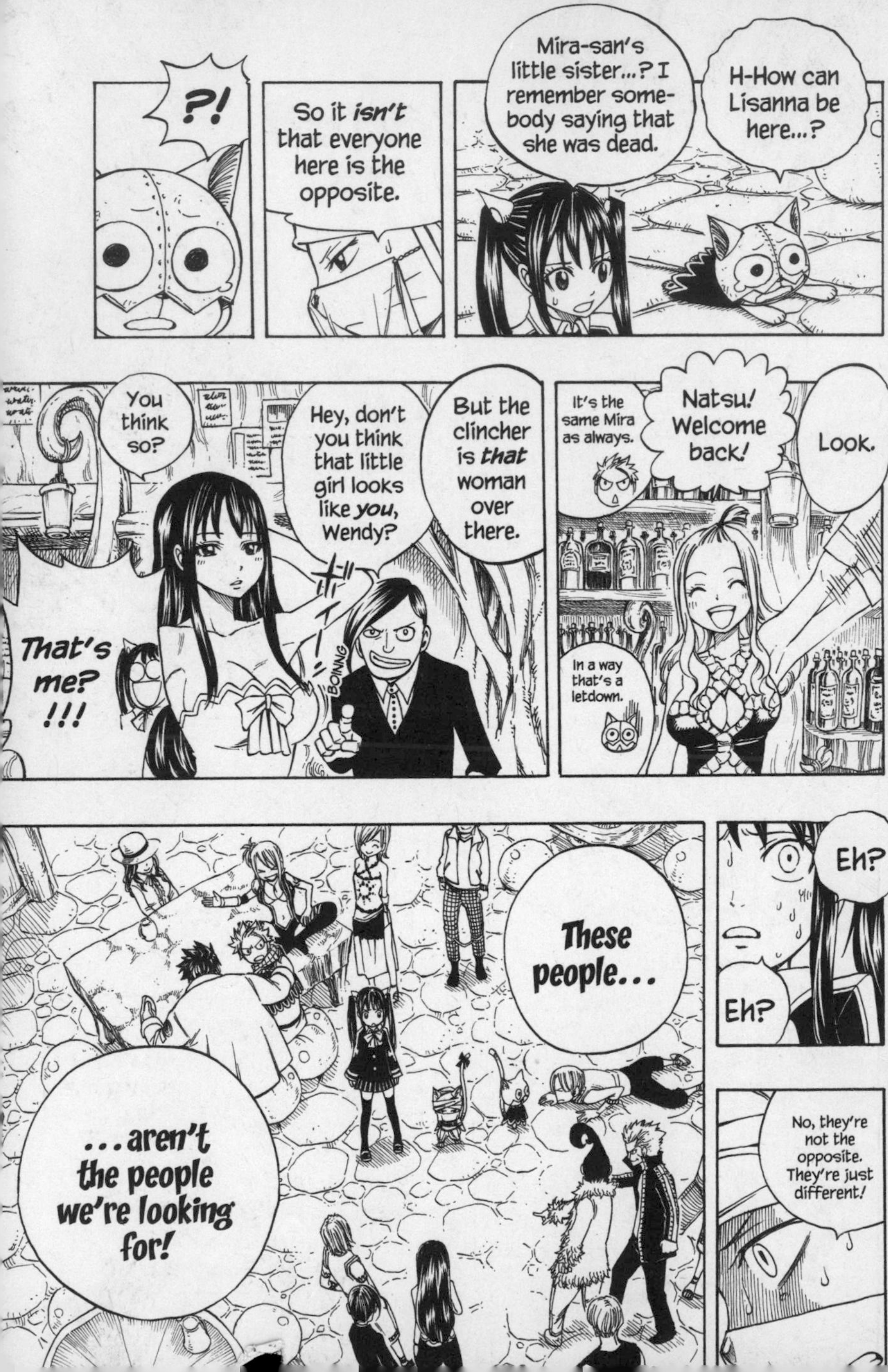
H-How can Lisanna be here...?
Mira-san's little sister...? I remember somebody saying that she was dead.
So it *isn't* that everyone here is the opposite.
?!
Look.
Natsu! Welcome back!
It's the same Mira as always.
In a way that's a letdown.
But the clincher is *that* woman over there.
Hey, don't you think that little girl looks like *you*, Wendy?
You think so?
BOINNG
That's me?!!!
Eh?
Eh?
No, they're not the opposite. They're just different!
These people...
...aren't the people we're looking for!

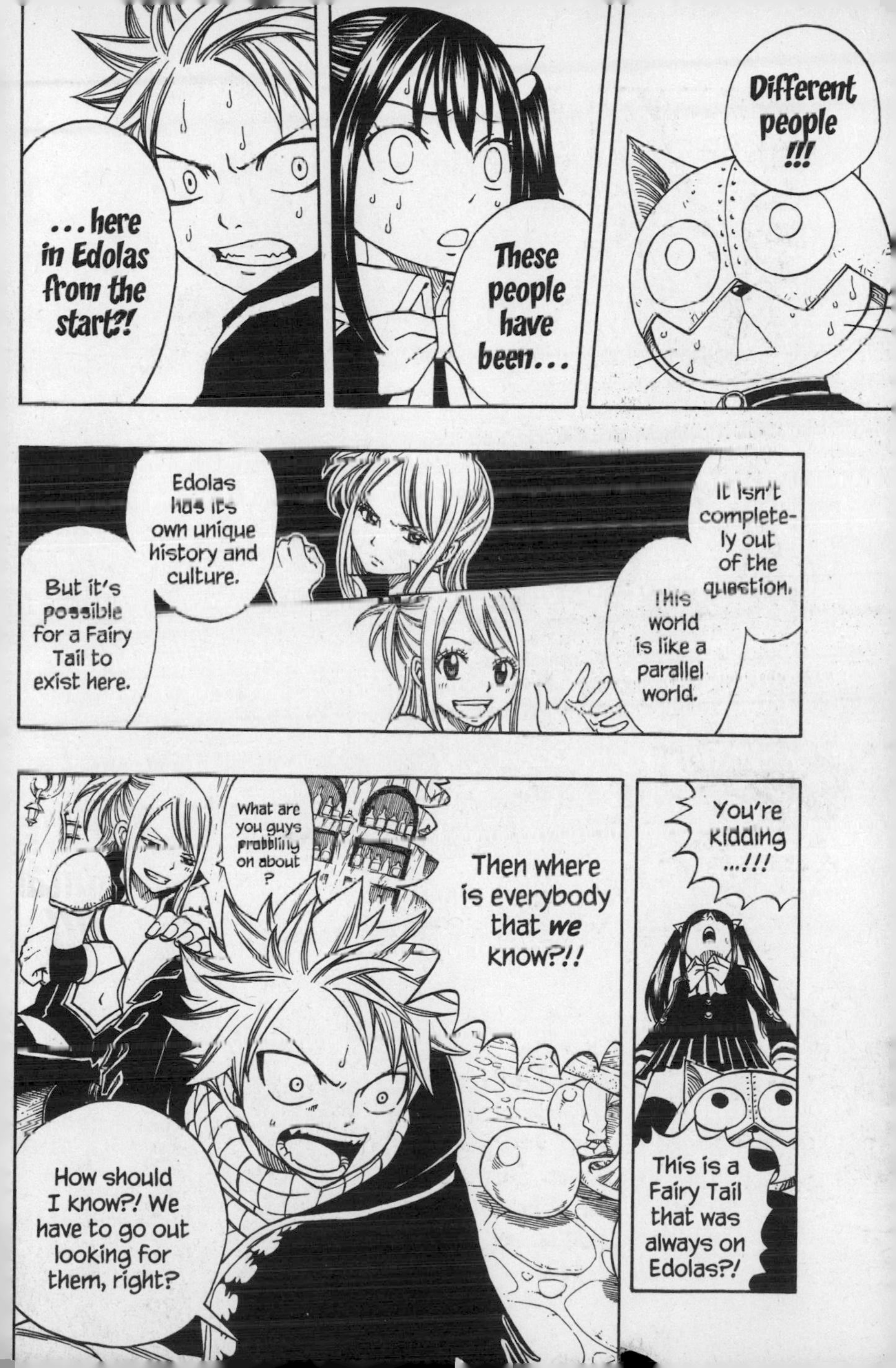
Different people !!!
These people have been...
...here in Edolas from the start?!
It isn't complete-ly out of the question.
This world is like a parallel world.
Edolas has its own unique history and culture.
But it's possible for a Fairy Tail to exist here.
You're kidding ...!!!
This is a Fairy Tail that was always on Edolas?!
Then where is everybody that *we* know?!!
What are you guys prattling on about ?
How should I know?! We have to go out looking for them, right?

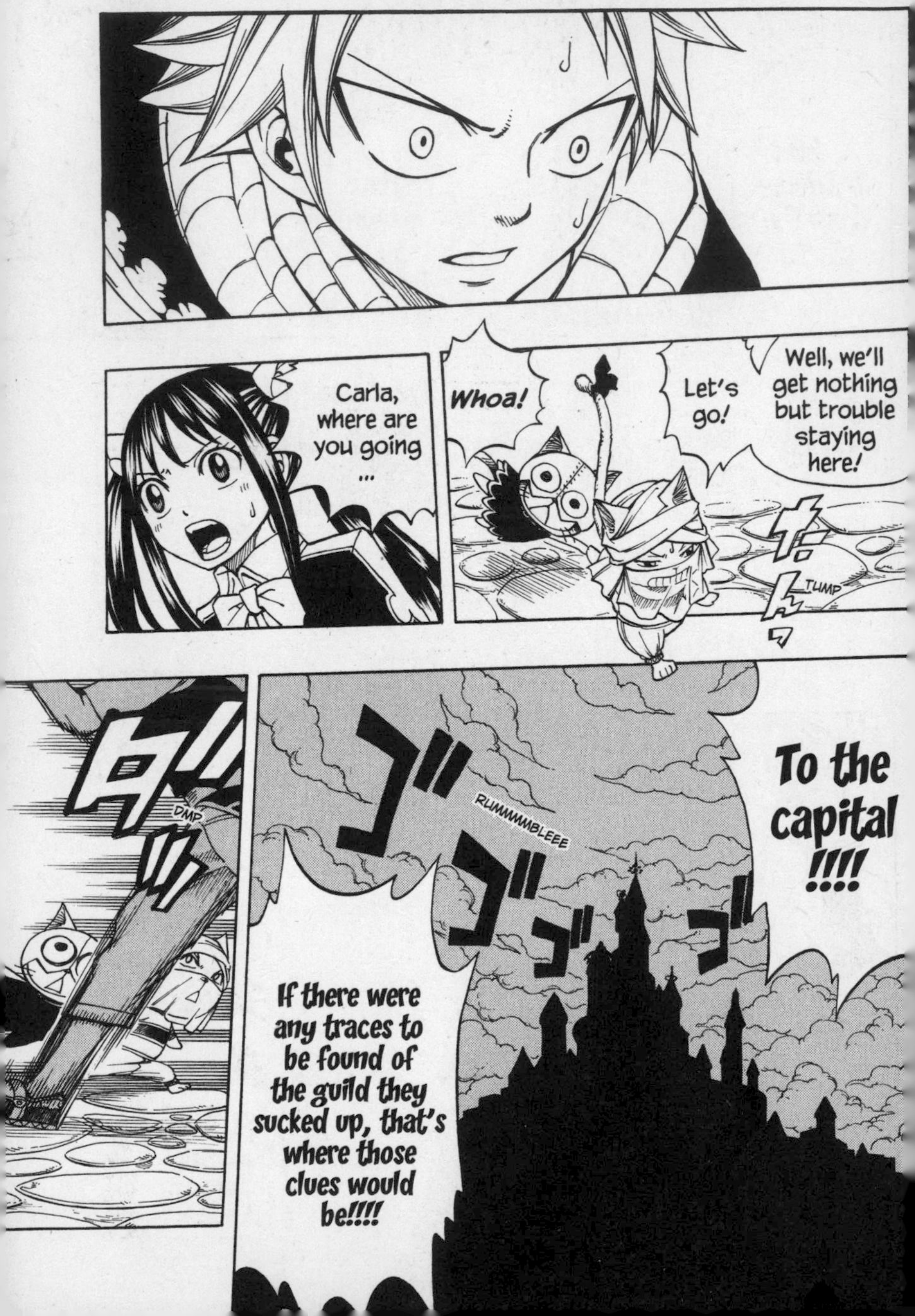
Well, we'll get nothing but trouble staying here!
Let's go!
Whoa!
TUMP
Carla, where are you going ...
To the capital!!!!
RUMMMMBLEEE
If there were any traces to be found of the guild they sucked up, that's where those clues would be!!!!
DMP

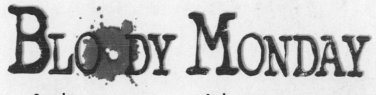

# BLOODY MONDAY

**Story by**
**Ryou Ryumon**    X    **Art by**
**Kouji Megumi**

Takagi Fujimaru may seem like a regular high school student, but behind the cheery facade lies a genius hacker by the name of Falcon.

When his father is framed for a murder, Falcon uses his brilliant hacking skills to try and protect his sister and clear his father's name.

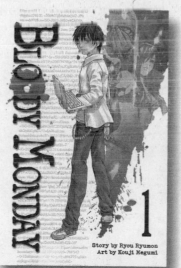

Story by Ryou Ryumon
Art by Kouji Megumi

*Special extras in each volume! Read them all!*

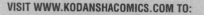

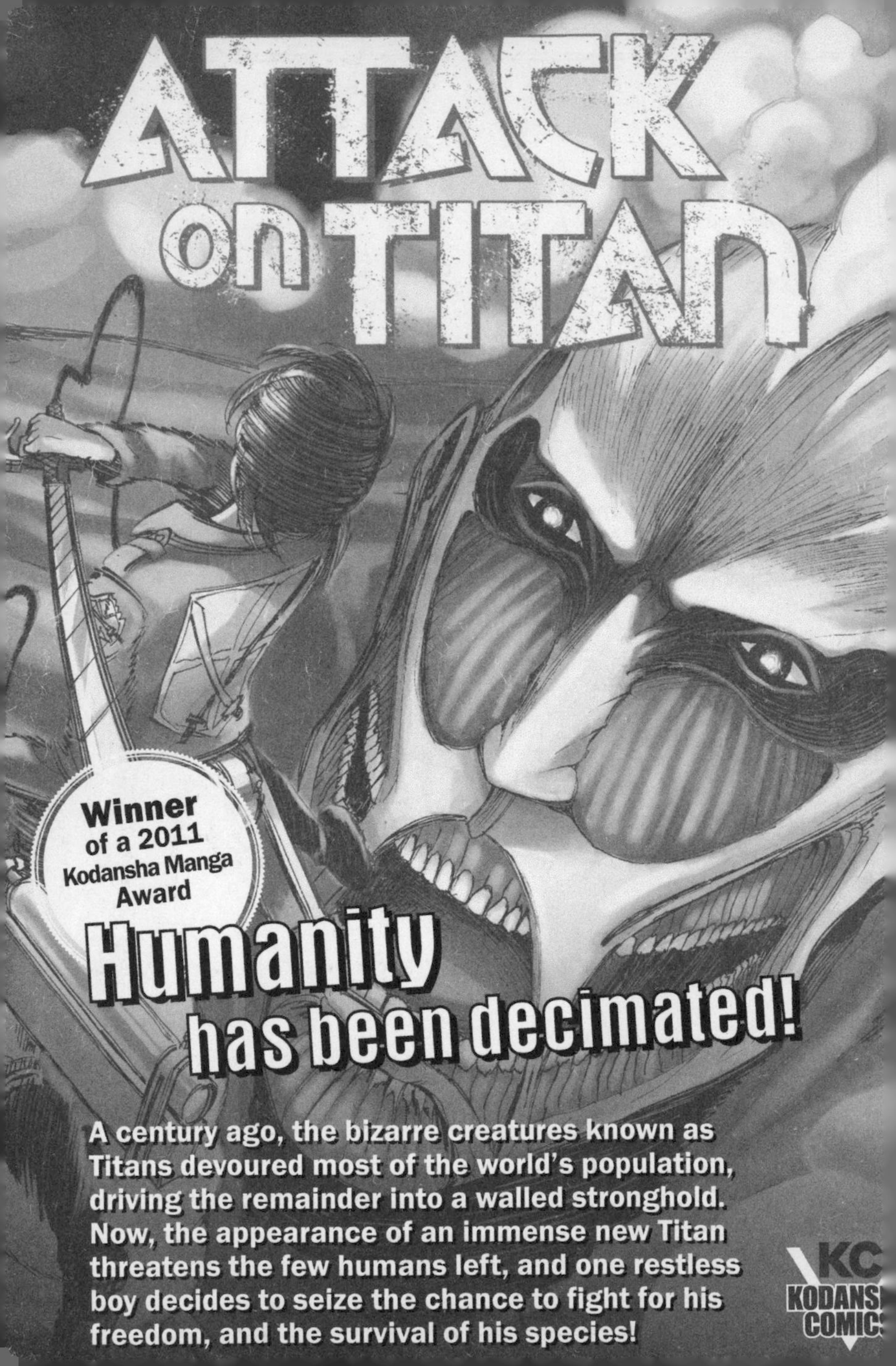
ATTACK on TITAN
Winner of a 2011 Kodansha Manga Award
Humanity has been decimated!
A century ago, the bizarre creatures known as Titans devoured most of the world's population, driving the remainder into a walled stronghold. Now, the appearance of an immense new Titan threatens the few humans left, and one restless boy decides to seize the chance to fight for his freedom, and the survival of his species!
KC
KODANSHA COMICS

A Kodansha Comics Trade Paperback Original

*Fairy Tail* volume 20 copyright © 2010 Hiro Mashima
English translation copyright © 2012 Hiro Mashima

Published in the United States by Kodansha Comics, an imprint of Kodansha USA Publishing, LLC., New York.

Publication rights for this English edition arranged through Kodansha Ltd., Tokyo.

First published in Japan in 2010 by Kodansha Ltd., Tokyo.

ISBN 978-1-612-62057-2

Printed in the United States of America.

www.kodanshacomics.com

9  8  7  6  5  4  3

Translator/Adapter: William Flanagan
Lettering: AndWorld Design

# TOMARE!

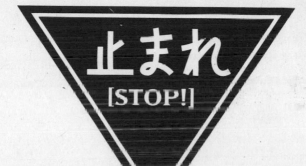

[STOP!]

You're going the wrong way!

Manga is a completely different type of reading experience.

To start at the *beginning,* go to the *end!*

That's right! Authentic manga is read the traditional Japanese way—from right to left, exactly the *opposite* of how American books are read. It's easy to follow: Just go to the other end of the book and read each page—and each panel—from right side to left side, starting at the top right. Now you're experiencing manga as it was meant to be!